United States Edition

2021 Year B

Workbook for Lectors, Gospel Readers, and Proclaimers of the Word®

Catherine Cory

Elizabeth Nagel

Peter O'Leary

Stephen S. Wilbricht, CSC

LTP

LITURGY
TRAINING
PUBLICATIONS

CONTENTS

(continued on next page)

Ordinary Time

This book was edited
by Victoria M. Tufano.
Christian Rocha was
the production editor,
Anna Manhart was the designer,
and Kari Nicholls was the
production artist.

Printed in the
United States of America

ISBN: 978-1-61671-552-6

WL21

In accordance with c. 827,
permission to publish was
granted on April 27, 2020, by
Most Rev. Ronald A. Hicks,
Vicar General of the Archdiocese
of Chicago. Permission to
publish is an official declaration
of ecclesiastical authority that
the material is free from doctrinal
and moral error. No legal
responsibility is assumed by
the grant of this permission.

MESSAGE AND PROCLAMATION

According to the *Catechism of the Catholic Church*, the liturgy is an "action" of the *whole Christ*, one that recapitulates the eternal drama in which "the Spirit and the Church enable us to participate whenever we celebrate the mystery of salvation in the sacraments" (1139). It is a celebration of the whole community: participative, connective, and joyful. Crucial to the celebration is the Liturgy of the Word, through which the Holy Spirit awakens faith, offering signs in the lectionary and the book of the Gospels; in procession, incense, and candles; and in the place of proclamation at the ambo—and instruction—through the proclamation itself of the Word of God to the faithfully assembled. As the *Catechism* puts it, "The Spirit makes present and communicates the Father's work, fulfilled by the beloved Son" (1155).

To read the Word of God is an act of proclamation. What is being proclaimed? The faith itself. *Kerygma* is the Greek word for proclamation; it appears multiple times in the New Testament, in St. Paul's letters and in the Acts of the Apostles, for instance, to refer to both the act and the content of proclaiming the good news. In Paul's First Letter to the Corinthians, he confesses, "When I came to you, brothers and sisters, *proclaiming* the mystery of God, I did not come with sublimity of words or of wisdom. For I resolved to know nothing while I was with you except Jesus Christ, and him crucified. I came to you in weakness and fear and much trembling, and my message and my *proclamation* were not with persuasive words of wisdom, but with a demonstration of spirit and power, so that your faith might rest not on human wisdom but on the power of God." "When I came to you, brothers and sisters, I did not come *proclaiming* the mystery of God to you in lofty words or wisdom. For I decided to know nothing among you except Jesus Christ, and him crucified. And I came to you in weakness and in fear and in much trembling. My speech and my *proclamation* were not with plausible words of wisdom, but with a demonstration of the Spirit and of power, so that your faith might rest not on human wisdom but on the power of God." (1 Corinthians 2:1–5; emphasis added). St. Paul doesn't want to be persuasive; rather, he wants his proclamation to reflect the spirit of God's power that fills him. When you proclaim, you reflect this spirit of the power of God.

In his Apostolic Exhortation *Evangelii gaudium*, Pope Francis insists that evangelization relies on a deeper understanding of proclamation. Francis refers to proclamation (he calls it *kerygma*, using the Greek term) as the "first announcement," whose essential confidence brings us deeper into the mystery of faith. (It is first because it is primary.) Francis is thinking of the importance of instruction when he writes, "All Christian formation consists of entering more deeply into the kerygma, which is reflected in and constantly illumines the work of catechesis, thereby enabling us to understand more fully the significance of every subject which the latter treats" (165). But this catechesis, which means simply a ministry of the Word (*catechesis*, which means "instruction," comes from the Greek word *katechein*, which means "echo"), has an instructive social element you involve yourself in whenever you attend Mass and whenever you participate as a proclaimer of the Word. Francis insists, "The kerygma has a clear social content: at the very heart of the Gospel is life in community and engagement with others" (177). Engagement with the community and deepening your life in that community are precisely what you accomplish as a lector, Gospel reader, and proclaimer of the Word.

Alpha and Omega

"I am the Alpha and the Omega." Thus says the Lord in the Revelation to John. Twice, in fact: in the opening chapter and in the twenty-second. It's one of the most potent and memorable phrases in all of the New Testament. Among its many interpretations and purposes, it might usefully serve as a motto for all proclaimers of the Word in the Church: lectors, deacons, and priests. One way to paraphrase this claim is that God is saying, "I am the alphabet."

Language, of course, is the medium you use as a lector, the instrument you play. Effective proclaiming is like effective piano playing. As every music teacher knows, some students are no good at playing the piano because they don't practice and don't have a good feel for the instrument. Other students are pretty good because they practice and have learned how to read music and to play the notes in the proper order. A few students are superb because they combine the discipline of practice with an intimate and immediately audible feel for the instrument, combining voicing, pauses, skill, and poise. Proclamation involves a similar skill set. Practice is important, but so is developing as good a feel for language—your instrument—as you can.

In the beginning was the Word, and the Word was with God, and the Word was God.

How do we develop a feel for language? One of the main ways that meaning is conveyed when modern English is spoken is through the interplay of syntax (the order of words in a sentence or phrase) and stress (the emphasis in speech that falls on one part of a word or phrase over another). Poetry is the literary form most attentive to syntax and stress. Poetry in English is qualitative, which means that it relies on the repetition of strong stresses in words to convey its patterns and meanings. This is called meter.

Scripture is organized by book, chapter, and verse. This system of organization is modern, coming into use in the sixteenth century. It was first used in English when the *Geneva Bible* was published in 1560. Verses refer, in the main, to sentences, since most of Scripture is written in prose. Some verses are poetic verse, including especially the Psalms but also the prophetic books in the Old Testament. Nevertheless, because the use and study of verse in English involve descriptive terminology, it is helpful to think about proclaiming the Word as a lector, deacon, or priest in terms of reading poetry aloud.

There are five basic metrical units in English, the names for which are all borrowed from Greek. A metrical unit is a pattern of stressed (DA) and unstressed (da) syllables. The five basic units, with examples of words that follow each pattern, are

iamb—da-DA (Detroit);

trochee—DA-da (London);

anapest—da-da-DA (Tennessee);

dactyl—DA-da-da (Arkansas);

and spondee—DA-DA (New York).

There are other meters, of course, but it's useful to have a sense of these five basic units when you are reading anything aloud, including Scripture, much of which, even in English translation, comes through as poetry.

You will note that the two longest of these metrical units have only three syllables. This means, practically speaking, that every two or three syllables, when you read something aloud, there should be a stress, an emphasis. Identifying these stresses does not exaggerate the sound of the phrase; instead, it enhances the phrase, highlighting its natural expressiveness.

Consider again "I am the Alpha and the Omega." This statement, one of the boldest of all in the New Testament, doesn't require any exaggeration or intensification on your part beyond identifying where the stresses in this statement lie. First, in the personal pronoun. Second, in the first syllable of Alpha. And third, in the second syllable of Omega. You could write the statement out this way, using capital letters to emphasize the stresses:

I am the ALpha and the oMEGa.

That captures the stresses. However, it doesn't entirely capture the most effective pace for proclaiming this statement.

Thinking about metrical units in English, you can identify where the pauses in this statement might usefully lie. The pauses in your speaking set the pace. Every two or three syllables, when speaking aloud, there is an opportunity for a pause, even if it's only a slight hesitation that allows you to enhance the stresses. We can use this symbol | to indicate pauses, however slight, and rewrite the statement from Revelation this way:

I | am the ALpha | and | the oMEGa.

An alternative reading would eliminate the third pause:

I | am the ALpha | and the oMEGa.

In the first version, the line has four beats:

1) I; 2) am the ALpha; 3) and; 4) the oMEGa.

The second version has three beats:

1) I; 2) am the ALpha; 3) and the oMEGa.

In the first version, the third pause, after "and," allows you to emphasize the parallel being drawn between the beginning and the end in the Lord's statement. In the second version, you speed ever so noticeably quicker to "Omega," which is the word in the verse imbuing it with ominous power.

Both versions are effective. Both, if you speak them aloud (as practice), can be suited to your speaking style. And both possible readings reinforce one of the most helpful strategies for effective proclaiming: read slowly enough that stresses and emphases can be heard by the congregation. A good rule of thumb, easy to remember, when reading anything aloud is this:

Read twice as loud and at half the pace that you normally speak.

Most lectors will be reading into a microphone, which means you need not increase your volume in the way you would without a microphone. However, the rule of thumb above can serve as a reminder that you are reading in front of an audience, your congregation, and the more clearly you proclaim, the more likely it is that they will pay attention. Like a teacher coming into a classroom and raising their voice above the level of the din or a coach blowing a whistle to

This is my commandment: love one another as I love you.

get the attention of the team, you can command the attention of your congregation by the pitch and volume of your voice. Don't be afraid to use it.

Likewise, read slowly. Depending on the architecture of your church, it's likely that your amplified voice will echo. Reading slowly allows your words to be heard and absorbed, rather than reflected and distorted.

Similarly, the more clearly you read, while paying attention to where the stresses lie in the passage from Scripture you are reading, the more intelligible and available your proclaiming will be. You do not need to act out any of the phrases by changing the pitch of your voice or feigning emotion. Scripture already contains all the drama and power required for its proper expression. You need merely to voice it.

"Less is more" might be a useful axiom for proclaiming, but you don't want to excuse yourself from the work of proclaiming, which requires your presence for maximum effect. Your presence includes your voice, which allows you to announce the Word of God, but also your attention, which shows you where the stresses and emphases in the passage you are proclaiming lie. Simone Weil, the twentieth-century activist and mystic, wrote, "Absolutely unmixed attention is prayer." The attention you bring to your proclaiming enables you then to pray the Word of God with your congregation.

Readings Old and New

The Liturgy of the Word typically consists of a reading from the Old Testament (during Easter Time, it is from the Acts of the Apostles), a reading from the New Testament (often one of the letters of Paul), and a reading from the Gospels. In the case of Year B, which this *Workbook* covers, most of the Gospel readings come from Mark.

Gospel readings during Ordinary Time tend to go more or less in order, in Year B, starting from the beginning of Mark and working toward the end. Readings on feast days and during the seasons of Advent, Christmas, Lent, and Easter are selected specifically for those Sundays and don't necessarily follow a sequential order. Year B also has a five-week stretch with readings from the Gospel of John, the famous "Bread of Life" discourse. This is owed in part to the brevity of Mark's Gospel, the shortest of the four. The first reading—again, typically from the Old Testament—is selected to harmonize with the Gospel reading.

The second reading—again, often from one of the letters of Paul, but not always—is more deliberately instructive. Usually, from week to week at Sunday Mass, you will notice that one Sunday's second reading picks up where the previous week's left off.

Each of these parts of Scripture can be proclaimed differently, with subtle but valuable effects. First readings tend to be more poetic than second readings. You can effectively infuse your first reading with forms of poetic attention, being mindful especially of pauses, but also of some of the other rhetorical features that make Scripture so rich. These include

anaphora, which is the use of the repetition of a word or phrase;

parallel structure, in which an entire phrase is repeated with slight variation;

the imperative voice, in which the speaker commands the audience to do something, usually to *listen,* to hear, and to *heed;*

and *the power of questions,* in which the speaker asks forceful questions not necessarily easy or comfortable to answer.

Magnify the LORD with me; let us exalt his name together.

Each of these rhetorical features serves to enhance the power of the words and phrases in the reading.

Consider the first reading for the Eighteenth Sunday in Ordinary Time, from the sixteenth chapter of Exodus. This reading concerns God's gift of manna to feed the grumbling Israelites wandering in the desert of Sinai. Toward the end of the reading, you find:

In the evening quail came up and covered
the camp.
In the morning a dew lay all about the camp,
and when the dew evaporated, there
on the surface of the desert
were fine flakes like hoarfrost on
the ground.

The use of "in the evening" and "in the morning" is an *anaphora.* The longer sentences they introduce are examples of *parallel structure.* The mysterious heart of the passage beats in the *question,* "What is this?" You'll also notice the use of alliteration—repetition of a consonant sound—in this passage, especially in the phrase, "fine flakes like hoarfrost," in which the sound of the letter *f* is repeated three times. Alliteration, like other forms of repetition, makes language more memorable. Recognizing these patterns can show you how best to read these verses.

The Gospel for the Eighteenth Sunday in Ordinary Time comes from the stretch of John's Gospel mentioned above, in which Jesus describes himself as the Bread of Life. Among other things, this Gospel reading signals to us that the Israelites' hunger in the desert will be fulfilled in Christ. In this respect, the experience of the Israelites prefigures the experience of those assembled to hear Jesus

preach. And just so, it prefigures our experience as worshippers listening to these passages from Scripture read aloud as part of the Liturgy of the Word at Mass, preparing us for the Liturgy of the Eucharist to follow, when we will be fed the Bread of Life.

The second reading for the Eighteenth Sunday in Ordinary Time offers a reading from Paul's Letter to the Ephesians, which is introduced three weeks earlier, on the Fifteenth Sunday in Ordinary Time. It's not connected the way the first reading and the Gospel are. It doesn't speak of or suggest anything about the Bread of Life. Instead, it's meant to immerse us in Paul's instructions to the members of the early Church in Ephesus, imagining ourselves in that audience and learning the imperative to "put on the new self, created in God's way in righteousness and holiness of truth." Where the first reading is often poetic, the second reading is typically instructive. It's also almost always a shorter reading. You should proclaim it as instruction. Read slowly, take your time presenting its argument, and emphasize its point, which will come in the last sentence or two of the reading.

First and second readings always conclude with the phrase "The Word of the Lord." Try to pause a moment before you read this conclusion. Likewise, don't rush through the phrase. It will blur, sounding like "Word Lord." Instead, break the phrase into two units, reading it like this: The WORD | of the LORD. It's effective to pause for two or three beats after you say this before stepping away from the ambo.

Preparation and Execution

It helps to practice. You should read through your assigned reading at least a few times, once silently to yourself to get its sense and two or three times aloud to get a feel for its rhythm and pace, as well as any unusual words, names, or place names. (The marginal pronunciation guides will help you with these.)

If you are assigned to proclaim the first reading, read the Gospel for that week as well. They will be connected in thematic ways. If you are assigned to proclaim the second reading, take a look at the previous week's second reading, as well as the following week's, to see where the second reading is coming from and where it is going. This will give you some context for the insights it contains.

For many of us, our main experience reading aloud comes from reading to children. Proclaiming Scripture is something different. When you practice reading aloud, it's better to read in as straightforward a way as possible than it is to try to dramatize your reading through inflection, pitch, or voicing in the way you might if you were reading something to a child. Scripture is unusually powerful in its expressiveness, symbolism, and language. If you read in a steady, evenly pitched, and articulate voice, its power will come through your reading. You will be during Mass the instrument for its power.

For many people, it can be a little intimidating to stand before a congregation and proclaim. You might find it helpful to place one of your index fingers in the margin of the lectionary to remind you of your place. You might also find it helpful to place your other hand on the ambo to steady yourself. This has the effect of giving you the appearance of an open posture.

As you read, try to look up from time to time and make eye contact. Choose faces in different places of the assembled congregation to focus on when you look up, sometimes close by, sometimes farther back, and sometimes from one side to the other. This simple gesture has an inclusive effect; you are not merely reading *to* the congregation, you are reading *for* it and *with* it. If you use your index finger to keep your place in the lectionary, you will not worry about getting lost whenever you look up.

That said, you are not performing. You don't need to smile unnecessarily, you don't need to emote beyond what the words themselves suggest, and you don't need somehow to exemplify the words in your comportment or your presentation. The words of Scripture are utterly endowed with power. You are the instrument to voice that power. A sincere and plainspoken proclamation will invariably convey that power to your fellow assembly members.

For the purposes of your proclaiming, you can usefully consider readings falling into three general forms: narrative, didactic, and exhortatory. (These designations are taken from Douglas Leal, author of *Stop Reading and Start Proclaiming!*, and an author for *Workbook* in previous years.)

A *narrative* reading tells a story, containing a plot. It moves from point to point and typically comes to a conclusion. Many of these stories, because of their repetition in the liturgy but also because of their importance to Christian thought, are very familiar. Take some pleasure in that familiarity while also encouraging your assembly to listen to the whole story, including all of its setup and context, which you can do by focusing on the pace of the story and its rhythm as accented in its language.

A *didactic* reading offers instruction, often leading to a specific point of teaching or faith. Paul's letters are typically didactic. He is trying to instruct members of the early Church on how to behave and what to believe. So much of what Paul writes is new to these communities, and therefore confusing. Paul's tone sometimes betrays his exasperation. He wants these followers to understand! When you read a didactic reading, imagine yourself not as the letter's writer (whether Paul or James or John or Peter, for instance) but as the recipient of that letter. Put yourself in the shoes of its hearer, which is exactly what you and your congregation are.

An *exhortatory* reading is one that makes an urgent appeal. (It comes from the word *exhort*, which comes from *ex-*, an intensifier, plus *hortari*, "to urge," and means to thoroughly urge or encourage.) Many of the writings from the prophets in the Old Testament are exhortatory, urging their listeners to change their lives or to prepare themselves for some divinely mandated change. Likewise, the Gospels contain exhortations when Jesus is preaching and even when he is talking to his disciples. An exhortatory reading is like God directly addressing us. When you proclaim an exhortatory reading, treat it as though it is intended for you personally. Imagine you are hearing it for the first time.

Participation

For inspiration, consider these words by Pierre Teilhard de Chardin, from *The Divine Milieu*, his "essay on the interior life."

> We may, perhaps, imagine that the Creation was finished long ago. But that would be quite wrong. It continues still more magnificently, and in the highest zones of the world. *Omnis creatura adhuc ingemescit et parturit.* And we serve to complete it, even by the humblest work of our hands. That is, ultimately, the meaning and value of our acts. Owing to the inter-relation between matter, soul, and Christ, we lead part of the being which He desires back to God *in whatever we do.* With each one of our *works,* we labor—atomically, but no less really—to build the Pleroma; that is to say, to bring to Christ a little fulfillment.

For Teilhard, "Pleroma" means the mysterious fullness of creation. The Latin phrase *omnis creatura adhuc ingemescit et parturit* refers to Romans 8:22, "all creation is groaning in labor pains until now." We are still in the process of creation; whenever you participate in the Mass, you are adding to that work. And whenever you proclaim at Mass, you are helping, by the humblest work of your voice, to bring to Christ a little fulfillment.

Peter O'Leary

The Authors

Catherine Cory is associate professor of theology at the University of St. Thomas in St. Paul, MN. She holds a doctorate in New Testament studies with subspecialties in Old Testament and early Church. Her research interests are in the Gospel of John and Revelation. She has edited and/or authored several books including *The Christian Theological Tradition*, *A Voyage through the New Testament*, and *Revelation* for the New Collegeville Bible Commentary series. In addition to her academic teaching at the undergraduate and graduate level, she enjoys doing adult education presentations at local parishes.

Elizabeth M. Nagel is a professor emerita of biblical exegesis at the University of Saint Mary of the Lake / Mundelein Seminary and a retired president of its Pontifical Faculty of Theology. She earned the licentiate (SSL) and doctorate (SSD) in Sacred Scripture at the Pontifical Biblical Institute and is the author of *Be a Blessing: A Spring of Refreshment on the Road of Daily Life* and a contributor to the *Paulist Biblical Commentary* (2018).

Peter O'Leary studied religion and literature at the Divinity School of the University of Chicago, where he received his doctorate. He has written several books of poetry, most recently, *Earth Is Best*, as well as two books of literary criticism, most recently *Thick and Dazzling Darkness: Religious Poetry in a Secular Age*. He teaches at the School of the Art Institute of Chicago and at the University of Chicago. He lives with his family in Oak Park, Illinois.

Stephen S. Wilbricht, CSC, is associate professor in the Religious Studies and Theology Department at Stonehill College in Easton, MA. He holds a doctorate in sacred theology from the Catholic University of America in Washington, DC, and has served in two parishes in the Southwest. He is the author of several books, including *Baptismal Ecclesiology and the Order of Christian Funerals* (LTP, 2018), *The Role of the Priest in Christian Initiation* (LTP, 2017), and *Rehearsing God's Just Kingdom: The Eucharistic Vision of Mark Searle* (Liturgical Press, 2013). He is also a team member for LTP's *Catechumeneon*.

The author's initials appear at the end of the Scripture commentaries.

An Option to Consider

The third edition of *The Roman Missal* encourages ministers of the Word to chant the introduction and conclusion to the readings ("A reading from . . . "; "The word of the Lord"). For those parishes wishing to use these chants, they are demonstrated in audio files that may be accessed either through the QR codes given here (with a smartphone) or through the URL indicated beneath the code. This URL is case sensitive, so be careful to distinguish between the letter l (lowercase L) and the numeral 1.

The first QR code contains the tones for the first reading in both a male and a female voice.

http://bit.ly/l2mjeG

The second QR code contains the tones for the second reading in both a male and a female voice.

http://bit.ly/krwEYy

The third QR code contains the simple tone for the Gospel.

http://bit.ly/iZZvSg

The fourth QR code contains the solemn tone for the Gospel.

http://bit.ly/lwf6Hh

A fuller explanation of this new practice, along with musical notation for the chants, is provided in a downloadable PDF file found at http://www.ltp.org /t-productsupplements.aspx. Once you arrive at this web page, scroll until you find the image of the cover of *Workbook*, click on it, and the PDF file will appear.

Recommended Works

Find a list of recommended reading and assistance in considering and implementing chanted introductions and conclusions to the readings in downloadable PDF files at http://www.ltp.org/products/details /WL21.

Pronunciation Key

bait = bayt	thin = thin
cat = kat	vision = VIZH*n
sang = sang	ship = ship
father = FAH-ther	sir = ser
care = kayr	gloat = gloht
paw = paw	cot = kot
jar = jahr	noise = noyz
easy = EE-zee	poison = POY-z*n
her = her	plow = plow
let = let	although = ahl-THOH
queen = kween	church = cherch
delude = deh-LOOD	fun = fuhn
when = hwen	fur = fer
ice = īs	flute = floot
if = if	foot = foot
finesse = fih-NES	

Shorter Readings

In the Scripture readings reproduced in this book, shorter readings are indicated by brackets and a citation given at the end of the reading.

FIRST SUNDAY OF ADVENT

LECTIONARY #2

READING I   Isaiah 63:16b–17, 19b; 64:2–7

A reading from the Book of the Prophet Isaiah

> **You**, Lord, are our **father**,
>   our **redeemer** you are named **forever**.
> Why do you let us **wander**, O Lord, from your **ways**,
>   and **harden** our **hearts** so that we **fear** you **not**?
> **Return** for the **sake** of your **servants**,
>   the **tribes** of your **heritage**.
> Oh, that you would **rend** the **heavens** and come **down**,
>   with the **mountains quaking** before you,
> while you wrought **awesome deeds** we could not **hope** for,
>   such as they had not **heard** of from of **old**.
> No ear has ever **heard**, no eye ever **seen**, any God but you
>   doing such **deeds** for those who wait for him.
> **Would** that you might **meet** us doing **right**,
>   that we were **mindful** of you in our ways!
> **Behold**, you are **angry**, and we are **sinful**;
>   all of us have **become** like unclean **people**,
>   all our **good deeds** are like polluted **rags**;
> we have all **withered** like **leaves**,
>   and our **guilt** carries us **away** like the **wind**.
> There is **none** who calls upon your name,
>   who **rouses** himself to **cling** to you;
> for you have **hidden** your face from us
>   and have **delivered** us up to our **guilt**. »

Isaiah = ī-ZAY-uh

An exhortatory reading. Most of this reading is delivered in a pleading and even accusatory tone. This will come through in reading; no need to play it up. The language itself is powerful. Trust in its rhythms.

Here the pleading tone becomes more penitent.

Slight pause here.

READING I The new Christian liturgical year begins with a fervent prayer for restoration. Although originally uttered in the context of the Hebrew people's return from captivity in Babylon in the sixth century BC, the words of the prophet Isaiah are just as powerful and poignant in our day. Great hope was certainly in the hearts of all of those called to journey back to the land of their ancestors. Yet their return was far from joyful. Instead, they found their Temple in ruins and their lands pillaged and burned. Even with this devastation before them, they called out in confidence to God, knowing that he alone could make their return a source of blessing.

A basic key to grasping the covenantal relationship between God and his chosen people Israel is the cycle of exile and return. Sin leads to the people's punishment, but banishment from grace allows the nation the opportunity to repent. In turn, God sees their repentance and chooses them as his own once again. This theological cycle of redemption is the foundation of the prophet's desire to summon the people as a whole back to Jerusalem despite its ravaged and forsaken condition. To "return" is to acknowledge the never-ending power of God to maintain and fortify the covenant, even in what appears to be a time of unsurmountable misfortune.

Isaiah calls out to God with questions: "Why do you let us wander, O Lord, from your ways, and harden our hearts so that we fear you not?" Recall here the wanderings of the Israelites in the desert and God's hardening of Pharaoh's heart (Exodus 7:3) so that the Israelites would have to work that much harder for their freedom. God desires a people who has to seek out his mercy and forgiveness. Pleading for God's

1

Shift your tone here; a little more uplifting.

Yet, O LORD, you are **our** father;
   we are the **clay** and you the **potter**:
   we are **all** the **work** of your **hands**.

For meditation and context:

RESPONSORIAL PSALM   Psalm 80:2–3, 15–16, 18–19 (4)

R. Lord, make us turn to you; let us see your face and we shall be saved.

O shepherd of Israel, hearken,
   from your throne upon the cherubim,
     shine forth.
Rouse your power,
   and come to save us.

Once again, O LORD of hosts,
   look down from heaven, and see;
take care of this vine,
   and protect what your right hand
     has planted,
   the son of man whom you yourself
     made strong.

May your help be with the man of your
   right hand,
   with the son of man whom you yourself
     made strong.
Then we will no more withdraw from you;
   give us new life, and we will call upon
     your name.

> **TO KEEP IN MIND**
> The responsorial psalm "has great liturgical and pastoral importance, since it fosters meditation on the Word of God," the *General Instruction on the Roman Missal* says. Pray it as you prepare.

Corinthians = kohr-IN-thee-uhnz

A didactic reading that expresses thanksgiving to God and to the community Paul is addressing.

READING II   1 Corinthians 1:3–9

A reading from the first Letter of Saint Paul to the Corinthians

Brothers and sisters:
Grace to you and **peace** from **God** our **Father**
   and the **Lord** Jesus **Christ**.

I give **thanks** to my God **always** on your **account**
   for the grace of God **bestowed** on you in **Christ** Jesus,
   that in him you were **enriched** in every way,
   with all **discourse** and all **knowledge**,
   as the **testimony** to **Christ** was **confirmed** among you,
   so that you are not **lacking** in any **spiritual gift**
   as you wait for the **revelation** of our **Lord** Jesus **Christ**.

awesome wonders on behalf of the people, Isaiah calls the nation to greater fidelity and a renewed hope that God will provide.

READING II Although the art of letter writing is threatened in today's world of emailing, texting, and face-to-face conversation over the internet, there remains a certain protocol about initial greetings in correspondence. Paul is a master letter writer! His opening salutations are words of gratitude for the members of the community to which he is writing. With artful prose, Paul wants the Christians of Corinth to know that they are grace filled as they listen to his words.

However, Paul begins with words of praise and thanksgiving so that he can later challenge the Corinthians in this same letter. This is a community known to possess many spiritual gifts and talents. The question for Paul is whether these spiritual gifts are being ordered to the building up of the Body of Christ. He is concerned that there is a good deal of self-righteousness as well as exclusion within this community. Thus, he instructs them to recognize that God's faithfulness is directly tied to their being called to "fellowship with his Son." There is much to be thankful for in God's grace at work in the community at Corinth, but the desire to share various and unique gifts for the sake of unity remains a great challenge.

GOSPEL The word "watch" is repeated several times in this short passage near the end of Mark's Gospel. Here Jesus compares "the watch" to the work of a gatekeeper who vigilantly remains alert at the door for his master's return. But what is the attitude of the gatekeeper, and what is the nature of his watch?

irreproachable = eer-rih-PROH-chuh-b*l
= without blame

Readings from Paul's letters tend to come to an instructive or uplifting conclusion, as here. Shift your tone in this direction.

He will keep you firm to the end,
    irreproachable on the day of our **Lord** Jesus **Christ**.
God is **faithful**,
    and by **him** you were **called** to **fellowship** with his **Son**,
Jesus Christ our **Lord**.

GOSPEL   Mark 13:33–37

A reading from the holy Gospel according to Mark

An exhortatory reading. Watchfulness and vigilance are the watchwords of Advent. This reading comes from the apocalyptic chapter in Mark's Gospel. The reading is infused with anticipatory power. Each use of the word "watch" and "watchful" intensifies this anticipation.

Jesus **said** to his **disciples**:
"Be watchful! Be **alert**!
You do not **know** when the **time** will **come**.
It is like a **man** traveling abroad.
He leaves **home** and places his **servants** in charge,
    each with his own **work**,
    and orders the **gatekeeper** to be on the **watch**.
Watch, therefore;
    you **do not know** when the **lord** of the **house** is coming,
    whether in the **evening**, or at **midnight**,
    or at **cockcrow**, or in the **morning**.

This is the core of the reading.

May he not come suddenly and find you **sleeping**.
What I say to you, I say to all: '**Watch**!'"

Is it one of fear at what his master might find when he comes home? Or is it one of great expectations, in which the gatekeeper is focused on a grand and celebratory reunion? Certainly, the true Christian attitude is the latter.

While he is forecasting his return in glory, Jesus also needs his friends to be by his side and to follow him faithfully to the cross. Throughout Mark's Gospel, the ones Jesus chose to be his disciples fail to understand what watching is all about; they fail to see Jesus for who he truly is. Thus, he orders them sternly to watch, to keep alert, and to

be ready when their service is needed. Yet we know that these are the men whom Jesus will find sleeping in the garden during his trial with agony and prayer.

The season of Advent is designed to be a time of fine-tuning our Christian attitude of hopeful, joyful watching. In the Northern Hemisphere, these days of waiting correspond to the darkest days of the year, a time that lures the human body into sluggishness. Yet that is not the posture of the Christian community. We are to hear and obey the summons of the Lord to be alert and watchful. Our watching constitutes

yearning for a world renewed by God and made perfect by his love and mercy. Using our gifts for others is the best way to stand ready and alert. S. W.

SECOND SUNDAY
OF ADVENT

LECTIONARY #5

READING I Isaiah 40:1–5, 9–11

Isaiah = ī-ZAY-uh

An exhortatory reading full of good news in poetic language. Let the language draw your recitation along.

expiated = EK-spee-ayt-*d = paid for

Slight pause.

A reading from the Book of the Prophet Isaiah

> **Comfort**, give **comfort** to my **people**,
> says your God.
> Speak **tenderly** to **Jerusalem**, and **proclaim** to her
> that her **service** is at an **end**,
> her **guilt** is expiated;
> indeed, she has **received** from the **hand** of the LORD
> **double** for all her sins.
>
> A **voice cries** out:
> In the desert **prepare** the **way** of the **LORD**!
> **Make straight** in the **wasteland** a **highway** for our God!
> Every **valley** shall be filled in,
> every **mountain** and **hill** shall be made **low**;
> the rugged **land** shall be **made** a **plain**,
> the rough **country**, a broad **valley**.
> Then the **glory** of the LORD shall be **revealed**,
> and all **people** shall **see** it together;
> for the **mouth** of the LORD has **spoken**.

TO KEEP IN MIND

If you are assigned to proclaim the first reading, read the Gospel for that week as well. They are connected in thematic ways.

READING I Chapter 40 of the Book of Isaiah begins the portion of Isaiah that is referred to by Scripture scholars as Deutero (meaning "Second") Isaiah. From chapters 40 to 55, the prophet speaks words of comfort to the people of Israel, who have just completed their time of exile in Babylon. Imagine having been torn away from your home and your community, forced into labor for a foreign people, adapting to a new way of life in a land not your own, and then being invited to return to your homeland, which had been occupied by others and destroyed in the process. The summons to return would undoubtedly be met with a certain fear and resistance. Many exiles had to say to themselves, "We're doing just fine in our new home; why would we ever want to go back there?"

Nevertheless, Isaiah reassures the people that no longer shall they feel punished by God. Instead, they will experience the reward of God's care. Once again, he will be a shepherd for his people. He will give them courage to make known the good news of their return to all the nations. As Israel rejoices once again in its chosen status, their joy will echo forth to all the world as an invitation to see the revelation of the Lord's glory. Freedom from exile is not only for the people of Israel; it is for the salvation of every nation. "Then the glory of the Lord shall be revealed, and all people shall see it together."

Deutero-Isaiah attempts here to balance words of comfort with the command to prepare the Lord's way. In their return from exile, the people are to make their pilgrimage homeward by imagining the world

4

Almost all of the words in this line are evenly emphasized. Notice the assonance (repeated S sound) in "Zion" and "tidings."

Slight emphasis here on "power."

recompense = REK-uhm-pens = reward for wrongs suffered

Go **up onto** a high **mountain**,
 Zion, **herald** of **glad tidings**;
cry out at the **top** of your **voice**,
 Jerusalem, **herald** of **good news**!
Fear **not** to cry **out**
 and say to the **cities** of Judah:
 Here is your God!
Here comes with **power**
 the Lord **God**,
 who **rules** by his **strong arm**;
here is his **reward** with **him**,
 his recompense **before** him.
Like a shepherd he **feeds** his **flock**;
 in his **arms** he **gathers** the **lambs**,
 carrying them in his **bosom**,
 and **leading** the **ewes** with **care**.

For meditation and context:

RESPONSORIAL PSALM   Psalm 85:9–10, 11–12, 13–14 (8)

R. Lord, let us see your kindness, and grant us your salvation.

I will hear what God proclaims;
 the Lord—for he proclaims peace to
 his people.
Near indeed is his salvation to those who
 fear him,
 glory dwelling in our land.

Kindness and truth shall meet;
 justice and peace shall kiss.
Truth shall spring out of the earth,
 and justice shall look down from heaven.

The Lord himself will give his benefits;
 our land shall yield its increase.
Justice shall walk before him,
 and prepare the way of his steps.

anew and by trusting that the Lord journeys with them. Images of straight highways, mountains made low, and valleys turned into plains are not simply for the prophet and his people of long ago. Instead, they represent the wonder of all that God is accomplishing for his people today. His is a strong arm that can do all things. Yet this is the tender shepherd who never lets his sheep go astray.

READING II The Second Letter of Peter is generally considered to be pseudepigraphical, meaning that Peter himself was not the author. In fact, scholars generally date the letter to have been written sometime between the very end of the first century until as late as AD 150. This means that the Church addressed by the author had been waiting for the Lord's return for a very long time. It must have become difficult for many followers to remain faithful given the fact that Christ's message of coming back seems to have

been misunderstood. For this reason, the author attempts to call the church to remain faithful by trying to make sense of time in God's eyes, comparing one day to a thousand years and a thousand years to a single day. God's Kingdom is surely beyond time. When we try to imagine the coming of God's Kingdom according to our experience of the ticking of the clock, the ordering of the day, and the turning of the pages on a calendar, we necessarily find ourselves confounded. Instead, Christian vigilance for the coming of that day must

READING II   2 Peter 3:8–14

A reading from the second Letter of Saint Peter

beloved = bee-LUHV-hud

A didactic reading that contains instruction. Proclaim it with that in mind.

This is the first point in Peter's letter.

Do not ignore this **one fact**, beloved,
    that with the **Lord one day** is like a thousand **years**
    and a thousand **years** like one **day**.
The Lord does not **delay** his **promise**, as some regard "**delay**,"
    but he is **patient** with you,
    not **wishing** that any should **perish**
    but that all should **come** to repentance.

This is the second point.

But the **day** of the **Lord** will **come** like a **thief**,
    and then the **heavens** will **pass away** with a mighty roar
    and the **elements** will be **dissolved** by **fire**,
    and the **earth** and everything **done on it** will be **found out**.

This is the third point. Focus on "holiness" and "devotion."

Since **everything** is to be **dissolved** in this way,
    what sort of **persons** ought you to **be**,
    conducting yourselves in **holiness** and **devotion**,
    waiting for and **hastening** the coming of the **day of God**,
    because of which the **heavens** will be **dissolved** in **flames**
    and the **elements** melted by **fire**.

This is the fourth point. With the word "but," Peter is shifting toward his conclusion.

But according to his **promise**
    we await new **heavens** and a new **earth**
    in which righteousness dwells.

And here is the conclusion. Slow your pace slightly with "at peace."

Therefore, beloved, since you **await** these things,
    be **eager** to be found without **spot** or **blemish** before him,
      at **peace**.

---

yield patience and repentance. In a sense, time for Christians is time beyond time.

Some who read these latter-day words issued to the Church might tremble in fear at the scene they convey—heavens passing away with a mighty sound and elements dissolved by fire—but those with a deep, abiding faith are able to hope in a new heaven and a new earth. Those of faith are able to live with devotion and fortitude and are capable of reaching out for God's mercy. Because the Lord does not delay in fulfilling his promise, the Church must be at peace and act as though he is there among them once again. Given the fact that many Christians in our world fail to understand the importance of the Lord's imminent return as a concrete reality, we must hear these words today as a challenge to act with justice and to be a people at peace.

GOSPEL On the Second Sunday of Advent we read of two iconic figures who embody the Advent attitude. First, the prophet Isaiah reveals the promise of a God who wishes to rebuild and restore relationship with Israel. Likewise, we are to hear the prophet challenging us to build up the world anew in God's redeeming grace. Second, John the Baptist takes center stage this Sunday, as we see clearly his attitudes of self-denial and humility. Mary, whom we will celebrate this week on the occasion of her Immaculate Conception, is yet another outstanding figure who combines all of these attitudes, as she humbly offers herself for the restoration of the world.

The very opening of Mark's Gospel is meant to place its readers into the mysterious environment of the desert. Deserts have been considered places of purification

GOSPEL   Mark 1:1–8

A reading from the holy Gospel according to Mark

The **beginning** of the **gospel** of **Jesus Christ** the **Son** of **God**.

As it is written in **Isaiah** the **prophet**:
> *Behold*, *I am sending my **messenger ahead** of you;*
>> *he will prepare your way.*
> *A **voice** of one **crying out** in the **desert**:*
>> *"**Prepare** the **way** of the **Lord**,*
>> *make **straight** his **paths**."*

John the Baptist **appeared** in the **desert**
  proclaiming a **baptism** of **repentance** for the
    forgiveness of **sins**.
People of the **whole** Judean countryside
  and all the **inhabitants** of Jerusalem
  were going **out** to him
  and were being **baptized** by him in the **Jordan River**
  as they **acknowledged** their sins.
John was clothed in **camel's hair**,
  with a leather **belt** around his **waist**.
He fed on **locusts** and **wild honey**.
And this is what he **proclaimed**:
  "One **mightier** than I is coming after me.
I am not **worthy** to **stoop** and **loosen** the thongs of his sandals.
I have **baptized** you with **water**;
  he will **baptize you** with the **Holy Spirit**."

A narrative reading. Here, John the Baptist's role as forerunner is directly related to Hebrew prophecy. John is like a figure out of antiquity, preparing for Christ's arrival. Treat the prophetic quotation and the words of John the Baptist as belonging to the same prefiguring intelligence.

John the Baptist's attributes are crucial to his authenticity as a prophet. Linger slightly on them.

The Holy Spirit is elemental like water but superior to it.

since time immemorial. Men and women ascetics attempt to escape the ways of the world by seeking out the desert's harshness. Deserts are places where only the unknown is certain. In deserts, one might walk for miles without finding a source for water, and encountering poisonous creatures is a constant anxiety. In deserts, light bounces off sand and rocks, playing tricks on the imagination. Thus, it is the desert where John the Baptist finds himself most at home. In the harsh environment of the desert, he chooses to live a completely austere life, with meager dress and a diet consisting of locusts and wild honey. He lives apart from the rest of the society in order to purify himself and to call others to the baptism of repentance.

John the Baptist is the precursor, the one who comes to prepare the way for the one who is to follow. Unlike those Jesus choses to be his disciples, John embodies the characteristics of a true disciple. It is clear from Mark's Gospel that his effort to herald the coming of God's Kingdom and the need for the people to respond with a complete change of life was very successful. Mark tells us that people from the whole countryside and those from the city of Jerusalem were going out to hear John and being baptized by him as they acknowledged their sins. The disciple's call is to attract people to embrace conversion. John is an undeniable success, but remains humble in his ministry. Every Christian is to embody the selfless outlook of John the Baptist, one who is willing to decrease so that the Lord himself may increase (John 3:6). S. W.

THE IMMACULATE CONCEPTION OF THE BLESSED VIRGIN MARY

LECTIONARY #689

READING I   Genesis 3:9–15, 20

A reading from the Book of Genesis

This reading contains some of the conclusion of one of the foundational narratives of our faith. Because it is a very familiar story, slow your recitation slightly to emphasize its richness.

After the man, **Adam**, had **eaten** of the **tree**,
   the Lord God **called** to the man and **asked** him,
      "Where are you?"
He answered, "I **heard** you in the **garden**;
   but I was **afraid**, because I was **naked**,
   so I **hid myself**."
Then he asked, "Who **told** you that you were **naked**?
You have **eaten**, then,
   from the **tree** of which I had **forbidden** you to **eat**!"

The shifting of blame from Adam to Eve and then from Eve to the serpent is crucial to the reading's drama. You can locate this shift in the repetition of the word "woman."

The man replied, "The **woman** whom you **put here** with me—
   she **gave me fruit** from the **tree**, and so I **ate** it."
The Lord God then asked the **woman**,
   "Why did you **do** such a **thing**?"
The woman answered, "The **serpent tricked me** into it,
   so I **ate** it."

Here, the scorn is heaped on the serpent. The punishment God metes out is as cruel as it is deserved.

Then the Lord God said to the **serpent**:
   "**Because** you have done this, you shall be **banned**
      from all the **animals**
      and from all the **wild creatures**;
   on your **belly** shall you **crawl**,
      and **dirt** shall you **eat**
      all the **days** of your **life**.

READING I The first eleven chapters of the Book of Genesis constitute a unit of Scripture known by scholars as the "primeval history." The characters and plot line of this unit are designed to answer such questions as: How did the world come into being? Why do such things as sin and death exist? Why does God choose to forgive in the case of rebellion?

The story chosen from Genesis for the Solemnity of the Immaculate Conception is the well-known story of the fall of Adam and Eve. At the heart of this story is the contrast between the beauty of God's abundant love symbolized by the Garden of Eden versus the ugliness of the curse that would plague the world and all subsequent generations of humanity. Prior to their act of disobedience against God, Adam and Eve lived at peace in the garden without pain, anxiety, shame, or fear. Such things were not a part of God's original plan of creation, Genesis suggests, but came about as a result of striving for the knowledge that belongs to God alone. We see here the human desire to grasp at being God rather than fully cooperating with God's designs.

The portion of the fall chosen to be read for today's liturgy focuses particularly on the severed relationship between the serpent and the woman. God puts "enmity" between them and commands that one will strike at the other. From this point forward, the humans will struggle with their stewardship of creation. No longer will all the creatures of the earth act as partners joined peaceably with their human counterparts. Instead, they will be at odds with one another. Furthermore, although not a part of the curse uttered by God in these verses, the verses that follow immediately suggest

8

enmity = EN-mih-tee = mutual hatred

I will put **enmity** between **you** and the **woman**,
    and between your **offspring** and hers;
he will **strike** at your **head**,
    while you **strike** at his **heel**."

The reading ends with Eve being named. The shift from "woman" to "Eve" feels significant. Convey this in your reading.

The man called his wife **Eve**,
    because she became the **mother** of **all** the **living**.

For meditation and context:

RESPONSORIAL PSALM Psalm 98:1, 2–3ab, 3cd–4 (1a)

R. Sing to the Lord a new song, for he has done marvelous deeds.

Sing to the LORD a new song,
    for he has done wondrous deeds;
His right hand has won victory for him,
    his holy arm.

The LORD has made his salvation known:
    in the sight of the nations he has
    revealed his justice.

He has remembered his kindness and his
    faithfulness
    toward the house of Israel.

All the ends of the earth have seen
    the salvation by our God.
Sing joyfully to the LORD, all you lands;
    break into song; sing praise.

READING II Ephesians 1:3–6, 11–12

Ephesians = ee-FEE-zhuhnz

A reading from the Letter of Saint Paul to the Ephesians

Brothers and sisters:

Blessed = BLES-uhd
Blessed = blesd
An exhortatory reading. Notice the three divisions: "Blessed be the God and Father . . . ," "In love he destined us . . . ," and "In him we were also chosen." Use these divisions to organize your reading.

Blessed be the **God** and **Father** of our **Lord** Jesus Christ,
    who has **blessed** us in Christ
    with **every spiritual blessing** in the **heavens**,
    as he chose us **in him**, before the **foundation** of the **world**,
    to be **holy** and without **blemish** before him.
In **love** he **destined us** for **adoption** to himself through
        Jesus Christ,
    in **accord** with the **favor** of his will,
    for the **praise** of the **glory** of his **grace**
    that he **granted** us in the **beloved**. »

Slight emphasis on "praise," "glory," and "grace."

---

that the pain of childbirth is the punishment for all women, and the curse of hard physical labor is to be the lot of all men. In a very real way, banishment from the Garden of Eden and distance from the direct presence of God result in a world that is governed by struggle on every level.

READING II Although the early Church was relatively silent about the topic of predestination, this reading from Ephesians certainly hints at the importance of God's choice in determining who is to receive his favor. The author states

that God "chose us in him (Christ), before the foundation of the world." It seems as though this act of choosing clearly suggests that some are chosen by God and others are not. We must ask ourselves, What does it mean for God to favor some over others?

However, what is really the author's concern is not to open a discussion regarding predestination, but rather to demonstrate how great is the need to bless God's name for all his many gifts, especially that of being called to be holy. The word for "blessing" in Hebrew is *berekah*, which is understood as a word of praise for God's

name. God provides a good gift, and we are to respond by blessing his holy name: "Blessed be the God and Father of our Lord Jesus Christ." How blessed is the name of our God "who has blessed us in Christ with every spiritual blessing in the heavens."

In the context of today's feast, it is good to ponder God's abundant blessing upon Mary, whom he predestined to be the mother of his Son by virtue of keeping her free from the corruption of Original Sin. Although talking about the blessing of Christ, one could easily replace his name with Mary's in this *berekah* prayer, for she

This is Paul's point.

You are assuring the assembly of this first hope.

A narrative reading of one of the most solemn passages in the Gospels, which is also one of the most frequently depicted by artists through the centuries. It's very easy to visualize as a result. Treat it like a pageant.

Because these words are so familiar from prayer, they can have a new life in the context of this reading.

In **him** we were also **chosen**,
  destined in accord with the **purpose** of the One
  who **accomplishes** all things according to the **intention**
    of his **will**,
  so that we might **exist** for the **praise** of his **glory**,
  we who **first hoped** in Christ.

GOSPEL   Luke 1:26–38

A reading from the holy Gospel according to Luke

The **angel Gabriel** was **sent** from God
to a **town** of **Galilee** called **Nazareth**,
  to a **virgin betrothed** to a man named **Joseph**,
  of the **house** of David,
  and the **virgin's name** was Mary.
And coming to her, he said,
  "**Hail**, **full** of **grace**! The **Lord** is with **you**."
But she was **greatly troubled** at what was **said**
  and **pondered** what sort of **greeting** this might be.
Then the **angel** said to her,
  "**Do not** be **afraid**, Mary,
  for you have found **favor** with God.

---

was likewise chosen by God "to be holy and without blemish before him."

We call Mary our Mother. The Letter to the Ephesians suggests that those chosen in Christ are destined to keep God's will and thereby "exist for the praise of his glory." We are invited to contemplate the mystery of Mary's Immaculate Conception, because in our Mother we see the perfect example of one who exists for nothing other than the praise of God's glory. In the Gospel passage that follows, the angel Gabriel proclaims Mary to be "full of grace."

Although we were not fashioned without sin, ours is the command to discover God's grace in every moment of our lives.

GOSPEL   The feast we celebrate is the Immaculate Conception of Mary, honoring Mary's sinlessness from the moment of her conception, a sinlessness that the Church understands remained intact for the rest of her life. Yet the Gospel passage we read today is Luke's account of the Annunciation, when the angel Gabriel appears to Mary and reveals

God's plan for her: "Hail, full of grace! The Lord is with you." We are led to ponder the grace of Mary's sinlessness by focusing on her humble response: "Behold, I am the handmaid of the Lord. May it be done to me according to your word."

Mary is the new Eve who is given the fullness of grace. However, unlike Eve, Mary remains obedient to God's voice throughout her life. It does us well to compare the deception of the serpent in the reading from Genesis to the fidelity of the angel in Luke. The serpent leads its victim astray,

"Most High" and "no end" share a rhythmical and thematic echo.

Behold, you will **conceive** in your womb and **bear** a son,
  and you shall **name him** Jesus.
He will be **great** and will be called **Son** of the **Most High**,
  and the **Lord God** will give him the **throne** of David
    his **father**,
  and he will **rule over** the house of **Jacob forever**,
  and of his **Kingdom** there will be **no end**."
But **Mary** said to the **angel**,
  "How can this **be**,
  since I have **no relations** with a **man**?"
And the **angel** said to her in **reply**,
  "The **Holy Spirit** will **come upon** you,
  and the **power** of the **Most High** will over**shadow** you.
Therefore the **child** to be **born**
  will be called **holy**, the **Son** of **God**.
And **behold**, Elizabeth, your relative,
  has **also conceived** a son in her old age,
  and this is the **sixth month** for her who was called **barren**;
  for **nothing** will be **impossible** for God."
Mary said, "**Behold**, I am the **handmaid** of the **Lord**.
May it be **done** to **me** according to **your word**."
Then the **angel departed** from her.

This is the good news that Gabriel delivers to Mary.
And Mary's declaration defines the role of all believers, including the Church.

TO KEEP IN MIND
Pause after you announce the book of the Bible at the beginning of the reading. Pause again after the reading, before you proclaim the concluding statement ("The Word of the Lord" or "The Gospel of the Lord").

---

while the angel opens Mary's eyes to the beauty of God's plan of salvation. Both Eve and Mary follow the message they are given. However, the underlying reason for the response is completely different. Eve picks the apple because she wants to grasp at being like God; Mary says yes to Gabriel's invitation in order to sacrifice herself for God. Undoubtedly, Mary deserved to be fearful at what the angel spoke, but she listened with intent and obeyed.

Furthermore, it is important to see that God's choice of Mary to be the bearer of his Son is such that the grandeur of his majesty is made manifest. God chooses the lowly virgin peasant girl in order to bring into the world the most precious gift of God's love, his only-begotten Son. If God had wanted, he could have come among us as a fully-grown person, or he could have been born into a family of wealth and status. Instead, his grace rested fully upon one who would have no influence or voice within her community, "for nothing will be impossible for God." As a faithful Jewish girl, Mary certainly was attuned to the working of God within her life. She spent her life discerning his movement in her life and was well prepared to offer herself as the chosen ark for God's Incarnation. Mary's sinlessness calls us to cooperate fully with God's will, making our response the giving of our whole selves. S. W.

THIRD SUNDAY OF ADVENT

LECTIONARY #8

READING I   Isaiah 61:1–2a, 10–11

Isaiah = ī-ZAY-uh

An exhortatory reading, filled with good news.

A reading from the Book of the Prophet Isaiah

The **spirit** of the **Lord GOD** is **upon** me,
    because the LORD has **anointed** me;
he has **sent me** to bring glad tidings to the **poor**,
    to **heal** the broken**hearted**,
to proclaim **liberty** to the **captives**
    and **release** to the **prisoners**,
to announce a **year** of **favor** from the LORD
    and a **day** of **vindication** by our **God**.

Slight emphasis on "God," "joy," and "soul," the heart of the reading.

I rejoice **heartily** in the LORD,
    in my **God** is the **joy** of my **soul**;
for he has **clothed me** with a **robe** of salvation
    and **wrapped me** in a **mantle** of justice,
like a **bridegroom** adorned with a **diadem**,
    like a **bride** bedecked with her **jewels**.

diadem = DĪ-uh-dem = crown

"Diadem," "bride," and "jewels": Note how these words echo each other sonically and thematically.

As the **earth** brings **forth** its **plants**,
    and a **garden** makes its **growth** spring up,
so will the Lord GOD make **justice** and **praise**
    spring up before all the **nations**.

READING I This proclamation of the prophet Isaiah most likely has a familiar ring to our ears because it is the passage that Jesus reads in the synagogue at the beginning of his ministry in the Gospel of Luke (Luke 4:16–19). However, Isaiah's prophecy predates Jesus by several centuries. These are challenging words directed to the nation of Israel upon its return from exile, which came to an end in 538 BC with the Persian victory over the Babylonians. The years following Israel's return to its cherished land proved to be very tumultuous. Not only did the recon-struction of the Temple mean a return to the religious requirement of animal sacri-fice, but also years of political instability when Israel was occupied first by the Greeks and then by the Romans. As a result, the Hebrew religion divided into competing sects that sought to win the people's loyalty.

This is the circumstance in which Isaiah appears, calling himself the "anointed." Freed from a captivity in a foreign land endured for more than forty years, the Hebrew people return to their land to find it destroyed and desecrated. Like their ances-tors before them in Egypt, they undoubtedly cried out, wondering why they had been led out of slavery only to experience such hun-ger and desolation. Isaiah works to reas-sure them that this is to be a time of favor for them by their God. A grand reversal will take place: "glad tidings" for the poor, "healing" for those who mourn, "liberty" for captives and prisoners, and a jubilee year for all!

Isaiah continues by articulating the attitude that Israel is to embrace, namely joy. "I rejoice heartily in the Lord, in my God is the joy of my soul." Even though the

For meditation and context:

RESPONSORIAL PSALM   Luke 1:46–48, 49–50, 53–54 (Isaiah 61:10b)

R. My soul rejoices in my God.

My soul proclaims the greatness of the Lord;
    my spirit rejoices in God my Savior,
for he has looked upon his lowly servant.
    From this day all generations will call
    me blessed.

The Almighty has done great things for me,
    and holy is his Name.

He has mercy on those who fear him
    in every generation.

He has filled the hungry with good things,
    and the rich he has sent away empty.
He has come to the help of his servant Israel
    for he has remembered his promise
    of mercy.

READING II   1 Thessalonians 5:16–24

A reading from the first Letter of Saint Paul to the Thessalonians

Brothers and sisters:
Rejoice **always**. **Pray** without **ceasing**.
In **all** circumstances give **thanks**,
    for **this** is the will of **God** for you in Christ **Jesus**.
Do not **quench** the **Spirit**.
Do not **despise** prophetic **utter**ances.
Test **everything**; retain what is **good**.
Refrain from every kind of **evil**.

May the **God** of **peace** make you **perfectly** holy
    and may you **entirely**, **spirit**, **soul**, and **body**,
    be preserved **blameless** for the **coming** of our Lord
        Jesus **Christ**.
The one who **calls you** is **faithful**,
    and he will **also** accomplish it.

A didactic reading. "Pray without ceasing" is one of the most mystical and compelling instructions in the New Testament. Paul is encouraging us to a life of total prayer.

Becoming perfectly and entirely holy, spirit, soul, and body, is the purpose of ceaseless prayer. Your reading can encourage the members of the assembly to want to accomplish this goal themselves.

temptation may be to look at the return to their destroyed and desolate land as a mistake, the prophet sees only potential and hope. He interprets this homecoming as a renewal of the covenant in which God will treat the nation as his espoused. Israel is to be like a bridegroom with a beautiful crown and a bride covered in jewels. Moreover, Israel's newfound fortune is to be a sign of justice for other nations to behold.

READING II The fifth chapter of his First Letter to the Thessalonians begins with Paul's admonition to the com-

munity to be sober and alert for the coming of the Lord. He contends that this vigilance is specifically tied to patience and caring conduct within the life of the community. The community at Thessalonica is called by Paul to work together to correct the reputation that circulates about them, as being idle busybodies (2 Thessalonians 3:11).

Paul then offers three basic Christian attitudes that are to serve as the foundation for holiness. First, followers of Jesus are to be people of joy: "Rejoice always." Second, they must be a people that prays always. Finally, disciples are a people of

thanks. Joy, prayer, and thanksgiving are to be the pattern of life for all who await the day of the Lord's return. With the fostering of these basic attitudes, Christians will be well suited for proper discernment. Guided by joy, prayer, and thanksgiving, the people will flourish in the Spirit and disciples will be able to sort out what is good and necessary for their spiritual welfare. In a world in which people proclaim themselves to have the message of truth or the formula for success, it is good to be reminded that joy, prayer, and a stance of thanks in Christ is the best route for discernment.

GOSPEL   John 1:6–8, 19–28

A reading from the holy Gospel according to John

A narrative reading with an anticipatory
focus on John the Baptist. What does
he know that others don't, and how does
he know these things?

A man named **John** was sent from **God**.
He came for **testimony**, to **testify** to the **light**,
　　so that all might **believe** through him.
He was not the **light**,
　　but came to **testify** to the **light**.

And this is the **testimony** of **John**.
When the **Jews** from **Jerusalem** sent **priests** and **Levites** to him
　　to ask him, "**Who are you?**"
　he **admitted** and did not **deny** it,
　　but **admitted**, "I am **not** the **Christ**."

This passage, with "Who are you,"
anticipates passages to be found in the
Gospels in which Jesus asks his disciples to
tell him what he is or who people say he is.
John (the evangelist) uses John the Baptist
imaginatively in this regard to show what he,
John the Baptist, is not and what Jesus who
comes will be.

So they asked him,
　　"What **are you** then? Are you **Elijah?**"
And he said, "I am **not**."
"Are you the **Prophet?**"
He answered, "**No**."
So they said to him,
　　"Who **are you**, so we can **give** an **answer** to **those** who **sent** us?
What do you have to **say** for yourself?"
He said:
　　"I am *the* **voice** *of one* **crying** *out in the* **desert**,
　　'*Make* **straight** *the* **way** *of the* **Lord**,'
　　as **Isaiah** the prophet said."
Some **Pharisees** were also sent.
They asked him,
　　"Why then do you **baptize**
　　if you are not the **Christ** or **Elijah** or the **Prophet?**"

Stress this line.

This passage from 1 Thessalonians
concludes with a prayer and a fervent affirmation of faith. Paul prays for the holiness
of the community and for their resolve to
live without fault. Then he reminds his hearers that God is the author of all this good
work and that it is God who will bring this
work to completion. So often the challenge
to live blamelessly with righteousness leads
to a puffed-up self, but it is God alone who
is at work within us, accomplishing all for
the well-being of his plan of salvation.

GOSPEL　The Third Sunday of Advent
is called by the Church
Gaudete Sunday, after the entrance anti-
phon, which begins "*Gaudete in Domino
semper: iterum dico, gaudete*" "Rejoice in
the Lord always; again I say, rejoice."
Today's liturgy calls for the accentuation of
the theme of joy. While we continue to
await joyfully the Lord's victorious return,
we draw nearer to our annual joyful celebration of his nativity. How does this passage from the opening of John's Gospel
correspond to the theme of joy? Quite

clearly, joy is manifested in John the
Baptist's testimony to the Messiah's coming. This ascetic has gathered a large following and has spent his days proclaiming
the need for the people's repentance and
their baptism into the Kingdom.

John knows full well that his ministry
is one of preparation. He freely acknowledges that he is not the Messiah whom the
people await, nor does he want to be considered a prophet who serves as a mouthpiece for God. And yet what a powerful
voice he is! He is the voice "crying out in

And slow down slightly with this line.

John answered them,
    "I **baptize** with **water**;
    but there is **one among you** whom you do not **recognize**,
    the one who is **coming after me**,
      whose **sandal strap** I am not **worthy** to **untie**."
This happened in **Bethany** across the **Jordan**,
    where **John** was **baptizing**.

PRAYERFUL READING, OR *LECTIO DIVINA*

1. *Lectio:* Read a Scripture passage aloud slowly. Notice what phrase captures your attention and be attentive to its meaning. Silent pause.

2. *Meditatio:* Read the passage aloud slowly again, reflecting on the passage, allowing God to speak to you through it. Silent pause.

3. *Oratio:* Read it aloud slowly a third time, allowing it to be your prayer or response to God's gift of insight to you. Silent pause.

4. *Contemplatio:* Read it aloud slowly a fourth time, now resting in God's Word.

---

the desert" commanding that crooked ways be made straight. John's ministry paves the way by creating an environment of reconciliation and new life that makes the region perhaps more ripe to hear and receive the Messiah when he comes. John's water baptism can be seen as a necessary cleansing of sorts. He serves to get the people focused on allegiance to God and his merciful love rather than service to any political power.

John the Baptist appears to us as a figure of great humility. Although his austere approach to the abandonment of worldly pleasures is not mentioned here in John's Gospel, his willingness to deny himself when courted with the temptation to embrace recognition and acclaim is clearly a profound expression of humility. When confronted with the question "Who are you?" it would have been quite understandable for the Baptist to say something like "I am the leader of a great spiritual revolution in the land." Instead he professes himself to be unworthy to perform the task of untying the sandals of the one who is to come after him.

We are to learn from John the virtue of joy. He was very much satisfied to take on the role of a precursor, of one who prepares the way and then steps aside for another to take over. In our world today such a figure is vital. If we seek to store up glory for ourselves in order to win the praise and attention of others, we miss the attitude of humility that leads to true joy. S. W.

FOURTH SUNDAY
OF ADVENT

LECTIONARY #11

READING I 2 Samuel 7:1–5, 8b–12, 14a, 16

A reading from the second Book of Samuel

A narrative reading with exhortations. Through the prophet Nathan, who has a vivid dream, God speaks directly to King David. The mood of this reading is anticipatory and uplifting.

This exclamation is what inspires Nathan's dream.

When **King David** was **settled** in his **palace**,
and the LORD had given him **rest** from his **enemies**
on every **side**,
he said to **Nathan** the prophet,
"Here I am **living** in a house of **cedar**,
while the **ark** of **God** dwells in a **tent**!"
Nathan **answered** the king,
"**Go**, do what**ever** you **have** in **mind**,
for the LORD is **with** you."
But that night the LORD spoke to Nathan and said:
"**Go**, tell my servant David, '**Thus says** the LORD:
Should you **build me** a **house** to **dwell** in?

When God begins to speak here to Nathan, you can shift your tone slightly from narration into exhortation. Much of what God says is in the future tense, which is more hopeful. You can shift your tone slightly with this shift into the future tense.

"'It was I who took you from the **pasture**
and from the **care** of the **flock**
to be **commander** of my people **Israel**.
I have **been with you** wherever you **went**,
and I have **destroyed** all your **enemies before** you.
And I will make you **famous** like the **great ones** of the **earth**.
I will **fix** a **place** for my **people Israel**;
I will **plant them** so that they may **dwell** in their **place**
without **further** disturbance.

READING I The first and second books of Samuel are part of the Old Testament known as the "Former Prophets." Also included in this category are Joshua, Judges, and Kings. Together they tell the theological history of Israel as it sought to hand over governance to a king. Samuel himself served as a figure of transition between the period of rule by judges to rule by a king. It was he who was chosen by God to anoint Saul as the first king of Israel (1 Samuel 9), and he will do the same for Saul's successor, King David (1 Samuel 16:1–13) years later. The transi-

tion to a peaceful monarchy was a difficult one, filled with rebellion against God, who wished to be understood as the true King of Israel. His power and wisdom were to be known as everlasting.

It is believed that King David ruled around the turn of the first millennium before Christ. It is also believed that David was a successful king, who governed with political savvy and strong military skills. Although best known for his youthful appearance in combat with Goliath (1 Samuel 17), David grew to become a shrewd leader. In today's passage from the Second Book of

Samuel, David can be seen basking in peace. He has successfully built up the city of Jerusalem as a political and economic center and feels confident in the Lord's blessing.

Nevertheless, this sense of security leads the king to ponder God's place in his success. For generations the Ark of the Covenant had been in a tent that had been moved throughout the desert and had finally come to rest in the city of Jerusalem. Now, David desires to build a more fitting dwelling place for God. David turns to the prophet Nathan to reveal his plan, and

Neither shall the **wicked continue** to afflict them as they **did**
of **old**,
since the **time** I first **appointed judges** over my **people Israel**.
I will give you **rest** from all your **enemies**.
The LORD also **reveals** to you
that he will **establish** a **house** for you.
And when your **time comes** and you **rest** with your **ancestors**,
I will **raise up** your heir **after** you, **sprung** from your **loins**,
and I will **make** his **king**dom **firm**.
I will be a **father** to him,
and he shall be a **son** to me.
Your **house** and your **kingdom** shall **endure forever** before me;
your **throne** shall stand **firm** forever.'"

To endure forever is the reassurance this reading offers.

For meditation and context:

RESPONSORIAL PSALM   Psalm 89:2–3, 4–5, 27, 29 (2a)

R. For ever I will sing the goodness of the Lord.

The promises of the LORD I will sing forever;
through all generations my mouth shall
proclaim your faithfulness.
For you have said, "My kindness is
established forever";
in heaven you have confirmed
your faithfulness.

"I have made a covenant with my chosen one,
I have sworn to David my servant:
forever will I confirm your posterity
and establish your throne for
all generations."

"He shall say of me, 'You are my father,
my God, the rock, my savior.'
Forever I will maintain my kindness
toward him,
and my covenant with him stands firm."

TO KEEP IN MIND

Pay attention to the pace of your reading. Varying the pace gives listeners clues to the meaning of the text. The most common error for proclaimers new to the ministry is speaking too fast.

Nathan immediately assures him that God will bless his decision: "Go, do whatever you have in mind, for the Lord is with you."

God is equally as quick to order Nathan to go back to David with the reminder that God alone can build a dwelling suitable for himself, as he has been the author of David's success. Every mark of power that David experiences comes from the hand of God. God commands Nathan to remind David: "It was I who took you from the pasture . . . have been with you wherever you went. . . . I will make you famous like the great ones of the earth." There is to

be no doubt that God is in charge. The prophecy ends with God declaring his intention to build a house for his people. While David may have been thinking about a dwelling place made by hands, God intends to build a house that is composed of a people made holy by his Law.

READING II   The sixteenth chapter is the last portion of Paul's Letter to the Romans, which he authored from Corinth between AD 57–58. It contains mostly greetings and encouragement to those in Rome who have responsibility over

its infant Christian community. At the very end of the letter, Paul adds words to strengthen the sense of his authority. First, he calls for the intensity of vigor among those who will follow the words of "his" gospel. Second, he commands the Romans to reveal to all the nations the "obedience of faith" owed to God through Christ Jesus.

Such a desire to articulate his authority as one who has been called to preach the Good News and to work for the establishment of the faithful should not come as a surprise. Paul has not yet journeyed to Rome at this point in his ministry, so this

READING II   Romans 16:25–27

A reading from the Letter of Saint Paul to the Romans

This is an exhortatory reading in one long sentence, built on parallels from the repetition of the word "according." Use "according" to organize your reading and to pace your breathing.

Brothers and sisters:
To **him** who can **strengthen** you,
    according to my **gospel** and the **proclamation** of Jesus Christ,
    according to the **revelation** of the **mystery kept secret**
      for **long** ages
    but **now manifested** through the **prophetic writings** and,
    according to the **command** of the eternal **God**,
    made **known** to **all nations** to bring about the **obedience**
      of faith,
    to the **only wise God**, through **Jesus Christ**
be **glory** forever and ever. Amen.

Pause if you need to in order to voice "Amen" fully.

GOSPEL   Luke 1:26–38

A reading from the holy Gospel according to Luke

A narrative reading of one of the most solemn passages in the Gospels, which is also one of the most frequently depicted by artists through the centuries. It's very easy to visualize as a result. Treat it like a pageant.

The **angel Gabriel** was **sent** from God
    to a **town** of **Galilee** called **Nazareth**,
    to a **virgin betrothed** to a man named **Joseph**,
    of the **house** of David,
    and the **virgin's name** was **Mary**.
And coming to her, he said,
    "**Hail, full** of **grace**! The **Lord** is **with** you."
But she was **greatly troubled** at what was **said**
    and **pondered** what sort of **greeting** this might be.
Then the **angel** said to her,
    "**Do not** be **afraid**, Mary,
    for you have found **favor** with God.

Because these words are so familiar from prayer, they can have a new life in the context of this reading.

---

letter is written from the position of an outsider. Nevertheless, as Paul has the truth of the Gospel on his side, the people of Rome would do well to hear his instructions and to follow them earnestly.

The Christian community at Rome will soon become an outstanding witness to the nascent religion throughout the world. Like members of the early Church, modern-day hearers of Paul's words are to take seriously the challenge to make known to all nations the obedience of faith. One of the major issues facing this early Christian

community was the issue of inclusion. How do those born under the Hebrew Law fit in with those Gentiles who are coming to faith via the Good News of Christ? Was circumcision under the former law necessary? We might do well today to ponder what the "obedience of faith" entails for our Christian communities. Do the nations of the world look at us and come to belief as a result of what they see? "To the only wise God, through Jesus Christ be glory forever and ever. Amen."

GOSPEL   The angel Gabriel plays a prominent role in the first chapter of Luke's Gospel. The name Gabriel means, "God is my strength." Indeed, God's strength is made abundantly clear in the announcements Gabriel makes. First, the angel appears to Zechariah and foretells that his wife, who is barren, will give birth to a son who is to be called John (Luke 1:5–25). Gabriel proclaims: "He will be a joy and a delight to you, and many will rejoice because of his birth" (Luke 1:14). Six months later, Gabriel appears to Mary and foretells

"**Behold**, you will **conceive** in your **womb** and **bear** a **son**,
    and you shall **name** him Jesus.
He will be **great** and will be called **Son** of the **Most High**,
    and the **Lord God** will give him the **throne** of **David**
        his father,
    and he will **rule over** the house of **Jacob** forever,
    and of his **kingdom** there will be **no end**."
But **Mary** said to the **angel**,
    "How can this **be**,
    since I have no **relations** with a man?"
And the **angel** said to her in **reply**,
    "The **Holy Spirit** will come **upon** you,
    and the **power** of the **Most High** will over**shadow** you.
Therefore the **child** to be **born**
    will be called **holy**, the **Son** of **God**.
And **behold**, Elizabeth, your relative,
    has **also conceived** a son in her old age,
    and this is the **sixth month** for her who was called **barren**;
    for **nothing** will be **impossible** for God."
Mary said, "**Behold**, I am the **handmaid** of the **Lord**.
May it be **done to me** according to **your word**."
Then the **angel** departed from her.

"Most High" and "no end" share a rhythmical and thematic echo.

This is the good news that Gabriel delivers to Mary.

And Mary's declaration defines the role of all believers, including the Church.

the birth of her Son who "will be called great and will be called the Son of the Most High" (Luke 1:32). These two announcements by Gabriel are meant to be seen as two sides of God's plan of salvation. While very similar, they also stand to make the distinction that John is to be the precursor for his cousin Jesus, whose kingdom will have no end.

These annunciation stories serve as a foretaste of what will be a predominant pattern in Luke's theology, namely that of reversal. In Luke's understanding of God's plan of salvation, the lowly are chosen by God in order to humble the mighty, and the poor are chosen to bear God's message to the rich who are stubborn of heart. Both Elizabeth and Mary fit this description perfectly. Elizabeth is barren and supposedly too old to bear a child; Mary is a peasant girl, whose status puts her at the margins of society. Both are women and therefore considered voiceless in the society of their day. Yet both women are chosen for a grand purpose. Both women cooperate with God's grace with little doubt. "For nothing will be impossible for God." The story of Mary's yes to the will of God is told on this Sunday immediately prior to the celebration of the Lord's birth because it is important for the Church to understand that salvation depends upon humanity's free will and cooperation with God. God's plan of salvation is not forced upon us; we must say yes to his designs. S. W.

THE NATIVITY OF THE LORD (CHRISTMAS): VIGIL

LECTIONARY #13

READING I   Isaiah 62:1–5

Isaiah = ī-ZAY-uh

An exhortatory reading. Notice the repetitions of the phrase "you shall." Pace your readings with each expression of "you shall" (or its variations) as a marker.

Notice the sound carried from "Zion's" to "silent" to "quiet."

A reading from the Book of the Prophet Isaiah

For **Zion's** sake I will **not** be **silent**,
    for **Jerusalem's** sake I will **not** be **quiet**,
until her **vindication shines forth** like the **dawn**
    and her **victory** like a burning **torch**.

Nations shall **behold** your **vindication**,
    and all the **kings** your **glory**;
you shall be **called** by a new **name**
    pronounced by the **mouth** of the LORD.
You shall be a **glorious crown** in the **hand** of the LORD,
    a **royal diadem** held by your God.
No more shall people call you "**Forsaken**,"
    or your land "**Desolate**,"
but you shall be called "**My Delight**,"
    and your land "**Espoused**."
For the LORD **delights** in you
    and makes your land his **spouse**.
As a young man marries a **virgin**,
    your **Builder** shall **marry** you;
and as a **bridegroom rejoices** in his **bride**
    so shall your God rejoice in **you**.

Give extra emphasis to each of these four names.

Even emphasis on all the words in this last line, with extra added on "you."

READING I   For the four weeks of Advent, especially during the Sunday liturgies, passages from Scripture have been chosen that instill in us attitudes of patient waiting and hopeful joy. During this time, when the light of the day can seem to be thwarted by the darkness of night, we have been striving to renew our hope in the Light of the World. We believe that this Light dawned upon the world historically in the person of Jesus and continues to burn brightly, leading us on to the day of God's triumphant victory, when all things will be gathered into one in him.

The prophecy of Isaiah was intended to herald a similar hope within the assembly of the Hebrew people as they returned from exile in Babylon in the sixth century BC. The conundrum of the Israelites during this period was detailed in the discussion of the passage from Isaiah 61, proclaimed on the Third Sunday of Advent. It is true that many of those exiled in Babylon found themselves prospering apart from Jerusalem. Many had come to discover that the essence of their religion need not be Temple sacrifice, rather, that God would be pleased with contrite hearts and a desire to

study his commands. Thus, a considerable portion of those living in the *diaspora*— outside Israel—resisted the call to return to their homeland.

Isaiah's call to come home was made difficult by the fact that foreign powers had devastated Jerusalem and its vicinities. The Temple had been leveled and the city destroyed. A place that had been the seal of God's promise to choose a people destined for holiness was now a sign of his rejection. Why would anyone want to return to such a place of misfortune? Isaiah answers by likening God to a bridegroom

For meditation and context:

RESPONSORIAL PSALM   Psalm 89:4–5, 16–17, 27, 29 (2a)

R. For ever I will sing the goodness of the Lord.

I have made a covenant with my
    chosen one,
  I have sworn to David my servant:
forever will I confirm your posterity
    and establish your throne for
    all generations.

Blessed the people who know the
    joyful shout;
  in the light of your countenance,
    O Lord, they walk.

At your name they rejoice all the day,
  and through your justice they are exalted.

He shall say of me, "You are my father,
  my God, the rock, my savior."
Forever I will maintain my kindness
    toward him,
  and my covenant with him stands firm.

READING II   Acts of the Apostles 13:16–17, 22–25

A reading from the Acts of the Apostles

When **Paul** reached Antioch in Pisidia and entered the synagogue,
  he stood up, motioned with his hand, and said,
    "**Fellow Israelites** and you others who are **God-fearing**, **listen**.
The God of this people **Israel** chose our **ancestors**
  and exalted the people during their **sojourn** in the land
    of Egypt.
With **uplifted arm** he led them **out** of it.
Then he removed **Saul** and raised up **David** as king;
  of him he testified,
    'I have found **David**, son of **Jesse**, a man after my own **heart**;
  he will carry out my **every** wish.'
From this man's descendants **God**, according to his **promise**,
  has brought to Israel a **savior**, **Jesus**.
John heralded his coming by proclaiming a **baptism** of **repentance**
  to **all** the people of Israel;
  and as John was completing his course, he would say,
    'What do you suppose that I **am**? I **am not he**.
Behold, one is coming **after** me;
  I am not **worthy** to unfasten the **sandals** of his **feet**.'"

Antioch = AN-tee-ahk
Pisidia = pih-SID-ee-uh
sojourn = SOH-jern (exile)

A didactic reading that sets up a prophetic succession, beginning with the Israelites in the desert and moving from David to John the Baptist, and finally to Jesus.

Though Paul is speaking in this reading, he is quoting the words of his predecessors. You can modulate your voice slightly to suggest this shift.

Paul concludes with John the Baptist's memorable phrase about Jesus. A slight emphasis on "sandals" and "feet" will remind the assembly whose words these are.

---

who takes delight in his bride. This description is filled with hope and promise. It is meant to help the newly returned people of Israel to see that God is making something new in restoring the covenant with them.

A great portion of this newness is the role that the nation will play, standing before other nations with the testimony of God's fidelity. At the outset of this passage, Isaiah makes this abundantly clear. He will not let his voice be silenced. God's victory must be revealed by the nation's desire to build up Jerusalem once again. As the Christian community gathers in vigil this night, the proclamation of God's victory ought to be welling up in every heart, preparing every member of the Church to proclaim from the peak of every mountain to the top of every house: God has come to save us.

| READING II | An important component of the Old Testament, as well as rabbinic reflection upon them, is the linking of an event back to a previous event or the tracing of relationships back through a family's bloodline. All of this is done in order to show that significant religious events and the appearance of a prophetic figure do not simply fall out of thin air; instead, they are part of a plan that God designed from the very beginning of creation.

The same concern for continuity was true for the early Church. The Apostles who believed themselves sent into the world with the Good News of Christ and his Resurrection knew that their preaching had to make connections with the past. This way of following after Jesus, while decidedly new, had to flow from the historical past that provided a foundation. When Paul entered the synagogue in Antioch in Pisidia

A whopper of a reading. Much of it is didactic before it shifts into a narrative. The first part of this reading is a performative, rhythmical incantation, one unusual name leading to the next. It goes from Abraham to David; from David to the Babylonian exile; from the Babylonian exile to Jesus. It's a folding screen with two hinges, each panel of the screen exactly the same size, and the image of Jesus' birth appears on its front.

Genealogy = jee-nee-OL-uh-jee
Abraham = AY-bruh-ham; Isaac = ī-zik
Judah = JOO-duh
Perez = PAYR-ez; Zerah = ZEE-rah

Only five women are included in this list.
Tamar = TAY-mahr
Hezron = HEZ-ruhn
Ram = ram
Amminadab = uh-MIN-uh-dab
Nahshon = NAH-shon
Salmon = SAL-muhn
Boaz = BOH-az
Rahab = RAY-hab
Obed = OH-bed
Jesse = JES-ee
Uriah = yoo-RI-uh
Rehoboam = ree-huh-BOH-uhm
Abijah = uh-BĪ-juh
Asaph = AY-saf
Jehoshaphat = jeh-HOH-shuh-fat
Joram = JOHR-uhm
Uzziah = yuh-ZĪ-uh
Jotham = JOH-thuhm
Ahaz = AY-haz

GOSPEL   Matthew 1:1–25

A reading from the holy Gospel according to Matthew

The book of the **genealogy** of **Jesus Christ**,
    the son of David, the son of Abraham.

Abraham became the father of **Isaac**,
    Isaac the father of **Jacob**,
    Jacob the father of **Judah** and his **brothers**.
Judah became the father of **Perez** and **Zerah**,
    whose mother was **Tamar**.
Perez became the father of **Hezron**,
    Hezron the father of **Ram**,
    Ram the father of **Amminadab**.
 Amminadab became the father of **Nahshon**,
    Nahshon the father of **Salmon**,
    Salmon the father of **Boaz**,
    whose mother was **Rahab**.
Boaz became the father of **Obed**,
    whose mother was **Ruth**.
Obed became the father of **Jesse**,
    Jesse the father of **David** the **king**.

David became the father of **Solomon**,
    whose **mother** had been the wife of **Uriah**.
Solomon became the father of **Rehoboam**,
    Rehoboam the father of **Abijah**,
    Abijah the father of **Asaph**.
Asaph became the father of **Jehoshaphat**,
    Jehoshaphat the father of **Joram**,
    Joram the father of **Uzziah**.
Uzziah became the father of **Jotham**,
    Jotham the father of **Ahaz**,
    Ahaz the father of **Hezekiah**.

as part of his missionary journey, he knew well that his Jewish audience, as well as the "God-fearers" (Gentile converts rooted in the teaching of the synagogue), needed to hear that his proclamation of Jesus was not merely a novelty but was securely based on Jewish roots.

Paul uses three important moments in history to claim the authenticity of Jesus. First, he points to God's plan of salvation in his freedom of the Israelites from slavery in Egypt. As described in the Book of Exodus, God led his people out of Egypt with his "mighty arm." Next, Paul reminds his hearers

of the establishment of David as King of Israel, the boy king who God knows "will carry out my every wish." Finally, Paul makes it clear that Jesus was born into this world from the royal line of David and was to be for Israel its savior.

There should be no doubt that Jesus has deep connections within the heart of the nation of Israel. Paul leaves no doubt that this recognition should be visible to all when he goes on to speak of John the Baptist's own testimony, who declares: "Behold, one is coming after me; I am not worthy to unfasten the sandals on his feet."

Paul's overall message is clear. The history of Israel manifests God's plan of salvation, for this there is no doubt. However, this history points to a new beginning in Jesus. God's promise is revealed in the one who has come to bring about a true and lasting freedom.

GOSPEL   Similar to Paul's approach to heralding the historical roots of Jesus in today's second reading, the beginning of Matthew's Gospel contains Jesus' genealogy. The word *genealogy* comes from the root word *genesis*, which

Hezekiah = hez-eh-KĪ-uh
Manasseh = muh-NAS-uh
Amos = AY-m*s
Josiah = joh-SĪ-uh
Jechoniah = jek-oh-NĪ-uh
Shealtiel = shee-AL-tee-uhl
Zerubbabel = zuh-ROOB-uh-b*l
Abiud = uh-BĪ-uhd
Eliakim = ee-LĪ-uh-kim
Azor = AY-sohr
Zadok = ZAD-uhk
Achim = AH-kim
Eliud = ee-LĪ-uhd
Eleazar = el-ee-AY-zer
Matthan = MATH-uhn

Hezekiah became the father of **Manasseh**,
  Manasseh the father of **Amos**,
  Amos the father of **Josiah**.
Josiah became the father of **Jechoniah** and his **brothers**
  at the time of the Babylonian **exile**.

After the Babylonian exile,
  Jechoniah became the father of **Shealtiel**,
  Shealtiel the father of **Zerubbabel**,
  Zerubbabel the father of **Abiud**.
Abiud became the father of **Eliakim**,
  Eliakim the father of **Azor**,
  Azor the father of **Zadok**.
Zadok became the father of **Achim**,
  Achim the father of **Eliud**,
  Eliud the father of **Eleazar**.
Eleazar became the father of **Matthan**,
  Matthan the father of **Jacob**,
  Jacob the father of **Joseph**, the husband of **Mary**.
Of her was born **Jesus** who is called the **Christ**.

Thus the total number of **generations**
  from **Abraham** to **David**
  is **fourteen** generations;
  from **David** to the Babylonian **exile**,
  fourteen generations;
  from the Babylonian **exile** to the **Christ**,
  fourteen generations.

Now [**this** is how the **birth** of Jesus **Christ** came about.
When his mother **Mary** was betrothed to **Joseph**,
  but before they **lived** together,
  she was found with **child** through the Holy **Spirit**.
Joseph her **husband**, since he was a **righteous man**,
  yet unwilling to expose her to **shame**,
  decided to **divorce** her quietly. »

Now that Jesus' genealogy has been established, the story of his birth can be told. The focus is Joseph, the second-to-last name in the genealogy. Attune the dynamics of your reading to the figure of Joseph, with whom the assembly is meant to identify.

---

simply means something's or someone's origins. The Book of Genesis, for instance, contains the cosmic and familial origins of Israel as God's Chosen People. Matthew begins his Gospel with the origins of Jesus because he wants his readers to be perfectly clear that Jesus is in continuity with Israel's past and God's promise of salvation.

Matthew writes at a very significant juncture in Israel's history. Scholars date the composition of this Gospel as immediately subsequent to the destruction of the Temple by the Romans in AD 70. Matthew's audience is decidedly Jewish, with a very

important decision on their hands: What are we to make of the covenant with God now that the Temple is no more? Matthew's answer: Come to believe that Jesus is the fulfillment of that covenant. Following after Jesus does not require the Temple; rather, it requires adherence to him through Baptism and by following his command. Fulfillment means that Jesus must be firmly situated within Jewish history. Thus, the importance of preceding the story of Jesus' nativity with his genealogy.

The proclamation of Matthew 1:1–25 in the context of the Vigil liturgy is some-

thing that many presiders avoid, choosing instead to read one of the other Gospel passages from the collection of Christmas Masses. This is unfortunate, as the four Christmas Masses, and the Gospel reading chosen for each, are meant to demonstrate a progression in understanding of the revelation of the mystery of the Incarnation, from Jesus' family tree (Vigil), to his birth announced by the angels under the stars (Night), to the shepherds' discovery of the infant Jesus (Dawn), to the theological reflection by John on the Word coming into the world as its true light (Day). The *genesis*

When the angel says here Joseph's name, it is a summons. Read it that way.

Such was his intention when, **behold,**
    the **angel** of the Lord appeared to him in a **dream** and said,
    "**Joseph**, son of David,
    do not be afraid to take Mary your wife into your **home.**
For it is **through** the Holy Spirit
    that this child has been **conceived in her.**
She will bear a **son** and you are to name him **Jesus,**
    because he will **save** his people from their **sins.**"
All this took place to **fulfill**
    what the Lord had said through the **prophet:**
        *Behold, the **virgin** shall conceive and bear a **son,***
          *and they shall name him **Emmanuel,***
    which means "**God** is **with** us."
When Joseph **awoke,**
    he **did** as the angel of the Lord had **commanded** him
    and took his **wife** into his **home.**
He had no **relations** with her until she bore a **son,**
    and he **named** him **Jesus.**]

[Shorter: Matthew 1:18–25 (see brackets)]

Joseph awaking is what happens to the assembly at this moment.

of Jesus plays an important role in setting the stage for the wonder of his birth and honors the names of all those who paved the way for his coming.

Upon the heels of the genealogy proper is Matthew's account of Jesus' birth (Matthew 1:18–25). We return to the time of Mary's being found to be with child and the angel's appearance to Joseph in a dream to care for Mary in his home as his wife. The angel foretells that "she will bear a son, and you are to name him Jesus." Jesus is to be the proper name of the child born into Joseph's home, who will come to be called in time "Emmanuel," meaning "God is with us." Just as the study of ancestry has popular appeal today, the hearing of Jesus' origins as the fullness of God's presence among us is significant for reminding us of our spiritual DNA. S. W.

THE NATIVITY OF THE LORD (CHRISTMAS): NIGHT

LECTIONARY #14

READING I Isaiah 9:1–6

A reading from the Book of the Prophet Isaiah

> The people who walked in **darkness**
>   have **seen** a great **light**;
> upon those who dwelt in the **land of gloom**
>   a **light** has **shone**.
> You have **brought** them abundant **joy**
>   and **great rejoicing**,
> as they **rejoice** before you as at the **harvest**,
>   as people make **merry** when dividing **spoils**.
> For the **yoke** that burdened them,
>   the **pole** on their shoulder,
> and the **rod** of their taskmaster
>   you have **smashed**, as on the day of **Midian**.
> For every **boot** that **tramped** in **battle**,
>   every **cloak rolled** in **blood**,
>   will be **burned** as fuel for flames.
> For a child is born to us, a **son** is given us;
>   upon his shoulder **dominion** rests.
> They name him **Wonder-Counselor, God-Hero,**
>   **Father-Forever, Prince** of **Peace. »**

Isaiah = ī-ZAY-uh

An exhortatory reading, one of great joy and mystery. Read with emphasis on the contrasts between light and gloom, battle and peace.

Take note here of the yoke, the pole, and the rod. These lines express parallel images in parallel constructions.

Midian = MID-ee-uhn

These names are the heart of this reading. Give them due emphasis.

READING I The Church has been guided throughout the season of Advent by the prophecy of Isaiah. His words challenge us to look forward to the dawning of that day when justice and peace shall reign. Tonight's reading speaks of the great rejoicing that is promised to a people who have suffered much and yet have remained faithful to their God.

Before arriving at that proclamation of peace, however, Isaiah speaks of the people dwelling in "the land of gloom." This image is carried over from the previous chapter, in which the prophet foretold the impending invasion of the Assyrian army. This would prove to be a horrific period for the people of the Promised Land, especially those who lived in the Northern Kingdom. It is particularly to these northern lands that the Messiah will come and usher in a time of healing and restoration. This is a Messiah who will destroy the means of oppression by foreign occupiers and who will restore the freedom of the people. Just as Gideon won a great victory over Midian (Judges 8), so too will the new king be favored with might and power.

Who is the Messiah who comes with the blessing of God to restore Israel's control over the land given to them by divine right? Isaiah speaks in the present tense: "For a child is born to us, a son is given us." It is very possible that Isaiah was referring to Hezekiah, who would follow his father, King Ahaz, in governing the land of Judah. Unlike his father, who was a weak and ineffective leader, Hezekiah would prove to be a just ruler. The very nature of this reign can be summed up in the names given to its leader: "Wonder-Counselor, God-Hero,

His dominion is **vast**
    and **forever** peaceful,
from David's **throne**, and over his **kingdom**,
    which he **confirms** and **sustains**
by **judgment** and **justice**,
    both **now** and **forever**.
The **zeal** of the LORD of **hosts** will **do** this!

Give each of the pairs in these three lines—confirms and sustains; judgment and justice; now and forever—equal emphasis.

For meditation and context:

RESPONSORIAL PSALM   Psalm 96:1–2, 2–3, 11–12, 13 (Luke 2:11)

R. Today is born our Savior, Christ the Lord.

Sing to the LORD a new song;
    sing to the LORD, all you lands.
Sing to the LORD; bless his name.

Announce his salvation, day after day.
    Tell his glory among the nations;
    among all peoples, his wondrous deeds.

Let the heavens be glad and the
    earth rejoice;
    let the sea and what fills it resound;
    let the plains be joyful and all that is
      in them!
Then shall all the trees of the forest exult.

They shall exult before the LORD,
    for he comes;
    for he comes to rule the earth.
He shall rule the world with justice
    and the peoples with his constancy.

READING II   Titus 2:11–14

A reading from the Letter of Saint Paul to Titus

Beloved:
The **grace** of God has appeared, saving **all**
    and training us to reject **godless ways** and **worldly desires**
    and to live **temperately**, **justly**, and **devoutly** in this age,
    as we await the blessed **hope**,
    the **appearance** of the **glory** of our great **God**
    and **savior** Jesus Christ,
    who gave himself for us to **deliver** us from all **lawlessness**
    and to **cleanse** for himself a **people** as his own,
    eager to do what is **good**.

Titus = TĪ-tuhs

An exhortatory reading, all in one long sentence, broken into three parts, beginning with "The grace of God," continuing with "the appearance of the glory," concluding with "who gave himself for us." Pace your reading accordingly.

Equal emphasis on these three adverbs.

Read the phrase "eager to do what is good" as a Christmas wish.

Father-Forever, Prince of Peace." Indeed, great hope is placed upon this child.

The passage concludes with a description of the kingdom over which this chosen one will reign. His reign will be "vast" and "forever peaceful." He will govern according to both "judgment and justice." Isaiah's prophecy is a grand and lofty description of a reign that perhaps only God could fulfill. Isaiah raises the expectations of the people to a new level: it is not just that a former age will be restored, but that something new and great will be accomplished by the one who is to come!

READING II   Paul's Letter to Titus is one of the three letters, along with First and Second Timothy, that are designated as the pastoral epistles. The main purpose of the Letter to Titus is to describe the ministerial responsibilities that belong to elders and bishops. It is believed that Titus served as the first bishop of Crete, where he remained until his death.

In this portion of his letter, Paul speaks of the day of the Lord's return and suggests that living "temperately, justly, and devoutly" is the necessary way to await this triumphal moment. Such advice must be placed in the context of Paul's overall concern for the governance of the fledging Church. Those in positions of leadership must provide a worthy example that is neither lofty nor inflated. Temperance, justice, and devotion are characteristics of one who puts others before the self.

For our purposes this night, the outset of this passage has particular significance: "The grace of God has appeared, saving all." We believe that Jesus entered the world to provide the perfect manifestation of God's grace, which may best be understood as God's presence. In his Son,

A narrative reading, divided into two parts. The first part tells the story of the census, moving Joseph and Mary from Nazareth to Bethlehem where Jesus will be born. The second part shifts to the shepherds visited by the angel of the Lord. Two vivid Christian images come from this reading: the manger of the Nativity and the heavenly host with the angel proclaiming glory to God, witnessed by the shepherds watching over their flocks. Both images come alive in this reading.

Caesar Augustus = SEE-zer aw-GUHS-tuhs
Quirinius = kwih-RIN-ee-uhs
Judea = joo-DEE-uh

Place emphasis on these lines by slowing your pace just slightly to draw attention to the image.

In this line, each word should have almost equal emphasis.

GOSPEL   Luke 2:1–14

A reading from the holy Gospel according to Luke

In those days a **decree** went out from Caesar Augustus
   that the **whole world** should be **enrolled**.
This was the **first** enrollment,
   when Quirinius was governor of Syria.
So **all went** to be **enrolled**, **each** to his own **town**.
And **Joseph too** went up from **Galilee** from the town of **Nazareth**
   to **Judea**, to the city of **David** that is called **Bethlehem**,
   because he was of the **house** and **family** of David,
   to be **enrolled** with **Mary**, his betrothed, who was with child.
While they were there,
   the time came for **her** to have her **child**,
   and she gave birth to her **firstborn son**.
She wrapped him in swaddling **clothes** and **laid** him in a **manger**,
   because there was **no room** for them in the inn.

Now there were **shepherds** in that region **living** in the fields
   and **keeping** the **night watch** over their flock.
The **angel** of the Lord appeared to them
   and the **glory** of the Lord **shone** around them,
   and they were **struck** with great **fear**.
The angel **said** to them,
   "**Do not be afraid**;
   for **behold**, I proclaim to you **good news** of **great joy**
   that will be for **all** the people.
For today in the city of **David**
   a **savior** has been **born** for you who is **Christ** and **Lord**. »

TO KEEP IN MIND
Smile when you share good news. Nonverbal cues like a smile help the assembly understand the reading.

whether as a newborn infant or the sacrificial Lamb on the cross, God's is with us. However, Paul makes clear that this grace continues in the Church as it is trained "to reject godless ways and worldly desires" and to await the days of Christ's coming with "the blessed hope." Grace is not something that is parceled out with some receiving more and others meriting less; it is an ongoing discovery of God's presence that is made possible through attachment to Christ.

GOSPEL   These fourteen verses of the second chapter of Luke's Gospel are composed in such a way as to announce the birth of Jesus between two contrasting bookends of sorts. Preceding the account of Jesus' birth is the description of the plan of human authority over the "whole world," namely the enrollment of Quirinius, who was a Roman official given control of Syria and the region of Judea. The purpose of any census is to have a certain amount of control over the people. After the description of the birth of Mary's child, a second bookend details the

shepherds receiving the message of an angel. The purpose of shepherds is to watch over and guide their flocks. Thus, both bookends are about establishing control. On the one hand, political authority seeks to control a people within a territorial border, on the other hand, the lowly shepherds are marked by God as the proper authority to spread the message of great joy for all peoples.

It is no mistake that Luke wants us to understand that the power of political officials pales in comparison to the might of God, a might which comes in the form of a

Give emphasis again to the word "manger."

Give slight emphasis to "praising" as a way of characterizing the image arising from the familiar words to follow: pure praise.

And **this** will be a **sign** for you:
> you will find an **infant wrapped** in swaddling clothes
> and **lying** in a **manger**."
And **suddenly** there was a multitude of the heavenly host with the angel,
> **praising** God and saying:
>> "**Glory** to God in the **highest**
>>> and on **earth peace** to those on whom his **favor** rests."

precious child. The Hebrew people thought that the Messiah would come as a royal figure, with the power to overturn worldly regimes and restore God's promise of a land flowing with milk and honey, prosperous in every way, and unconquerable in its national security. But such is not the way of the God of surprises, who delights the shepherds with the song of the angels: "Glory to God in the highest and on earth peace to those on whom his favor rests." Clearly, the favor of God rests upon those who care for others rather than upon those who seek gain for their own prowess and personal security.

There is no missing Luke's theology in this passage. Within the first few verses of his Gospel, Jesus has been given the titles "savior" and the one who is "Christ and Lord." Through the message of the angels, the epiphany of God's love for the world is made manifest. He may be wrapped in swaddling clothes and lying in a manger, but our eyes are meant to see the King of Kings and the Lord of Lords. God's love is thoroughly cosmic, for in the encounter between the angels and the shepherds, heaven and earth are united under one authority. God's grace and the promise of his peace permeate all of creation. S. W.

THE NATIVITY OF THE LORD (CHRISTMAS): DAWN

LECTIONARY #15

READING I   Isaiah 62:11–12

A reading from the Book of the Prophet Isaiah

> **See**, the LORD **proclaims**
>   to the **ends** of the earth:
> **say** to daughter Zion,
>   your **savior** comes!
> Here is his reward with him,
>   his **recompense before** him.
> They shall be **called** the holy **people**,
>   the **redeemed** of the LORD,
> and you shall be called "**Frequented**,"
>   a **city** that is **not forsaken**.

Isaiah = ī-ZAY-uh

A short, exhortatory reading, usefully read as a poem, which is to say slowly and with emphasis on the highlighted words.

recompense = REK-uhm-pens = compensation for wrongs suffered

The word "redeemed" is focal in this reading.

Frequented= FREE-kwen-t*d

For meditation and context:

RESPONSORIAL PSALM   Psalm 97:1, 6, 11–12

R. A light will shine on us this day: the Lord is born for us.

The LORD is king; let the earth rejoice;
   let the many isles be glad.
The heavens proclaim his justice,
   and all peoples see his glory.

Light dawns for the just;
   and gladness, for the upright of heart.
Be glad in the LORD, you just,
   and give thanks to his holy name.

READING I   In keeping with the natural progression in the four Mass settings for the Lord's Nativity, the Liturgy of the Word at the Mass at Dawn opens with the continuation of Isaiah's prophecy from the Vigil Mass. Recall that the original context for this section of Isaiah is the Israelite's return from their Babylonian captivity. Not only was their return to the ruins of the Promised Land an act of trust in their God, but their migration spoke volumes to the neighboring nations. The people around them must have thought how foolish it was to leave a situation of prosperity only to set up shop once again in a place of dashed hopes!

The Lord was in fact using the return of the Hebrews to proclaim his power and might to the entire world. In the verse immediately prior to this brief passage, Isaiah announces: "Pass through, pass through the gates! . . . Build up, build up the highway!" The nation that has been set free from captivity is now to be the major contractor in building a new world. For this reason, they will be called "the holy people, the redeemed of the Lord." The newness of Israel is seen in the name that it is given, namely "Frequented." No longer will this be a nation that is forgotten and despised, but now it will be a bright light to the world. We hear this prophecy at the dawning of Christmas morn. Like those returning to a new land, the Church sees itself reborn in the dawning of Christ as the true light of the world.

Titus = TĪ-tuhs

A short didactic reading, in one long sentence. After the initial "Beloved," the lines of the reading form natural pairs. Read each pair of lines as a thought, proceeding from one to the next, offering advice, and concluding with a message of hope.

The rhythm of this line provides this reading with its reverberant note, so allow yourself to slow slightly as you come to this conclusion.

TO KEEP IN MIND

Pause to break up separate thoughts, set apart significant statements, or indicate major shifts. Never pause in the middle of a thought. Your primary guide for pauses is punctuation.

READING II   Titus 3:4–7

A reading from the Letter of Saint Paul to Titus

Beloved:
When the **kindness** and generous **love**
    of **God** our savior appeared,
not **because** of any righteous deeds we had done
    but because of his mercy,
he **saved us** through the **bath** of rebirth
    and **renewal** by the Holy **Spirit**,
whom he **richly poured out** on **us**
    through **Jesus** Christ our **savior**,
so that we might be **justified** by his **grace**
    and become **heirs** in **hope** of eternal **life**.

READING II   Paul's Letter to Titus also served as the second reading for the Mass at Night for the Nativity of the Lord. This is one of the three pastoral letters that are written under Paul's name to be guidelines for the pastoral care of the infant Church. The author of this letter is particularly concerned with the behavior and charisms of elders and bishops.

    The method of this letter is quite simple. A theology of God's graciousness and kindness in Christ Jesus is first presented so that readers may wish to embody this same approach in their dealings with other members of the community. Paul presents an understanding of God's grace that is based upon God's pure love. God's "kindness and generous love" did not flow into our world because of anything we humans did to deserve it, but rather, justification by God's grace comes about because of God's great mercy. In turn, it is to be understood that we are to act mercifully towards one another in order to embody the kindness that comes from God.

    Another theological key to this passage is the author's understanding of Baptism. He calls it the "bath of rebirth and renewal." It is through Baptism that we become, as Paul writes, "heirs in hope of eternal life." Not only is Baptism meant to cleanse us from our former ways and give us a new birth, it is also the mark of discipleship and our commission to show others our hope that God will grant us our inheritance of life eternal. The beauty of Christmas morning ought to rekindle our desire, rooted in Baptism, to be ambassadors of hope in a world that is often trapped in darkness.

GOSPEL   Luke 2:15–20

A reading from the holy Gospel according to Luke

When the **angels** went away from them to **heaven**,
   the **shepherds** said to one another,
   "Let us **go**, then, to **Bethlehem**
   to **see this thing** that has taken place,
   which the **Lord** has made **known** to us."
So they went in **haste** and found **Mary** and **Joseph**,
   and the **infant lying** in the manger.
When they **saw** this,
   they made **known** the message
   that had been **told them** about this child.
All who heard it were **amazed**
   by what had been **told** them by the **shepherds**.
And **Mary** kept all these things,
   reflecting on them in her **heart**.
Then the **shepherds** returned,
   glorifying and **praising** God
   for **all** they had **heard** and **seen**,
   just as it had been **told** to them.

A short narrative reading that concludes the Nativity story. While the focus is on the infant Jesus lying in the manger, the eyes through which we see him are those of the shepherds. The shepherds modeled Christian devotion from the beginning of our faith.

manger = MAYN-jer

Amazement is the primary emotion of this story.

The shepherds' glorifying and praising are to be our own.

GOSPEL Luke's narrative of the Lord's birth continues where it left off at the Night Mass. The angel has now returned to his heavenly home, leaving the shepherds to determine the meaning of the news imparted to them. Recall the angel's song praising God's name: "Glory to God in the highest and on earth peace to those on whom his favor rests." Given their lives as lowly shepherds, they had to ask each other "How could it be that God's favor rests on us?" Nevertheless, they trusted in the message and ran off "in haste," most likely abandoning their flocks in the field, in order to find the proof for the angel's song.

Luke suggests that their discovery of the child lying in the manger immediately leads to their testifying to the message of the angel and the "multitude of the heavenly host." In effect, these shepherds are the first disciples of the Lord. Even though they have not specifically been called by him, they are the first ones to broadcast the truth that through this child amazing things will take place. Even Mary is mystified by their words. It is no mistake that God has chosen those of a humble background to have the privilege of announcing his coming into this world.

As with so many figures in the Gospels who encounter Jesus and experience a great life change as a result, we do not know what becomes of the shepherds. We are simply told that they "returned" and that they praised God for what they had been shone. Like the humble shepherds, we contemplate the angel's message and peer into the manger, but how does such evidence of God's abundant love for the world enhance our commitment to spreading that message of love? S. W.

THE NATIVITY OF THE LORD (CHRISTMAS): DAY

LECTIONARY #16

READING I   Isaiah 52:7–10

Isaiah = ī-ZAY-uh

An exhortatory reading of great joy. In reading this, you are bringing glad tidings to the assembly.

A reading from the Book of the Prophet Isaiah

How **beautiful** upon the **mountains**
    are the **feet** of him who **brings glad tidings**,
announcing **peace**, bearing good **news**,
    announcing **salvation**, and saying to Zion,
    "Your **God** is **King!**"

"Hark" is a word with rich Christmas associations. Allow it to resonate in your reading.

Hark! Your sentinels **raise** a cry,
    together they **shout** for **joy**,
for they see **directly**, before their **eyes**,
    the LORD restoring Zion.
Break out together in song,
    O ruins of Jerusalem!
For the LORD comforts his **people**,
    he **redeems** Jerusalem.
The LORD has bared his holy arm
    in the **sight** of all the **nations**;
all the **ends** of the **earth** will **behold**
    the **salvation** of our **God**.

Allow "salvation" to resonate here. This word is the key to the whole reading.

READING I In keeping with the other first readings chosen for the Christmas Masses, the first reading for the Mass of the Day is from the prophecy of Isaiah. He proclaims Israel's obligation to serve as an ambassador of God's marvelous deeds. Isaiah suggests going to high places, such as mountaintops and sentinel towers, to proclaim all that God has done on its behalf. There is a definite urgency to getting the message out into the world; there is no holding back here, no room for timidity or cowardice. The work of announcing peace and salvation, bring-ing glad tidings and good news must be done now!

Imagine the challenge that these words must have been for the people. Upon their return, the people who had been in exile found the land and the cities desolate and uninhabitable. They surely had to focus their energy on rebuilding the nation. Instead, Isaiah wants them to focus on the work of proclaiming God's guiding hand in the work of restoration: "The Lord has bared his holy arm in the sight of all the nations." Just as when the Israelites were free from Egyptian captivity and God gave them a circuitous route out of the land of slavery in order to show his power and might to all of Egypt (Exodus 13:17), here in Isaiah's prophecy, God's desire to be noticed by the entire world is abundantly clear.

It may be tempting for a people who consider themselves to be chosen by God to turn in on themselves and simply give thanks that they are not like others in this world. However, this is not the point of God's special care. It is a gift that comes with a responsibility: proclaiming that salvation has dawned upon the earth. Adherence to the good news of God's

For meditation and context:

RESPONSORIAL PSALM   Psalm 98:1, 2–3, 3–4, 5–6 (3c)

R. All the ends of the earth have seen the saving power of God.

Sing to the LORD a new song,
    for he has done wondrous deeds;
his right hand has won victory for him,
    his holy arm.

The LORD has made his salvation known:
    in the sight of the nations he has
        revealed his justice.
He has remembered his kindness and
    his faithfulness
    toward the house of Israel.

All the ends of the earth have seen
    the salvation by our God.
Sing joyfully to the LORD, all you lands;
    break into song; sing praise.

Sing praise to the LORD with the harp,
    with the harp and melodious song.
With trumpets and the sound of the horn
    sing joyfully before the King, the LORD.

READING II   Hebrews 1:1–6

A reading from the Letter to the Hebrews

Brothers and sisters:
In times **past**, God **spoke** in **partial** and **various** ways
    to our **ancestors** through the **prophets**;
    in these **last days**, he has **spoken to us** through the **Son**,
    whom he **made heir** of all **things**
    and through **whom** he created the **universe**,
    who is the **refulgence** of his **glory**,
        the very **imprint** of his being,
    and who **sustains all things** by his **mighty** word.
    When he had **accomplished** purification from sins,
    he **took** his **seat** at the right **hand** of the **Majesty** on high,
    as **far superior** to the angels
    as the **name** he has **inherited** is more **excellent** than theirs.

For to **which** of the **angels** did **God** ever **say**:
    You are my son; *this day I have begotten* **you**?
Or **again**:
    I will be a **father** *to him, and he shall be a* **son** *to me?*
And **again**, when he **leads** the firstborn into the **world**, he says:
    Let **all** *the angels of God* **worship** *him.*

A didactic reading of poetic and argumentative power about the nature and glory of Christ. The reading consists of a long and poetic setup that yields to an argumentative call-and-response. Allow the setup to gather tension in your reading that the call-and-response releases.

refulgence = ree-FUHL-j*nts = radiance or brilliance

"Universe," "refulgence," and "glory": This is celestial language to characterize the Son.

The call-and-response is like a small theater piece.

---

entrance into this world is not simply insurance upon which to rest, but rather, is a commissioning to "go, tell it on the mountains, over the hills and everywhere!"

READING II | The Letter to the Hebrews was written to people of Jewish background, as the title suggests. The contents of the letter as a whole are in keeping with an internal debate within Christianity between the "Judaizers," who argued that Gentiles must embrace Judaism prior to Baptism, and the "Antimonians," who insisted that those of Jewish back-

ground must reject the Law of the Old Testament.

The letter opens with today's passage, which acknowledges a change in God's means of revelation. Those of the previous Law (the Hebrews) were recipients of a divine message that was communicated "in partial and various ways." They did not receive the fullness of divine revelation. However, "in these last days," God has revealed himself fully in his Son. It is important to note that the author in no way intends to overturn or discard the method that God previously chose to communicate

himself; rather, the fullness of God's love has been made new. We have listened carefully during the season of Advent to the wisdom of the prophets, especially Isaiah, and continue to believe that this prophecy contains wisdom concerning God's plan of salvation for us today, but far superior is the dawning of the Lord's coming into this world.

This excerpt from the Letter to the Hebrews reads as though it was likely used as a liturgical hymn regarding faith in God's design of the universe through his Son. The one chosen to be the "heir of all things" is

GOSPEL John 1:1–18

A reading from the holy Gospel according to John

[In the **beginning** was the **Word**,
  and the **Word** was with **God**,
  and the Word **was** God.
He **was** in the beginning **with** God.
All things came to be **through** him,
  and **without him nothing** came to be.
What came to be **through him** was **life**,
  and **this life** was the **light** of the human **race**;
  the light **shines** in the **darkness**,
  and the **darkness** has not overcome it.]
A man named **John** was sent from God.
He came for **testimony**, to testify to the **light**,
  so that all might believe **through him**.
He was **not** the light,
  but came to **testify to** the light.
[The **true light**, which enlightens **everyone**,
  was **coming** into the world.
  He was **in** the world,
  and the **world** came to be **through** him,
  but the **world** did not **know** him.
  He **came** to what was his **own**,
  but his **own people** did not **accept** him.

An exhortatory reading that is one of the pillars of Christian theology. The emphases in the opening verses are crucial to that theology.

Linger a little at the contrast between light and darkness.

This passage about John links his testimony with the light.

TO KEEP IN MIND
Be careful not to swallow your words. Articulate carefully, especially at the end of lines.

---

to be praised as the perfect reflection of God: the "refulgence of his glory," the "very imprint of his being," the one who "sustains all things by his mighty word." Jesus is no mere prophet who has been called by God to impart words of challenge for the purpose of conversion; instead, he shares in God's majesty, "far superior to the angels." A Jewish audience would no doubt have been taken aback by the radical nature of these words; those keepers of God's covenant understood the words of this letter to imply a new way of inheritance. By choosing to quote Psalm 2:7—"You are my son;

this day I have begotten you"—the author makes no doubt that "in these last days," God has done something decidedly new in the revelation that emanates from his beloved Son.

GOSPEL | Today's Gospel reading from John, when placed in the context and flow of the four Masses designated for the Lord's Nativity, may be considered to be the theological stamp on the Church's celebration of the mystery of the Incarnation. Since John's Gospel is the last of the four Gospels to be composed

(near the end of the first century), it has a very high Christology. This means that the divinity of Jesus is emphasized over his humanity. John's Gospel does not have an infancy narrative; instead, Jesus first appears as a fully grown man and is designated from the start of his ministry as the "Christ," or the "anointed" one of God. In keeping with this theology, John's prologue opens not on earth but in the heavens: "In the beginning was the Word, and the Word was with God, and the Word was God."

For those who prefer the nativity story, complete with shepherds and angels

The Word becoming flesh is the heart of this reading.

But to those who **did** accept him
    he gave **power** to become **children** of God,
    to those who **believe** in his **name**,
    who were born **not** by natural generation
    nor by **human choice** nor by a man's **decision**
    but of **God**.
      And the **Word** became **flesh**
      and made his **dwelling among** us,
      and we **saw** his **glory**,
      the **glory** as of the **Father's only** Son,
      full of **grace** and **truth**.]

And once again, John testifies. His testimony yields revelation. Give proper emphasis to the word "revealed" at the end of the reading.

John **testified** to him and **cried out**, saying,
    "This was **he** of **whom** 1 **said**,
    'The one who is coming **after** me ranks **ahead** of me
    because he existed **before** me.'"
From his **fullness** we have **all** received,
    grace in place of **grace**,
    because while the **law** was given through **Moses**,
    grace and **truth** came through Jesus **Christ**.
No one has ever **seen** God.
The only **Son**, God, who is at the Father's side,
    has **revealed** him.

[Shorter: John 1:1–5, 9–14 (see brackets)]

and a manger, these words from the start of John's Gospel may seem less than warm and fuzzy. But that is precisely John's point—to remind Christian believers of the seriousness of the Incarnation, the Word made flesh. So often, Christians mistakenly limit the liturgical purpose of Christmas to the celebration of Jesus' birthday. Christmas is more than the opportunity to ruminate on the innocence of the child Jesus lying among the sheep and the cattle; it is meant to hone our attention on the wonder of God's desire to become one with humanity and thus all of creation. The celebration of the Incarnation revolves around the awesome truth that God did not simply choose to save the world from afar, but instead, God wanted to experience what his creation experiences. God's glory does not remain hidden, but in fact becomes intermingled with humanity so that our destiny is a sharing in Christ's divinity.

Furthermore, John's prologue introduces the symbol of Christ as the Light of the World. In these days of winter, in which the daylight will continue to grow stronger, the Church reminds us that only Jesus offers the world true light. Even though much of the world does not know him, and even his own would reject him, his light reveals the fullness of God's grace. S. W.

THE HOLY FAMILY OF JESUS, MARY, AND JOSEPH

LECTIONARY #17

READING I   Genesis 15:1–6; 21:1–3

A reading from the Book of Genesis

The **word** of the Lord came to **Abram** in a vision, saying:
   "**Fear not**, Abram!
      I am your **shield**;
      I will make your **reward** very great."
But Abram said,
   "O Lord GOD, what **good** will your **gifts** be,
   if I keep on being **childless**
   and have as my **heir** the **steward** of my house, Eliezer?"
Abram continued,
   "**See**, you have given me no **offspring**,
   and so one of my **servants** will be my **heir**."
Then the **word** of the LORD came to him:
   "**No**, that one shall **not be** your heir;
   your **own issue** shall be your **heir**."
The Lord took Abram outside and said,
   "**Look up** at the sky and count the stars, if you can.
Just so," he added, "shall your **descendants** be."
Abram put his **faith** in the LORD,
   who **credited** it to him as an act of **righteousness**.

A narrative reading in two parts, beginning with Abraham's visionary conversation with God (when he was still Abram), and concluding with the fulfillment of God's promise to Abraham to give Sarah a child. The first half of the reading goes from the word of the Lord to an act of righteousness. The second half names Abraham and Isaac, but focuses on Sarah.

Eliezer = el-ee-AY-zer

Five places of emphasis to note: "Fear not," "O Lord God," "See," "No," and "Look up."

Give emphasis to "descendants" and "righteousness."

There are options for today's readings. Contact your parish staff to learn which readings will be used.

READING I | **Genesis.** Abraham is considered the "father of faith" for Jews, Christians, and Muslims. Abram was chosen by God to be the foundation of a people that would be destined for greatness. History has shown us the bitter disagreement among the peoples who claim to be the rightful heirs of God's promise to Abraham. Perhaps this dispute over an inheritance would be better resolved by concentrating more upon the way in which Abraham grows and matures in his faith and love of God, regardless of God's reward for him. Abraham's overall faith journey is full of surprises and depends upon his willingness to trust and to obey God's command.

Today's installment from Genesis begins with God detecting not Abraham's faith but his fear: "Fear not, Abram!" Abram clearly tells God that his fear is based upon a dismal forecast for the future: What will become of his name if he has no children to carry on his line? God replies with a sacrament of sorts. God instructs him to gaze upon the stars in the night sky and to see in their immeasurable number the vastness of Abraham's legacy. God uses the massiveness of the cosmos to depict Abraham's lineage.

Then the story in the lectionary jumps ahead five chapters to God gifting Abraham's elderly wife with fertility; Sarah becomes pregnant and bears a son named Isaac. We ought to know that a major part of Abraham's journey of faith has been omitted here in creating this passage. Genesis 16 contains the story of the birth of Ishmael.

Sarah's name is repeated three times in this second part. Be sure to give them due emphasis.

The **LORD** took note of **Sarah** as he had **said** he would;
   he **did** for her as he had **promised**.
Sarah became **pregnant** and bore Abraham a **son** in his old age,
   at the **set time** that God had **stated**.
Abraham gave the name **Isaac** to this son of his
   whom Sarah **bore** him.

Or:

READING I   Sirach 3:2–6, 12–14

Sirach = SEER-ak; SĪ-ruhk

A didactic reading in which each set of phrases offers advice.

A reading from the Book of Sirach

God sets a father in **honor** over his children;
   a mother's **authority** he **confirms** over her sons.
Whoever **honors** his father **atones** for sins,
   and **preserves** himself from them.
When he **prays**, he is **heard**;
   he stores up **riches** who reveres his **mother**.
Whoever **honors** his father is **gladdened** by children,
   and, when he **prays**, is **heard**.
Whoever **reveres** his father will live a **long life**;
   he who **obeys** his father brings **comfort** to his mother.

Note the parallels established by the repetition of the word "whoever." The word "and" serves a similar purpose. Each of these teachings is meant to be equal.

My son, take **care** of your father when he is old;
   grieve him **not** as **long** as he lives.
Even if his **mind** fail, be **considerate** of him;
   revile him not all the **days** of his **life**;
kindness to a father will not be **forgotten**,
   firmly planted against the **debt** of your sins
   —a **house** raised in justice to **you**.

The advice in the second section, beginning here, is more familial, the words of a father to his son. You can proclaim it in this spirit.

Abraham and Sarah lose faith that God's promise would hold true for them. As a result, Abraham has relations with Hagar, Sarah's maidservant, and is given his first-born son. God's displeasure in Abraham's taking the matter into his own hands results in God providing Abraham with a second chance and the opportunity to learn from his lack of obedience. Just as with our father in faith, growth in trust and obedience often requires of us the willingness to forgive and to accept forgiveness, to give and to offer a second chance.

Sirach. Also known as the Book of Ecclesiasticus, the Book of Sirach contains wisdom literature written by the Jewish scribe Ben Sira between the years 200 and 175 BC. Because of its late authorship, this book is not contained within the Jewish canon, and thus does not appear in the authoritative canon used by the churches of the Reformation. However, the Catholic Church maintains the tradition of gleaning profound insight from the scribe's worldview.

The book of Sirach is essentially a book of collected ethical teachings. The themes of this book are very similar to those found in Proverbs and are similar in their poetic nature. Sirach's basic intent is to strengthen everyday relationships to manifest wisdom, which can be equated with the fear of God. In other words, bettering relationships between husband and wife, parents and children, the young and the old, the rich and the poor ultimately leads to an improvement in the reverence paid to God and to God's will.

The author's desire for right relationship is abundantly clear in today's short passage: a father is to be honored by his children, and a mother is to have authority

For meditation and context:

RESPONSORIAL PSALM   Psalm 105:1–2, 3–4, 5–6, 8–9 (7a , 8a)

R. The Lord remembers his covenant for ever.

Give thanks to the LORD, invoke his name;
     make known among the nations
         his deeds.
Sing to him, sing his praise,
     proclaim all his wondrous deeds.

Glory in his holy name;
     rejoice, O hearts that seek the LORD!
Look to the LORD in his strength;
     constantly seek his face.

You descendants of Abraham, his servants,
     sons of Jacob, his chosen ones!
He, the LORD, is our God;
     throughout the earth his
         judgments prevail.

He remembers forever his covenant
     which he made binding for a thousand
         generations
which he entered into with Abraham
     and by his oath to Isaac.

Or:

For meditation and context:

RESPONSORIAL PSALM   Psalm 128:1–2, 3, 4–5 (1)

R. Blessed are those who fear the Lord and walk in his ways.

Blessed is everyone who fears the LORD,
     who walks in his ways!
For you shall eat the fruit of your handiwork;
     blessed shall you be, and favored.

Your wife shall be like a fruitful vine
     in the recesses of your home;
your children like olive plants
     around your table.

Behold, thus is the man blessed
     who fears the LORD.
The LORD bless you from Zion:
     may you see the prosperity of Jerusalem
     all the days of your life.

READING II   Hebrews 11:8, 11–12, 17–19

A reading from the Letter to the Hebrews

Brothers and sisters:
By **faith** Abraham **obeyed** when he was called to go **out**
     to a place
     that he was to **receive** as an **inheritance**;
     he went **out**, not **knowing** where he was to go.

A didactic reading, unified by the repetition of the phrase "By faith" three times. Use the repetition to direct your reading, with each claim building on the intensity of the last.

over her sons. Paying due homage to one's parents, says Sirach, "atones for sins," and thus reveals wisdom (or the fear of the Lord). Sirach's teaching on family life may be particularly important in today's world, where families are quite fragile and are stretched to the limit by outside-the-house obligations and commitments. Sirach calls each member of the household to develop concern, respect, honor, and kindness within the relationships that constitute the family, an ancient teaching that has contemporary import.

READING II   **Hebrews.** The Letter to the Hebrews is believed to have been written several years before the destruction of the Temple in Jerusalem in the year AD 70. It is clear that the author (possibly Paul) was steeped in the milieu of Second Temple rabbinic dialogue, in which rabbis would interpret a contemporary event based on its consistency with a pattern found in Hebrew Scripture. The author's primary purpose in writing the letter is to convince his audience that Jesus truly is the long-awaited Messiah, who comes as a priest rather than as a prince. The Letter to

the Hebrews examines figures from the Hebrew Scriptures that point to such an understanding of the chosen Messiah.

Abraham certainly fulfills this expectation. Three times in today's readings, Abraham is described according to his "faith." In verse 8, Abraham's faith is demonstrated by recalling the initial call God made to him to set out from his native land "not knowing where he was to go." Verses 11 and 12 recall Abraham's strong faith when God promised that he, who was "as good as dead," and his barren wife would be the parents of an immeasurable number

By **faith** he received **power** to generate,
    even though he was **past** the normal **age**
    —and **Sarah** herself was **sterile**—
    for he **thought** that the one who had made the **promise**
       was **trustworthy**.
So it was that there came **forth** from one man,
    himself as good as **dead**,
    descendants as **numerous** as the **stars** in the **sky**
    and as **countless** as the **sands** on the **seashore**.

By faith Abraham, when put to the **test**, offered up **Isaac**,
    and he who had **received** the promises was **ready** to offer his
       only son,
    of whom it was said,
    "Through **Isaac descendants** shall **bear** your name."
He reasoned that **God** was able to raise **even** from the dead,
    and he received Isaac **back** as a **symbol**.

Or:

READING II   Colossians 3:12–21

A reading from the Letter of Saint Paul to the Colossians

Brothers and sisters:
[Put on, as God's chosen ones, **holy** and **beloved**,
    heartfelt **compassion**, **kindness**, **humility**, **gentleness**,
       and **patience**,
    bearing with one another and **forgiving** one another,
    if one has a **grievance** against another;
    as the **Lord** has forgiven **you**, so must you also do.
And over **all these** put on **love**,
    that is, the **bond** of perfection.
And let the **peace** of Christ control your **hearts**,
    the **peace** into which you were also **called** in one body.

Abraham's faith, according to the writer of Hebrews, gives him life, in the form of Isaac, whom he nearly sacrificed. The writer of Hebrews clearly intends to honor Abraham for the virtue of his faith.

Colossians = kuh-LOSH-uhnz

A didactic reading that speaks of the virtues of building community.

Each of these qualities is worthwhile, deserving emphasis.

---

of descendants. Finally, verses 17 and 19 depict Abraham's ultimate act of faith: the willingness to follow through on God's command to slaughter his son, Isaac. Not only would this sacrifice be incredibly torturous for any father to make, but in the case of Abraham, it also put in jeopardy the future of the great nation promised to him by God.

In all three of these moments in the saga of Abraham, we are left to ponder his battle with demons during what must have been extremely painful instances of discernment. Over and over again, he must

have been tempted to count himself as completely foolish for believing in the word that God sent him. Abandoning homeland, trusting in providence to provide, obediently willing to sacrifice his child—it is no wonder that Jews, Christians, and Muslims all refer to Abraham as our "father in faith."

Colossians. It is generally agreed upon by scholars that Paul wrote this letter to the Christians in Colossae, a city of Asia Minor east of Ephesus, when he was imprisoned in Rome between the years AD 60 and 61. Paul had never visited the city, but he had received word that this fledgling

community was struggling with a heresy that was being taught by some that Jesus was not truly divine. In countering this teaching, he writes: "For in him dwells the whole fullness of the deity bodily" (Colossians 2:9). Paul wants the Colossians to understand that Jesus is fully divine.

Chapter 3 of the letter consists of a series of exhortations based on baptismal theology. Thus, not only is Jesus to be understood as being fully divine, but those baptized into him are also to see themselves as "raised with Christ" and therefore able to have their hearts set on things

This passage concludes with a note of thanksgiving, a feeling to guide the community as it builds.

And be **thankful**.
Let the word of Christ **dwell** in you richly,
    as in all wisdom you **teach** and **admonish** one another,
    singing **psalms**, **hymns**, and spiritual **songs**
    with **gratitude** in your hearts to God.
And whatever you **do**, in **word** or in **deed**,
    do **everything** in the name of the Lord **Jesus**,
    giving **thanks** to God the Father **through** him.]

A challenging passage to proclaim: it reinforces codes of conduct common to Greco-Roman society but which Paul typically disdains. (Most scholars of early Christianity regard these verses as added later by someone other than the original author, likely a scribe.) Probably best to read this in a neutral tone.

Wives, be **subordinate** to your husbands,
    as is proper in the Lord.
Husbands, love your **wives**,
    and avoid any **bitterness** toward them.
Children, obey your **parents** in everything,
    for this is **pleasing** to the Lord.
Fathers, do not **provoke** your children,
    so they may not become **discouraged**.

[Shorter: Colossians 3:12–17 (see brackets)]

GOSPEL   Luke 2:22–40

A reading from the holy Gospel according to Luke

A vivid narrative reading, filled with prophetic signs and wonders fulfilled in the birth of Christ.

[When the **days** were **completed** for their **purification**
    according to the **law** of Moses,
    they took him up to **Jerusalem**
    to **present** him to the **Lord**,]
    just as it is **written** in the **law** of the Lord,
*Every **male** that opens the **womb** shall be **consecrated**
      to the Lord,*
    and to offer the **sacrifice** of
*a **pair** of turtledoves or **two young** pigeons,*
    in **accordance** with the **dictate** in the **law** of the Lord.

The sacrifice alluded to in these opening verses is meant to suggest to the assembly something of the sacrifice to come when Jesus is crucified.

---

above. Those baptized into Christ are to see themselves united as equals, for as Paul states in the verse immediately preceding our reading today: "Here there is not Greek and Jew, circumcision and uncircumcision, barbarian, Scythian, slave, free; but Christ is all and in all" (Colossians 3:11).

It must seem to Paul that the Christian community in Colossae needs further instruction on what is involved in "putting on" the new outlook of Christian discipleship. To be baptized into Christ means to embrace all that the Christ-life entails: "heartfelt compassion, kindness, humility,

gentleness, and patience." Unity in Christ demands that his members treat one another with perfect love, striving for peace and self-control. Maintaining the outlook of Christ by the members of his body leads to the welling up of worship and praise, with the singing of psalms and hymns and other songs of gratitude.

The final exhortation of this reading, which the lectionary suggests may be omitted for pastoral reasons, is more specifically designated toward the keeping of peaceful relations within the family. The first line may often cause discomfort in the

assembly, as Paul writes: "Wives, be subordinate to your husbands." Although such language may sound overly patriarchal to our ears, Paul follows this up with a command for husbands to "love" their wives. In the framework of baptismal relationships, Paul is not concerned here with power but rather with peace, striving for familial relationships that mirror the pattern of life of those who "were also called in one body."

GOSPEL | The second chapter of Luke's Gospel consists of three very separate, yet interrelated

Simeon = SIM-ee-uhn

Simeon's prophetic vision is fulfilled when he lays eyes on Jesus. His amazement is Luke's amazement.

Pause a moment at "revealed."
Anna's story is meant to echo Simeon's.
Phanuel = FAN-yoo-el

Pause a moment at "redemption of Jerusalem."

Now there was a **man** in Jerusalem whose **name** was **Simeon**.
This man was **righteous** and **devout**,
    awaiting the **consolation** of Israel,
    and the **Holy Spirit** was upon him.
It had been **revealed** to him by the Holy Spirit
    that he should **not see death**
    before he had seen the **Christ** of the **Lord**.
He **came** in the Spirit into the **temple**;
    and when the **parents** brought in the **child** Jesus
    to perform the **custom** of the **law** in regard to him,
    he took him into his **arms** and **blessed God**, saying:
        "**Now**, Master, you may let your servant go
            in **peace**, according to your word,
        for my **eyes** have **seen** your **salvation**,
            which you **prepared** in **sight** of all the peoples,
        a **light** for revelation to the **Gentiles**,
            and **glory** for your people **Israel**."
The child's father and mother were **amazed** at what was said
        about him;
    and Simeon blessed them and said to Mary his mother,
    "**Behold**, this child is **destined**
    for the **fall** and **rise** of **many** in Israel,
    and to be a **sign** that will be contradicted
    —and you yourself a **sword** will pierce—
    so that the **thoughts** of many **hearts** may be **revealed**."
There was also a **prophetess**, Anna,
    the daughter of **Phanuel**, of the tribe of **Asher**.
She was **advanced** in years,
    having lived **seven years** with her husband after her marriage,
    and then as a **widow** until she was eighty-four.
She never **left** the temple,
    but worshiped night and day with **fasting** and **prayer**.
And coming forward at that very time,
    she gave **thanks** to God and **spoke** about the child
    to all who were awaiting the **redemption** of Jerusalem. »

stories. It begins with the birth of Jesus (vv. 1–21), proceeds to his presentation in the Temple (vv. 22–40), and concludes with his being lost in the temple at the age of twelve (vv. 41–52). The chapter opens with the proclamation of a census by Caesar Augustus and ends with the statement, "The child grew and became strong, filled with wisdom; and the favor of God was upon him." The three sections of this chapter form a triptych of prophecy and revelation: the picture on the left, an icon of the shepherds heralding the Lord's birth; the picture on the right, an image of proph-

ecies of Simeon and Anna declaring Jesus to be Israel's salvation; and the central image, Jesus making his identity known by teaching the elders in the Temple. Taken together, these three sections demonstrate the growth that takes place in Jesus—not just his physical growth but also his development as the world's Savior. While Caesar Augustus is interested in charting numbers for the growth of the Roman Empire, Jesus appears as one who will call men and women to be counted for God's Kingdom.

Today's reading of the presentation of the Lord in the Temple concerns the rite of

consecration that was obligatory for Hebrew parents. This is a ritual purification that is meant to conclude the birthing process, which included the rite of redeeming the firstborn son (Exodus 13:12–15). The animal generally required for the sacrifice was a lamb, but because Mary and Joseph were poor, they were allowed to offer "a pair of turtledoves or two young pigeons." What is important here for Luke is that the parents of Jesus follow the prescribed law. God's prior revelation to them (in the form of the shepherds visiting the manger) might have led Mary and Joseph to see the miraculous

The ordinariness of the child growing strong is the outcome of prophetic signs and wonders the reading focuses on.

[When they had **fulfilled** all the prescriptions
    of the **law** of the **Lord**,
    they returned to **Galilee**,
    to their own town of **Nazareth**.
The child **grew** and became **strong**, **filled** with wisdom;
    and the **favor** of God was **upon** him.]

[Shorter: Luke 2:22, 39–40 (see brackets)]

> **TO KEEP IN MIND**
> As you prepare your proclamation, make choices about what emotions need to be expressed. Some choices are evident from the text, but some are harder to discern. Understanding the context of the Scripture passage will help you decide.

nature of this birth as placing the child above the standards of the law, but still, they did not neglect to follow the ordinary, age-old custom to dedicate their son to God.

Verses 25 to 38 serve to stamp the revelation announced by the shepherds' visitation to Jesus, as the prophet Simeon and the prophetess Anna declare the uniqueness of this baby boy. They put words to what the shepherds adored in silence. As Simeon holds Jesus in his arms and blesses God, Luke writes that Mary and Joseph were amazed at what he said about the child. Likewise, Anna approaches the child, thanks God, and prophesies about Jesus in relation to the redemption of Israel. These two figures, both wise and aged, both trustworthy representatives of the Temple establishment, leave no doubt that the child Jesus is to be "light for revelation to the Gentiles, and glory for your people Israel." S. W.

MARY, THE HOLY MOTHER OF GOD

LECTIONARY #18

READING I   Numbers 6:22–27

A reading from the Book of Numbers

The **LORD** said to **Moses**:
  "**Speak** to Aaron and his sons and **tell** them:
  This is how you shall bless the Israelites.
Say to them:
    The **LORD** bless you and **keep** you!
    The **LORD** let his face **shine** upon
      you, and be **gracious** to you!
    The **LORD** look upon you **kindly** and
      give you **peace**!
So shall they **invoke** my name upon the **Israelites**,
  and I will **bless** them."

A didactic reading, built on advice that God gives to Moses. The verbs "speak," "say," and "invoke" are crucial, as are repetitions of "The Lord." Use these repetitions to guide your proclamation.

Note how the word "bless" is repeated.

Note how "bless" echoes in "peace."

For meditation and context:

RESPONSORIAL PSALM   Psalm 67:2–3, 5, 6, 8 (2a)

R. May God bless us in his mercy.

May God have pity on us and bless us;
  may he let his face shine upon us.
So may your way be known upon earth;
  among all nations, your salvation.

May the nations be glad and exult
  because you rule the peoples in equity;
  the nations on the earth you guide.

May the peoples praise you, O God;
  may all the peoples praise you!
May God bless us,
  and may all the ends of the earth
    fear him!

READING I   The blessing prayer that God commands Moses to have Aaron proclaim to the Israelites is well known by Christians. In fact, it is one of the options for the prayer over the people to be used at the end of Mass. While the words of this blessing may be familiar to us, it is good to remember the context in which it was first uttered.

In the story of Israel's exodus from Egypt and sojourn to the Promised Land, this prayer for peace and prosperity is heard as the people are preparing to leave Mount Sinai and to embark on their forty years of wandering through the desert. The benediction itself was not meant to be a one-time prayer, but rather a prayer of blessing used by the Israelites on a daily basis to help ensure their safe passage.

This benediction for a successful journey may be broken down according to the six benefits that God will provide for his people. Verse 24 reassures the Israelites that he will "bless" and "keep" them. The word "bless," as in other cases of the Jewish *berakah*, suggests that God's countenance overshadows those whom he protects. Verse 25 refers to the Lord letting his face "shine" upon his chosen ones and being "gracious" to them. Clearly, the favor of the Lord is with those who are attentive to him. Finally, verse 26 requests the Lord's face to "look upon" his people, as he is asked to "give" them his peace. These six aspects of God's benevolent goodness are meant to evoke the generosity of God's care for those who have declared themselves willing to be led on pilgrimage by grace into the land flowing with milk and honey.

READING II   Galatians 4:4–7

A reading from the Letter of Saint Paul to the Galatians

Brothers and sisters:
When the **fullness** of time had come, God sent his Son,
    born of a woman, **born** under the law,
    to ransom those **under** the law,
    so that we might **receive** adoption as sons.
As **proof** that you are **sons**,
    God sent the **Spirit** of his Son into our hearts,
    crying out, "**Abba**, Father!"
So you are **no longer** a slave but a **son**,
    and if a **son** then also an **heir**, **through** God.

A didactic reading in which Paul connects the members of the early church in Galatia directly to Jesus. He does so in three sentences, introduced by "when," "as," and "so." In short order, he builds his argument and then concludes it.

The conclusion of Paul's argument, that we are no longer slaves but sons and heirs of God, is truly radical. It deserves some astonishment and emphasis.

TO KEEP IN MIND
Recognize how important your proclamation of the Word of God is. Prepare well and take joy in your ministry.

READING II It is believed that the addressees of Paul's letter to the Galatians were a group of Celtic Christians in northern Galatia who were wrestling with the Mosaic Law, which required circumcision in order to be a true disciple. Paul attempts to dismantle the chains of this law by suggesting that life in Christ is not meant to be burdensome, but freeing. Probably the most often quoted verse of Galatians is 3:28: "There is neither Jew nor Greek, there is neither slave nor free person, there is not male and female; for you are all one in Christ Jesus."

This same theme of freedom in Christ is found in today's short reading. Here Paul suggests that God chose a particular time in history ("when the set time had fully come") to follow through on his plan of salvation. Just as Paul had said several verses prior that in Christ there is neither slave nor free, now he suggests that a Christian's true identity (not by birth under the law but by Baptism into Christ) is that of being an adopted child of God. In others words, Christians must see themselves as close to God as God is close to his very own Son whom he has sent into the world. How is

God able to recognize those who have been adopted? Not by the mark of circumcision, but rather through the gift of the Spirit who inhabits the hearts of Christians and calls out to God with words of intimacy: "*Abba*, Father!"

What makes this reading so fitting for proclamation on the feast day of Mary, Mother of God, is the promise of an inheritance that Paul makes known in verse 7: God has made each of us "no longer a slave but a son, and if a son then also an heir." What does it mean to be an heir? Quite simply, it means discovering the freedom of

JANUARY 1, 2021 ■ MARY, THE HOLY MOTHER OF GOD 45

A short narrative reading that concludes the Nativity story. While the focus is on the infant Jesus lying in the manger, the eyes through which we see him are those of the shepherds. The shepherds modeled Christian devotion from the beginning of our faith.

Amazement is the primary emotion of this story.

The shepherds' glorifying and praising are to be our own.

GOSPEL   Luke 2:16–21

A reading from the holy Gospel according to Luke

The **shepherds** went in haste to **Bethlehem** and found **Mary**
    and **Joseph**,
  and the infant **lying** in the manger.
When they **saw** this,
  they made **known** the message
  that had been **told** them about this child.
All who heard it were **amazed**
  by what had been **told** them by the **shepherds**.
And **Mary** kept all these things,
  reflecting on them in her **heart**.
Then the **shepherds** returned,
  glorifying and **praising** God
  for **all** they had **heard** and **seen**,
  just as it had been **told** to them.

When eight days were **completed** for his circumcision,
  he was named **Jesus**, the name **given** him by the **angel**
  before he was **conceived** in the **womb**.

being called God's child. Just as Mary discovered true freedom in hearing and obeying God's will, so too do those adopted by God discover lasting freedom in following his Son.

| GOSPEL | Today's Gospel passage presents two very different reactions to the birth of Jesus. On the one hand, we see the shepherds filled with amazement as they run off to broadcast their discovery. On the other hand, we see the response offered by Mary. Luke states that "Mary kept all these things, reflecting

on them in her heart." Surely, she was no less convinced of God's gift in the birth of Jesus than were the shepherds; rather, she clearly wanted to contemplate the depths of what this birth might mean for the world.

Luke proceeds to suggest that as faithful Hebrew parents, Mary and Joseph follow through on the custom of having their son circumcised on the eighth day after his birth, when he is given the name "Jesus." As Mary continued to contemplate the nature of her son's birth, her quiet meditation not only leads to her demonstration of obedience to the ancient law but

also reveals her ongoing fiat to God's plan of salvation. Rather than naming the child according to her own desires, she selflessly follows the word of God, surrenders her own will, and makes way for the one who "will be great and will be called Son of the Most High" (Luke 1:32). Today, we are invited to meditate upon the gentle, humble, contemplative spirit of Mary as a means of echoing the announcement of peace made by the angel: "Glory to God in the highest heaven, and on earth peace to people of good will" (Luke 2:14). S. W.

THE EPIPHANY OF THE LORD

LECTIONARY #20

READING I Isaiah 60:1–6

A reading from the Book of the Prophet Isaiah

Isaiah = ī-ZAY-uh

An exhortatory reading filled with rich and poetic images and phrases. Radiance, light, gift giving, and praise guide this prophetic passage. Let these words guide your reading.

This passage is addressed to Jerusalem, but because it is written in the second person, it allows you to speak directly to the assembly. "Raise your eyes and look about. . . . "

dromedaries = DROM-eh-dayr-ees = single-humped camels
Midian= MID-ee-uhn
Ephah = EE-fuh
The camels and the gifts they carry prefigure the magi. Present this passage as a prelude to the Epiphany story.

Rise up in splendor, Jerusalem! Your **light** has **come**,
    the **glory** of the **Lord shines** upon you.
See, **darkness** covers the earth,
    and **thick clouds cover** the peoples;
but upon **you** the LORD **shines**,
    and **over** you appears his **glory**.
Nations shall walk by your **light**,
    and **kings** by your **shining radiance**.
Raise your eyes and **look** about;
    they all **gather** and **come** to you:
your **sons come** from **afar**,
    and your **daughters** in the **arms** of their **nurses**.

Then you shall be **radiant** at what you **see**,
    your **heart** shall **throb** and over**flow**,
for the **riches** of the sea shall be **emptied** out before you,
    the **wealth** of nations shall be **brought** to you.
Caravans of **camels** shall **fill** you,
    dromedaries from **Midian** and **Ephah**;
all from **Sheba** shall come
    bearing **gold** and **frankincense**,
    and **proclaiming** the **praises** of the **LORD**.

READING I The Book of the Prophet Isaiah is generally interpreted according to what biblical scholars believe to be three distinct sections, perhaps written at three different times: *Proto-Isaiah* (Chapters 1—39), *Deutero-Isaiah* (Chapters 40—55), and *Trito-Isaiah* (Chapters 56—66). Today's reading is taken from the third section of Isaiah and is its thematic heart, proclaiming the reclaimed beauty of Jerusalem after the years of darkness spent in exile. Thus, there is no wonder why Isaiah was important for Jews in the Second Temple era (roughly 450 BC to AD 70). Isaiah heralds with great joy: "Rise up in splendor, Jerusalem!"

Indeed, the prophet announces to the people a message of vindication—"upon you the Lord shines and over you appears his glory." However, he does not intend his words to be overly triumphalist. The reestablished radiance of Jerusalem comes with a hefty responsibility. While the people are meant to rebuild and reclaim their national status, they are now to recognize that nations will be guided by the way in which they serve the Lord. In other words, the prosperity of Jerusalem is not for its own sake but so that God's light will radiate throughout the world. A renewed Jerusalem is a Jerusalem that will profit all the nations.

READING II The entire season of Christmas, which centers on the mystery of the Incarnation, is devoted to contemplating the awesomeness of God's revelation. That God reveals himself in ancient times through moments of personal encounter—such as in the classic tale of Moses and the Burning Bush (Exodus 3:1–15) or in the silent breeze that communicates his presence to Elijah at the mouth

For meditation and context:

RESPONSORIAL PSALM Psalm 72:1–2, 7–8, 10–11, 12–13 (11)

R. Lord, every nation on earth will adore you.

O God, with your judgment endow the king,
    and with your justice, the king's son;
he shall govern your people with justice
    and your afflicted ones with judgment.

Justice shall flower in his days,
    and profound peace, till the moon be
    no more.
May he rule from sea to sea,
    and from the River to the ends of
    the earth.

The kings of Tarshish and the Isles shall
    offer gifts;
    the kings of Arabia and Seba shall
    bring tribute.
All kings shall pay him homage,
    all nations shall serve him.

For he shall rescue the poor when he
    cries out,
    and the afflicted when he has no one
    to help him.
He shall have pity for the lowly and the poor;
    the lives of the poor he shall save.

Ephesians = ee-FEE-zhuhnz

A didactic reading in which Paul emphatically includes the Gentile members of the early church in Ephesus into the community of believers. It's in two long sentences, emphasizing revelation and the gospel respectively.

Emphasize "Gentiles," "coheirs," "members," and "copartners" as part of the "same body."

READING II Ephesians 3:2–3a, 5–6

A reading from the Letter of Saint Paul to the Ephesians

Brothers and sisters:
You have **heard** of the **stewardship** of God's **grace**
    that was given to me for your **benefit**,
    namely, that the **mystery** was made known to me by **revelation**.
It was not made known to **people** in other **generations**
    as it has **now** been revealed
    to his **holy apostles** and **prophets** by the **Spirit**:
    that the **Gentiles** are **coheirs**, **members** of the **same** body,
    and **copartners** in the **promise** in Christ **Jesus** through
       the **gospel**.

A narrative reading that tells a rich and mysterious story, one that includes astrology and betrayal, providing a vivid context for the world into which Jesus was born.

The arrival of the magi sets the scene. Their desire to pay homage to the newborn king prepares the way for our own worship.

GOSPEL Matthew 2:1–12

A reading from the holy Gospel according to Matthew

When **Jesus** was born in **Bethlehem** of **Judea**,
    in the **days** of King **Herod**,
    behold, **magi** from the **east** arrived in Jerusalem, saying, **»**

---

of a cave (1 Kings 19:9–13)—there is no doubt. However, God's revelation becomes even closer in Jesus, a revelation perpetuated through the sending of the Holy Spirit.

Today's reading from Ephesians, which scholars generally agree was penned by someone other than Paul, declares that he, Paul, is a steward of God's grace. Unlike instances of revelation in the Old Testament that served to carve out a people from among the nations, the grace that the author of this letter describes is distributed universally. In other words, revelation is understood in terms of drawing people into

Christ in order to unite them into one body. Thus, the author unequivocally declares that "the Gentiles are coheirs" of the covenant revealed long ago and renewed in Jesus Christ. The author will continue in this chapter of Ephesians to describe himself as a "servant of the Gospel" whose mission is to "preach to the Gentiles the boundless riches of Christ" (Ephesians 3:7–8). Clearly, the grace revealed here is no cheap grace, but one requiring unfailing commitment and self-sacrifice.

GOSPEL It is important to remember the contents of chapter 1 of Matthew in order to situate and interpret the first twelve verses of this second chapter. Chapter 1 opens with the detailed genealogy of Jesus and proceeds to foretell the Lord's birth through the angel speaking to Joseph in a dream. In other words, in this rendition of Jesus' birth, there is no manger and no shepherds, no dramatic infancy narrative. Instead, Matthew is primarily interested in establishing that Jesus is born in the line of David; he is not an outsider but is thoroughly Jewish. This is important

homage = HOM-ij

Herod's trouble represents doubt and deception, which the subsequent verses elaborate.

"**Where** is the newborn **king** of the **Jews**?
We saw his **star** at its **rising**
　and have **come** to do him **homage**."
When King Herod heard this,
　he was greatly **troubled**,
　and **all Jerusalem** with him.
Assembling all the chief priests and the scribes of the people,
　he **inquired** of them **where** the Christ was to be **born**.
They said to him, "In **Bethlehem** of **Judea**,
　for **thus** it has been **written** through the **prophet**:
　　And **you**, **Bethlehem**, *land of* **Judah**,
　　　are by **no means least** *among the* **rulers** *of Judah;*
　　since from **you** *shall* **come** *a* **ruler**,
　　　who is to **shepherd** *my people* **Israel**."
Then **Herod** called the magi **secretly**
　and ascertained from them the **time** of the star's **appearance**.
He sent them to Bethlehem and said,
　"**Go** and search **diligently** for the **child**.
When you have **found** him, bring me **word**,
　that **I too may go** and do him homage."
After their **audience** with the king they set out.
And **behold**, the **star** that they had seen at its rising
　　preceded them,
　until it **came** and **stopped over** the place where the **child was**.
They were **overjoyed** at seeing the star,
　and on entering the house
　they saw the child with **Mary** his mother.
They **prostrated** themselves and did him **homage**.
Then they **opened** their treasures
　and offered him gifts of **gold**, **frankincense**, and **myrrh**.
And having been **warned** in a **dream** not to **return** to Herod,
　they **departed** for their country by **another** way.

Pause slightly after "stopped."

prostrated = PROS-tray-t*d

Awe and wonder authenticate the magi and their prophetic visions. Their gifts are utterly precious. And their dream of warning is impossible to ignore. Don't sell their departure short. It's what makes this passage so vivid.

to Matthew because he writes in the aftermath of the Temple's destruction (AD 70) with the objective to convince Jews and Jewish Christians that Jesus is the fulfillment of the law.

　Chapter 2 of Matthew's Gospel opens with a question spoken by foreigners (i.e., non-Jews): "Where is the newborn king of the Jews?" It is significant that the magi are from the far east (to be read as "the ends of the earth"). King Herod, who was king of Judea, is greatly troubled by this and plots the demise of the rival king. Matthew's objective here is to highlight, from the outset of the Messiah's birth, the rejection by his own that he will experience during his lifetime. In Matthew's Gospel, the way in which Jesus preaches the fulfillment of the law will continually be viewed as a threat to continuity. For example, as he will say in chapter 5: "Do not think that I have come to abolish the Law or the Prophets; I have not come to abolish but to fulfill them" (Matthew 5:17). Again, the Gospel is constructed so that we are to see from his very birth that Jesus' mission will be frustrated and even thwarted by those within his own family. Thus, it is the Gentiles from the far east who pay homage to the baby king. Herod's plan of destruction is overturned when a dream instructs the magi to return home. Far removed from Bethlehem of Judea, these seekers surely continued to testify to God's wondrous deeds. S. W.

THE BAPTISM OF THE LORD

LECTIONARY #21

READING I   Isaiah 55:1–11

A reading from the Book of the Prophet Isaiah

Isaiah = ī-ZAY-uh

An exhortatory reading of grandeur and power. Its argument makes use of the imperative voice in verbs such as "heed" and "seek." These are the words of the Lord that you are speaking directly to the assembly.

> Thus says the LORD:
> All you who are **thirsty**,
>   **come** to the **water**!
> You who have no **money**,
>   **come**, receive **grain** and **eat**;
> **come**, without paying and without **cost**,
>   drink **wine** and **milk**!
> Why spend your **money** for what is not **bread**,
>   your **wages** for what fails to **satisfy**?
> **Heed** me, and you shall **eat** well,
>   you shall **delight** in rich fare.
> Come to me **heedfully**,
>   **listen**, that you may have **life**.

The renewal of the everlasting covenant is what unifies this whole reading. The promise of this covenant is what compels the Lord to tell the people to listen.

Place even stress on all the words in this line.

> I will **renew with you** the everlasting **covenant**,
>   the **benefits** assured to David.
> As I made him a **witness** to the **peoples**,
>   a **leader** and **commander** of nations,
> so shall you summon a nation you knew not,
>   and **nations** that knew you **not** shall run to you,
> because of the LORD, your **God**,
>   the **Holy One** of Israel, who has **glorified** you.
>
> **Seek** the LORD while **he** may be found,
>   **call** him while he is **near**. »

There are options for today's readings. Contact your parish staff to learn which readings will be used.

READING I   **Isaiah 55.** The Old Testament is filled with stories of prophecies that warn against the failure to seek conversion and follow the way of the Lord. Take, for example, Moses' battle with Pharaoh in Exodus (Exodus 5). Moses helps to forecast God's displeasure with Pharaoh's hard-heartedness in Egypt's gradual demise through the ten plagues. Likewise

the message of Jonah to the Ninevites is equally severe: "Forty days more, and Nineveh will be overthrown" (Jonah 3:4). Isaiah, too, chastises the pride of Samaria, likening its people to those whose lives have been ravaged by drunkenness. Indeed, the Old Testament prophets understood clearly that reform and change of heart were necessary for the reception of God's Word.

However, in this reading from Isaiah, the words of the prophet come in the form of an invitation rather than a warning. Rather than accentuating gloom and doom,

Isaiah proclaims the bounty of a God who freely gives. "Come, buy wine and milk without money and without cost." What an attractive summons! God promises the gifts of fortification without needing to be reimbursed! At least not financially. Instead, he wants one thing: for the people to listen to him. God makes his desire known: "Come to me heedfully, listen, that you may have life."

From the initial invitation to come to the water (representing the fullness of life that God promises) Isaiah proceeds in verses eight to eleven to describe more

Let the **scoundrel** forsake his way,
and the **wicked man** his thoughts;
let him **turn** to the LORD for **mercy**;
to our **God**, who is **generous** in **forgiving**.
For my **thoughts** are not your **thoughts**,
nor are your ways **my ways**, says the LORD.
As **high** as the heavens are above the **earth**
so **high** are my ways above your ways
and my **thoughts** above your **thoughts**.

For **just** as from the heavens
the **rain** and **snow** come **down**
and **do not** return there
till they have **watered** the **earth**,
making it **fertile** and **fruitful**,
giving **seed** to the one who **sows**
and **bread** to the one who **eats**,
so shall my word be
that goes **forth** from my **mouth**;
my **word** shall not **return** to me **void**,
but shall **do my will**,
achieving the end for which I **sent** it.

Or:

The rain and the snow, and the fertility they increase, are signs of God's word, similarly fertile.

Even stresses on these words.

Again, even stresses.

TO KEEP IN MIND
The words in bold are suggestions for ways to express the meaning of the reading. Consider using them as you practice the reading, then choose to stress them or to find your own way of proclaiming.

fully what this listening might look like. First, listening to God entails the recognition that God's ways are beyond human comprehension. Thus, listening to God requires the suspension of human expectations. Second, listening means that one is able to see that God's actions in this world successfully achieve his intentions: "My word shall not return to me void, but shall do my will, achieving the end for which I sent it. Although the world may fail to see the way in which God plants the seeds of his kingdom, those who listen to him reap the benefits of its growth.

Isaiah 42. The first four verses of today's reading constitute the first of Isaiah's four Suffering Servant songs. These poems were written to describe God's intention to send a Messiah, meaning the "anointed" one, who would usher in a kingdom of lasting peace. Rather than mentioning the context of suffering, this first poem introduces the Messiah as the one who pleases God. He will work tirelessly for the dawning of justice and will not be discouraged.

Verses six and seven shift from an introduction of the Messiah to God's speaking directly to his servant and commissioning him to be a "light for the Gentiles." This servant, governed by the Spirit, will not exhibit power through the destruction of life, but rather, he will be one to heal and overturn the evil of this world, such as giving sight to the blind, setting captives free, and illuminating the way of those trapped in darkness.

God's covenant with Israel comes very much into play when reflecting on the ministry of the Messiah. The people redeemed from slavery in Egypt, led into the Promised Land by God's angel, and then subjected to captivity in Babylon

READING I   Isaiah 42:1–4, 6–7

A reading from the Book of the Prophet Isaiah

Thus says the LORD:
Here is my **servant** whom I uphold,
   my **chosen one** with whom I am **pleased**,
upon whom I have **put** my spirit;
   he shall bring forth **justice** to the **nations**,
not crying **out**, not **shouting**,
   not making his **voice heard** in the **street**.
A bruised reed he shall not break,
   and a **smoldering wick** he shall not **quench**,
until he establishes **justice** on the **earth**;
   the **coastlands** will wait for his **teaching**.

I, the LORD, have **called** you for the **victory** of justice,
   I have **grasped you** by the hand;
I **formed** you, and **set** you
   as a **covenant** of the people,
   a **light** for the nations,
to open the **eyes** of the **blind**,
   to bring out **prisoners** from **confinement**,
   and from the **dungeon**, those who live in **darkness**.

Isaiah = ī-ZAY-uh

An exhortatory reading in which the Lord identifies his servant, characterizing his virtues in terms of his humility and preparedness, followed by a passage in which the Lord shifts from talking about his chosen servant in the third person ("he") to the second person ("you"), which allows you to direct your proclamation to the gathered assembly. Take advantage of this shift in pronouns.

Even stresses on the words in this line, which present a compelling image. A bruised reed is easy to break; why isn't the chosen servant breaking the reed?

Emphasize "grasped you" and "formed you."

The passage ends with images of dire things the Lord will use "you" to correct.

For meditation and context:

RESPONSORIAL PSALM   Isaiah 12:2–3, 4bcd, 5–6 (3)

R. You will draw water joyfully from the springs of salvation.

God indeed is my savior;
   I am confident and unafraid.
My strength and my courage is the LORD,
   and he has been my savior.
With joy you will draw water
   at the fountain of salvation.

Give thanks to the LORD, acclaim his name;
   among the nations make known his deeds,
   proclaim how exalted is his name.

Sing praise to the LORD for his
   glorious achievement;
   let this be known throughout all
   the earth.
Shout with exultation, O city of Zion,
   for great in your midst
   is the Holy One of Israel!

Or:

---

surely struggled with the way God revealed Israel as his chosen people. If chosen, then why not powerful and mighty in stature? If chosen, why did Israel experience so much suffering throughout its history? The same could be asked of God's servant. If called "for the victory of justice" and led by God's hand, why must the Messiah suffer? The answer boils down to faithfulness. Just as the Suffering Servant trusts unconditionally in the will of God, so must Israel learn that God desires most of all a listening, obedient heart.

READING II | **Acts.** Due to the vision he received in a trance earlier in this tenth chapter of Acts, Peter recognizes that God does not show favoritism. While he was alone praying, he realized he was hungry and was shown, in his vision, a variety of living creatures that could serve as food. When he utters words of resistance, calling these animals unclean, or profane, a voice says to him, "What God has made clean, you are not to call profane." (Acts 10:9–16). As Peter is left to ruminate on the vision, he is approached by a group of men requesting that he come

with them to the house of Cornelius. Because Cornelius is a Roman centurion, he is to be considered unclean according to Jewish customs. However, Peter makes the connection between this invitation to enter Cornelius' house and his dream and concludes, "God has shown me that I should not call any person profane or unclean" (Acts 10:28).

Fast-forward to today's reading. Peter is standing before a large crowd gathered in the house of Cornelius. These verses are part of a short catechesis that Peter imparts regarding the person of Jesus Christ, whom

For meditation and context:

RESPONSORIAL PSALM   Psalm 29:1–2, 3–4, 3, 9–10 (11b)

R. The Lord will bless his people with peace.

Give to the LORD, you sons of God,
  give to the LORD glory and praise,
give to the LORD the glory due his name;
  adore the LORD in holy attire.

The voice of the LORD is over the waters,
  the LORD, over vast waters.

The voice of the LORD is mighty;
  the voice of the LORD is majestic.

The God of glory thunders,
  and in his temple all say, "Glory!"
The LORD is enthroned above the flood;
  the LORD is enthroned as king forever.

A somewhat complex exhortatory reading in that it makes claims about love in terms of obedience, and obedience in terms of faith. The reading divides in two. The first part focuses on love and keeping the commandments. The second part insists on the life of the Spirit that testifies of the Son.

"Commandments" is repeated three times and then followed by the word "burdensome." Be sure to stress the word "not" before "burdensome." And then emphasize the word "victory" to diffuse any lingering connection.

Allow the repetition of "water and blood" to resonate. Likewise the repetitions of "Spirit," "three," and "testify" (and its variants) that dominate the second part of this reading.

READING II   1 John 5:1–9

A reading from the first Letter of Saint John

Beloved:
Everyone who believes that **Jesus** is the **Christ** is **begotten**
    by God,
  and everyone who loves the **Father**
  loves also the one **begotten** by him.
In this way we **know** that we **love** the children of **God**
  when we **love God** and **obey** his commandments.
For the **love** of **God** is **this**,
  that we **keep** his **commandments**.
And his **commandments** are not **burdensome**,
  for whoever is **begotten** by God **conquers** the world.
And the **victory** that conquers the world is our **faith**.
Who indeed is the **victor** over the world
  but the one who believes that **Jesus** is the Son of God?

This is the one who came through water and blood, **Jesus Christ**,
    not by water alone, but by water and blood.
The **Spirit** is the one who **testifies**,
  and the **Spirit** is truth.

God anointed "with the Holy Spirit and power" (Acts 10:38). Peter's preaching begins with the admission that God does not show favoritism. Thus, the reader is able to see how Peter himself comes to the recognition that the preaching of Christ is not meant to be exclusive in any way. As he continued to describe for the crowd the mission that Jesus left to his followers, the Holy Spirit "fell upon all who were listening to the word" (Acts 10:44). Although the circumcised visitors to Cornelius' house find it difficult to believe that the Spirit would descend upon the Gentiles in the room,

Peter is quick to see God's indiscriminate grace, and orders that all be baptized (Acts 10:48).

The transformation of Peter's worldview, from one of seeing the need to distinguish the clean from the unclean to one of recognizing God's goodness extending to all of creation is particularly important in our articulation of a theology of Baptism. While it may be tempting to think of Baptism as making a person more "holy," it is really meant to be a sacrament that helps us to live into the unity of Christ that God desires for the whole world. Baptism is

a social leveler that breaks down divisions between male and female, Jew and Greek, slave and freeperson (Galatians 3:28). God does not show favoritism.

1 John. The three letters of John are believed to have been written at the close of the first century AD. They represent the time of transition from the Apostolic Period to the time of the infant institutional Church. Like so many of the New Testament epistles, the First Letter of John was written to several churches who were battling heresies that proposed that Jesus was not truly God. Some in the community

So there are **three** that **testify**,
    the **Spirit**, the **water** and the **blood**,
    and the **three** are of **one accord**.
If we **accept** human testimony,
    the testimony of **God** is surely greater.
Now the testimony of **God** is **this**,
    that he has **testified** on **behalf** of his **Son**.

Or:

_____

READING II   Acts of the Apostles 10:34–38

A reading from the Acts of the Apostles

Peter proceeded to speak to those gathered
    in the **house** of Cornelius, saying:
    "In **truth**, I see that **God** shows no **partiality**.
Rather, in every nation whoever **fears** him and acts **uprightly**
    is **acceptable** to him.
You know the **word** that he sent to the **Israelites**
    as he proclaimed **peace** through Jesus **Christ**,
        who is **Lord** of all,
    what has **happened** all over **Judea**,
    beginning in Galilee after the **baptism**
    that John preached,
    how God **anointed** Jesus of Nazareth
    with the **Holy Spirit** and **power**.
He went about doing **good**
    and healing all those oppressed by the devil,
    for **God** was **with** him."

TO KEEP IN MIND
Make eye contact with the assembly. This helps keep the assembly engaged with the reading.

An exhortatory reading in a narrative context, spoken by Peter to some early apostles of Jesus. This reading expresses ancient convictions of the earliest members of the faith.

"Peace," "Christ," and "Lord" express a unified vision of things.

Even emphasis on the words of this line.

Even emphasis here as well, characterizing Jesus' powers.

believed themselves to be above the law and therefore not susceptible to accusations of immorality. John's reproach calls them to return to the basic Commandments, especially the prescription to "love one another" (1 John 3:11).

In this portion of the letter, John argues that keeping the commands of God is the essential way that people can be assured that they are God's children. Rather than seeing the commands of God as a heavy burden, disciples of Jesus are to understand them as a way "to conquer the world." John makes it abundantly certain

that conquering the world cannot be done according to one's own design and one's own spiritual prowess, rather only "the one who believes that Jesus is the Son of God" can do this.

Verses 6–9 of this chapter continue by spelling out the evidence for this assertion of faith. The three forms of testimony are water, blood, and the Spirit. Tradition holds that John understands the water to be a symbol for Jesus' purity and the blood to be a symbol for his sufferings. The Spirit recognizes both the spotlessness of Jesus' mission and the fullness of his sacrifice.

Likewise, disciples are to strive for purity in their relations and complete dedication in their faith.

GOSPEL   Many theologians have struggled to make sense of Jesus' baptism by John in the Jordan. The general question they debate is, if Jesus is the Son of God, was it necessary that he be baptized? In some ways, John's own words in the first two verses of this Gospel reading would suggest that the answer to this question is no, as he is quite clear that the power and the authority of the one who is

A narrative reading that emphasizes John the Baptist as the precursor to Jesus in two parts. The first focuses on John the Baptist's ministry foretelling the coming of Jesus; the second focuses on Jesus' baptism at the hands of John the Baptist. These scriptural prefigurations are like theological rhymes.

Even emphasis on the words of this line.

Likewise, even emphasis on these words.

GOSPEL   Mark 1:7–11

A reading from the holy Gospel according to Mark

This is what John the Baptist proclaimed:
  "One **mightier** than I is coming **after** me.
I am not worthy to **stoop** and **loosen** the thongs of his sandals.
I have baptized you with water;
  he will **baptize** you with the **Holy Spirit**."

It happened in those days that **Jesus** came from **Nazareth**
    of Galilee
  and was **baptized** in the **Jordan** by **John**.
On coming up out of the water he saw the **heavens** being
    torn **open**
  and the **Spirit**, like a **dove**, descending **upon** him.
And a voice came from the heavens,
  "**You** are my beloved **Son**; with you I am well **pleased**."

to come after him are far greater than his own. However, it is necessary to acknowledge the nature of the baptism performed by John. He sought to prepare hearts for the coming of God's Kingdom; thus, his baptism was a visible means of sealing conversion. While Jesus may not have needed any sort of conversion, his willingness to be baptized represents his total allegiance to the Kingdom. In the water, Jesus himself becomes the very sign of the dawning of the Kingdom. What John has been pointing to has now been fully revealed in Jesus.

For this reason, the Holy Spirit plays a particularly important role at the baptism of the Lord. First of all, John states in verse 8 that "he will baptize you with the Holy Spirit." This suggestion of the Spirit as the gift of Baptism must be connected to what Jesus experiences in the Jordan in verses 10–11. As he emerges from the water, he sees the Spirit descend upon him and he hears a heavenly voice declare: "You are my beloved Son; with you I am well pleased." The seeing of the Spirit and the hearing of the voice ratify this relationship.

It is not the sealing of conversion, but the acknowledgement of love. This moment in Jesus' life reassures him that everything he does from this point forward in making God's Kingdom a reality, he does not do alone. This is what makes John's prophetic words about Jesus baptizing with the Spirit so true; the mission of Jesus is not simply to convert hearts but to establish a relationship in which his followers believe themselves to be beloved by God. S. W.

SECOND SUNDAY IN ORDINARY TIME

LECTIONARY #65

READING I   1 Samuel 3:3b–10, 19

A reading from the first Book of Samuel

Samuel was **sleeping** in the **temple** of the LORD
    where the **ark** of **God** was.
The LORD called to Samuel, who answered, "**Here** I am."
Samuel ran to **Eli** and said, "**Here** I am. You **called** me."
"I did not **call** you," Eli said. "Go **back** to **sleep**."
So he went back to **sleep**.
Again the LORD called Samuel, who **rose** and went to **Eli**.
"**Here** I am," he said. "You **called** me."
But Eli answered, "I did not call you, my son. Go back to **sleep**."

At that time Samuel was not **familiar** with the LORD,
    because the LORD had not **revealed** anything to him as yet.
The LORD called Samuel **again**, for the **third** time.
Getting up and going to Eli, he said, "**Here** I am. You **called** me."
Then Eli **understood** that the LORD was calling the youth.
So he said to Samuel, "Go to **sleep**, and if you are **called**, reply,
    '**Speak**, LORD, for your **servant** is **listening**.'"
When Samuel went to **sleep** in his place,
    the LORD **came** and revealed his **presence**,
    calling out as before, "Samuel, **Samuel!**"
Samuel answered, "**Speak**, for your servant is **listening**."

Samuel **grew** up, and the LORD was **with** him,
    not permitting any **word** of his to be without **effect**.

A rich narrative reading that connects vocation directly to the power of dreams.

Eli = EE-lī

This opening section involves repetitions of the phrases "Here I am," "You called me," and "Go back to sleep." There is no need to overemphasize any of these phrases. Nevertheless, allow their ordinariness to shift into something more extraordinary in your voicing of them as the reading proceeds.

Here, Eli's understanding increases our anticipation that something powerful will happen to Samuel.

Give this second utterance of the word "listening" additional resonance.

READING I The calling of prophets in the Old Testament always involves some sort of grand drama. Genesis 12 depicts Abraham, at the age of seventy-five, leaving the land of Harran with his elderly wife and every cherished possession in response to God's invitation to make of him a great nation. Moses hears the voice of God coming from a burning bush when he is given the call to liberate the Israelites from their Egyptian slavery (Exodus 3). The Old Testament suggests that God chooses unlikely characters who hesitate to obey his command.

While the calling of Samuel is surely dramatic—the call comes to a youth born of Hannah long after her childbearing years had come to an end—Samuel's response to God is anything but hesitant. Since childhood, Samuel had been under the tutelage of the temple priests and had spent many a night watching over the Ark of the Covenant. In many respects, the young boy is well positioned to hear the voice of God. Simply trying to discern the voice, Samuel consistently answers: "Here I am. You called me."

It takes three tries for God to break through to Samuel and help him realize that it is not the high priest Eli calling him. In fact, it is Eli who alerts Samuel to the nature of the call, instructing Samuel to modify his response ever so slightly: "Speak, Lord, for your servant is listening." Two important facets of discerning God's call are evident in Samuel's story. First, Eli helps him discern. Discernment is best done when the project involves a variety of perspectives and not simply one's own thinking. Second, Samuel announces to the Lord that he is listening. A selfless prophet is one who

For meditation and context:

RESPONSORIAL PSALM   Psalm 40:2, 4, 7–8, 8–9, 10 (8a and 9a)

R. Here am I, Lord; I come to do your will.

I have waited, waited for the LORD,
  and he stooped toward me and
    heard my cry.
And he put a new song into my mouth,
  a hymn to our God.

Sacrifice or offering you wished not,
  but ears open to obedience you gave me.
Holocausts or sin-offerings you sought not;
  then said I, "Behold I come."

"In the written scroll it is prescribed for me,
to do your will, O my God, is my delight,
  and your law is within my heart!"

I announced your justice in the
    vast assembly;
  I did not restrain my lips, as you,
    O LORD, know.

READING II   1 Corinthians 6:13c–15a, 17–20

Corinthians = kohr-IN-thee-uhnz

A didactic reading about avoiding immorality.

The body is the focus of this reading. The word is repeated several times. Paul's argument involves an insistence on the goodness of the body and his proscription against treating the body immorally. Keep your emphasis on the body while you read.

A reading from the first Letter of Saint Paul to the Corinthians

Brothers and sisters:
The body is not for **immorality**, but for the **Lord**,
  and the **Lord** is for the **body**;
    God **raised** the Lord and will also raise **us** by his power.

Do you not **know** that your **bodies** are **members** of **Christ**?
But whoever is **joined** to the Lord becomes one **Spirit** with him.
Avoid immorality.
Every other **sin** a person commits is **outside** the body,
  but the **immoral** person sins against his **own** body.
Do you not **know** that your body
  is a temple of the Holy Spirit **within** you,
    whom you **have** from God, and that you are **not** your own?
For you have been **purchased** at a **price**.
Therefore **glorify** God in your **body**.

Slight emphasis on "glorify."

> **TO KEEP IN MIND**
> Read the Scripture passage and its commentary in *Workbook*. Then read it from your Bible, including what comes before and after it, so that you understand the context.

truly listens to the voice of God at all times. Because of his humility and desire to serve the Lord, the Lord blessed Samuel, "not permitting any word of his to be without effect."

READING II It is generally accepted that Paul's correspondence to the Corinthians took place in the middle of the first century AD. Furthermore, it is widely known that the Christian community at Corinth had a host of problems that Paul, as an ambassador of Christ, felt obliged to address. At the very top of the list was the issue of a sort of spiritual pride that led

many in the community to divorce the body from the spirit, meaning that the body could participate in immoral acts without damage to the spirit.

In this section of his letter, Paul attends to this egotism on the part of the Corinthians. He frames his message in terms of belonging: because Baptism grafts members onto Christ, there is no aspect of the body that can be used for any other purpose than for glorifying God. The image of the body is important in Paul's writing, and here he wishes to claim a holistic understanding of it. Instead of thinking of the brain

(and therefore wisdom) as the sole locus of spiritual gifts, Paul declares the entire body to be a "temple of the Holy Spirit." Simply put, sexual immorality (*porneia*), physical licentiousness, prostitution, and any form of desecration of the body have no place in Paul's very incarnational theology.

GOSPEL Unlike the synoptic Gospels, which record the baptism of Jesus as a firsthand occurrence, the Gospel of John relies upon the testimony of the Baptist to reveal Jesus' true nature: "Now I have seen and testified that he is the

A narrative reading about a moment early in Jesus' ministry when he began to accumulate followers. In this account, John the Baptist is the one who initiates others to follow Jesus, with the words "Behold, the Lamb of God." Allow that imperative to resonate.

Allow the various names to resonate as well, including "Rabbi."

This conviction that Jesus is the messiah comes very early in the Gospel of John.

Cephas = SEE-fuhs

GOSPEL   John 1:35–42

A reading from the holy Gospel according to John

John was standing with two of his disciples,
   and as he watched **Jesus** walk by, he said,
   "**Behold**, the **Lamb** of **God**."
The two disciples **heard** what he said and **followed** Jesus.
Jesus **turned** and saw them following him and said to them,
   "What are you **looking for**?"
They said to him, "**Rabbi**"—which translated means **Teacher**—,
   "where are you **staying**?"
He said to them, "**Come**, and you will **see**."
So they **went** and **saw** where Jesus was staying,
   and they **stayed** with him that day.
It was about four in the afternoon.
Andrew, the brother of Simon **Peter**,
   was one of the two who heard John and followed Jesus.
He first **found** his own brother **Simon** and told him,
   "We have found the **Messiah**" —which is translated **Christ**—.
Then he **brought** him to Jesus.
Jesus **looked** at him and said,
   "You are **Simon** the son of **John**;
   you will be called **Cephas**"—which is translated **Peter**.

Son of God." (John 1:34). The next day, after Jesus was baptized, John spots him walking by the Jordan and makes his identity known once again: "Behold, the Lamb of God." Thus, from the words of the Prologue that announce Jesus as the Word that "became flesh" (v. 14) and the "true light" that has come into the world (v. 9) to the testimony of John the Baptist, hearers of John's Gospel come to know the Lord's nature.

It is clear from the very start that following Jesus is worthwhile. The two disciples on the river's shore hear the words of the Baptist, and they follow Jesus without question. In fact, it is Jesus who questions them: "What are you looking for?" This question is really the foundational stamp of John's Gospel that is posed to all seekers. Rather than answering Jesus' question head-on, the two question Jesus: "Where are you staying?" It is significant that the disciples are unable to answer Jesus and want more contextual information about his circumstances. Unlike us, who have been told who Jesus is, they remain puzzled.

"Come, and you will see." Like the basic question "What are you looking for?" this is directed as much to us as it is to the two disciples. What did they discover when they went to where Jesus was staying? Certainly, it was enough to convince them that they had found the long-awaited Messiah. The evangelist's theological agenda is clearly revealed within these opening verses of the Gospel: seek, and you will see. S. W.

THIRD SUNDAY
IN ORDINARY TIME

LECTIONARY #68

READING I Jonah 3:1–5, 10

A reading from the Book of the Prophet Jonah

Jonah = JOH-nuh
Nineveh = NIN-uh-vuh

A narrative reading with the scope of an epic but the purpose of a parable. Be sure to stress the enormous largeness of Nineveh to give proper context to the parabolic quality of the reading.

The first part of the reading tells the story of Jonah's journey. It concludes with the people of Nineveh heeding his warning. Emphasize "all," "great," and "small" in this line.

The second, shorter part of the reading depicts God's mercy but also, as a shadow, the harshness of his judgment, which he doesn't act on, thanks to Jonah.

TO KEEP IN MIND

Pause after you announce the book of the Bible at the beginning of the reading. Pause again after the reading, before you proclaim the concluding statement ("The Word of the Lord" or "The Gospel of the Lord").

The **word** of the LORD came to **Jonah**, saying:
   "**Set out** for the great **city** of **Nineveh**,
   and announce to it the **message** that I will **tell** you."
So **Jonah** made ready and **went** to **Nineveh**,
   according to the LORD's **bidding**.
Now Nineveh was an **enormously large** city;
   it took **three days** to go through it.
Jonah began his **journey** through the city,
   and had gone but a **single day's walk** announcing,
   "**Forty days more** and Nineveh shall be **destroyed**,"
when the people of Nineveh **believed** God;
   they proclaimed a **fast**
   and **all** of them, **great** and **small**, put on **sackcloth**.

When God **saw** by their actions how they **turned** from their
      evil **way**,
   he **repented** of the evil that he had **threatened** to do to them;
   he did **not** carry it out.

READING I The selection of these verses from the Book of Jonah clearly emphasizes the theme of repentance. Not only do the people of Nineveh repent of the evil, but God himself repents of his desire to destroy Nineveh when he sees the people's resolve to change their lives. What is omitted from this telling of the story is Jonah's repentance—the best-known part of the tale—when he spends three days and three nights in the belly of a fish after he had tried to flee from God's command to summon the Ninevites to conversion (Jonah 1:2).

Clearly, the author of Jonah wishes to distinguish the Ninevites' response to God's word from that of Jonah's. Whereas Jonah attempts to run away from God, the people of Nineveh immediately respond with concrete actions that demonstrate their willingness to undergo transformation. It took somewhat longer for Jonah, but even this sluggish prophet comes to his senses, accepts the Lord's bidding and boldly makes his way through the streets of the city announcing forty days to prepare for the coming of God's wrath.

It is somewhat unfortunate that our lectionary eliminates verses 6 to 9 of chapter 3, for it contains the extensive efforts to which the inhabitants of Nineveh, including its animals, are willing to go to make up for their sins. It is the king of Nineveh himself who is the first to don sackcloth and proceeds to sit in a pile of ashes, and it is he who commands that the people and the livestock be marked with a sign of repentance.

One might be tempted to see in verse 10 of chapter 3 a fitting conclusion to the story of Jonah. However, this is not the

For meditation and context:

RESPONSORIAL PSALM   Psalm 25:4–5, 6–7, 8–9 (4a)

R. Teach me your ways, O Lord.

Your ways, O Lord, make known to me;
teach me your paths,
guide me in your truth and teach me,
    for you are God my savior.

Remember that your compassion, O Lord,
    and your love are from of old.

In your kindness remember me,
    because of your goodness, O Lord.

Good and upright is the Lord;
    thus he shows sinners the way.
He guides the humble to justice
    and teaches the humble his way.

Corinthians = kohr-IN-thee-uhnz

A short, intense, exhortatory reading, built on rhetorical negations that intensify the urgency of the opening line of the reading.

Use the parallels of these lines to guide your reading, concluding slightly more slowly with the words "passing away."

READING II   1 Corinthians 7:29–31

A reading from the first Letter of Saint Paul to the Corinthians

I **tell** you, brothers and sisters, the time is running **out**.
From **now on**, let those having wives **act** as not **having** them,
    those **weeping** as **not** weeping,
    those **rejoicing** as **not** rejoicing,
    those **buying** as **not** owning,
    those **using** the world as **not** using it **fully**.
For the world in its **present** form is **passing** away.

A narrative reading that depicts the time when Jesus was gathering his first disciples. It begins with Jesus preaching his message of repentance and belief. But this shifts to the Sea of Galilee and the fishermen who were his first followers.

GOSPEL   Mark 1:14–20

A reading from the holy Gospel according to Mark

After **John** had been **arrested**,
    Jesus came to **Galilee** proclaiming the **gospel** of God:
    "**This** is the time of **fulfillment**.
The **kingdom** of **God** is at **hand**.
Repent, and **believe** in the **gospel**." »

case. Instead of an ending that triumphs the wonder of God's mercy, chapter 4 shows Jonah's anger at God for having saved the Ninevites. After having been released from the belly of a fish, it is most unfortunate that Jonah persists in failing to recognize the abundance of God's compassion.

 The seventh chapter of Paul's First Letter to the Corinthians contains the author's guidelines for marriage and sexual morality. Among his suggestions is the recommendation that a person's present state of life

ought to be the accepted way of life for the future. In other words, if a person is unmarried, it is better to remain unmarried and refrain from all sexual relations. Why? Because Christ's return is imminent: "Brothers, everyone should continue before God in the state in which he was called" (1 Corinthians 7:24).

In his exhortation on the passing of time, Paul uses the word *kairos*, which has the connotation in Greek of an opportune moment. This is the time for God's will to be done, meaning that the Lord's return is near. Thus, while working to maintain one's

present state of life, the Corinthians are charged by Paul to not be lured by the ways of the world. In other words, the attitudes of the community are not to reflect those of the surrounding society but must be rooted in the coming fruition of God's Kingdom. Although to human eyes the world and all it contains may look permanent and fulfilling, "the world in its present form is passing away."

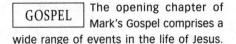 The opening chapter of Mark's Gospel comprises a wide range of events in the life of Jesus.

As he passed by the Sea of **Galilee**,
    he saw **Simon** and his brother **Andrew** casting their **nets**
        into the sea;
    they were **fishermen**.
Jesus said to them,
    "Come **after** me, and I will make you **fishers** of **men**."
Then they **abandoned** their nets and **followed** him.
He walked along a little **farther**
    and saw **James**, the son of **Zebedee**, and his brother **John**.
They **too** were in a boat mending their **nets**.
Then he **called** them.
So they **left** their father **Zebedee** in the boat
    along with the hired men and **followed** him.

"Fishers of men." One of Scripture's truly resonant phrases.

Emphasis on these names.
Zebedee = ZEB-uh-dee

Emphasis on "called" and "followed."

From the Lord's baptism in the Jordan to his time of fasting and prayer in the desert and on to Galilee, where he proclaims the Kingdom, calls his first disciples, and heals many who are sick or possessed, it is clear that Mark intends to demonstrate that Jesus is very busy!

But Mark clearly intends something more significant than Jesus having a huge agenda. This opening chapter is structured in such a way as to impress upon hearers that the Good News of the Kingdom deserves one's immediate attention. In other words, responding to the invitation to "repent, and believe in the gospel" is not something that can be put off until tomorrow. While Jesus is silent during his own baptism and says nothing as he is tempted by Satan in the desert (in Mark's version), his very first words in Mark's Gospel are: "This is the time of fulfillment. The kingdom of God is at hand." These words deserve our complete attention and a response that is radical and full of faith.

Such is the response of Simon and Andrew, James, and John as they hear the summons: "Come after me, and I will make you fishers of men." Like the fish they hope to catch, these four disciples are lured by Jesus. Their reaction is radical and demonstrates complete faith. Not a question is asked as they leave their nets to follow him. From the very first chapter of his Gospel, Mark leaves no doubt that following after Jesus and proclaiming the Kingdom of God calls for a conversion of heart that begins, not tomorrow, but right now! S. W.

FOURTH SUNDAY IN ORDINARY TIME

LECTIONARY #71

READING I Deuteronomy 18:15–20

Deuteronomy = doo-ter-AH-nuh-mee

Horeb = HOHR-eb

An exhortatory reading in which Moses uses the words of God to authorize his prophecy. Moses' prophetic authority comes directly from God. He uses the phrase "raise up" twice in this passage: once in his own words and once in God's. As the reading progresses, emphasize this raising up of authority by shifting your tone slightly toward urgency and increasing your pace very slightly to match the shift in tone.

These last two claims of God serve as a warning to the Israelites.

Emphasize "die" with finality.

A reading from the Book of Deuteronomy

Moses spoke to all the people, saying:
"A **prophet** like **me** will the Lord, your God, raise up for you
from **among** your own **kin**;
to **him** you shall **listen**.
This is **exactly** what you **requested** of the Lord, your God,
at **Horeb**
on the day of the **assembly**, when you said,
'Let us not **again** hear the **voice** of the Lord, our God,
nor **see** this great **fire** any more, lest we **die**.'
And the Lord said to me, '**This** was well **said**.
I will **raise up** for them a **prophet** like you from among their **kin**,
and will put **my** words into his **mouth**;
he shall tell them **all** that I **command** him.
Whoever will not **listen** to my words which he speaks
in my name,
I **myself** will make him **answer** for it.
But if a prophet **presumes** to speak in my name
an oracle that I have **not** commanded him to speak,
or speaks in the name of **other gods**, he shall **die**.'"

READING I Today's reading from Deuteronomy represents Moses' cautionary words to the Israelites concerning the authority of prophets, or leaders, who will follow in his footsteps. These words from Moses occur near the end of his life, when Israel is about to end their forty years of wandering in the desert. Moses cautions them not to be swayed by the allure of the power of those who perform sorcery (Deuteronomy 18:10–11), but rather discern well the intentions of those who claim to speak on God's behalf.

As a result, we glean several important characteristics for those who might call themselves prophets. First, Moses instructs the people that God will appoint a prophet from their own ranks. God chose the inarticulate Moses because he was an insider who understood well the oppression of the Israelites. Second, it is necessary that a prophet humbly acknowledge the message proclaimed as coming from God: "I . . . will put my words into his mouth; he shall tell them all that I command him." Finally, Deuteronomy suggests

to us that, while it may be difficult to determine whether or not the prophet is speaking God's word, God promises to reveal the truth: "But if a prophet presumes to speak in my name an oracle that I have not commanded him to speak . . . he shall die." For those fortunate enough to have a prophet sent to them, the challenge is to listen deeply to hear God speaking.

For meditation and context:

RESPONSORIAL PSALM   Psalm 95:1–2, 6–7, 7–9 (8)

R. If today you hear his voice, harden not your hearts.

Come, let us sing joyfully to the LORD;
    let us acclaim the rock of our salvation.
Let us come into his presence
        with thanksgiving;
    let us joyfully sing psalms to him.

Come, let us bow down in worship;
    let us kneel before the LORD who made us.

For he is our God,
    and we are the people he shepherds,
        the flock he guides.

Oh, that today you would hear his voice:
    "Harden not your hearts as at Meribah,
    as in the day of Massah in the desert,
where your fathers tempted me;
    they tested me though they had seen
        my works."

READING II   1 Corinthians 7:32–35

Corinthians = kohr-IN-thee-uhnz

A reading from the first Letter of Saint Paul to the Corinthians

Brothers and sisters:
I should like you to be **free** of **anxieties**.
An **unmarried** man is anxious about the things of the **Lord**,
    how he may **please** the Lord.
But a **married** man is anxious about the things of the **world**,
    how he may **please** his **wife**, and he is **divided**.
An unmarried **woman** or a **virgin** is anxious about the **things**
        of the **Lord**,
    so that she may be **holy** in **both** body and **spirit**.
A **married** woman, on the other hand,
    is anxious about the **things** of the **world**,
    how she may please her **husband**.
I am telling you this for your own **benefit**,
    not to impose a **restraint** upon you,
    but for the sake of **propriety**
    and adherence to the Lord without **distraction**.

A didactic reading in which Paul is telling the members of the early Church in Corinth about the conditions of marriage. His intentions are generous; he wants to alleviate their anxiety. But there is not getting around the preachiness of this reading. He addresses four types of people: unmarried men, married men, unmarried women, and married women. Treat each of these types of people as points of equal concern to Paul.

TO KEEP IN MIND
If you are assigned to proclaim the second reading, take a look at the previous week's second reading, as well as the following week's, to see where the second reading is coming from and where it is going.

READING II — Paul's ideas of how to be free of anxieties may strike us as outdated. To say that being married or unmarried constitutes whether a person will be anxious about serving the Lord or preoccupied with the things of the world does not really fit into a contemporary worldview. For this reason, the Second Vatican Council reminds us that all Christians—married or unmarried, religious or lay—are called to a life of holiness, and therefore, all of us are called to be "anxious about the things of the Lord."

Nevertheless, it is important to acknowledge Paul's exhortation in the milieu in which he was writing. His worldview was such that the Lord's return was on the horizon and that the people of his day should not make major life changes in anticipation of being ready for this cataclysmic event. Preparing for this overturning of life as we know it should draw the attention of all—married or unmarried—so that we would work to make that anxiety our primary joy.

Although Paul's teaching may be viewed as rigorous, his primary concern is to help the Corinthians see the need to create a loving order in which all members of the community could flourish in their pursuit of clinging to the Lord "without distraction." We know that Paul understood the community at Corinth to be riddled with divisions. "For the sake of propriety," the Apostle to the Gentiles is concerned that a harmony rooted in eschatological hope will win the day and that the many anxieties of life, like the world itself, will pass away.

GOSPEL   Mark 1:21–28

A reading from the holy Gospel according to Mark

Capernaum = kuh-PER-nee-*m; kuh-PER-n*m

A narrative reading of Jesus expelling an unclean spirit. From early in the Gospel of Mark, this passage begins with an expression of Jesus' authoritative teaching, followed by him being mocked by a man with an unclean spirit, whom Jesus coaxes out of the man. It's a scene with vivid language. Savor it.

Emphasis on "authority," "unclean spirit," "destroy," "rebuked," and "convulsed."

This last sentence anticipates the speed at which the fame of Jesus grows.

Then they came to Capernaum,
    and on the sabbath **Jesus** entered the synagogue and **taught**.
The people were **astonished** at his teaching,
    for he taught them as one having **authority** and **not** as
        the scribes.
In their synagogue was a man with an **unclean spirit**;
    he cried out, "What have you to do with **us**, Jesus of Nazareth?
Have you **come** to **destroy** us?
I know who you are—the **Holy** One of **God**!"
Jesus **rebuked** him and said,
    "**Quiet**! Come **out** of him!"
The unclean spirit **convulsed** him and with a loud **cry** came
    out of him.
All were **amazed** and asked one another,
    "What **is** this?
A **new** teaching with **authority**.
He commands even the unclean **spirits** and they **obey** him."
His **fame** spread everywhere throughout the **whole**
      region of Galilee.

GOSPEL One of the primary means of interpreting the Gospel of Mark, which gained scholarly acceptance in the early 1900s, is something called the "messianic secret." This theory contends that the author of Mark's Gospel portrays the disciples and those closest to Jesus as failing to understand his identity as God's Son. It is not until his death on the cross that a Roman soldier (a foreigner and Gentile) recognizes who Jesus is and announces: "Truly this man was the Son of God" (Mark 15:39). Another important characteristic of the theory of the messianic

secret, unique to Mark, is that demons are able to see who Jesus truly is. We see this at work in today's reading as the demon declares: "I know who you are—the Holy One of God!"

Understanding Mark's desire to conceal Jesus' identity helps us appreciate the way in which the Lord has to struggle to claim authority with his teaching and with his proclamation of God's Kingdom. The city of Capernaum in Galilee is the place where Jesus launches his ministry. Here Jesus assumes the role of a rabbi as he enters the synagogue on the Sabbath and

teaches with authority "and not as the scribes." What makes Jesus' teaching fundamentally different from that of the scribes is demonstrated by what happens next: Jesus heals a man possessed with an unclean spirit. By his actions, Jesus teaches the fundamentals of God's Kingdom. In Jesus, the Law is actualized in his extension of God's mercy. The people are amazed by what they see and hear. They may not understand precisely who Jesus is, but they see for themselves that the coming of the Kingdom is at hand. S. W.

FIFTH SUNDAY
IN ORDINARY TIME

LECTIONARY #74

READING I   Job 7:1–4, 6–7

A reading from the Book of Job

Job spoke, saying:
> Is not man's life on earth a **drudgery**?
>> Are not his days those of **hirelings**?
> He is a **slave** who longs for the **shade**,
>> a **hireling** who waits for his **wages**.
> So I have been assigned **months** of **misery**,
>> and **troubled nights** have been **allotted** to me.
> If in bed I say, "**When** shall I arise?"
>> then the night drags on;
>> I am **filled** with **restlessness** until the **dawn**.
> My days are **swifter** than a **weaver's shuttle**;
>> they come to an **end** without **hope**.
> **Remember** that my life is like the **wind**;
>> I shall not see **happiness** again.

Job = johb

An exhortatory, misery-inducing reading. Job is miserable. Emphasize "drudgery," "hirelings," "slave," "misery," and "troubled nights." Pretty much everyone can relate to these words in some fashion.

Even emphasis on the words of this line.

Allow this poetic image to resonate.

TO KEEP IN MIND
If you are assigned to proclaim the first reading, read the Gospel for that week as well. They are connected in thematic ways.

READING I The Book of Job is part of the "Writings" collection in the Old Testament. Its storyline follows the framework of a theodicy, an argument in which the existence of suffering and evil in this world are scrutinized according to the presumption that God is a caring God. In other words, it attempts to answer the question, if God is loving, then why does evil exist? In the story of Job, his three friends, Eliphaz, Bildad, and Zophar, dialogue with Job and try to destroy his trust in God's ability to right what appears to be a situation of injustice. Since Job's prosper-ity and good fortune have suddenly been replaced by poverty and suffering, they argue that surely he must have sinned against God.

Today's reading is taken from Job's first response to Eliphaz, who suggests that Job is being punished. However, Job's approach to his situation is to decipher that no one on earth is truly able to understand the workings of God. In this response, he takes up the concept of the passing of time. Job describes life as a "drudgery," composed of "months of misery" and nights that drag on. And yet, life is so very short, for as he states: "My days are swifter than a weaver's shuttle, they come to an end without hope." We are tempted to read Job's speech as one of complete despair, but he does not blaspheme God's name for his design of the world. Job's torment is a solemn lament. He does not expect God to correct what may feel like an injustice but he wants to register his frustration before God. Job refuses to reject God and, over the course of time, comes to discover the wisdom of knowing that God's ways are ultimately inscrutable.

For meditation and context:

RESPONSORIAL PSALM   Psalm 147:1–2, 3–4, 5–6 (3a)

R. Praise the Lord, who heals the brokenhearted.
or
R. Alleluia.

Praise the LORD, for he is good;
 sing praise to our God, for he is gracious;
 it is fitting to praise him.
The LORD rebuilds Jerusalem;
 the dispersed of Israel he gathers.

He heals the brokenhearted
 and binds up their wounds.

He tells the number of the stars;
 he calls each by name.

Great is our Lord and mighty in power;
 to his wisdom there is no limit.
The LORD sustains the lowly;
 the wicked he casts to the ground.

Corinthians = kohr-IN-thee-uhnz

A didactic reading in which Paul asserts his role as a preacher, using a language of obligation and recompense, of slavery and freedom.

recompense = REK-uhm-pens

Emphasize "stewardship."

READING II   1 Corinthians 9:16–19, 22–23

A reading from the first Letter of Saint Paul to the Corinthians

Brothers and sisters:
If I preach the **gospel**, this is no reason for me to **boast**,
 for an **obligation** has been **imposed** on me,
 and **woe** to me if I do **not** preach it!
If I do so **willingly**, I have a **recompense**,
 but if **unwillingly**, then I have been entrusted with
  a **stewardship**.
What then is my **recompense**?
That, when I **preach**,
 I offer the gospel free of charge
 so as not to make full use of my **right** in the gospel.

Although I am **free** in regard to all,
 I have made myself a **slave** to all
 so as to win over as **many** as possible.
To the **weak** I became **weak**, to win **over** the weak.
I have become **all** things to **all**, to save at least **some**.
All this I do for the **sake** of the **gospel**,
 so that **I too** may have a **share** in it.

With "Although," Paul is building his argument in this passage to its rhetorical conclusion in which his earnestness cannot be denied. Voice Paul's earnestness as your own.

READING II | One of the identifying characteristics of the Corinthian Christians—one that is a chief concern for Paul—is their pride. This is an infant church that is filled with many spiritual gifts (1 Corinthians 12–13), but Paul leaves no doubt that jealousy over how these gifts should be used has created division. The same is true in their treatment of the poor; Paul condemns the Corinthians for celebrating the Lord's Supper before those who must labor are able to arrive. He instructs them that they should all eat together when they gather (1 Corinthians

11:33). Whether the issue is the failure to use spiritual gifts properly or the exclusion of the poor from worship, the Corinthians need to be taught the lesson of humility.

Thus, we see in today's reading that Paul wishes to describe himself in this very light: a man who has been humbled by the call to preach the Gospel. First, he makes it abundantly clear that preaching is not a matter of self-aggrandizement. Like Paul, therefore, the Corinthians must see the Gospel as a matter of "stewardship." Those who are entrusted with spreading the Good News have a tremendous duty that makes

no room for boasting. Second, Paul makes himself a model of humility for the Corinthians by calling himself a slave. He writes, "I have become all things to all." Paul does not mean to say that he is wishy-washy; he wants the Corinthians to understand that the preaching of Christ does not discriminate—it is Good News for all people.

GOSPEL | Jesus has just commenced his ministry at the synagogue in Capernaum, where his teaching astonished the people who recognized his preaching as something new. In the syna-

A narrative passage in which Jesus casts out demons and cures illness. Jesus' supernatural powers are what made his divinity initially visible to his followers. We are seeing Jesus through their eyes. Though he wants to preach, it's these spectacular exorcisms that capture people's attention at first.

Give equal emphasis to all these names.

Though Simon's mother-in-law goes unnamed, give her a place as well.

GOSPEL   Mark 1:29–39

A reading from the holy Gospel according to Mark

On leaving the **synagogue**
    Jesus entered the house of **Simon** and **Andrew** with **James**
       and **John**.
Simon's mother-in-law lay **sick** with a **fever**.
They immediately **told** him about her.
He **approached**, grasped her hand, and **helped** her up.
Then the fever **left** her and she **waited** on them.

When it was **evening**, after sunset,
    they brought to him **all** who were **ill** or **possessed** by **demons**.
The **whole town** was gathered at the door.
He cured **many** who were **sick** with various **diseases**,
    and he drove out many **demons**,
       not permitting them to **speak** because they **knew** him.

Rising very early before dawn, he **left**
    and went off to a **deserted** place, where he **prayed**.
Simon and those who were with him **pursued** him
    and on **finding** him said, "Everyone is **looking** for you."
He told them, "Let us go on to the nearby **villages**
    that I may preach there **also**.
For **this purpose** have I come."
So he went into their **synagogues**,
    preaching and driving out **demons** throughout the **whole**
       of Galilee.

This closing passage depicts Jesus wanting some solitude to recharge his depleted powers. You might contrast this mood with the urgency of Simon and the others.

gogue he expelled a demon, and now in Simon's house, Jesus raises up Simon's sick mother-in-law. The setting of a house is important for Mark; it appears throughout the gospel as an important place for teaching and healing. This first house that Jesus enters in Mark's Gospel seems to be a place of little rest for Jesus. Although Jesus and the disciples will all be the beneficiaries of the healed woman's hospitality, everyone in the area soon hears of his great power and presses in upon the door of the house.

Mark shows us a brief respite from the chaos of this scene as Jesus sets out by himself to a secluded place where he can pray. Mark says nothing about the details of the journey or the place of refuge itself, but immediately returns to the scene of Jesus being pursued by those in need. "Everyone is looking for you." Simon tells Jesus. Jesus responds by telling Simon that it's time to move on to the rest of Galilee to fulfill his purpose. Perhaps Mark is suggesting here that while Jesus' need for solitary prayer is important and necessary, the needs of the

Kingdom call for his immediate attention. We are meant to see that there is little time for rest when the Kingdom is to be preached and the sick are to be healed. S.W.

SIXTH SUNDAY IN ORDINARY TIME

LECTIONARY #77

READING I   Leviticus 13:1–2, 44–46

A reading from the Book of Leviticus

The LORD said to **Moses** and **Aaron**,
   "If someone has on his skin a **scab** or **pustule** or **blotch**
   which appears to be the **sore** of **leprosy**,
   he shall be brought to **Aaron**, the **priest**,
   or to one of the priests among his **descendants**.
If the man is **leprous** and **unclean**,
   the priest shall **declare** him unclean
   by reason of the **sore** on his head.

"The one who **bears** the **sore** of leprosy
   shall keep his **garments rent** and his **head bare**,
   and shall **muffle** his **beard**;
   he shall cry out, '**Unclean, unclean**!'
As long as the sore is on him he shall **declare** himself unclean,
   since he is in **fact** unclean.
He shall dwell **apart**, making his abode **outside** the camp."

Leviticus = lih-VIT-ih-kuhs

Aaron = AYR-uhn

A didactic reading, focused on leprosy. Modern-day leprosy, also called Hansen's disease, is not the same thing as the leprosy named in Scripture, which referred to a variety of skin conditions that involved ruptures or lesions. Because such skin conditions threatened ritual purity, they were a topic of ongoing concern in Scripture.

Emphasize these words to signify what leprosy is.

leprous = LEP-ruhs

"Unclean." This word is key.

Isolation is the solution to the problem. Emphasize this because it will be contrasted in the Gospel reading.

READING I   The Book of Leviticus is the third book of the Old Testament and largely contains the code of conduct belonging to priests of the tribe of Levi. While the second book, Exodus, has a lengthy list of instructions given to Moses on how to construct the tabernacle, Leviticus is designed to provide for its ongoing maintenance. It is particularly concerned with the behavior and ritual purity of those responsible for offering sacrifice on behalf of the community of Israel.

Purity is an important dimension of Hebrew Law because it represents wholeness. When God created the world in Genesis, he designed it to be utterly complete. Similarly, the Tabernacle in the middle of the Israelite camp was to be understood as a physical representation of the wholeness of God. Thus, when something was deemed scarred or impure, it was determined to be lacking in wholeness. Holiness and wholeness are one and the same in the Hebrew worldview. For this reason, those who suffer from leprosy or from any other severe form of skin disease had to be distanced from the camp. This isolation was understood not so much as a punishment (although disease, in general, was usually seen as the result of sin) but as a necessary precaution to ensure the holiness of the people. For the people to be God's holy people they had to be whole and without blemish.

For meditation and context:

RESPONSORIAL PSALM   Psalm 32:1–2, 5, 11 (7)

R. I turn to you, Lord, in time of trouble, and you fill me with the joy of salvation.

Blessed is he whose fault is taken away,
   whose sin is covered.
Blessed the man to whom the LORD imputes
   not guilt,
   in whose spirit there is no guile.

Then I acknowledged my sin to you,
   my guilt I covered not.
I said, "I confess my faults to the LORD,"
   and you took away the guilt of my sin.

Be glad in the LORD and rejoice, you just;
   exult, all you upright of heart.

READING II   1 Corinthians 10:31—11:1

A reading from the first Letter of Saint Paul to the Corinthians

Brothers and sisters,
Whether you **eat** or **drink**, or **whatever** you do,
   do **everything** for the glory of **God**.
Avoid giving **offense**, whether to the **Jews** or **Greeks** or the
      church of **God**,
   just as **I** try to please **everyone** in every way,
   not seeking my **own** benefit but that of the many,
   that they may be **saved**.
Be **imitators** of me, as **I** am of **Christ**.

A brief exhortatory reading in which Paul advises against excess and sets himself up as a model for following Christ.

Almost even emphasis on the words of this line, with a little extra for "saved."

This last line summarizes Paul's instruction.

> **TO KEEP IN MIND**
> Be careful not to swallow your words. Articulate carefully, especially at the end of lines.

READING II   Much of Paul's correspondence with the Christians in Corinth deals with their moral conduct. One of the issues that concerns Paul the most is this church's participation in sacrifice to idols. Although they may claim to be followers of Christ, many within the Christian community at Corinth seem to have no trouble consuming meat that had been previously offered to an idol of a pagan god (1 Corinthians 10:20). Paul warns them sternly that those who gather around the table of the Lord can have nothing to do with the "table of demons" as well (1 Corinthians 10:21). He concludes with the instruction that is often uttered as part of a table prayer today: "Whether you eat or drink, or whatever you do, do everything for the glory of God."

Many could justifiably argue that meat is meat, and even if it were dedicated to a name contrary to Christ, it should not be wasted. For the spiritually mature such may be the case, but what about potential scandal? Paul wants no one in the community to be alarmed. Thus, all moral decisions can boil down to the basic question: What displays unequivocal dedication to God's glory? To highlight God's glory at the expense of one's self-interest is precisely the example that Paul believes that he has shown the Corinthians. Thus, they would be very wise to be "imitators" of him, for he imitates Christ.

GOSPEL   Mark 1:40–45

A reading from the holy Gospel according to Mark

A **leper** came to **Jesus** and kneeling down **begged** him and said,
  "If you **wish**, you can make me **clean**."
Moved with **pity**, he stretched out his **hand**,
  touched him, and **said** to him,
  "I **do** will it. **Be made clean**."
The leprosy left him **immediately**, and he was made **clean**.
Then, warning him **sternly**, he **dismissed** him at once.

He **said** to him, "See that you tell **no one** anything,
  but **go**, show yourself to the **priest**
  and **offer** for your cleansing what Moses **prescribed**;
  that will be **proof** for them."

The man went away and began to **publicize** the whole matter.
He **spread** the report abroad
  so that it was **impossible** for Jesus to enter a town **openly**.
He remained **outside** in **deserted** places,
  and people kept **coming** to him from **everywhere**.

A narrative reading in which Jesus shifts his cures from demon possession to leprosy. The opening passage shows Jesus doing the unthinkable: touching a person with leprosy. Not only is there the danger of contagion, Jesus is also deliberately opening himself to ritual impurity, which was strictly forbidden in Jewish society.

The second section expresses Jesus' wish not to advertise what he had done for the leper, which leads to the third section, in which news of Jesus' deed spreads quickly, obliging him to avoid crowds.

Use the subjects of these three sections to pace your reading.

GOSPEL   The leper in today's Gospel clearly suffers from the visible impairment described in Leviticus. Due to the affliction found on his skin, the law restricts this man from participation in the community; he is to be regarded as untouchable. While many in the society of his day may have rushed to label this individual as unclean, his most visible characteristic is his display of humility and faith, as he kneels before Jesus and begs him: "If you wish, you can make me clean." The intense desire on the part of this sick man is matched by Jesus' equally intense desire to heal him. Mark testifies that the disease left him "immediately."

As Jesus makes his way throughout Galilee, the signs of people being cast out from society were all around him. As he proclaimed the nearness of God's kingdom, these situations stood as contradictions to the wholeness—and holiness—of God's creation. This could be the reason that Jesus instructs the man to remain silent about his healing. Jesus may recognize that he will have many more people to make whole before the majority of the people will come to understand his mission.

Nevertheless, Mark suggests that the man could not keep quiet, but instead "began to publicize the whole matter." While the result of broadcasting his healing far and wide served as an act of disobedience toward Jesus, it may have had a missionary purpose for the broader world. Not only did it serve to draw more and more people to Jesus, but it certainly helped to open Jesus' eyes, at this early stage in announcing the kingdom, that there was much work to be done in restoring creation to its original sinless beauty. Thus, "people kept coming to him from everywhere." S. W.

ASH WEDNESDAY

LECTIONARY #219

READING I Joel 2:12–18

A reading from the Book of the Prophet Joel

Even **now**, says the LORD,
    return to me with your **whole heart**,
    with **fasting**, and **weeping**, and **mourning**;
Rend your **hearts**, not your **garments**,
    and **return** to the LORD, your **God**.
For **gracious** and **merciful** is **he**,
    slow to anger, **rich** in kindness,
    and **relenting** in punishment.
Perhaps he will **again** relent
    and leave **behind** him a **blessing**,
Offerings and **libations**
    for the LORD, your **God**.

Blow the trumpet in **Zion**!
    proclaim a fast,
    call an assembly;
Gather the people,
    notify the congregation;
Assemble the elders,
    gather the children
    and the **infants** at the breast;
Let the **bridegroom** quit his **room**
    and the **bride** her **chamber**.

Joel = JOH-*l
rend = tear

An exhortatory reading in which Joel in his role as prophet becomes the mouthpiece for the Lord; it is as if God is addressing the people directly in this reading. Proclaim this reading like Joel himself, letting your voice be the instrument for this highly charged and poetic language to come to life. No need to exaggerate or emote; the language is filled to the brim with feeling. Proclaim with a sure and steady voice and that vibrancy will come through.

This reading makes use of frequent parallels. Give the words in pairs emphasis: "hearts" and "garments"; "gracious" and "merciful"; "slow" and "rich"; "offerings" and "libations."

The energy picks up with a series of imperative verb forms. These words are highly charged—God is telling the assembly directly what to do. "Blow," "proclaim," "call," "gather," "notify," "assemble," "let."

READING I The short Book of Joel is constructed in response to a great drought and a concurrent plague of locusts that afflicted the land in the prophet's time. At the outset of the book (1:1—2:17), the prophet laments a nation that has appeared to have lost God's blessing. He then assures the people that if they repent, God will richly reward them (2:18–32). Finally, the book concludes with the promise that God will pass judgment on Israel's enemies (3:1–21).

The section of Joel that opens the Liturgy of the Word on Ash Wednesday every year represents the prophet's call to an entire nation to "return to the Lord." He envisions such a return not only through the outward gestures of fasting, weeping, and mourning, but also with the interior movement of the heart. Thus, while the Lord will be able to discern the hearts of individuals who desire repentance, the need for a public and communal display of rededication on the part of the nation should not be overlooked. Rather, the prophet calls for the blowing of the trumpet (the *shofar*, or ram's horn, representing Abraham's faith) to summon the people together as one in an assembly. Young and old, and even those with life situations that usually take precedence—the entire nation—Joel calls to gather to demonstrate a corporate fidelity that will certainly lead to the bestowal of God's blessings.

In addition to the actions of gathering, weeping, and performing other signs of regret and reverence, the prophet calls the priests of the people to utter prayers on their behalf: "Spare, O Lord, your people, and make not your heritage a reproach." Here, Joel speaks of the future effect of the nation's display of repentance. Securing

Between the **porch** and the **altar**
  let the **priests**, the **ministers** of the LORD, **weep**,
And say, "**Spare**, O LORD, your **people**,
  and make **not** your **heritage** a **reproach**,
  with the **nations** ruling **over** them!
Why should they **say** among the **peoples**,
  '**Where** is their **God**?' "

Then the LORD was stirred to **concern** for his **land**
  and took **pity** on his **people**.

Allow for a slight pause between the question and the final expression in the reading.

For meditation and context:

RESPONSORIAL PSALM Psalm 51:3–4, 5–6ab, 12–13, 14 and 17 (3a)

R. Be merciful, O Lord, for we have sinned.

Have mercy on me, O God,
  in your goodness;
  in the greatness of your compassion
  wipe out my offense.
Thoroughly wash me from my guilt
  and of my sin cleanse me.

For I acknowledge my offense,
  and my sin is before me always:

"Against you only have I sinned,
  and done what is evil in your sight."

A clean heart create for me, O God,
  and a steadfast spirit renew within me.
Cast me not out from your presence,
  and your Holy Spirit take not from me.

Give me back the joy of your salvation,
  and a willing spirit sustain in me.
O Lord, open my lips,
  and my mouth shall proclaim your praise.

READING II   2 Corinthians 5:20—6:2

Corinthians = kohr-IN-thee-uhnz

An exhortatory reading in which Paul seeks to impress upon the members of the early Church at Corinth the importance of reconciliation with God in preparation to receive God.

The phrasing in this statement, "he made him to be sin," is a little peculiar. Practice it a few times and sound it out. It's not an expression we commonly use in relation to sin. "Be" is paralleled with "know." Emphasize those two words to anchor your proclamation.

A reading from the second Letter of Saint Paul to the Corinthians

Brothers and **sisters**:
We are **ambassadors** for **Christ**,
  as if **God** were appealing **through** us.
We **implore** you on behalf of **Christ**,
  be **reconciled** to God.
For **our** sake he made him to **be** sin who did not **know** sin,
  so that we might become the **righteousness** of **God** in **him**. »

God's blessing once again will prevent other nations from looking at Israel and questioning the power and authority of God.

It is helpful to recognize the cosmic nature of Joel's prophecy. This passage ends with the statement that "the Lord was stirred to concern for his land and took pity on his people." The Lord cares not only for his people but for the land as well. Thus, the prophet clearly demonstrates that repentance is far more than an individual act or a personal turning toward the Lord; it involves the entire nation and all of creation as well.

READING II Paul's call to the Corinthians here is quite simply to "be reconciled to God." However, in order to give those words greater weight, he needs to establish his own authority. Thus, he likens himself and possibly Timothy or other coworkers to "ambassadors for Christ." An ambassador is someone who has more than the ability to represent the thinking and the agenda of another. He or she is someone who has demonstrated the leadership skills of gaining the trust of those to whom the ambassador has been sent. In this way,

Paul is appealing to the Corinthians as a voice that is fully trustworthy and has been proven to be effective.

However, the important thing is that Paul does not come alone. The plural use of the word "we" is not to be missed: "we are ambassadors," "we implore you," "working together . . . we appeal to you." Just as the call for reconciliation is issued to a community, Paul understands the work of growing in "righteousness" to be task of people united. But even this work is something that can only be accomplished by Christ, he who became "sin who did not know sin."

The exhortation of the reading resolves in Paul's use of the word "acceptable." In its first appearance, you do not need to emphasize it. When it reappears, be sure to give it extra emphasis.

Working **together**, then,
  we **appeal** to you not to **receive** the grace of God in **vain**.
For he **says**:

  In *an acceptable time I **heard** you,
    and on the day of salvation I **helped** you.*

Behold, **now** is a **very acceptable time**;
  behold, **now** is the **day** of **salvation**.

GOSPEL   Matthew 6:1–6, 16–18

A reading from the holy Gospel according to Matthew

A didactic reading in which Jesus provides advice for how to approach the practices of almsgiving, prayer, and fasting. Each section of advice is constructed very similarly, creating parallel expressions. Don't let them become formulaic in your proclamation. Each of these practices is important to Jesus for bringing us closer to God.

Almsgiving comes first.

Jesus said to his disciples:
  "Take **care** not to **perform** righteous deeds
  in order that people may **see** them;
  otherwise, you will have **no** recompense from your
    heavenly Father.
When you give **alms**,
  do **not** blow a **trumpet** before you,
  as the **hypocrites** do in the **synagogues** and in the **streets**
  to win the **praise** of others.
Amen, I say to you,
  they have **received** their **reward**.
But when **you** give alms,
  do not let your **left** hand know what your **right** is doing,
  so that your **almsgiving** may be **secret**.
And your **Father** who sees in secret will **repay** you.

Emphasis on "left," "right," "secret," "Father," and "repay."

TO KEEP IN MIND
Use the pitch and volume of your voice to gain the attention of the assembly.

Thus, the reconciliation called for by Paul is one of acknowledging the sacrifice of the Lord's death on the cross and receiving God's grace.

When will such reconciliation occur? Paul wants the Corinthians to waste no time: "Behold, now is a very acceptable time; behold, now is the day of salvation." Heard on the threshold of the doorway that opens the Church to the season of Lent, these words challenge Christians today to refrain from hesitation in working together for the rediscovery of God's grace. Like Paul, all who are baptized into Christ are

fashioned as "ambassadors for Christ," as those chosen to embody the sacrifice of the cross in a spirit of complete and total selflessness.

GOSPEL   Context is a very important issue for the proclamation of today's Gospel. It is heard in the midst of a public assembly that begins the Lenten season as a people united by the very visible display of ashes worn on the forehead as an act of penance. In Matthew's Gospel, Jesus tells his disciples to avoid forms of public displays of piety. Yet the Christian

community chooses to set itself apart from the rest of the world by showing the mark of ashes for all to see. Are we modern-day hypocrites, like the scribes and the Pharisees of Jesus' day who "neglect their appearance, so that they may appear to others to be fasting"? We hope the answer is no as we contemplate deeper the intention of Jesus' cautionary prescriptions for religious duties.

Today's reading from Matthew is part of Jesus' teaching to his disciples that is considered his preaching debut: the Sermon on the Mount (Matthew 5:1—7:29). Jesus'

Next comes prayer. The wording is very similar to that in the almsgiving section. Emphasis on "inner," "secret," "Father," "secret," and "repay."

"When you **pray**,
　do **not** be like the **hypocrites**,
　who love to **stand** and **pray** in the **synagogues** and on
　　street corners
　so that **others** may **see** them.
Amen, **I** say to you,
　they have **received** their **reward**.
But when **you** pray, **go** to your inner **room**,
　close the door, and **pray** to your **Father** in **secret**.
And your **Father** who sees in **secret** will **repay** you.

And finally comes fasting. Once again, similar wording. This time, emphasis on "head," "face," "appear," "Father," "hidden," and "repay."

"When you **fast**,
　do not look **gloomy** like the **hypocrites**.
They **neglect** their **appearance**,
　so that they may **appear** to others to be **fasting**.
Amen, I say to you, they have **received** their **reward**.
But when you **fast**,
　anoint your **head** and wash your **face**,
　so that you may not **appear** to be **fasting**,
　except to your **Father** who is **hidden**.
And your **Father** who sees what is **hidden** will **repay** you."

instruction on kingdom living begins with the Beatitudes, continues into a new interpretation of the law, and concludes with clues on how to discern true disciples from false prophets. The instructions on almsgiving, prayer, and fasting in secret occupy the middle portion of Jesus' preaching.

When considering the Beatitudes, we can see right away that the righteous actions to be performed by those deserving of God's blessing are all very public: bearing poverty in spirit, acting with gentleness, mourning, striving for righteousness, showing mercy, exhibiting purity of heart,

peacemaking, and being persecuted for the sake of justice. These outward dispositions are meant to be viewed by others so that they too might change their worldview. They are all performed so that the world might be awakened to the greatness of the kingdom of heaven. The Beatitudes are the attempt by Jesus to instruct his disciples on the importance of performing acts of charity and justice for the sake of God's future blessing, not for some temporal reward in the here and now. Likewise, the disciplines of almsgiving, fasting, and prayer must always be focused on God and a future joy.

How easy it is to use the performance of these core practices as a measure for spiritual achievement. One is tempted to start out on the first day of Lent with an agenda for personal improvement. However, that is not what kingdom living requires. It is not about trying to appear worthy before God, as much as it is about living selflessly for others. When almsgiving, fasting, and prayer are conducted in such a way as to lose the self for others, then they are rightly directed for the fruition of God's kingdom. God will see what others cannot. S. W.

FIRST SUNDAY OF LENT

LECTIONARY #23

READING I   Genesis 9:8–15

A reading from the Book of Genesis

Genesis = JEN-uh-sihs

A narrative reading that tells a very familiar story, one that forms the headwaters of our faith.

God said to **Noah** and to his **sons with** him:
"**See**, I am now **establishing** my covenant with **you**
  and your descendants **after** you
  and with **every living creature** that was **with** you:
  all the **birds**, and the various tame and wild **animals**
  that were **with** you and came **out** of the ark.
I will establish my covenant with you,
  that **never again** shall **all** bodily creatures be **destroyed**
  by the **waters** of a **flood**;
  there shall **not** be another **flood** to devastate the **earth**."

Note the repetitions of the word "covenant," which is the core of this reading. Give each repetition equal emphasis.

God added:
"**This** is the sign that I am **giving** for **all** ages to come,
  of the **covenant** between **me** and **you**
  and every living creature **with** you:
  I set my **bow** in the **clouds** to **serve** as a **sign**
  of the covenant between me and the **earth**.
When I bring **clouds** over the **earth**,
  and the bow **appears** in the **clouds**,
  I will **recall** the covenant I have **made**
  between **me** and **you** and **all living beings**,
  so that the **waters** shall **never again** become a flood
  to **destroy all** mortal beings."

The rainbow is a sign of God's will arching over creation.

Give equal emphasis to "me" and "you" and "all living beings."

READING I What is God's relationship with the world? Is God active in the workings of the universe, or does God maintain complete distance? The Hebrew people crafted a very clear answer to this quandary. God desires to be in relationship with his people through the establishment of a covenant, a permanent bond calling for mutual fidelity. The most well known of the covenants are those created by God with Abraham (Genesis 17:1–14) and with Moses (Exodus 19—24). However, perhaps not so well known, but no less significant, is the covenant made by God with Noah, which we encounter in today's reading from Genesis.

Noah is best known for his construction of an ark that would serve to carry the remnant of creation carved out by God after he vowed to destroy "the wickedness of human beings" (Genesis 6:5). The forty days spent by Noah riding on the waters of the flood, like the forty days Moses would spend on the mountain with God, represent the time of preparation necessary to receive fully the promise of a new creation. When Noah disembarks from the ark and discovers the beauty of the earth and its newly dried land, he immediately erects an altar and makes a sacrifice from every kind of clean animal on the ark (Genesis 8:20). Noah's sacrifice signals his reverence and trust in God, who smells the sacrifice and wishes to bless Noah for all he has done to contribute to the work of salvation.

Thus, God establishes a covenant with Noah: "never again shall all bodily creatures be destroyed by the waters of a flood." The sign of God's promise is the rainbow, guaranteeing an end to every storm that threatens the well-being of the world. God asks nothing of Noah in return, thereby demonstrating

For meditation and context:

RESPONSORIAL PSALM Psalm 25:4–5, 6–7, 8–9 (10)

R. Your ways, O Lord, are love and truth to those who keep your covenant.

Your ways, O LORD, make known to me;
    teach me your paths,
guide me in your truth and teach me,
    for you are God my savior.

Remember that your compassion, O LORD,
    and your love are from of old.

In your kindness remember me,
    because of your goodness, O LORD.

Good and upright is the LORD,
    thus he shows sinners the way.
He guides the humble to justice,
    and he teaches the humble his way.

READING II   1 Peter 3:18–22

A reading from the first Letter of Saint Peter

Beloved:
Christ **suffered** for sins **once**,
    the **righteous** for the sake of the **unrighteous**,
    that he might **lead** you to **God**.
Put to **death** in the **flesh**,
    he was brought to **life** in the **Spirit**.
In it he also went to **preach** to the spirits in **prison**,
    who had once been **disobedient**
    while **God** patiently waited in the **days** of **Noah**
    during the **building** of the ark,
    in which a **few persons**, eight in all,
    were **saved** through **water**.
This prefigured **baptism**, which saves you **now**.
It is **not** a removal of dirt from the body
    but an **appeal** to God for a **clear** conscience,
    through the **resurrection** of Jesus **Christ**,
    who has gone into **heaven**
    and is at the **right hand** of God,
    with **angels**, **authorities**, and **powers** subject to him.

A didactic reading in which Peter defines Baptism in its spiritual terms—not merely in terms of cleansing but as part of a foreordained salvation.

Note the contrasts in this passage between righteousness and unrighteousness, life and death. Give them emphasis as you move into the passage about work and Noah's patience.

Beginning with "not," this conclusion clarifies the meaning of Baptism, finishing with a potent celestial vision. Give the "not," therefore, its emphasis.

the totality of his love for every aspect of existence. This primeval story suggests that creation constantly receives God's enduring mercy and not his vengeful wrath.

| READING II | The First Letter of Peter contains material used for baptismal catechesis in the early Church. The author joins the suffering of Christ with the new life that is bestowed in Baptism. Just as Christ was "brought to life in the Spirit," so is Baptism understood as the means through which those who have been washed in its water might be led to God.

Peter employs the image of the ark to discuss God's patience as he waited for Noah to complete the ark's construction and to allude to God's patience in waiting for sinners to turn to Baptism. In addition, Peter points to the number of Noah's family—"eight in all"—as a symbol of the new creation that God establishes after the flood. Those baptized in Christ are a new creation and are resurrected into life eternal.

Peter continues by guaranteeing that Baptism constitutes more than a mere physical washing, but enacts a complete renovation of "conscience." By participating

in the Resurrection of Christ through the act of Baptism, one is able to view the powers of the world differently. The "angels, authorities, and powers" that are subject to Christ are incapable of distracting the baptized from the work accepting the gift of salvation entails.

| GOSPEL | Each year, the First Sunday of Lent confronts us with the story of Jesus being tempted in the desert by Satan. Mark's account contains a variety of characters that are important in contemplating the nature of Jesus'

A narrative reading with an exhortation in its conclusion. The story of the temptation of Christ in the desert never gets old.

"This," "fulfillment," "kingdom," "repent," "believe": These are the watchwords of Lent. Give them each equal emphasis.

GOSPEL   Mark 1:12–15

A reading from the holy Gospel according to Mark

The **Spirit** drove **Jesus** out into the **desert**,
    and he **remained** in the desert for **forty days, tempted**
        by **Satan**.
He was among **wild beasts**,
    and the **angels ministered** to him.

After **John** had been **arrested**,
    Jesus came to **Galilee** proclaiming the **gospel** of God:
    "**This** is the time of **fulfillment**.
The **kingdom** of God is at hand.
Repent, and **believe** in the gospel."

PRAYERFUL READING, OR *LECTIO DIVINA*

1. *Lectio:* Read a Scripture passage aloud slowly. Notice what phrase captures your attention and be attentive to its meaning. Silent pause.

2. *Meditatio:* Read the passage aloud slowly again, reflecting on the passage, allowing God to speak to you through it. Silent pause.

3. *Oratio:* Read it aloud slowly a third time, allowing it to be your prayer or response to God's gift of insight to you. Silent pause.

4. *Contemplatio:* Read it aloud slowly a fourth time, now resting in God's Word.

---

temptation. First mentioned is the Spirit who is responsible for driving Jesus into the desert for the duration of forty days. Next appears Satan, who is mentioned simply as tempting Jesus. Also in the story are the wild beasts, who certainly represent the mystery of nature. Finally, there appear the angels, who are responsible for ministering to the Lord. Although Mark does not spell out the parameters of the temptation, the forty-day period clearly denotes a time of reconstruction and reorientation. Just as Noah assisted in providing the means by which God was able to reconstruct creation,

so is this forty-day period a time that allows Jesus to see the world in a new way. Similar to the way in which Noah was accompanied by remnants of creation—animals of every sort—Jesus is "among wild beasts" as he prepares himself for the task of proclaiming the kingdom, the beauty of creation as God intended it to be.

At the end of his time of testing, Jesus appears with a new sense of authority. Very shortly after his inaugural appearance in Galilee, he proclaims boldly: "This is the time of fulfillment. The kingdom of God is at hand. Repent, and believe in the gospel."

Jesus will back up these words with the visible manifestations of power through numerous cures and the calling of disciples. Mark soon suggests that the proclamation and the revelation of the kingdom is a matter of great urgency. Thus, the brief story of Jesus in the desert suggests that God's power is more than ready to be revealed. Rather than a future forecast, the kingdom of God is now. "This is the time of fulfillment. The kingdom of God is at hand." S. W.

SECOND SUNDAY OF LENT

LECTIONARY #26

READING I   Genesis 22:1–2, 9a, 10–13, 15–18

A reading from the Book of Genesis

God put **Abraham** to the **test**.
He called to him, "**Abraham**!"
"**Here** I am!" he replied.
Then God said:
   "**Take** your son **Isaac**, your only one, whom you **love**,
     and go to the land of **Moriah**.
There you shall offer him up as a **holocaust**
     on a **height** that I will point out to you."

When they came to the **place** of which God had **told** him,
     Abraham built an **altar** there and arranged the **wood** on it.
Then he **reached** out and took the **knife** to **slaughter** his son.
But the LORD's messenger called to him from heaven,
     "**Abraham**, **Abraham**!"
"**Here** I am!" he answered.
"Do not lay your **hand** on the **boy**," said the messenger.
"Do not do the **least thing** to him.
I know now how **devoted** you are to **God**,
     since you did not **withhold** from me your own beloved **son**."
As **Abraham** looked about,
     he spied a **ram** caught by its **horns** in the **thicket**.
So he went and took the ram
     and offered it up as a **holocaust** in place of his **son**. »

Genesis = JEN-uh-sihs
A narrative reading of considerable power. Because this is such a dramatic tale, you might be inclined to proclaim in a dramatic manner. This can have an unwanted "community theater" effect. The language of this reading is so inherently dramatic, you can focus your proclamation on pace and emphasis more memorably.

Moriah = moh-Rī-uh

"Holocaust" is a loaded word, repeated twice in this reading. Give the word its due emphasis.

The power of this reading erupts from the word "slaughter." Take your time reading this line, slowing slightly as you read "slaughter."

READING I Today's reading from the Book of Genesis depicts why Abraham is known as the "Father of Faith." The movement of this tale is horrific, yet from the beginning to the end of this scene, there seems to be a complete absence of emotion. Abraham's response to God in the words "Here I am!" seems to be void of any feeling whatsoever. We might question why Abraham did not struggle to defend his son's life.

It is important to keep in mind what Isaac represents. Not only does he exist to engender the affection between a father and a son, he also stands as the gateway to the future. Since God had promised the aged Abraham that he would carve out a great nation from among Abraham's descendants (Genesis 12:2), the death of Isaac would nullify God's covenant with Abraham. Thus, in the act of sacrificing his only son, Abraham would not only lose his family but also the future of the people to whom God had pledged his faithfulness.

Note that God summons Abraham to make his sacrifice at the location of Mount Moriah. Mountains in the Old Testament are understood to be sacred sites that provided a worthy setting for God's revelation. When Abraham ascends the mountain with his son, God is able once again to speak words of blessing. God accepts Abraham's obedient faith and provides the ram by which Abraham is able to offer an oblation. Then God reiterates his promise to make of Abraham a great nation, with "descendants as countless as the stars of the sky and the sands of the seashore."

READING II Read on the heels of the story of Abraham's willingness to sacrifice his own son, this short

God's messenger is relaying this declaration of God to Abraham. Though it is not the direct speech of God, it feels like it. The declaration resolves in the word "obeyed." Slow your reading to emphasize the word.

Again the LORD's messenger **called** to Abraham from heaven
    and **said:**
"I **swear** by **myself, declares** the LORD,
that because you **acted** as you **did**
in not withholding from me your **beloved** son,
I will **bless** you **abundantly**
and make your **descendants** as **countless**
    as the **stars** of the **sky** and the **sands** of the **seashore;**
your **descendants** shall take possession
    of the **gates** of their **enemies,**
and in your **descendants** all the **nations** of the earth
    shall find **blessing—**
all this because you **obeyed** my **command.**"

For meditation and context:

RESPONSORIAL PSALM   Psalm 116:10, 15, 16–17, 18–19 (9)

R. I will walk before the Lord, in the land of the living.

I believed, even when I said,
  "I am greatly afflicted."
Precious in the eyes of the LORD
  is the death of his faithful ones.

O LORD, I am your servant;
  I am your servant, the son of your
    handmaid;
  you have loosed my bonds.

To you will I offer sacrifice of thanksgiving,
  and I will call upon the name of the LORD.

My vows to the LORD I will pay
  in the presence of all his people,
in the courts of the house of the LORD,
  in your midst, O Jerusalem.

TO KEEP IN MIND
The responsorial psalm "has great liturgical and pastoral importance, since it fosters meditation on the Word of God," the *General Instruction on the Roman Missal* says. Pray it as you prepare.

READING II   Romans 8:31b–34

A reading from the Letter of Saint Paul to the Romans

Brothers and sisters:
If God is **for** us, who can be **against** us?
He who did not **spare** his own **Son**
    but **handed** him over for us **all,**
    how will he not **also** give us **everything else** along with him?

An exhortatory reading in which Paul uses a series of questions to bring us to an understanding of Christ's interceding power. The questions frame the mystery of this intercession as much as they suggest answers.

passage from Paul's correspondence with the fledgling community of Christians at Rome suggests that God's favor, God's fidelity, resides with those who benefit from Christ's intercession at the Father's right hand. Most likely written in the mid-50s AD, during a particularly volatile period of unrest between Jewish and Gentile Christians in the city of Rome, this section of Paul's letter emphasizes the promise of salvation for those who are in Christ—no power on heaven or on earth is able to destroy this gift. Paul wants the Romans to be confident in all that God has done in handing over his

own Son. If God is capable of permitting the suffering and death of his beloved, then surely God will not fail to provide for those who have been chosen through Christ.

Paul uses legalistic terminology to fortify his proposition that the death and Resurrection of Christ serves to claim all those in the Church for eternal life. If those outside of Christ bring "charges" against the church, surely God will "acquit." Human condemnation against those who believe has no power over God's desire to set free and proclaim innocent. As the Romans heard Paul's rhetorical questions—"If God

is for us, who can be against us?" "It is God who acquits us, who will condemn?" —they were certainly reassured that the sacrifices entailed in maintaining the faith in the midst of persecution were worth the costs. There could be no successful prosecution waged against them.

GOSPEL   The story of the Transfiguration must be understood as a theophany, a visible manifestation of God's glory. Because Jesus is accompanied on the mountain by Peter, James, and John, the dramatic change in the Lord's appear-

These two rhetorical questions allow Paul to introduce Christ's death as an implicit answer. The second question, because it follows a straightforward declaration, can get swallowed. Give the question its place by slowing your reading at "who will condemn."

Who will bring a **charge** against God's **chosen ones?**
  It is **God** who acquits us, who will **condemn?**
Christ Jesus it is who **died**—or, rather, was **raised**—
  who also is at the **right hand** of God,
  who indeed inter**cedes** for us.

GOSPEL   Mark 9:2–10

A reading from the holy Gospel according to Mark

A narrative reading of the Transfiguration, one of the most beautiful and mysterious of Gospel scenes, giving us a brief glimpse of the light of heaven.

Jesus took Peter, James, and John
  and led them up a **high** mountain **apart** by **themselves.**
And he was trans**figured** before them,
  and his clothes became **dazzling white,**
  such as **no fuller** on earth could **bleach** them.
Then Elijah **appeared** to them along with **Moses,**
  and they were **conversing** with **Jesus.**
Then **Peter** said to Jesus in **reply,**
  "**Rabbi,** it is **good** that we are **here**!

Peter's reply, earnest though it be, is also a little funny because he is clueless. Here you can let a little comedy seep into this austere scene by enjoying Peter's cluelessness.

Elijah = ee-LĪ-juh

Let us make **three tents:**
  one for **you,** one for **Moses,** and one for **Elijah.**"
He hardly **knew** what to say, they were so **terrified.**
Then a **cloud** came, casting a **shadow** over them;
  from the **cloud** came a **voice,**
  "**This** is my beloved **Son. Listen** to him."
Suddenly, looking around, they no longer saw **anyone**
  but **Jesus alone with** them.

When God speaks, he echoes his words at Jesus' baptism. Here, Jesus is being baptized in the heavenly light of creation.

As they were coming **down** from the **mountain,**
  he charged them not to relate what they had seen to **anyone,**
  except when the Son of Man had **risen** from the dead.
So they **kept** the matter to **themselves,**
  questioning what **rising** from the **dead meant.**

Part of the mystery of this passage is Jesus' desire to keep it secret. You don't need to play this up, but you can allow yourself to sound a little puzzled by this request as you read it.

ance is intended to be witnessed and carried forth to others. Just as Moses appears to the Israelites with his face transfigured (Exodus 34:29–35), giving witness to the intimate relationship he shares with God, so does the Transfiguration of Jesus testify to God's intimacy with his Son. The Transfiguration of Jesus is not a dramatic revelation to be contained on the mountaintop; it is meant to be taken out into the world.

And what, precisely, is that revelation? The presence of Moses and Elijah, who bear witness to this theophany, suggests that Jesus, as well as his foreshadowed suffering and death, is meant to be in keeping with all that has taken place in the Law and the Prophets. Jesus does not stand for a new plan of salvation; rather, he is to be understood as continuing the mission of the forerunners. And who is this Jesus? Just as the divine voice broke through the heavens to reveal Jesus as the "beloved Son" at the time of his baptism in the Jordan (Mark 1:11), so here does the voice repeat the introduction and the command: "This is my beloved Son. Listen to him." With the utterance of these words, Moses and Elijah depart, leaving the three disciples alone with Jesus. From all that they have seen and heard, Peter, James, and John should have no doubt that Jesus is God's Son, a relationship of unbreakable intimacy. What remains for them to understand is how Jesus' Transfiguration in glory is tied to his future death and Resurrection. Concerning this quandary, Mark writes: "So they kept the matter to themselves, questioning what rising from the dead meant." S. W.

THIRD SUNDAY OF LENT

LECTIONARY #29

READING I Exodus 20:1–17

A reading from the Book of Exodus

Exodus = EK-suh-duhs

A powerful didactic reading, very familiar to your congregation. The four sections of the reading divide the Ten Commandments for emphasis. You can treat each of the four sections with almost equal emphasis, though the first and third provide the richest detail. The first section provides the first commandment, with its confession that the Lord is a jealous God. Give that claim the emphasis it deserves, since obedience is the message of the reading.

[In **those** days, God delivered **all** these commandments:
 "**I**, the LORD, am your **God**,
 who **brought** you out of the land of **Egypt**, that **place** of **slavery**.
You shall not have other gods besides **me**.]
You shall not carve **idols** for yourselves
 in the shape of **anything** in the sky **above**
 or on the earth **below** or in the waters beneath the **earth**;
 you shall not bow **down** before them or **worship** them.
For I, the LORD, your God, am a **jealous** God,
 inflicting **punishment** for their fathers' **wickedness**
 on the **children** of those who **hate** me,
 down to the **third** and **fourth generation**;
 but bestowing **mercy** down to the **thousandth** generation
 on the children of those who **love** me and keep
  my **commandments**.

The second commandment. Focus here on the repetition of "name."

["You **shall not** take the **name** of the LORD, your God, in **vain**.
For the LORD will not leave **unpunished**
 the **one** who takes his **name** in vain.

The third commandment. This passage rehearses the story of creation. Give emphasis, then, to the word "remember" at its beginning, as well as "seventh day" and "sabbath."

"**Remember** to keep **holy** the sabbath **day**.]
Six days you may **labor** and do all your **work**,
 but the **seventh day** is the **sabbath** of the LORD, your God.

There are options for today's readings. Contact your parish staff to learn which readings will be used.

READING I The Decalogue, commonly referred to as the Ten Commandments, is part of a larger collection of regulations known as the Covenant Code (Exodus 21—23). This body of law concerns such matters as right conduct with slaves, issues of theft, mistreatment of animals, and religious requirements in general. The point of the Covenant Code is to ensure the proper functioning of the newly formed Israelite society as it gradually learns to adjust to life outside the confines of Egypt and Pharaoh's oppressive regime.

At the forefront of this law is what will be seen to require the greatest amount of adjustment on the part of the Israelites: how to understand their relationship with God. Because the environment of polytheistic Egypt exposed the Hebrews to the possibility of developing an allegiance to many gods, it was necessary for the Lord to make it clear that he alone is God. Thus, he reveals that he, and he alone, is responsible for delivering the Israelites from the hands of the Egyptians. As a result, the people are to honor him alone. God goes so far as to refer to himself as "jealous," from whom both blessing and mercy are passed down through the generations. At the outset of the law, God lets Israel know that their relationship with him has lasting consequences; it will prove to be a relationship filled with both fortune and failure.

From the perspective of developing a right relationship between the people and their patron (the *Lord*, the word used to translate the four Hebrew letters expressed

No work may be **done** then either by **you,** or your **son** or **daughter,**
    or your **male** or female **slave,** or your **beast,**
    or by the **alien** who **lives** with you.
In six days the LORD made the **heavens** and the **earth,**
    the **sea** and all that is in them;
    but on the **seventh day** he **rested.**
That is why the LORD has blessed the **sabbath day** and made
    it **holy.**

The remaining seven commandments, which go quickly. Emphasize "shall not," since most of these are restrictive commandments.

["**Honor** your **father** and your **mother,**
    that you may have a **long life** in the **land**
    which the LORD, your God, is **giving** you.
You **shall not** kill.
You **shall not** commit **adultery.**
You **shall not** steal.
You **shall not** bear false **witness** against your **neighbor.**
You **shall not** covet your neighbor's **house.**
You **shall not** covet your neighbor's **wife,**
    nor his **male** or female **slave,** nor his **ox** or **ass,**
    nor anything **else** that **belongs** to him."]

[Shorter: Exodus 20:1–3, 7–8, 12–17 (see brackets)]

For meditation and context:

RESPONSORIAL PSALM   Psalm 19:8, 9, 10, 11 (John 6:68c)

R. Lord, you have the words of everlasting life.

The law of the LORD is perfect,
  refreshing the soul;
the decree of the LORD is trustworthy,
  giving wisdom to the simple.

The fear of the LORD is pure,
  enduring forever;
the ordinances of the LORD are true,
  all of them just.

The precepts of the LORD are right,
  rejoicing the heart;
the command of the LORD is clear,
  enlightening the eye.

They are more precious than gold,
  than a heap of purest gold;
sweeter also than syrup
  or honey from the comb.

in English as YHWH, the unknowable Name of God), the law demands keeping "holy" the sabbath day. The sabbath harkens back to God's original creation, when perfect order triumphed over chaos and all things understood themselves in right relationship. Keeping the sabbath is an opportunity for the Israelites to honor God's name by seeking to put things back together the way he intended them. For instance, by not laboring on this day, humans allow for the created world to once again magnify the beauty of the Creator. In a similar way, the law demands the honoring of parents and

prohibits killing, committing adultery, stealing, lying about one's neighbor, and coveting either their goods or their wives; this is for the purpose of securing relationships as intended by God. Thus, in a very few words, God commands the way of right relationship not as a means of restriction but rather as a way of discovering true freedom.

READING II   How can the ultimate display of God's power be demonstrated by a sign of human weakness? For those without the gift of faith, the death of Jesus on a cross is seen as

complete humiliation, a great and lofty plan destroyed before its completion, and utter foolishness as a way of life for those who follow Christ.

For believers in Corinth, this debate was particularly pertinent. Corinth was a community divided over the expression of spiritual gifts. Paul devotes a major portion of this letter to the Corinthians to warning them to avoid ranking one another according to such things as the gifts of prophecy, speaking in tongues, and healing. All spiritual gifts were to be directed to the one body of Christ, the Church, and placed under

A didactic reading in which Paul is trying to persuade the members of the early church at Corinth—which consisted of Gentiles—to understand the new thing that Christ's crucifixion brought to life, utterly different from what they already know.

This reading relies on parallels. Initially, there are parallels between the Jews (like Paul himself) and the Greeks (or Gentiles, like the Corinthians). Be sure to make these parallels clear by adding emphasis to the words "Jews" and "Greeks."

In the last portion of the reading, the emphasis shifts to a pair of parallels relying on comparisons of God to humans. "Foolishness" and "wisdom," "weakness" and "strength" are the attributes to emphasize.

READING II 1 Corinthians 1:22–25

A reading from the first Letter of Saint Paul to the Corinthians

Brothers and sisters:
Jews demand **signs** and **Greeks** look for **wisdom**,
    but we **proclaim** Christ **crucified**,
    a **stumbling block** to **Jews** and **foolishness** to **Gentiles**,
    but to **those** who are **called**, Jews and **Greeks alike**,
    Christ the **power** of God and the **wisdom** of God.
For the **foolishness** of God is **wiser** than human **wisdom**,
    and the **weakness** of God is **stronger** than human **strength**.

GOSPEL John 2:13–25

A reading from the holy Gospel according to John

A narrative reading of great power. Because Jesus' anger is on display in this passage, you might feel it appropriate to read with an angry tone. That's not necessary. The language conveys Jesus' anger more than adequately. Read this at an even pace and the anger will come through powerfully.

Since the **Passover** of the Jews was **near**,
    Jesus went **up** to Jerusalem.
He found in the temple area those who sold **oxen**, **sheep**,
    and **doves**,
    as well as the **money changers** seated there.
He made a **whip** out of **cords**
    and drove them **all out** of the **temple area**, with the **sheep**
        and **oxen**,
    and spilled the **coins** of the **money** changers
    and **overturned** their **tables**,
    and to **those** who sold **doves** he said,
    "Take these **out** of here,
    and stop making my Father's **house** a **marketplace**."
His disciples recalled the **words** of Scripture,
    *Zeal for your house will **consume** me.*
At this the **Jews** answered and said to him,
    "What **sign** can you show us for **doing** this?"

Read these words with a slow intensity.

the umbrella of love. Spiritual gifts are not provided by God so that individuals may puff themselves up; rather, spiritual gifts are given so that the body may be united in Christ. Furthermore, all spiritual gifts fall under the virtue of love: "Love is patient, love is kind. It is not jealous, [love] is not pompous, it is not inflated, it is not rude, it does not seek its own interests, it is not quick-tempered, it does not brood over injury" (1 Corinthians 13:4–5).

For Paul, there can be no greater expression of love than the cross of Christ.

Thus, the spiritually mature are able to see in acts of self-surrender "the power of God and the wisdom of God." While the Corinthians may be tempted to believe that power and wisdom are found in the discovery and developing of spiritual gifts, it is instead to be discovered in self-emptying love.

The cross of Christ, "a stumbling block to the Jews and foolishness to Gentiles," is no less a sign of scandal and contradiction in our contemporary society than it was in the days of Paul. In our society of rampant individualism and aggressive materialism,

so many people who adorn themselves with jewelry or tattoos in the form of a cross know nothing of the sacrifice it entails. The "foolishness of God" resides in giving oneself totally for the life of others. In a world in which we are taught the skills of self-preservation over and against the needs of others, the truth of the cross remains a message of folly and weakness. Yet for those who are able to practice the kind of love that is nailed to a cross there is the assurance that the "weakness of God is stronger than human strength."

Part of the mystery of this passage lies in Jesus' sense that the temple he is destroying will be his body. When John shares this claim, it still comes as a surprise.

Jesus answered and said to them,
    "**Destroy** this temple and in **three days** I will **raise** it up."
The Jews said,
    "**This temple** has been under **construction** for forty-six **years**,
    and you will **raise it up** in three **days**?"
But he was **speaking** about the **temple** of his **body**.
Therefore, when he was **raised** from the **dead**,
    his disciples **remembered** that he had **said** this,
    and they **came** to believe the **Scripture**
    and the **word** Jesus had **spoken**.

The conclusion speaks to Jesus' acknowledgment that people are beginning to believe in him but that they might not yet fully understand. This condition reflects your congregation's.

While he was in **Jerusalem** for the feast of **Passover**,
    many began to **believe** in his **name**
    when they **saw** the signs he was **doing**.
But **Jesus** would not trust himself to them because he **knew**
        them all,
    and did not need **anyone** to testify about **human** nature.
He **himself** understood it **well**.

GOSPEL The second chapter of John's Gospel contains two dramatic examples of divine power that are displayed in the person of Jesus. First, the wedding at Cana, when Jesus turns water into wine (John 2:1–12), is the inaugural miracle in John's Gospel. As a foreshadowing of the kingdom to come, the wedding feast at Cana serves to demonstrate the abundance of the kingdom. In a symbolic gesture, Jesus demonstrates that those who wait patiently for the manifestation of the kingdom will not be disappointed.

This miracle is followed by the account of Jesus cleansing the Temple. While the Jews who hear Jesus believe that he is threatening the destruction of the physical Temple in Jerusalem, Jesus is foretelling his death and subsequent Resurrection, by which God will provide new life in abundance.

The actions of Jesus changing water into wine and spilling the coins and overturning the tables of the money changers are meant to be read together as two great signs of things to come. However, the Jews in John's Gospel require something more. They are incapable of seeing that Jesus

views the world in a way far different from their perspective. The dual settings of the wedding feast and the Temple precincts hint at key factors of the human heart which the preaching of the kingdom seeks to overturn, namely, fear and greed. The guests at Cana were fearful that the wine was running out, while the money changers in the Temple greedily took advantage of pilgrims to Jerusalem. As Jesus participated in this particular Passover feast in Jerusalem, he becomes fully aware of the drawbacks of human nature. S. W.

THIRD SUNDAY OF LENT, YEAR A

LECTIONARY #28

READING I Exodus 17:3–7

A reading from the Book of Exodus

In **those** days, in their **thirst** for **water**,
  the people **grumbled** against **Moses**,
  saying, "**Why** did you ever make us leave **Egypt**?
Was it just to have us **die** here of thirst
  with our **children** and our **livestock**?"
So **Moses** cried out to the LORD,
  "What shall I **do** with this **people**?
A little more and they will **stone** me!"
The LORD answered Moses,
  "Go over **there** in front of the **people**,
  along with some of the **elders of Israel**,
  holding in your **hand**, as you go,
  the **staff** with which you **struck** the river.
I will be **standing** there in front of you on the **rock** in Horeb.
Strike the **rock**, and the **water** will flow **from** it
  for the **people** to **drink**."
This Moses did, in the presence of the elders of Israel.
The place was called **Massah** and **Meribah**,
  because the **Israelites** quarreled there
  and **tested** the LORD, saying,
  "Is the **LORD** in our **midst** or **not**?"

Exodus = EK-suh-duhs

A narrative reading which is essentially a dialogue involving the Israelites, Moses, and the Lord. It is inherently dramatic; you need mainly emphasize when the different speakers begin to speak.

Moses is exasperated here.

The words of the Lord are meant to placate Moses' exasperation. But they are also instructions. Read them in this spirit.

Horeb = HOHR-eb

Massah = MAS-uh
Meribah = MAYR-ih-bah

The passage concludes with a naming of the place where this happened, but in the form of a question. The question does not shed the most generous light on the Israelites. Be sure to give emphasis to the word "not."

There are options for today's readings. Contact your parish staff to learn which readings will be used.

READING I Water plays an important role in the Exodus story. One can rightly surmise that water symbolizes freedom for the Israelites in the context of their liberation from Egyptian captivity and in their developing relationship with God throughout the desert. Recall the birth of Moses and his release from Pharaoh's clutches, as his mother hides him in a papyrus basket and sets him afloat down the Nile River (Exodus 2:1–10). The water of the Nile comes into play again when the adult Moses confronts Pharaoh with the Ten Plagues, the first being the turning of the water into blood (Exodus 7:14–25). Certainly, the most dramatic mention of water in Exodus takes place when Moses parts the Red Sea, allowing the Israelites to pass through to safety and escaping the pursuit of the Egyptians one last time (Exodus 14:15–31). Surely, as Moses progressed in his understanding of God's choosing him as the shepherd of the Israelites with the job of molding them into God's Chosen People, he had to be struck by the powerful role water would play in their prolonged pilgrim journey.

In today's reading from Exodus, the Israelites have moved beyond the marshy region of the Red Sea into the arid desert of Sin. In the previous chapter, chapter 16, which takes place two weeks after they had departed from Egypt, the Israelites began to grumble against Moses and Aaron when they started to run out of food and became hungry. How very quickly they abandoned a sense of awe and gratitude for God's might in releasing them from bondage. Instead,

For meditation and context:

TO KEEP IN MIND

On the Third, Fourth and Fifth Sundays of Lent, the readings from Year A are used when the Scrutinies—prayers for purification and strength—are celebrated with the elect, those who will be baptized at the Easter Vigil.

An exhortatory reading in which Paul provides a clear sense of how faith progresses from the proof of God's love evident in Christ's death. As is often true in Paul's letters, he gets right to the point. You should allow yourself to read this passage in the same spirit.

The tone shifts slightly here, especially at "disappoint." Despite the difficulty of what Christ accomplished, his success means victory, giving us hope.

The words in this line should have almost equal emphasis, especially "proves," "love," and "us."

RESPONSORIAL PSALM   Psalm 95:1–2, 6–7, 8–9 (8)

R. If today you hear his voice, harden not your hearts.

Come, let us sing joyfully to the Lord;
  let us acclaim the Rock of our salvation.
Let us come into his presence with
    thanksgiving;
  let us joyfully sing psalms to him.

Come, let us bow down in worship;
  let us kneel before the Lord who
    made us.

For he is our God,
  and we are the people he shepherds, the
    flock he guides.

Oh, that today you would hear his voice:
  "Harden not your hearts as at Meribah,
    as in the day of Massah in the desert.
Where your fathers tempted me;
  they tested me though they had seen
    my works."

READING II   Romans 5:1–2, 5–8

A reading from the Letter of Saint Paul to the Romans

Brothers and sisters:
Since we have been **justified** by faith,
  we have **peace** with God through our **Lord** Jesus Christ,
  through whom we have gained **access** by faith
  to this **grace** in which we **stand**,
  and we **boast** in hope of the **glory** of God.

And **hope** does **not** disappoint,
  because the **love** of God has been **poured out** into our hearts
  through the **Holy Spirit** who has been **given** to us.
For **Christ**, while we were still **helpless**,
  died at the appointed time for the **ungodly**.
Indeed, only with **difficulty** does one **die** for a just **person**,
  though perhaps for a **good person** one might even find **courage**
    to die.
But **God proves** his **love** for us
  in that while we were **still sinners** Christ **died** for us.

they complained profusely: "If only we had died at the Lord's hand in the land of Egypt, as we sat by our kettles of meat and ate our fill of bread!" (Exodus 16:3). God responds by providing manna for them to eat.

In today's passage, the Israelites are raising their complaint to Moses yet again. Thirst has consumed them, and they cry out in desperation. In what appears to be exasperation, Moses cries out to God for help: "What shall I do with this people?" (Exodus 17:4). The Lord displays no hint of losing heart with the Israelites; instead he patiently explains to Moses what he can do

to alleviate their thirst. Just as he did at the Red Sea, Moses is to use his staff to strike a rock from which water will flow to quench the people's thirst.

Today's reading contains a theme that runs throughout the Book of Exodus. Even though God proves himself faithful in providing for the needs of his people, their fidelity is weak; they are easily distracted from God's providence. However, this ultimately provides the means for God to display his greatest show of might, bestowing the gift of mercy in abundance (Exodus 34:6–7). God's mercy may be likened to a stream of flowing

water that never runs dry and always makes possible the flourishing of new life.

READING II Paul beautifully states that "the love of God has been poured out into our hearts." This is grace. Grace may be defined simply as presence. Thus, God's presence resides in our hearts through the working of the Holy Spirit. Paul's way of describing grace here suggests that it is given by God in abundance and is not earned or merited.

Scripture is full of stories of people throughout the ages turning away from this

Samaria = suh-MAYR-ee-uh
Sychar = SĪ-kahr

A lengthy reading with a rich narrative progression. The focus of this reading is on the transformation of the Samaritan woman, who presents herself to Jesus as a skeptic but becomes a true believer by the end of the reading. Her conversion is presented in slight contrast to the work of Jesus' disciples, who themselves are skeptical of the Samaritan woman, mostly out of prejudice. Allow the rich social and spiritual realities of this passage to resonate in your proclamation.

At this point the dialogue between Jesus and the Samaritan woman begins. Distinguish between their words by slightly adjusting the pitch of your voice for each speaker.

Samaritan = suh-MAYR-uh-tuhn

The rhythm of this line is emphatic. Notice the stresses.

cistern = SIS-tern

These words of Jesus are the core of his exchange with the Samaritan woman.

GOSPEL   John 4:5–42

A reading from the holy Gospel according to John

[Jesus came to a town of **Samaria** called Sychar,
     near the **plot** of land that **Jacob** had given to his son **Joseph**.
Jacob's well was **there**.
Jesus, tired from his **journey**, sat down there at the **well**.
It was about **noon**.

A woman of **Samaria** came to draw **water**.
Jesus said to her,
     "**Give me** a **drink**."
His disciples had gone into the **town** to buy **food**.
The Samaritan woman **said** to him,
     "How can **you**, a **Jew**, ask **me**, a **Samaritan woman**,
          for a **drink**?"
—For Jews use **nothing** in common with **Samaritans**.—
Jesus answered and said to her,
     "If you **knew** the gift of **God**
     and who is **saying** to you, 'Give me a **drink**,'
     you would have **asked** him
     and he would have **given** you living **water**."
The woman **said** to him,
     "**Sir**, you do not even have a **bucket** and the cistern is **deep**;
     where then can you **get** this **living** water?
Are you **greater** than our father **Jacob**,
     who **gave** us this cistern and **drank** from it **himself**
     with his **children** and his **flocks**?"
Jesus answered and said to her,
     "Everyone who **drinks** this water will be **thirsty** again;
     but whoever drinks the water **I** shall give will **never** thirst;
     the water **I** shall give will **become** in him
     a spring of water **welling up** to **eternal** life."

gift. God approaches people with love and mercy, and still there are those who reject God's grace. Paul reminds his hearers that we were once like this: "we were still helpless." Those who choose to dwell apart from God are indeed "helpless," but the gift of Christ's sacrifice for all sinners overturns this situation. Christ's death continues to manifest God pouring himself out for the reconciliation and peace of all the world.

Such a free gift of justification cannot be chosen or enacted by anyone; this act must come from God alone. Thus, Paul suggests that our only means of boasting, or of

claiming anything on our own, is to "hope in the glory of God." Our realization of the overflowing of grace into our world is through hope: never rejecting God's abundance of love and trusting that no situation of despair will end in defeat. God's love conquers all. As Paul writes: "hope does not disappoint." Hope is thus the true hallmark of Christian faith. Like the grace of God, which flows freely and overflows like a torrent, hope continues even in the face of darkness and sin. The sacrifice of Christ has produced the outpouring of grace into the human heart; there is nothing that can con-

tain our boasting in that hope which endures forever.

GOSPEL   The fourth chapter of John's Gospel, which we hear almost in its entirety this Sunday, is designed around baptismal imagery. It is not just the "living water" that Jesus speaks of that makes this chapter baptismal in nature; rather, it is the encounter between Jesus and the Samaritan woman in general: his invitation to her personally to come to faith and the call to deepen that faith in worship make this a grace-filled moment of

The woman **said** to him,
"Sir, **give** me this **water**, so that I may **not** be thirsty
or have to keep **coming** here to draw **water**."]

Jesus said to her,
"Go **call** your husband and come **back**."
The woman answered and said to him,
"I do not **have** a husband."
Jesus answered her,
"You are **right** in saying, 'I **do not** have a **husband**.'
For you have had **five** husbands,
and the one you have **now** is **not** your husband.
What you have **said** is **true**."
The woman said to him,
["**Sir**, I can see that you are a **prophet**.
Our **ancestors worshiped** on this mountain;
but you people say that the place to worship is in **Jerusalem**."
Jesus said to her,
"**Believe** me, woman, the **hour** is coming
when you will **worship** the Father
neither on this **mountain** nor in **Jerusalem**.
You people **worship** what you do not **understand**;
we worship **what** we understand,
because **salvation** is from the **Jews**.
But the hour is coming, and is **now** here,
when **true worshipers** will worship the Father in **Spirit**
and **truth**;
and indeed the Father **seeks** such people to **worship** him.
God is **Spirit**, and those who **worship** him
must **worship** in **Spirit** and **truth**." »

With these words, the Samaritan woman's skepticism shifts into belief.

initiation into God's kingdom. While it is not Jesus' intention to baptize the Samaritan woman, the actions of this encounter are undeniably immersion into a faithful following of his mission.

It is important to recognize where and when this conversation between Jesus and the woman takes place. First, the land of Samaria is located between Galilee and Judea. The Samaritans were considered unorthodox by the Jews, strangers to the law, and thus unclean. It was unwarranted for Jews to interact with Samaritans. Second, the location for the exchange

between Jesus and the Samaritan woman is at a well. In fact, it is no ordinary well, but one that is believed to have been the property of Jacob's family. Wells, at this time, were considered sacred places where the divine was known to break into the human domain. Finally, the timing of the encounter is significant as it takes place in the noonday sun. Women usually drew water in the early morning, before the heat of the day; John the Evangelist seems to suggest that this woman is unafraid of exposing herself to the heat as well as to the light of the truth.

When Jesus encounters the woman, he is alone; his disciples have gone into town to buy supplies for the continuation of their journey. Jesus breaks the silence by instructing the woman, "Give me a drink." When she questions his command, due to gender differences and religious law, he offers that he has "living water" to give, not ordinary water from a cistern. It is clear that the woman wants this water but does not know where to find it. From John's baptismal perspective in this chapter, the discovery of this "living water," this source of life, comes when one keeps company with

And here, Jesus reveals himself as the Messiah. Emphasize "he" and "speaking" to express the revelation.

The return of the disciples reinforces the "problem" of Jesus interacting with a Samaritan woman (something Jewish custom ordinarily forbad); it also marks a slight excursion, because the disciples want Jesus to eat while he has a lesson he wants to convey to them.

The woman said to him,
    "I **know** that the Messiah is **coming**, the one called
        the **Christ**;
    when he **comes**, he will tell us **everything**."
Jesus said to her,
    "I am **he**, the one **speaking** with you."]

At that moment his **disciples** returned,
    and were **amazed** that he was talking with a **woman**,
    but still no one said, "What are you looking for?"
    or "Why are you talking with her?"
The woman left her **water** jar
    and went into the **town** and said to the **people**,
    "Come see a **man** who told me **everything** I have **done**.
Could he possibly **be** the **Christ**?"
They went out of the town and **came** to him.
Meanwhile, the disciples urged him, "**Rabbi, eat**."
But he said to them,
    "I have **food** to eat of which you do not **know**."
So the disciples said to one another,
    "Could **someone** have brought him something to **eat**?"
Jesus said to them,
    "My **food** is to do the **will** of the one who **sent** me
        and to **finish** his **work**.
Do you not say, 'In **four** months the **harvest** will **be** here'?
I tell you, look **up** and see the fields **ripe** for the **harvest**.
The **reaper** is already **receiving** payment
    and **gathering crops** for eternal **life**,
        so that the **sower** and **reaper** can rejoice **together**.
For **here** the saying is **verified** that '**One sows** and another **reaps**.'

Jesus, who tells the woman, "The water I shall give will become in him a spring of water welling up to eternal life." Jesus speaks on a spiritual plane, which the woman, slow to understand at first, gradually comprehends. The woman displays a sense of urgency as she demands this "living water" from Jesus in order to be thirsty no more. However, faith in Jesus is not a gift imparted all at once; it is a process that takes time as deeper insight is provided.

When Jesus reveals to the woman his knowledge that the woman has had five husbands and is living in an adulterous state, she is given the opportunity to profess a faith statement of sorts. She first proclaims Jesus to be a prophet and next witnesses to her belief in the coming of the Messiah, who "will tell us everything." Before Jesus utters the line that identifies himself as the Messiah, it should be clear to the hearers of John's Gospel that Jesus demonstrates the ability to "tell us everything." He is indeed the Messiah. Although the woman is not given the chance to affirm her belief in Jesus as Lord, since the disciples have returned and seemingly interrupt the intimate conversation, it should be evident to us that the woman has indeed been "baptized" in "living water." She has come to faith and is now able to be an evangelist herself, as she tells everyone in the town: "Come see a man who told me everything I have done."

The Gospel passage ends with an eschatological tone—a look toward the fulfillment of the kingdom. When Jesus' disciples encourage him to eat in order to sustain himself for the journey ahead, Jesus

I sent you to **reap** what you have not **worked** for;
> **others** have done the **work**,
> and you are **sharing** the fruits of **their** work."

[Many of the **Samaritans** of that town began to **believe** in him
> because of the **word** of the woman who **testified**,
> "He told me **everything** I have **done**."
When the **Samaritans** came to him,
> they invited him to **stay** with them;
> and he **stayed** there two **days**.
Many more began to **believe** in him because of his **word**,
> and they **said** to the woman,
> "We no longer **believe** because of your **word**;
> for we have **heard** for **ourselves**,
> and we know that this is **truly** the savior of the **world**."]

[Shorter: John 4:5–15, 19b–26, 39a, 40–42 (see brackets)]

The conclusion returns us to the Samaritan woman; not only does she believe in Jesus, she is able to convert the other Samaritans because of her conviction. The words of the assembled Samaritans are spoken directly to the congregation's own faith.

implies that he is filled with a different kind of food, the satisfaction of gathering people into the kingdom. His worldview is one of seeing the world as ripe for the reaping of "crops for eternal life." Just as he has made a disciple out of the woman at the well, Jesus sees that there is much work in sowing the seeds of faith and in reaping a bountiful harvest of believers. This is an ingathering that extends far beyond the land of Jerusalem and includes the most unlikely of outsiders. John leaves no doubt that the "living water" that one finds in Jesus produces the gift of new life in abundance in this world and the hope of eternal life in the world to come. S. W.

FOURTH SUNDAY OF LENT

LECTIONARY #32

READING I 2 Chronicles 36:14–16, 19–23

Chronicles = KRAH-nih-k*ls
Judah = JOO-duh

A narrative reading describing the Babylonian exile, which resulted from infidelities of the ancient Israelites. The reading begins with of moral condemnation but leads to promise when the Persian king, Cyrus, makes a place for them. The reading switches, then, from condemnation to promise (if not yet deliverance).

This section focuses on the way the Israelites mocked God's messengers, who tried to set them straight. Shed light on all the details by pacing your reading through this passage. Give "palaces afire" and "destroyed" a little extra emphasis.

Chaldeans = kahl-DEE-uhnz; kal-DEE-unhz

A reading from the second Book of Chronicles

In **those** days, all the **princes** of **Judah**, the **priests**, and the **people**
    added **infidelity** to **infidelity**,
    practicing all the abominations of the nations
    and **polluting** the LORD's **temple**
    which he had **consecrated** in **Jerusalem**.

Early and **often** did the LORD, the **God** of their **fathers**,
    send his **messengers** to them,
    for he had **compassion** on his people and his **dwelling** place.
But they **mocked** the messengers of **God**,
    despised his warnings, and **scoffed** at his **prophets**,
    until the **anger** of the LORD against his **people** was so **inflamed**
    that there was **no** remedy.
Their enemies burnt the **house** of God,
    tore down the **walls** of Jerusalem,
    set all its **palaces afire**,
    and **destroyed** all its precious **objects**.
Those who escaped the sword were carried **captive** to **Babylon**,
    where they became **servants** of the **king** of the **Chaldeans**
        and his **sons**
    until the **kingdom** of the **Persians** came to **power**.

There are options for today's readings. Contact your parish staff to learn which readings will be used.

READING I First and Second Chronicles serves as a two-volume history of Israel from after the death of Saul through the time of the Babylonian Exile. Critical to the history contained in the first book is the construction of the Temple by Solomon and its subsequent administration under the leadership of various kings. Throughout the pages of this history, the chronicler clearly details the central role that the Temple would play in the success and the fall of Jerusalem.

Today's reading from Second Chronicles provides a glimpse into the destruction that occurs as the result of infidelity. The history of the people of Israel is such that, time and time again, prophets are sent by God to remind them of the need for faithfulness. Yet, over and over, the nation veers from the commitment that the proper functioning of the Temple entails. Instead, every dimension of the nation—"all the princes of Judah, the priests, and the people"—participates in "polluting the Lord's temple."

Despite the warnings that prophets provided, Israel fails to repent, and their enemies easily take advantage of their weakness. The Temple is destroyed, every precious artifact is stolen, and the people are forced into slavery in a foreign land, Babylon. The history suggests that freedom finally is restored to Israel when Cyrus becomes the king of Persia.

The importance of keeping this history alive in writing is that Israel believes that its flourishing in every age comes down to resisting infidelity. Although the Temple will be rebuilt as the people return from exile,

Jeremiah = jayr-uh-Mī-uh

Cyrus = Sī-ruhs
The appearance of King Cyrus in the third section of the reading lightens the tone. Again, not quite deliverance but a sense of promise that you can convey by quickening your pace ever so slightly.

All this was to **fulfill** the word of the LORD spoken by **Jeremiah**:
 "Until the **land** has retrieved its lost **sabbaths**,
  during all the **time** it lies **waste** it shall have **rest**
  while **seventy years** are fulfilled."

In the **first year** of **Cyrus**, king of **Persia**,
  in order to **fulfill** the word of the LORD spoken by **Jeremiah**,
  the LORD inspired King **Cyrus** of **Persia**
  to issue this proclamation **throughout** his kingdom,
  both by word of **mouth** and in **writing**:
 "Thus says **Cyrus**, king of **Persia**:
  All the **kingdoms** of the **earth**
  the LORD, the **God** of **heaven**, has **given** to me,
  and he has also **charged** me to build him a **house**
  in **Jerusalem**, which is in **Judah**.
  Whoever, therefore, among you **belongs** to any part
   of his **people**,
  let him **go up**, and may his **God** be with him!"

For meditation and context:

RESPONSORIAL PSALM   Psalm 137:1–2, 3, 4–5, 6 (6ab)

R. Let my tongue be silenced, if I ever forget you!

By the streams of Babylon
 we sat and wept when we
  remembered Zion.
On the aspens of that land
 we hung up our harps.

For there our captors asked of us
 the lyrics of our songs,
and our despoilers urged us to be joyous:
 "Sing for us the songs of Zion!"

How could we sing a song of the LORD
 in a foreign land?
If I forget you, Jerusalem,
 may my right hand be forgotten!

May my tongue cleave to my palate
 if I remember you not,
if I place not Jerusalem
 ahead of my joy.

---

history shows that it will be destroyed once again and never be rebuilt. The Temple may not stand today, but contemporary Jews see the human heart and the study of God's law as the dual locale for the expression of fidelity. While burnt offerings may no longer comprise Israel's sacrifice, the call comes to keep the heart free from every pollution and truly consecrated to the Lord.

READING II The Letter to the Ephesians is considered to be part of the Deutero-Pauline corpus, meaning that

along with 1 and 2 Timothy and the Letter to Titus, the author of this letter is considered to be someone other than Paul. The major theme of this relatively short letter concerns the work of promoting the unity of the body of Christ. Today's reading from Ephesians, however, deals less with unity and more on the free gift of God's mercy and grace.

The author of Ephesians opens chapter 2 with the acknowledgement that the sinful ways of life prior to attachment to Christ are to be considered the things of death. "Following the wishes of the flesh

and the impulses" (Ephesians 2:3) is equated with a former life that one rejects in coming to obedience in Christ. The decision to leave this world behind requires the element of human choice. However, this choice is initiated by the grace of God. Paul suggests that we do not come to new life by any merit of our own, but only because God's mercy makes possible the turn from sinful ways to new life in Christ.

The theology contained in this passage is a form of realized eschatology, meaning that salvation is not something yet to be attained but rather is lived in the

Ephesians = ee-FEE-zhuhnz

An exhortatory reading in which Paul instructs the Ephesians about the nature of grace, the source of our salvation.

The title "Christ Jesus" is used three times in this passage. The first time it's used, place the emphasis on Christ; the other two times, place the emphasis on "Jesus."

These final two lines have comparable rhythm to them: three stresses apiece. The last line: that WE should LIVE in THEM.

Nicodemus = nik-uh-DEE-muhs

This exhortatory reading includes a passage that has become something of a cliché, with placards posted prominently at sporting events. The best strategy for conveying the message of this reading is to read it as straightforwardly as possible, without embellishment or drama. Let the words speak for themselves.

READING II   Ephesians 2:4–10

A reading from the Letter of Saint Paul to the Ephesians

Brothers and sisters:
God, who is **rich** in **mercy**,
  because of the **great love** he **had** for us,
  even when we were **dead** in our **transgressions**,
  brought us to **life** with **Christ**—by **grace** you have
    been **saved**—,
  raised us up **with** him,
  and **seated** us with him in the **heavens** in **Christ** Jesus,
  that in the **ages** to **come**
  he might show the **immeasurable riches** of his **grace**
  in his **kindness** to us in Christ **Jesus**.
For by **grace** you have been **saved** through **faith**,
  and this is not from **you**; it is the **gift** of **God**;
  it is not from **works**, so no one may **boast**.
For we are his **handiwork**, created in Christ **Jesus** for the
    good works
  that **God** has **prepared** in **advance**,
  that **we** should **live** in **them**.

GOSPEL   John 3:14–21

A reading from the holy Gospel according to John

Jesus said to Nicodemus:
  "Just as **Moses** lifted up the **serpent** in the **desert**,
  so must the Son of **Man** be lifted up,
  so that **everyone** who believes in him may have **eternal** life."

present age. God has bestowed his mercy "because of the great love he had for us," and as a result "raised us up with" Christ. Furthermore, the Letter to the Ephesians states that salvation is experienced as a participation in the Ascension of Christ, as God has "seated us with him in the heavens." How beautiful such exaltation makes those who have been led from death to life. Paul calls Christians the "handiwork" of God, a creation made possible by the grace received in faith. What incredible mercy God delivers for those who turn to his Son.

GOSPEL Today's excerpt from the conversation between Jesus and Nicodemus takes place very early in John's Gospel. Jesus has just cleansed the Temple by overturning the money changers' tables and has foretold his death and Resurrection through the symbolism of the destruction and restoration of the Temple; now his dialogue with Nicodemus reveals the very purpose for which he was born. Jesus tells Nicodemus: "For God so loved the world that he gave his only Son, so that everyone who believes

in him might not perish but might have eternal life." John 3:16 can be understood as a thesis statement of sorts for the entirety of John's Gospel. Belief is key to Johannine theology; it can be summed up as "believe, and you will be saved."

Nicodemus has come to Jesus at night, John 3:2 tells us. He has come to Jesus in darkness and encounters a light that provides the truth. After teaching Nicodemus on the necessity of being "born from above" (John 3:3), Jesus uses the image of Moses lifting a serpent high on a pole for

John 3:16 are the watchwords of Christian witness. Let your conviction arise from the words themselves.

John's dualities of light and darkness, truth and wickedness, form a core of Christian theology. Nevertheless, these expressions are easy to misunderstand. Don't shy away from the words "wicked" and "evil"; likewise, don't overemphasize the words "light" and "truth." As above, let the words speak for themselves.

TO KEEP IN MIND
When you proclaim the Word, you participate in catechizing the faithful and those coming to faith. Understand what you proclaim so those hearing you may also understand.

For God **so loved** the **world** that he gave his **only** Son,
    so that **everyone** who believes in him might not **perish**
    but might have **eternal** life.
For God did not send his **Son** into the **world** to **condemn**
    the world,
    but that the **world** might be **saved through** him.
Whoever **believes** in him will **not** be **condemned**,
    but whoever does not **believe** has already been **condemned**,
    because he has not **believed** in the name of the **only Son**
    of God.
And **this** is the **verdict**,
    that the **light** came into the **world**,
    but **people** preferred **darkness** to light,
    because their **works** were **evil**.
For everyone who does **wicked** things **hates** the light
    and does not come **toward** the light,
    so that his **works** might not be **exposed**.
But whoever **lives** the truth comes to the **light**,
    so that his works may be clearly **seen** as done in **God**.

the healing of the people as a parallel to his own being raised high on the cross in order that people may lift up their eyes to him and come to belief. Thus, not only does Jesus draw people out of darkness, but his death will also be a source of healing as people gaze upon the cross and contemplate the true sacrifice that it entails.

Like the reading from Ephesians read just before this Gospel today, this selection from John's Gospel is an example of realized eschatology. The contrast is created between the present situation of those who believe versus those who do not: "Whoever believes in him will not be condemned, but whoever does not believe has already been condemned." Just as no one is able to prevent the sun from rising and shining brightly in the sky, casting its light in every corner of the world, so too is no one able to escape being judged according to their reception or denial of the light of Christ. In many ways, this portion of John's Gospel makes salvation appear to be very neat and tidy—simply make the choice to believe in the Son of Man and you will be favorably judged. Living in the light means lifting your eyes to the cross and believing "in the name of the only Son of God." For John, salvation is not an other-worldly reality; it is the result of faith lived in the present day. S. W.

FOURTH SUNDAY OF LENT, YEAR A

LECTIONARY #31

READING I   1 Samuel 16:1b, 6–7, 10–13a

A reading from the first Book of Samuel

The LORD said to **Samuel**:
  "Fill your **horn** with **oil**, and **be** on your **way**.
I am **sending** you to **Jesse** of **Bethlehem**,
  for I have **chosen** my king from among his **sons**."

As Jesse and his sons **came** to the **sacrifice**,
  Samuel looked at **Eliab** and thought,
  "**Surely** the LORD's anointed is **here before** him."
But the LORD said to Samuel:
  "**Do not judge** from his **appearance** or from his **lofty** stature,
  because I have **rejected** him.
Not as **man sees** does **God see**,
  because **man** sees the **appearance**
  but the LORD looks into the **heart**."
In the same way **Jesse** presented seven **sons** before **Samuel**,
  but **Samuel** said to **Jesse**,
  "The LORD has not chosen any **one** of these."
Then Samuel asked Jesse,
  "Are **these** all the **sons** you **have**?"
Jesse replied,
  "There is still the **youngest**, who is **tending** the **sheep**."
Samuel said to Jesse,
  "**Send** for him;
  we will not **begin** the sacrificial **banquet** until he **arrives** here."

Samuel = SAM-yoo-uhl
Jesse = JES-ee
Eliab = ee-LĪ-uhb

A narrative reading with a dramatic conclusion, in which Samuel, chosen by the Lord and endowed with power, is sent among the sons of Jesse to find and anoint a new king. Samuel's power is the ability to recognize this king, whose appearance, when Samuel sees him at last, thrills him. The words themselves convey the drama of this reading compellingly.

Emphasize the parallel: not as man sees does God see.

Samuel cannot see the chosen king among the sons. Subtle emphasis on "one."

There are options for today's readings. Contact your parish staff to learn which readings will be used.

READING I   As so often happens throughout Old Testament, the story of David's anointing by Samuel as King of Israel is a story of divine reversal, whereby God selects the most unlikely candidate as his chosen servant. The key to this reading is the reminder that God gives the job to Samuel after rejecting the most likely candidate, Eliab, the eldest son of Jesse who makes a great appearance due to his "lofty stature." God suggests to Samuel that his requirements for a king do not follow the apparent wisdom of human thinking: "Not as man sees does God see, because man sees the appearance but the Lord looks into the heart." How true this message is! How easily people make mistakes by judging on appearances and failing to probe what lies beneath the surface.

The commissioning of Samuel to seek out, call forward, and anoint a new king for Israel takes place shortly after God rejects the kingship of Saul (1 Samuel 15:35). The reason for God removing Saul as king is very important for the future history of Israel. If Israel was to be guided by a king other than God, then it was expected that this king would approximate divinity. While Saul was indeed a successful leader according to human judgment, he failed to make proper sacrifice to God. Instead of choosing offerings that were the choicest fruits and the best of the herd, Saul settled for a less than desirable sacrifice (1 Samuel 15:9). This represented a misuse of authority on Saul's part; he failed to give God what was his due.

ruddy = RUHD-ee = having a reddish complexion

Jesse **sent** and had the young man **brought** to them.
He was **ruddy**, a youth **handsome** to behold
    and making a **splendid** appearance.
The LORD said,
    "**There**—anoint **him**, for **this** is the **one**!"
Then **Samuel**, with the **horn** of oil in hand,
    anointed **David** in the presence of his **brothers**;
    and from that day on, the **spirit** of the LORD **rushed**
      upon David.

Samuel can see the chosen king at last. Equal emphases on "There," "anoint," "this," and "one."

For meditation and context:

RESPONSORIAL PSALM   Psalm 23:1–3a, 3b–4, 5, 6 (1)

R. The Lord is my shepherd; there is nothing I shall want.

The LORD is my shepherd; I shall not want.
    In verdant pastures he gives me repose;
beside restful waters he leads me;
    he refreshes my soul.

He guides me in right paths
    for his name's sake.
Even though I walk in the dark valley
    I fear no evil; for you are at my side
with your rod and your staff
    that give me courage.

You spread the table before me
    in the sight of my foes;
you anoint my head with oil;
    my cup overflows.

Only goodness and kindness follow me
    all the days of my life;
and I shall dwell in the house of the LORD
    for years to come.

TO KEEP IN MIND
On the Third, Fourth and Fifth Sundays of Lent, the readings from Year A are used when the Scrutinies—prayers for purification and strength—are celebrated with the elect, those who will be baptized at the Easter Vigil.

Ephesians = ee-FEE-zhuhnz

READING II   Ephesians 5:8–14

A reading from the Letter of Saint Paul to the Ephesians

Brothers and sisters:
You were **once darkness**,
    but now you are **light** in the **Lord**.
Live as **children** of **light**,
    for **light** produces every kind of **goodness**
    and **righteousness** and **truth**.
Try to **learn** what is **pleasing** to the **Lord**. **»**

An exhortatory reading in which Paul tries to convince the Ephesians to live as children of the light. The concluding exhortation, after "Therefore," (next page) is the culmination of this reading.

While God chooses to put an end to Saul's line of kingship in Israel, he has no intention of ending the monarchy itself. He turns to the family of Jesse, from which the nation will renew itself. Making such a radical shift in leadership (a new family and the youngest of the family) may appear to be a risky move on God's part. However, once again, in keeping with God's pattern of selecting the lowly in order to overturn the authority of the mighty, the selection of David coincides perfectly with the mysterious ways of God. We need only to ponder the many ways in which David's character

will grow and mature from his roots as a lowly shepherd. Not only will he prove his strength by destroying the mighty Goliath (1 Samuel 17:40–51), but he will provide proper worship for God, especially by delighting him with the many songs we know as psalms (see 1 Samuel 22:1–51). David's strength will be found not only in military might but in his deference to divine authority as displayed in proper worship.

Although David is not officially anointed in a public ceremony until later (2 Samuel 5:1–5), today's reading witnesses to the prophet's anointing of the young David,

upon whom "the spirit of the Lord rushed" and remained for all time. In the Christian process of initiation, anointing with oil is understood to communicate the indwelling of the Holy Spirit. Oil not only serves to heal the body, but it is also used to highlight strength. Such was the purpose for its use in setting apart a king who was to be commissioned with authority as the people's leader. In a Christian initiatory context, oil is used in the Sacrament of Baptism to indelibly mark the neophyte in the image Christ. In Confirmation, oil is used once again to not only visibly manifest a chosen

Take no **part** in the fruitless works of **darkness**;
　　rather **expose** them, for it is **shameful** even to **mention**
　　the things done by them in **secret**;
　　but **everything** exposed by the light becomes **visible**,
　　for **everything** that becomes visible is **light**.
Therefore, it says:
　　"**Awake**, O sleeper,
　　and **arise** from the **dead**,
　　and **Christ** will give you **light**."

Take note of the parallels and shifts in these lines: from "everything" to "visible," and then "everything" to "light."

"Awake," "arise," and "light" are the focal points of these final lines. Don't rush through them.

GOSPEL　John 9:1–41

A reading from the holy Gospel according to John

[As Jesus passed by he saw a man **blind** from **birth**.]
His disciples asked him,
　　"**Rabbi**, who **sinned**, this **man** or his **parents**,
　　that he was **born blind**?"
Jesus answered,
　　"Neither **he** nor his **parents** sinned;
　　it is so that the **works** of God might be made **visible**
　　　　through him.
We have to do the **works** of the one who sent me while it is **day**.
Night is coming when **no one** can **work**.
While I am in the **world**, I am the **light** of the **world**."
When he had **said** this, [he **spat** on the ground
　　and made **clay** with the **saliva**,
　　and **smeared** the clay on his **eyes**, and said to him,
　　"**Go wash** in the **Pool** of **Siloam**"—which means **Sent**—.
So he **went** and **washed**, and came back **able** to see.

His neighbors and those who had seen him **earlier**
　　as a **beggar** said,
　　"Isn't this the one who used to **sit** and **beg**?"

Rabbi = RAB-ī

This is a complex narrative reading with many characters, each with different motivations, as well as several scene changes. In this reading, Jesus upturns traditional rabbinic understanding of blindness as a punishment for immorality. It also relies on a defiant tone to make its point. Keep this in mind as you proclaim.

This line has an anticipatory, prophetic quality, characteristic of John's Gospel.

These details of Jesus' healing powers are interesting; don't rush through them. Siloam = sih-LOH-uhm

---

status but to suggest through the sense of smell that the Holy Spirit has "rushed upon" the candidate with wisdom and strength. In the Sacrament of Holy Orders, the candidate's hands are anointed with chrism to signal Christ's connection to the hands of the one who will stand at the altar to make an offering on the people's behalf. Thus, oil serves to make visible God's choice of men and women whose election was made not according to appearances but by his having looked into the heart.

READING II　A characteristic motif of Paul's writings, as well as of the social world in which Paul lived, is the contrast between honor and shame. To shame a person was to exercise control over that individual, while to honor another was to express one's allegiance. Honor and shame functioned particularly well in the context of the family; parents readily taught their children of the importance of bringing honor to the household and avoiding shame. Thus, Paul will warn the Christian household in Rome: "Let us live honorably as in the daylight: no drunken orgies, no promiscuity or licentiousness, and no wrangling or jealousy" (Romans 13:13).

　　Here, in his letter to the Ephesians, Paul makes the contrast between living in darkness and living as "children of light." While the former brings shame, the latter is a way of life that has tremendous positive consequences for the honor of the entire Christian community at Ephesus. Paul says that living together as light in the Lord exhibits at least three characteristics: goodness, righteousness, and truth. For

Any expression of "I am" in John's Gospel is freighted with authority.

Some said, "It **is**,"
  but others said, "**No**, he just **looks** like him."
He said, "**I am**."]
So they said to him, "How were your **eyes** opened?"
He replied,
  "The man called **Jesus** made **clay** and anointed my **eyes**
  and told me, 'Go to **Siloam** and **wash**.'
So I **went** there and washed and was able to **see**."
And they said to him, "Where **is** he?"
He said, "I don't **know**."

The (formerly) blind man's tone here is somewhat exasperated.

[They brought the one who was once blind to the **Pharisees**.
Now Jesus had made **clay** and opened his **eyes** on a **sabbath**.
So then the **Pharisees** also asked him **how** he was able to **see**.
He **said** to them,
  "He put **clay** on my **eyes**, and I **washed**, and now I can **see**."
So some of the Pharisees said,
  "This man is **not** from God,
  because he **does not keep** the **sabbath**."
But others said,
  "How can a sinful man do such **signs**?"
And there was a **division** among them.
So they said to the blind man again,
  "What do you have to **say** about him,
  since he **opened** your **eyes**?"
He said, "He is a **prophet**."]

Once again, the man who had been blind has to explain his story, this time to the Pharisees. His exasperation mounts to defiance when he proclaims Jesus a prophet.

Now the Jews did not **believe**
  that he had been **blind** and gained his **sight**
  until they **summoned** the parents of the one who had **gained**
    his sight.
They asked them,
  "Is this your **son**, who you say was born **blind**?
How does he now **see**?"
His parents answered and said,
  "We **know** that this is our son and that he was born **blind**. »

the author, these not only continue to bring honor to those baptized into Christ, but they also serve to unite the community as one. Where goodness, righteousness, and truth prevail, the community is able to live honorably, without attempting to hide itself from the Lord.

Thus, Paul will continue in his letter to suggest the need to expose the things of darkness to the light. Although the human tendency is to keep hidden those things that may lead to shame, the notion here is that exposure to the light will heal them.

The light not only exposes what is caught up in darkness, it has the power to overwhelm, so that "everything that becomes visible is light."

Finally, Paul equates the darkness to death and challenges those outside the realm of Christ's light to awaken and receive the gift of light. For those in the final weeks of preparing for the waters of Baptism, the call to hear Christ inviting them into the light may be particularly poignant. The celebration of the scrutiny rite today will serve to remind them that the ways that constitute

living in darkness are often subtle but no less deserving of the healing that exposure to the light will provide. However, not only the elect, but all members of the Church will certainly hear in these words from Ephesians the call to ongoing conversion. "Awake, O sleeper, and arise from the dead, and Christ will give you light."

GOSPEL   Today's reading from the Gospel of John constitutes the entirety of the ninth chapter, which in the Bible immediately follows the story of

Because the Pharisees don't believe the man who had been blind, they question his parents. Crucially, they repeat that he is of age and can speak for himself. Their tone is defiant. They believe their son.

We do not **know** how he sees **now**,
    nor do we know who **opened** his eyes.
Ask him, he is of **age**;
    he can **speak** for **himself**."
His parents said this because they were **afraid**
    of the **Jews**, for the **Jews** had already **agreed**
    that if anyone **acknowledged** him as the **Christ**,
    he would be **expelled** from the **synagogue**.
For this **reason** his parents said,
    "He is of **age**; **question** him."

So a second time they **called the man** who had been blind
    and said to him, "**Give God** the praise!
We **know** that this man is a **sinner**."
He replied,
    "If he is a **sinner**, I do not **know**.
One thing I **do know** is that I was **blind** and now I **see**."
So they said to him,
    "What did he **do** to you?
    How did he open your **eyes**?"
He answered them,
    "I told you already and you did not **listen**.
Why do you want to hear it **again**?
Do you **want** to become his **disciples, too**?"
They **ridiculed** him and said,
    "**You** are that man's disciple;
    we are disciples of **Moses**!
We **know** that God **spoke** to **Moses**,
    but we do not **know** where this one is **from**."
The man answered and said to them,
    "This is what is so **amazing**,
    that you do not **know** where he is **from**, yet he **opened** my **eyes**.
We know that **God** does **not** listen to sinners,
    but if one is **devout** and does his **will**, he listens to **him**.
It is **unheard** of that **anyone** ever opened the eyes of a person
        born **blind**.

Exasperation and defiance.

The Pharisees cannot believe his temerity. This disbelief intensifies to the point where they throw him out because he has the gall to try to teach them. Ridiculous as they are, don't ridicule the Pharisees with your tone of voice.

the scribes and the Pharisees presenting an adulterous woman to Jesus for his judgment and his use of the occasion as an opportunity to reveal himself to be the "light of the world" (John 7:12). In this encounter with the man blind since birth, Jesus is able to demonstrate that darkness has no place in the kingdom of God. If the light has entered the world, then blindness stands as a contradiction to the reception of God's grace.

Thus, the story begins with the age-old dilemma: is bodily illness or disease a curse that comes from sin committed either in the present or as something handed down through the generations? Jesus answers this quandary by turning the condition of the man's blindness into a positive trait—it is through his blindness that God is able to work wonders in him for others to see. While society may want to exclude the blind man from participation in all of its dealings and relationships, Jesus suggests that the man plays a missionary role in the kingdom. He says to the man: "While I am in the world, I am the light of the world." Clearly, the presence of blindness in his midst is simply unacceptable for Jesus. It contradicts the existence of God's kingdom.

Added to this is the recognition that the blind man does not ask to be healed. Instead, Jesus initiates the healing process without a plea coming from either the man or any other intercessor. Jesus spits on the ground, makes clay with his saliva, and applies the clay to the man's eyes. Step one of the healing process is complete. But Jesus requires something more. He desires that the man demonstrate his own cooperation, which he has the freedom to withhold. Therefore, Jesus sends the man off to

Jesus validates the belief of the man who had been blind.

> If this man were **not** from God,
>   he would **not** be able to do **anything**."
> [They **answered** and said to him,
>   "You were born **totally** in sin,
>   and are **you** trying to teach **us**?"
> Then they **threw** him out.
>
> When Jesus heard that they had **thrown him out**,
>   he found him and said, "Do you **believe** in the Son of **Man**?"
> He answered and said,
>   "Who **is** he, sir, that I may believe in **him**?"
> Jesus said to him,
>   "You have **seen** him,
>   and the one **speaking** with you is **he**."
> He said,
>   "I **do believe**, Lord," and he **worshiped** him.]
> Then Jesus said,
>   "I **came** into this world for **judgment**,
>   so that **those** who do not **see** might **see**,
>   and **those** who do **see** might become **blind**."

The reading concludes with a crucial inversion: blindness to sight, sight to blindness. The sin tradition indicated in the blind man has been shifted to the Pharisees. When we believe something blindly, are we believing or are we blind?

> Some of the Pharisees who were with him **heard** this
>   and said to him, "**Surely** we are not also blind, **are** we?"
> Jesus said to them,
>   "If you were **blind**, you would have no **sin**;
>   but now you are saying, 'We **see**,' so your **sin** remains."

[Shorter: John 9:1, 6–9, 13–17, 34–38 (see brackets)]

wash himself. In other words, the blind man has an important role to play in his healing; he is asked to cooperate with grace.

A powerful transformation takes place in the blind man after he returns with his newfound sight. Up to this point, he has said nothing, but now, he uses his words to testify to Jesus having "anointed" his eyes and giving him the gift of sight. The man who is perceived at the outset of the story to be blind because of some sin now becomes a disciple and stands as a primary witness to the power in Jesus that frustrates and frightens the religious authori-

ties. Rather than seeing the tremendous good that Jesus is doing in overturning the people's suffering, the scribes and the Pharisees continue to reject the possibility that his is the work of God. "This man is not from God, because he does not keep the Sabbath." Soon, however, the man is able to come to deeper insight: "If this man were not from God, he would not be able to do anything." The questioning leads to exhaustion on the part of the religious establishment, who, after recognizing that the man has been teaching them, throw him out from their midst! The evangelist

has painted here a situation that overturns expectations: the man born blind, who comes to see the truth, is able to express faith, while those who consider themselves to be fully knowledgeable of the workings of the law prove themselves to be blind and faithless. When the man who now sees professes his belief in Jesus—"I do believe, Lord"—Jesus is given the opportunity to once again define his mission as the light of the world: "I came into this world for judgment, so that those who do not see might see and those who do see might become blind." S. W.

FIFTH SUNDAY OF LENT

LECTIONARY #35

READING I   Jeremiah 31:31–34

A reading from the Book of the Prophet Jeremiah

The days are **coming**, says the LORD,
    when I will **make** a new **covenant** with the house of **Israel**
    and the house of **Judah**.
It **will not be like** the covenant I made with their **fathers**
    the day I **took** them by the **hand**
    to lead them **forth** from the land of **Egypt**;
    for they **broke** my covenant,
    and I had to **show myself** their **master**, says the LORD.
But this is the covenant that I will **make**
    with the house of **Israel** after those days, says the LORD.
I will place my law **within** them and **write** it upon their **hearts**;
    I will be their **God**, and they shall be my **people**.
No **longer** will they have need to teach their friends
    and relatives
    how to **know** the LORD.
All, from least to greatest, shall **know me**, says the LORD,
    for I will **forgive** their evildoing and **remember** their sin
      no more.

Jeremiah = jayr-uh-MĪ-uh

An exhortatory reading hearkening to the better days to come. The tone of this reading is anticipatory, corrective, and moving toward jubilance.
Here Jeremiah, channeling the Lord, voices old grievances.

At this point, the tone shifts to something more promising.

The reading concludes with the promise of forgiveness. Emphasis on "remember."

There are options for today's readings. Contact your parish staff to learn which readings will be used.

READING I Today's reading from the Book of the Prophet Jeremiah has long served as a foundational text for biblical literature. It represents a section of prophecy based on hope and the promise of restoration for Israel. Chapters 30 to 33 of Jeremiah are considered to be a book in and of themselves, the Book of Consolation. The basic theme of this section of Jeremiah's prophecy is to restore the people's faith in God's desire to make of them his beloved people.

The verses immediately prior to verse 31 in chapter 31 speak of individual responsibility for sin. Instead of having to repent for the sinfulness of a former generation, God's renewed vision is that each person will be judged according to the sins they have committed. This is important precisely because it connects to God's instruction that he will place the law within individuals and write it on their hearts (v. 33). This is not to say that the House of Israel is not to be cognizant of its social sin, but rather, God acknowledges here that writing the law upon stone tablets was insufficient for each member of the household to interiorize the law. Thus, the renewal of the covenant demands a greater personal appropriation of the demands of the law. God wishes to chose a people of conviction.

Not only does this prophecy demonstrate God's desire to place the law deep within the bones of his people, it suggests that he wishes to have a greater personal relationship with them. Verse 34 states that the ways of the Lord will not have to be passed on through teaching; rather, the

RESPONSORIAL PSALM   Psalm 51:3–4, 12–13, 14–15 (12a)

R. Create a clean heart in me, O God.

Have mercy on me, O God, in your
        goodness;
    in the greatness of your compassion wipe
        out my offense.
Thoroughly wash me from my guilt
    and of my sin cleanse me.

A clean heart create for me, O God,
    and a steadfast spirit renew within me.
Cast me not out from your presence,
    and your Holy Spirit take not from me.

Give me back the joy of your salvation,
    and a willing spirit sustain in me.
I will teach transgressors your ways,
    and sinners shall return to you.

READING II   Hebrews 5:7–9

A reading from the Letter to the Hebrews

In the **days** when Christ **Jesus** was in the **flesh**,
    he offered **prayers** and **supplications** with loud cries and tears
    to the one who was able to **save** him from death,
    and he was **heard** because of his **reverence**.
Son though he was, he learned **obedience** from what he **suffered**;
    and when he was made **perfect**,
    he became the **source** of eternal **salvation** for **all** who
        obey him.

GOSPEL   John 12:20–33

A reading from the holy Gospel according to John

Some **Greeks** who had come to worship at the **Passover** Feast
    came to **Philip**, who was from Bethsaida in Galilee,
    and asked him, "**Sir**, we would like to see **Jesus**." ❯❯

A brief didactic reading that provides a lesson on obedience. The tone throughout is instructive.

From this point forward, the reading is using Jesus to model our own behavior, hard to achieve but worth aspiring to. Place emphases on "suffering," "perfect," and "all."

Though part of a narrative, this passage includes extensive exhortations. Jesus is anticipating his death in these passages, something the disciples and those who are following him are not yet prepared to understand. Nevertheless, he means to prepare them. In John's Gospel, Jesus' expressions are often otherworldly; don't be too stern when you proclaim these passages.

"least to greatest" will come to know the Lord. How? Through the forgiveness of their sins. God will prove himself to be abundant in mercy. He shall "remember their sin no more." Clearly, these are verses of consolation for a people returning from exile.

READING II These short verses from the Letter to the Hebrews are situated within a portion of the text that depicts Christ as the compassionate high priest who, even from his place in the heavenly sanctuary, is able to sympathize with humanity. Just as Jesus does not give himself glory, but rather receives it from

the Father, so too is the high priest responsible for interceding for us.

The element that shines forth most radiantly in this passage is Jesus' complete and total share in humanity, "in the days when Christ Jesus was in the flesh" (v. 7). His humanity is recognized in the trusting obedience he displays in offering prayers and supplications. And just like sinful humanity, he made these prayers with "loud cries and tears." The author suggests that such actions on Jesus' part were possible "because of his reverence." We should see here that the depth of lament that

Jesus exhibits reveals that his human suffering was very real.

Yet another mark of the high priest's connection to humanity is the statement that Jesus "learned obedience from what he suffered" (v. 8). The prayer of Jesus led him to understand God's will. Jesus, just like every human person, had to feel in his body the pains of suffering, and he had to learn how to make sense of that suffering. While suffering tempts people to wallow in self-pity, it can also lead people to focus on the needs of others. This is what Jesus learned. His perfection came when he was able to empty himself on the cross for the sake of

A metaphor. Simply present it.

Note the repetitions of "whoever." These will anchor the claims Jesus is making.

Philip went and told Andrew;
    then **Andrew** and **Philip** went and told **Jesus**.
Jesus answered them,
    "The **hour** has **come** for the Son of **Man** to be **glorified**.
Amen, amen, I say to you,
    unless a **grain** of **wheat falls** to the ground and **dies**,
    it **remains** just a grain of **wheat**;
    but if it **dies**, it produces **much fruit**.
Whoever **loves** his life **loses** it,
    and whoever **hates** his life in this world
    will **preserve** it for eternal **life**.
Whoever **serves** me must **follow** me,
    and where **I am**, there also will **my servant be**.
The **Father** will honor **whoever** serves me.

Here, Jesus is channeling his confidence. Do the same by speaking these lines straightforwardly.

"I am **troubled** now. Yet what should I **say**,
'**Father**, **save** me from this **hour**'?
But it was for **this purpose** that I came to **this hour**.
Father, **glorify** your name."
Then a **voice** came from **heaven**,
    "I have **glorified** it and will **glorify** it again."
The crowd there heard it and said it was **thunder**;
    but others said, "An **angel** has **spoken** to him."
Jesus answered and said,
    "**This voice** did not come for my sake but for **yours**.
Now is the time of **judgment** on this **world**;
    now the ruler of this world will be **driven out**.
And when I am **lifted up** from the **earth**,
    I will draw **everyone** to myself."
He said this indicating the **kind** of **death** he would **die**.

Thunder is the supernatural voice in the passage; Jesus hears it foretelling the purpose of his death. The mysterious reverberation.

the world's salvation. Thus, this passage ends with the subtle cue that Christians who follow in the footsteps of Jesus are to learn obedience from their suffering, emptying themselves for the good of others.

GOSPEL Jesus' discourse on his imminent death and future glorification opens with outsiders to Jerusalem, most likely Gentiles, seeking to find him. Because these visitors had come to participate in the Passover, it is possible that they were in the process of converting to Judaism. But they are to have a different purpose in John's narrative; because these Gentiles wish to "see" Jesus, they represent the universality of Jesus' mission. The events concerning Jesus that are about to take place during these Jewish high holy days are meant to be shared with the world beyond Jerusalem.

Furthermore, the seeking out of Jesus from the Gentile world causes Jesus to announce that the hour for his glorification has now arrived. This "hour" can be interpreted in a variety of ways. First, Jesus subtly compares his future death on the cross to a grain of wheat that falls to the earth in order to produce new life (v. 26). That which willingly gives up life will discover it anew in abundance. Second, the "hour" is also seen as turmoil. Jesus reveals that he is "troubled," and yet, understood in relationship to the Father's will, this moment of trouble will give way to glorification (v. 27). Finally, this "hour" is a time of judgment (v. 28). Jesus forecasts that his future death and Resurrection will draw everyone to himself and defeat the powers of evil in the world. This verse harkens back to the purpose of the visitors from Greece inquiring where they might find Jesus: the death of the Lord and his glorification by the Father is meant for the salvation of all the world. S. W.

FIFTH SUNDAY OF LENT, YEAR A

LECTIONARY #34

READING I   Ezekiel 37:12–14

A reading from the Book of the Prophet Ezekiel

Thus says the LORD God:
 O my people, I will **open** your **graves**
  and have you **rise** from them,
  and bring you **back** to the land of **Israel**.
Then you shall **know** that I am the LORD,
  when I **open** your graves and have you **rise** from them,
  O my people!
I will **put** my spirit **in** you that you may **live**,
  and I will **settle** you upon your **land**;
  thus you shall **know** that I am the LORD.
I have **promised**, and I will **do** it, says the LORD.

RESPONSORIAL PSALM   Psalm 130:1–2, 3–4, 5–6, 7–8 (7)

R. With the Lord there is mercy and fullness of redemption.

Out of the depths I cry to you, O LORD;
  LORD, hear my voice!
Let your ears be attentive
  to my voice in supplication.

If you, O LORD, mark iniquities,
  LORD, who can stand?
But with you is forgiveness,
  that you may be revered.

I trust in the LORD;
  my soul trusts in his word.
More than sentinels wait for the dawn,
  let Israel wait for the LORD.

For with the LORD is kindness
  and with him is plenteous redemption;
and he will redeem Israel
  from all their iniquities.

Ezekiel = ee-ZEE-kee-uhl

An exhortatory reading in which a small number of promises are repeated and varied a few times to impressive effect. Focus on the phrase "O my people," which includes all the feelings of care and connection that motivate this reading.

This line rephrases the opening lines. Slow down very slightly to signal the repetition.

Emphasize "promised" and "do" to conclude the exhortation.

For meditation and context:

TO KEEP IN MIND
On the Third, Fourth and Fifth Sundays of Lent, the readings from Year A are used when the Scrutinies—prayers for purification and strength—are celebrated with the elect, those who will be baptized at the Easter Vigil.

There are options for today's readings. Contact your parish staff to learn which readings will be used.

READING I   Ezekiel was perhaps born roughly thirty years before the destruction of the Temple in 586 BC and the subsequent exile of the Hebrew people to the land of Babylon. It is during the time of captivity that Ezekiel receives visions and the call to announce the Lord's desire to restore the former glory of Israel.

In the vision found in today's reading, Ezekiel sees the restoration of Israel depicted by the opening of graves. This is truly the language of resurrection: "O my people, I will open your graves and have you rise from them, and bring you back to the land of Israel" (v. 12). Earlier, Ezekiel painted Israel as a desert land filled with dry bones (vv. 1–11). Death has totally overwhelmed the people; there is nothing here that is filled with life. Yet the hope that Ezekiel impresses upon his hearers is that from the dryness of death will come the promise of future life: "I will put my spirit in you that you may live." Just as God breathed his spirit into his human creation at the outset of the world (Genesis 2:7), so here do we see God re-creating humanity by breathing new life into what was dead.

The subtext in Ezekiel's prophecy is that the gift of resurrection and the people's return to the land once theirs will be accomplished by the work of the Lord. Over and over the Lord takes responsibility for saving his people. "I have promised, and I will do it, says the Lord" (v. 14). The Lord will follow through on his promise to restore the bond of the covenant with

READING II Romans 8:8–11

A reading from the Letter of Saint Paul to the Romans

Brothers and sisters:
Those who are in the **flesh cannot** please **God**.
But you are **not** in the flesh;
  on the **contrary**, you are in the spirit,
  if only the **Spirit** of God dwells in you.
Whoever does not **have** the Spirit of **Christ** does not **belong**
    to him.
But if **Christ** is **in** you,
  although the **body** is dead because of **sin**,
  the **spirit** is alive because of **righteousness**.
If the **Spirit** of the one who raised **Jesus** from the **dead** dwells
    in you,
  the One who raised **Christ** from the dead
  will give **life** to your mortal bodies **also**,
  through his Spirit dwelling in **you**.

Paul's didactic reading contrasts the flesh and the spirit. In Paul's letters, the spirit is superior to the flesh, which desires, fades, and dies, while the spirit lives. This can make it challenging to read him to an assembly, each member of whom is in the flesh, in a body. However you regard this aspect of Paul's thinking, proclaim this reading as straightforwardly as you can.

The sense of life is decidedly in the spirit, but it can enter the mortal body, too. Emphasize the phrase "give life."

Israel in which they recognize him as their God. Having been immersed in the polytheistic worldview of the Babylonians for several decades, the people's commitment to worshipping God alone must be restored; this is necessary for the reconstruction of Jerusalem and the flourishing of the people.

READING II After having completed two chapters dealing with deliverance from sin, death, and the Law, Paul devotes the eighth chapter of his correspondence with the Romans to a positive appraisal of the Christian life. He does this by employing the dichotomy of "flesh" (*sarx*), understood as the person enslaved by the powers of sin, and "spirit" (*pneuma*), the person who "is alive because of righteousness" (Romans 8:10). To live "in the flesh" means to live completely for oneself, whereas to live with the Spirit dwelling in you is to live for God.

The entirety of the Christian life is truly focused on the indwelling of the Holy Spirit and the enactment of spiritual gifts. Paul writes several lines after today's passage: "[I]f by the Spirit you put an end to the misdeeds of the body you will live" (Romans 8:13). The Holy Spirit is the first fruit of Christ's Resurrection, and therefore, wherever death to self is transcended by life directed to God and others, the Spirit is active and is fully operational.

Those who have been baptized do not wait solely for a future moment of redemption; rather, salvation is taking place right now for those who have been grafted onto Christ. Phrases such as "you are not in the flesh," "you are in the spirit," and "Christ is in you," make certain that the Christian is seen by God not as being in any lingering sin but rather as being in the fullness of the

Lazarus = LAZ-uh-ruhs
Bethany = BETH-uh-nee
A long and complex narrative reading energized by the intense emotions of the figures in the story. The outcome of this story is well known. Its mysteries reside in the power over death that Jesus demonstrates, as well as his declarations about himself ("I am the resurrection and the life"). There are also the curious details that texture the imagination, such as the days Lazarus has been dead and the potential stench of his corpse. You can linger on these details in your proclamation.

These are the four main characters in the story.

Rabbi = RAB-ī

Emphasize the relationships between walking and day, walking and night, the light, and stumbling.

GOSPEL   John 11:1–45

A reading from the holy Gospel according to John

Now a man was **ill**, **Lazarus** from Bethany,
  the village of **Mary** and her sister **Martha**.
Mary was the one who had **anointed** the Lord with perfumed **oil**
  and **dried** his feet with her **hair**;
  it was her brother **Lazarus** who was **ill**.
So [the sisters sent word to Jesus saying,
  "**Master**, the one you **love** is **ill**."
When Jesus **heard** this he said,
  "This **illness** is not to **end** in death,
  but is for the **glory** of God,
  that the **Son** of God may be glorified **through** it."
Now Jesus loved **Martha** and her **sister** and **Lazarus**.
So when he **heard** that he was **ill**,
  he remained for **two days** in the place where he **was**.
Then **after** this he said to his disciples,
  "Let us go **back** to Judea."]
The disciples said to him,
  "**Rabbi**, the Jews were just trying to **stone** you,
  and you want to go **back** there?"
Jesus answered,
  "Are there not **twelve hours** in a day?
If one **walks** during the **day**, he does not **stumble**,
  because he **sees** the **light** of this **world**.
But if one **walks** at **night**, he **stumbles**,
  because the **light** is not in him."
He said this, and then told them,
  "Our friend **Lazarus** is **asleep**,
  but I am going to **awaken** him." »

Spirit. Salvation occurs today. Yet this is not to abandon the attitude of hope for the appearance of some long-awaited future glory. This is the very essence of the last sentence of today's reading: "If the Spirit of the one who raised Jesus from the dead dwells in you, the One who raised Christ from the dead will give life to your mortal bodies also, through his Spirit dwelling in you."

To summarize this brief excerpt of Paul's theology: Baptism causes one to switch allegiances from sin to God, thereby bringing about the death of life in the flesh in order to live fully in the spiritual realm.

GOSPEL   The story of the raising of Lazarus takes place immediately after Jesus made several claims to being the Son of God. He retreats to the far side of the Jordan River to escape the religious authorities who wanted to arrest him. Thus, the story begins with Martha and Mary, Lazarus' sisters, sending word to Jesus that their brother is gravely ill. This provides Jesus with the opportunity to proclaim that this illness will prove to be the means through which Jesus' true identity will be made known and is for the glory of God. In some ways, John the Evangelist

plunges us into the cosmic realm whereby the evil forces of this world (represented by those seeking to put Jesus to death) and the power of God's glory are at war with each other. Jesus is very certain that the outcome will testify to the victory of God.

At first, Jesus' reaction to the news that his friend is very ill might surprise us. He makes the decision to stay where he was for two more days. His delay in returning to Bethany allows Lazarus to die and be buried. If Jesus were to have returned when Lazarus was merely dying, his return to life may not have had the same effect on the

So the disciples said to him,
   "**Master**, if he is **asleep**, he will be **saved**."
But **Jesus** was talking about his **death**,
   while they **thought** that he meant **ordinary sleep**.
So then Jesus said to them clearly,
   "**Lazarus** has **died**.
And I am **glad** for you that I was not **there**,
   that you may **believe**.
Let us **go** to him."
So **Thomas**, called **Didymus**, said to his fellow disciples,
   "Let us **also** go to **die** with him."

[When Jesus **arrived**, he found that **Lazarus**
   had already been in the **tomb** for four days.]
Now Bethany was near **Jerusalem**, only about **two miles** away.
And many of the **Jews** had come to **Martha** and **Mary**
   to **comfort them** about their **brother**.
[When **Martha** heard that **Jesus** was coming,
   she went to **meet** him;
   but **Mary** sat at home.
Martha said to Jesus,
   "**Lord**, if you had **been** here,
   my **brother** would not have **died**.
But even **now** I know that what**ever** you ask of **God**,
   God will **give** you."
Jesus said to her,
   "Your **brother** will **rise**."
Martha said to him,
   "I **know** he will rise,
   in the **resurrection** on the last **day**."
Jesus told her,
   "**I** am the **resurrection** and the **life**;
   whoever **believes** in me, **even if he dies**, will **live**,
   and **everyone** who lives and **believes** in me will **never** die.

Didymus = DID-uh-muhs = twin

This exchange, concluding with "everyone who lives and believes in me will never die," expresses the core of this reading. Read it with care, allowing for Jesus' striking expression that he is the resurrection and the life to arise directly, even irrefutably, from this exchange.

crowds of people who witness Jesus raising Lazarus from the dead. The last line of this reading is therefore critical to the purpose of the passage: "Now many of the Jews who had come to Mary and seen what he had done began to believe in him."

Jesus knows that waiting for Lazarus' death and burial will allow him to perform the miracle that will draw many people over to his side, thereby waging an even greater threat to the religious establishment. In addition, the evangelist wants to leave no doubt that Lazarus is dead and that his raising will be far greater than

resuscitation, shown by the detail that Lazarus has been dead for four days and that the stone had been rolled over the entrance to the tomb.

There are two important dimensions of Johannine eschatology that are represented in this story. Both are knitted together when Jesus makes the proclamation: "I am the resurrection and the life; whoever believes in me, even if he dies, will live, and everyone who lives and believes in me will never die." For John, the one who believes in Jesus has already died and is on the journey from death to life, with final

resurrection as the confirmation of what has already occurred. Thus, the raising of Lazarus is meant to symbolize the resurrection of Christians. What happens to him will happen to all those who put their faith in Jesus.

The first to express such faith in Jesus is Martha. She makes three faith statements that are meant to be the utterances of every believing Christian, and when taken today, reveal the sense of *anamnesis* in which the past, the present, and the future coincide. First she declares her faith regarding the past: "Lord, if you had been

Do **you** believe this?"
She said to him, "**Yes**, Lord.
I have **come** to **believe** that you are the **Christ**, the Son of God,
    the one who is **coming** into the world."]

When she had **said** this,
    she went and called her sister Mary **secretly**, saying,
    "The **teacher** is here and is **asking** for you."
As soon as she **heard** this,
    she rose **quickly** and **went** to him.
For Jesus had not yet come into the village,
    but was **still** where Martha had **met** him.
So when the **Jews** who were **with her** in the house **comforting** her
    saw Mary get up **quickly** and go **out**,
    they **followed** her,
    presuming that she was going to the **tomb** to **weep** there.
When Mary came to where Jesus was and saw him,
    she **fell** at his feet and **said** to him,
    "**Lord**, if you had **been** here,
    my **brother** would not have **died**."
When Jesus saw her **weeping** and the **Jews** who had come with
        her **weeping**,
    [he became **perturbed** and deeply **troubled**, and said,
    "**Where** have you **laid** him?"
They said to him, "Sir, **come** and **see**."
And Jesus wept.
So the Jews said, "See how he **loved** him."
But some of them said,
    "Could **not** the one who opened the **eyes** of the **blind** man
    have done **something** so that this man would not have **died**?"

So **Jesus**, perturbed again, **came** to the tomb.
It was a **cave**, and a **stone** lay across it.
Jesus said, "**Take away the stone**." »

Even emphasis on the words in this line.

Even emphasis here as well.

Mary repeats the same words as her sister Martha. Repeat them yourself plainly.

perturbed = per-TERBD = agitated and upset

Jesus weeping over Lazarus is a foretaste of his own Passion.

From here to the conclusion of the reading, Jesus is in complete command. He has an audience, to whom he relates his miracle. Take note of the rhythm of the words, "Take away the stone."

here, my brother would not have died. But even now I know that whatever you ask of God, God will give you." Next, Martha declares her hope for the future: "I know he will rise, in the resurrection on the last day." After Jesus declares that he is "the resurrection and the life," Martha professes her faith in the present moment: "Yes, Lord. I have come to believe that you are the Christ, the Son of God, the one who is coming into the world."

Although Lazarus still lies buried behind the stone, Martha's faith is fully alive. John uses the extension of an invita-tion to Mary to come and see Jesus as the opportunity to have many Jews follow her in order to witness to the miracle about to be performed. Upon arriving at the burial site, Mary greets Jesus with the very words that her sister had earlier: "Lord, if you had been here, my brother would not have died." However, Mary omits a very impor-tant caveat; she fails to make the state-ment of faith made by her sister—"But even now I know that whatever you ask of God, God will give you." Furthermore, Mary approaches Jesus with a different disposi-tion that Martha had; Mary falls to her knees before the feet of Jesus and, along with the Jews who had accompanied her, was weeping. John tells us that Jesus sees this display of grief and "became perturbed and deeply troubled." Clearly, Mary and the Jewish crowd do not articulate the faith in Jesus that Martha does.

The Jewish audience perceives Jesus' weeping as a sign of his love for his friend, which would be a purely natural percep-tion; however, they fail to perceive that his tears are for the failure of those who have been given so many opportunities yet fail to see that he is the Messiah of God. John

Even emphasis on this line with a slight additional emphasis on "believe."

Martha, the dead man's sister, said to him,
  "**Lord**, by now there will be a **stench**;
  he has been **dead** for **four days**."
Jesus said to her,
  "Did I not tell you that if you **believe**
  you will see the **glory** of God?"
So they **took away** the **stone**.
And Jesus raised his eyes and said,
  "**Father**, I thank you for **hearing** me.
I know that you **always** hear me;
  but because of the **crowd** here I have **said** this,
  that they may **believe** that you **sent** me."
And when he had **said** this,
  he cried out in a **loud voice**,
  "**Lazarus**, come **out**!"
The dead man came **out**,
  tied **hand** and **foot** with **burial** bands,
  and his **face** was wrapped in a **cloth**.
So Jesus said to them,
  "**Untie** him and let him **go**."

Now **many** of the Jews who had come to **Mary**
  and seen what he had **done** began to **believe** in him.]

[Shorter: John 11:3–7, 17, 20–27, 33b–45 (see brackets)]

tells us that Jesus became "perturbed again" as he came to the tomb and ordered the stone to be rolled away. How frustrated Jesus has become with the people's unwillingness to believe. Even Martha now displays some degree of doubt as she declares: "Lord, by now there will be a stench, he has been dead for four days." After attempting to bolster Martha's fledgling faith, Jesus raises his eyes and prays that this miracle may produce faith: "Father, I thank you for hearing me. I know that you always hear me; but because of the crowd here I have said this, that they may believe that you sent me." With that, Jesus commands Lazarus to "come out!" and gives the instructions to untie him. While the story acknowledges that "many" came to believe, the reality is that the opposition against Jesus gains strength, "So Jesus no longer went about openly among the Jews." S. W.

PALM SUNDAY OF THE PASSION OF THE LORD

LECTIONARY #37

GOSPEL AT THE PROCESSION   Mark 11:1–10

A reading from the holy Gospel according to Mark

When **Jesus** and his disciples drew near to **Jerusalem**,
    to Bethphage and Bethany at the **Mount** of Olives,
    he sent **two** of his disciples and said to them,
    "**Go** into the village **opposite** you,
    and immediately on entering it,
    you will find a **colt tethered** on which **no one** has ever **sat**.
Untie it and bring it **here**.
If anyone should **say** to you,
    '**Why** are you doing this?' reply,
    'The **Master** has **need** of it
    and will **send** it **back here** at once.'"
So they went off
    and found a **colt** tethered at a **gate** outside on the **street**,
    and they **untied** it.
Some of the **bystanders** said to them,
    "What are you **doing**, untying the **colt**?"
They answered them just as **Jesus** had **told** them to,
    and they **permitted** them to **do** it.
So they **brought** the colt to **Jesus**
    and put their **cloaks** over it.
And he **sat** on it. »

Bethphage = BETH-fuh-jee
Bethany = BETH-uh-nee

A narrative reading that initiates Holy Week. The "When" that begins the reading enters us into the mystery of this time. Treat this reading like the beginning of a great story that will play out over the course of Holy Week. Though the reading is dramatic, most of it is direct; Jesus speaking to two disciples.

The colt is mentioned three times. By this third time, the colt is being untied. Give a little extra weight to the words "doing" and "colt."

Even emphasis on the words in this line, with a little extra added to "cloaks."

There are options for today's readings. Contact your parish staff to learn which readings will be used.

PROCESSION GOSPEL All of the Gospels report the triumphal entry of Jesus into Jerusalem several days before he will be put to death. It is important to each of the evangelists to underscore the humility of a king who comes riding a lowly colt. In fact, the colt is really the central character of these ten verses. Jesus gives his disciples specific instructions to find a particular colt at a designated location; the people question the disciples as to why they are untying and taking the colt; finally, the disciples place their own cloaks over it. All of this is done to draw the prophecy of Zechariah to the forefront: "Behold: your king is coming to you, a just savior is he, humble, and riding on a donkey, on a colt, the foal of a donkey." "(Zechariah 9:9). The humility of this king is so great that he will not even ride upon a donkey but rather upon the offspring of a donkey.

Unlike the account of the triumphal entry in Matthew and Luke, Mark makes no mention of a vast multitude. Instead, he refers simply to "many people." Since Mark's reporting of the story is the first of the synoptics to be written, we may do well to reframe our imagination's portrayal of Jesus' journey from Bethpage and Bethany to Jerusalem on this day. It is likely that the historical event took place without much fanfare. Moreover, because Jesus' entrance into the holy city took place simultaneously with the arrival of a throng of pilgrims to Jerusalem to celebrate the Passover feast, it may very well have occurred unnoticed. It is even possible that the scene of waving

Many people spread their **cloaks** on the road,
    and others spread **leafy branches**
    that they had **cut** from the **fields**.
Those preceding him as well as those following kept crying out:
    "**Hosanna!**
        Blessed is he who **comes** in the name of the **Lord!**
        Blessed is the kingdom of our father **David** that is to **come!**
    Hosanna in the **highest!**"

Or

GOSPEL AT THE PROCESSION   John 12:12–16

A reading from the holy Gospel according to John

When the **great crowd** that had come to the **feast** heard
    that **Jesus** was coming to **Jerusalem**,
    they took **palm branches** and went out to meet him,
        and cried **out:**
        "**Hosanna!**
        Blessed is he who **comes** in the **name** of the **Lord,**
            the **king** of **Israel.**"
Jesus found an **ass** and **sat** upon it, as is written:
    Fear no more, O daughter Zion;
    see, your king comes, seated upon an ass's colt.
His **disciples** did **not** understand this at first,
    but when **Jesus** had been **glorified**
    they **remembered** that these things were **written** about him
    and that they had **done** this for him.

A narrative reading that has an exhortatory quality in its memory of scriptural reality.

This line has an intrinsically poetic quality, almost song-like. You can deliver it with some bounce.

Give almost even emphasis to the words in this line, a little extra on "Fear."

Land on the word "him."

palm branches and the singing of Psalm 118 with shouts of "Hosanna!" may have been part of a traditional pilgrim chant prayed by those passing through the gates of the sacred city.

Whatever the case may be, the liturgical use of this Gospel passage to accompany the pilgrim church on its entrance into the atmosphere of Holy Week is of principal importance. These sacred days are meant to rehearse in our lives the central mystery of our faith, the Paschal Mystery of Christ's suffering, death, and Resurrection. Thus, in the week ahead, joy mingles with tragedy,

and betrayal stands alongside hope. Just as the people outside Jerusalem welcomed Jesus with great anticipation of his power, so are we invited to see that ultimate power resides in humility and obedience to God's will. "Hosanna in the highest!"

READING I This reading constitutes the third of the four "Suffering Servant" songs of Isaiah. It is likely that these verses were sung among the Hebrew people during the years of exile in Babylon (late sixth century BC) in recognition of the suffering they endured in their expulsion

from their land. While they certainly looked forward to the day when a savior would come who would take their suffering upon himself and release them permanently from bondage, they understood themselves as a nation struggling to be faithful to God as they endured the many trials and afflictions that accompanied exile.

It is important to observe the way this song acknowledges the work of God that undergirds the one who serves by suffering. First, God provides the servant with "a well-trained tongue" in order to prophesy. Second, God opens the ear of the one who

LECTIONARY #37

READING I   Isaiah 50:4–7

A reading from the Book of the Prophet Isaiah

The **Lord GOD** has **given** me
  a **well-trained** tongue,
that I might **know** how to speak to the **weary**
  a **word** that will **rouse** them.
Morning after **morning**
  he opens my **ear** that I may **hear**;
and I have not **rebelled**,
  have not turned **back**.
I gave my back to **those** who **beat** me,
  my **cheeks** to those who **plucked** my beard;
my face I did not **shield**
  from **buffets** and **spitting**.

The Lord GOD is my **help**,
  therefore I am not **disgraced**;
I have set my **face** like **flint**,
  knowing that I shall **not** be put to **shame**.

Isaiah = ī-ZAY-uh

A short and powerful exhortatory reading in which Isaiah asserts his trust in God.

Note the poetic rhythm that begins with the phrase "Morning after morning."

buffets = BUF-its = slaps

Give "not" and "shame" equal emphasis. These last lines can be read with conviction.

For meditation and context:

RESPONSORIAL PSALM   Psalm 22:8–9, 17–18, 19–20, 23–24 (2a)

R. My God, my God, why have you abandoned me?

All who see me scoff at me;
  they mock me with parted lips, they wag
    their heads:
"He relied on the LORD; let him deliver him,
  let him rescue him, if he loves him."

Indeed, many dogs surround me,
  a pack of evildoers closes in upon me;
they have pierced my hands and my feet;
  I can count all my bones.

They divide my garments among them,
  and for my vesture they cast lots.
But you, O LORD, be not far from me;
  O my help, hasten to aid me.

I will proclaim your name to my brethren;
  in the midst of the assembly I will
    praise you:
"You who fear the LORD, praise him;
  all you descendants of Jacob,
    give glory to him;
  revere him, all you descendants of Israel!"

> **TO KEEP IN MIND**
> The attention you bring to your proclaiming enables you to pray the Word of God with the assembly.

presses forward and refuses to "turn back." The song ends by acclaiming the Lord as "my help." Thus, speaking to the weary, resisting the temptation to rebel against the oppressor, having the beard plucked, and setting the face "like flint" against "buffets and spitting" are all possible because the Lord remains committed and faithful to his servant. We Christians can easily see in the suffering endured by this servant the suffering of Jesus. Throughout all he endured, Jesus turned to his Father as his help. We can so easily hear the Lord testify in prayer: "Morning after morning he opens my ear

that I may hear; and I have not rebelled, have not turned back" (Isaiah 50:5).

READING II This hymn is sung throughout the year at Evening Prayer on Sundays. It praises Christ for his willingness to empty himself of divine power in order to become "obedient to the point of death." The hymn is sung on a regular basis because it contains the primary description of what it means to be Christlike. One cannot claim to be a follower of Christ if he or she is not willing to empty oneself for the sake of others.

Thus, we hear this Philippians reading each year in the context of Palm Sunday. How is it possible that Jesus Christ rejected "equality with God"? The ancient Scriptures are filled with stories of men and women who want nothing more than to strive for equality with God. Think of the story of Adam and Eve. They ate from the Tree of Knowledge in the center of the Garden because that they wanted to become like God, to be able to see the world as God sees it, and to relish the power of divinity. How can it be that Jesus gives this up?

READING II   Philippians 2:6–11

A reading from the Letter of Saint Paul to the Philippians

Christ **Jesus**, though he was in the **form** of God,
   did not regard **equality** with God
   something to be **grasped**.
Rather, he **emptied** himself,
   taking the form of a **slave**,
   coming in **human** likeness;
   and found **human** in appearance,
   he **humbled** himself,
   becoming **obedient** to the point of **death**,
   even **death** on a **cross**.
Because of this, God **greatly** exalted him
   and **bestowed** on him the name
   which is above **every** name,
   that at the name of **Jesus**
   every **knee** should **bend**,
   of those in **heaven** and on **earth** and **under** the earth,
   and every **tongue** confess that
   Jesus Christ is Lord,
   to the **glory** of God the **Father**.

Philippians = fih-LIP-ee-uhnz

An exhortation in which Paul seems to quote to the members of the Church at Philippi an early Christian hymn, whose focus is the *kenosis*, or emptying, mentioned in the fourth line of the reading. It's an utterly mysterious presentation of the power of Jesus' Incarnation. When you get to "emptied," give the word extra emphasis.

Give emphasis and rhythm to the words "human," "human," and "humbled."

Even emphasis on these four words: "Jesus Christ is Lord."

GOSPEL   Mark 14:1—15:47

The Passion of our Lord Jesus Christ according to Mark

The **Passover** and the Feast of **Unleavened Bread**
   were to take place in **two days'** time.
So the **chief priests** and the **scribes** were seeking a **way**
   to **arrest** him by **treachery** and put him to **death**.
They said, "**Not** during the **festival**,
   for **fear** that there may be a **riot** among the **people**."

An intensely powerful narrative reading of the story at the core of our faith. It is as dramatic as a novel, told with unusual economy and speed. But it also lingers on vivid scenes, vivid moments. Although the reading is dramatic, its drama is inherent in the language and the pacing of the story. You may have an instinct to intensify the drama by "acting out" some of the voices and scenes. Better to avoid that by allowing the language to dictate the drama. You need mainly to stay focused.

The author of the hymn answers in two ways: first, to learn obedience, and second, to exalt God. Thus, both the mystery of the Incarnation and the Paschal Mystery are alluded to here. Jesus "emptied himself," became a "slave," and was found to be "human in appearance." We have to guard against reading any sort of theology in which Jesus' divinity is merely masked by a human body. We can be assured of the total assumption of the human nature when we hear of his obedience. As a means of accepting the complete obedience of Jesus, the hymn states that

God "greatly exalted him," by giving him a name that would call for the bowing low of every creature of the cosmos. When the profession "Jesus Christ is Lord" rings out throughout the universe, God's name is given further glory. Profession of that name echoes our willingness to be self-emptying and our desire to glorify God above all things.

PASSION The final line of chapter 13, immediately prior to beginning of Mark's account of the Passion, contains Jesus' warning his disciples to "stay awake" (13:37). With this warning in mind,

chapter 14 opens with Mark setting the stage for the chaos that is about to ensue. The first part of this backdrop is the timing: the Passover and the Feast of Unleavened Bread are only two days away. This should be a time of preparation and joyful expectation. Instead, the chief priests and the scribes are plotting a way to put Jesus to death. A mixture of evil intent amongst the preparations for a festival are meant to permeate the Lord's Passion.

Mark continues this mood as the story moves to the house of Simon the leper in Bethany. How could it be that a leper was

Bethany = BETH-uh-nee
spikenard = SPĪK-nahrd

Whether this Gospel is proclaimed by one person or divided among several, avoid theatricality. Proclaim boldly, clearly, and slowly.

Almost even emphasis on the words in this line and on the one that follows.

This scene of the woman who brings the expensive spikenard sets the tone for the whole Passion. Let the line "costly genuine spikenard" anchor your reading of this passage.

Iscariot = ih-SKAYR-ee-uht

Pause slightly at this break.

The beginning line of the next passage with almost even emphasis on all the words.

When he was in **Bethany** reclining at **table**
    in the **house** of Simon the **leper**,
    a woman came with an alabaster **jar** of perfumed **oil**,
    costly genuine spikenard.
She **broke** the alabaster jar and **poured** it on his **head**.
There were some who were **indignant**.
"Why has there been this **waste** of perfumed **oil**?
It could have been **sold** for more than three hundred days' **wages**
    and the **money** given to the **poor**."
They were **infuriated** with her.
Jesus said, "Let her **alone**.
Why do you make **trouble** for her?
She has done a **good thing** for me.
The **poor** you will always have **with you**,
    and whenever you **wish** you can do **good** to them,
    but you will not **always** have **me**.
She has **done** what she **could**.
She has **anticipated** anointing my **body** for **burial**.
Amen, I say to you,
    wherever the **gospel** is proclaimed to the **whole world**,
    what she has **done** will be **told** in memory of her."

Then **Judas Iscariot**, one of the **Twelve**,
    went off to the **chief priests** to hand him **over** to them.
When they **heard him** they were **pleased**
    and promised to **pay** him **money**.
Then he **looked** for an opportunity to hand him **over**.

On the first day of the Feast of Unleavened Bread,
    when they **sacrificed** the Passover lamb,
    his disciples said to him,
    "Where do you want us to **go**
    and **prepare** for you to **eat** the Passover?" »

providing for a meal, as lepers in this society were shunned? Since this setting is going to be the place where Jesus will come to recognize the infidelity of a close disciple, it is very possible that Mark wants us to see that a leper can be a more faithful disciple than those who have journeyed with Jesus throughout his years of ministry.

Regardless, our attention is meant to be focused on the unnamed woman who approaches Jesus with oil and pours it over his head. This act of kindness, no doubt a foreshadowing of anointing Jesus' body in preparation for burial, causes dissension

amongst the disciples. When Jesus scolds the disciples to leave the woman alone, he tells them "you will not always have me." This woman performs an act of selflessness that Jesus declares "will be told in memory of her."

The next person introduced into this scene is Judas Iscariot. He stands in direct contrast to the woman who anointed Jesus. While she is extravagant in her expression of care for Jesus, Judas is greedy. Instead of honoring Jesus' body, Judas will treat it as a means for making money. Another point of contrast here is the

identification of Judas as "one of the Twelve" while Mark, the earliest Gospel, does not identify the woman. Perhaps we are meant to assume that the woman who anointed Jesus had been an outsider to the group, while Judas is intimately joined to Jesus' circle of friends. This makes his act of turning Jesus in to the authorities all the more sinful.

The Passion narrative now moves to the day on which the Passover lambs are to be sacrificed and other preparations are to be made for the celebration of the Passover feast. It is quite certain that Mark understands Jesus' final meal with his

Emphasis on "follow."

The power of this passage arises from Jesus' certainty about this betrayal. Read this passage straightforwardly, without a judgmental tone, to enhance this certainty.

The words of institution, which the priest proclaims at every Mass. Read them with the same reverence.

He sent two of his disciples and said to them,
    "**Go** into the **city** and a man will meet you,
    carrying a jar of **water**.
Follow him.
Wherever he **enters**, say to the master of the house,
    'The **Teacher** says, "Where is my **guest room**
    where I may **eat** the **Passover** with my **disciples**?"'
Then he will show you a **large upper room** furnished and ready.
Make the preparations for us **there**."
The disciples then went **off**, entered the **city**,
    and found it **just** as he had **told** them;
    and they **prepared** the Passover.

When it was **evening**, he came with the **Twelve**.
And as they **reclined** at table and were **eating**, Jesus said,
    "**Amen**, I say to you, one of you will **betray** me,
    one who is **eating** with me."
They began to be **distressed** and to say to him, one by one,
    "Surely it is not **I**?"
He said to them,
    "One of the **Twelve**, the one who **dips** with me
        into the **dish**.
For the **Son** of **Man** indeed **goes**, as it is written of him,
    but **woe** to that man by whom the **Son** of **Man** is **betrayed**.
It would be **better** for that man if he had never been born."

While they were **eating**,
    he took **bread**, said the blessing,
    broke it, and gave it to them, and said,
    "**Take** it; this is my **body**."
Then he took a **cup**, gave thanks, and **gave** it to them,
    and they all **drank** from it.
He **said** to them,
    "This is my **blood** of the **covenant**,
    which will be **shed** for **many**.

disciples to occur during a Passover meal. For John, it is more of a final farewell meal, set on the night before the feast itself, the same time that the Passover lambs are being slaughtered, Mark and the other Synoptic Gospels wish to emphasize the theology of liberation and deliverance that are celebrated as the themes of Passover.

When Jesus is asked by the disciples where they are to prepare the meal, he provides details that suggest predetermined knowledge about the event itself. He provides them with information that seems very much like clues meant to direct them

on a hunt. Just as Jesus had given directions to his disciples regarding his entry into Jerusalem, here, too, he takes on the characteristic of a mighty prophet who is able to forecast the future. Mark tells us that the disciples "found it just as he had told them."

The sun has set, and the festival of the Passover has begun. Just as at the meal earlier in the week at the house of Simon the leper, the Last Supper begins with tension. Jesus and the Twelve have all reclined around the table, which signals their fraternity and desire to celebrate as a united

household. However, Jesus makes the revelation that one of his disciples sharing this very dinner with him will betray him (14:18). Because enemies did not share meals with one another in antiquity, this accusation is a very powerful statement regarding a betrayal of the meal's nature.

Although Jesus had foretold of suffering as he made his way to Jerusalem with his disciples, their refusal one after another to accept their part in the betrayal of Jesus is apparent. "Surely it is not I?" In Mark's account of the supper, the betrayer continues to share in the meal, even after Jesus

Amen, I say to you,
　I shall not **drink again** the **fruit** of the **vine**
　until the **day** when I drink it **new** in the kingdom of **God**."
Then, after singing a **hymn**,
　they went out to the **Mount** of Olives.

Pause slightly after this line.

Then Jesus said to them,
　"**All of you** will have your **faith shaken**, for it is **written**:
　　*I will **strike** the shepherd,*
　　　*and the **sheep** will be dispersed.*
But after I have been **raised up**,
　I shall go **before** you to **Galilee**."
Peter said to him,
　"Even though **all** should have their faith shaken,
　mine **will not be**."
Then Jesus said to him,
　"Amen, I say to **you**,
　this **very night** before the **cock crows twice**
　you will deny me **three times**."
But he vehemently replied,
　"Even though I should have to **die** with you,
　I will not **deny** you."
And they **all** spoke similarly.

Peter's challenged faith, and his defense of its fidelity, stands for our own. No need to dress this up. The whole congregation relates to Peter's reactions.

Almost even emphasis on the words in this line.

Gethsemane = geth-SEM-uh-nee

Then they came to a place named **Gethsemane**,
　and he said to his **disciples**,
　"**Sit here** while I **pray**."
He took with him **Peter**, **James**, and **John**,
　and began to be **troubled** and **distressed**.
Then he said to them, "My **soul** is sorrowful even to **death**.
Remain here and keep **watch**." ≫

This is the scene of the "agony in the garden." There is exasperation and fear on Jesus' part, but also tenderness. The scene moves fairly quickly.

has made his announcement. Completing the act of eating before committing the deed of betrayal is important here and corresponds with the words of Psalm 41: "Even my trusted friend, who ate my bread, has raised his heel against me." For Mark, the act of handing Jesus over to the authorities to be condemned is a clear mark of treachery, but the very act of eating together with the betrayer makes this disloyalty all the more grave.

Leaving aside the tension, Mark turns his focus to the meal itself. We see in Mark 14:22–25 the indication of a liturgical for-mula that was clearly known by the time of the Gospel's, but in Mark's account, Jesus makes no pronouncement that his disciples are to repeat this blessing as a means of remembering him. Instead, Mark interprets this act as a foreshadowing of his death and Resurrection: "I shall not drink again the fruit of the vine until the day when I drink it new in the kingdom of God" (14:25). For Mark, this supper is to teach the disciples again what they continually have failed to understand: Jesus must suffer and die.

With the meal completed by the sing-ing of a hymn, Jesus and the disciples leave for the Mount of Olives. At some point along the way, Jesus returns to the theme of betrayal. Referring to the prophecy found in the Book of Zechariah 13:7, Jesus sug-gests to them that they will be "dispersed" on account of their lack of faith. This scat-tering, he tells them, will be brought about by his death, "But after I have been raised up, I shall go before you to Galilee" (14:28). Without being direct, Jesus indicates that even though his disciples will find their faith tested and end up abandoning him, he will never abandon them. Once again, we see in Mark that the disciples simply do not

He **advanced** a little and **fell** to the ground and **prayed**
    that if it were **possible** the hour might **pass by him**;
    he said, "**Abba**, **Father**, all things are **possible** to you.
Take this cup **away** from me,
    but not what I will but what **you** will."
When he **returned** he found them **asleep**.
He said to Peter, "**Simon**, are you **asleep**?
Could you **not keep watch** for **one hour**?
Watch and **pray** that you may not **undergo** the **test**.
The **spirit** is willing but the **flesh** is weak."
Withdrawing again, he **prayed**, saying the same thing.
Then he **returned** once more and found them **asleep**,
    for they **could not** keep their eyes **open**
    and **did not** know what to **answer** him.
He returned a **third time** and said to them,
    "Are you **still sleeping** and taking your **rest**?
It is **enough**. The **hour** has **come**.
Behold, the Son of Man is to be handed **over** to sinners.
Get **up**, let us **go**.
See, my betrayer is at **hand**."

Then, while he was still **speaking**,
    Judas, one of the **Twelve**, **arrived**,
    accompanied by a **crowd** with **swords** and **clubs**
    who had **come** from the **chief priests**,
    the **scribes**, and the **elders**.
His **betrayer** had arranged a **signal** with them, saying,
    "The **man** I shall **kiss** is the **one**;
    arrest him and lead him away **securely**."
He **came** and immediately went over to him and said,
    "**Rabbi**." And he **kissed** him.
At **this** they laid **hands** on him and **arrested** him.

The scene of Jesus' betrayal and arrest is filled with drama that the language amply conveys. No stage whispers or undue emphases necessary.

understand. Peter's profession that he will remain faithful even if none of the others do gives Jesus the opportunity to predict that Peter will deny him three times. Both Jesus and Peter utter words similar to those of a prophet, but only those of Jesus are filled with certainty. The disciples in Mark's account are understood to have abandoned Jesus, whereas Jesus will forgive and stay true to his followers.

Arriving at the Mount of Olives, Jesus takes Peter, James, and John apart from the rest of the disciples and becomes "troubled and distressed." These are the same three

who witnessed Jesus' Transfiguration. Instead of seeing Jesus in glory, they behold him in anguish. No doubt, Jesus wants to impress upon them that his imminent suffering is not tangential to his mission but rather reveals the depths of his commitment to the kingdom of God. To heighten the intimacy of his prayer, Mark moves Jesus slightly away from the three disciples so that he might ask his Father ("Abba") to "Take this cup away from me," but only if his Father wills it. Jesus is focused on his Father's will until the very end.

After the time of prayer Jesus discovers the three disciples asleep upon his return. Addressing Peter specifically, Jesus commands him to keep watch "and pray that you may not undergo the test." A second and a third time Jesus departs from them to pray in secret, returning to find them asleep each time. The amount of time that Jesus spends in prayer, as well as the time that his disciples use for sleep, is roughly three hours. The darkness of this "hour" is to match the darkness of the hour in which Jesus dies upon the cross.

The scene of the naked boy is striking. Pause after "naked."

One of the **bystanders** drew his **sword,**
    struck the **high priest's** servant, and cut off his **ear.**
Jesus said to them in **reply,**
    "Have you come **out** as against a **robber,**
    with **swords** and **clubs,** to **seize** me?
Day after day I was **with** you teaching in the temple area,
    yet you did not **arrest** me;
    but that the **Scriptures** may be **fulfilled.**"
And they all **left him** and **fled.**
Now a **young man** followed him
    wearing **nothing** but a **linen cloth** about his **body.**
They **seized** him,
    but he **left** the cloth **behind** and ran off **naked.**

The drama intensifies here; Jesus is on trial. The language itself provides all the drama. Allow it to speak for itself by moving confidently through this passage.

They led Jesus **away** to the high **priest,**
    and all the **chief priests** and the **elders** and the **scribes**
        came **together.**
Peter followed him at a **distance** into the high priest's **courtyard**
    and was **seated** with the guards, **warming** himself at the **fire.**
The chief priests and the entire **Sanhedrin**
    kept trying to obtain **testimony** against **Jesus**
    in order to **put him** to **death,** but they found **none.**
Many gave false witness **against** him,
    but their testimony did not **agree.**
Some took the stand and testified **falsely** against him,
    alleging, "We **heard** him say,
    'I will **destroy** this temple made with **hands**
    and within **three days** I will build **another**
    not made with hands.'"
Even so their testimony did not **agree.**
The high priest **rose** before the assembly and questioned **Jesus,**
    saying, "Have you no **answer?**
What are these men **testifying against** you?"
But he was silent and answered **nothing.**
Again the high priest asked him and said to him,
    "Are you the **Christ,** the son of the **Blessed** One?" »

Mark's account of Jesus' arrest is succinct. Although there is certainly the crowd carrying "swords and clubs" along with the chief priests, the scribes, and the elders, the emphasis is on Judas and his act of betrayal. By reminding us that Judas is "one of the Twelve," Mark wants his reader to be aware that just as Judas betrayed the friendship of Jesus by sharing bread with him at the Last Supper while he was plotting to hand him over, now he further betrays Jesus with a gesture used to signal friendship—the greeting of a kiss. We are meant to see this kiss with all the ugliness

it conveys. Judas even calls Jesus "Rabbi" as he signals with a kiss the one to be arrested.

As the "crowd with swords and clubs" approaches Jesus to arrest him, an unnamed bystander is seen striking the high priest's servant and cutting his ear off, providing Jesus the opportunity to reveal that all of this chaos is taking place in order that the Scriptures may be fulfilled. Jesus does not simply surrender to his assailants; he fulfills Scripture.

While Jesus is faithful to his mission, everyone flees from the scene, including a young man dressed only in a linen cloth. He

attempts to run away but is seized and then escapes, leaving the cloth behind. A great deal of effort has been made by scholars attempting to interpret the symbolism of this stranger and his nakedness. Perhaps the best that can be made of the nakedness is that everything is laid bare when confronted with the choice of whether to stay with Jesus or to abandon him in his moment of need.

The next station of Jesus' Passion occurs at the house of the high priest. Peter is there "at a distance," warming himself at a fire in the high priest's courtyard. There is

Even emphasis to all the words in this line.

Then Jesus answered, "I **am**;
    and 'you will **see** the Son of **Man**
        seated at the **right hand** of the **Power**
        and coming with the clouds of heaven.' "
At that the high priest tore his garments and said,
    "What **further** need have we of **witnesses**?
You have **heard** the **blasphemy**.
What do you **think**?"
They all **condemned** him as deserving to **die**.
Some began to **spit** on him.
They **blindfolded** him and struck him and said to him,
    "**Prophesy!**"
And the guards **greeted** him with **blows**.

Prophesy = PROF-uh-sī = verb, to speak a prophecy. Don't say PROF-uh-see, which is the noun.

Shifting to the scene of Peter's betrayal, proclaim with the feeling that Peter's imperfections reflect the assembly's.

Nazarene = NAZ-uh-reen

While **Peter** was **below** in the **courtyard**,
    one of the high priest's **maids** came along.
Seeing Peter **warming** himself,
    she looked **intently** at him and said,
    "**You too** were with the **Nazarene, Jesus**."
But he **denied** it saying,
    "I neither **know** nor **understand** what you are **talking** about."
So he went **out** into the outer **court**.
Then the cock **crowed**.
The **maid** saw him and began again to **say** to the bystanders,
    "This man is **one** of them."
Once again he **denied** it.
A little later the **bystanders** said to **Peter** once more,
    "**Surely** you are **one** of them; for **you too** are a **Galilean**."
He began to **curse** and to **swear**,
    "I do not **know** this man about whom you are **talking**."
And immediately a cock **crowed** a **second** time.

great tension in the air as the chief priests and the Sanhedrin are going about attempting to amass evidence sufficient to convict Jesus of a criminal offense. Many people step forward to give testimony, which proves to be false and insufficient. Having heard enough from faulty witnesses, the high priest stands up to question Jesus directly. Mark leaves no doubt that there is insufficient testimony against Jesus except for the one who knows the truth, Jesus himself. The high priest attempts to break Jesus' silence by asking him directly, "Are you the Christ, the son of the Blessed One?" Jesus has no option but to respond

with the truth: "I am." Then Jesus quotes the prophecy of Daniel (7:13) to underscore his messianic mission: "'you will see the Son of Man seated at the right hand of the Power and coming with the clouds of heaven.'" The evidence that Jesus presents is more than enough to convict him under Jewish law (Leviticus 24:16). To the ears of the high priest and the crowd gathered around him, Jesus utters words of blasphemy.

It takes them no time at all to pronounce him guilty. Those gathered proceed to spit at Jesus and to strike at him. Perhaps the greatest blow, however, is Peter's act of denial, which plays out over

the next several verses. Standing within high priest's courtyard, Peter denies any association with Jesus and even denying ever hearing the man they are talking about. In Mark's Gospel, Peter and the disciples may be weak in their faith and their allegiance to Jesus, but they are not beyond rehabilitation. We know that in the Resurrection, Jesus will restore his friendship with them.

Having found Jesus guilty of blaspheming the name of God, the Jewish authorities now hand him over to the Roman establishment to carry out the necessary punishment. Since Pilate's major role as the Roman

Even emphasis on "down" and "wept."
Pause.
The narrative shifts back to Jesus' trial.
The pace picks up just slightly.

Slow the pace for this line.

Barabbas = buh-RAB-uhs

Same emphasis as previously for "King of the Jews."

Then **Peter** remembered the word that Jesus had **said** to him,
   "Before the **cock crows twice** you will deny me **three** times."
He broke **down** and **wept**.

As soon as **morning** came,
   the **chief priests** with the **elders** and the **scribes**,
   that is, the **whole Sanhedrin**, held a **council**.
They **bound** Jesus, led him **away**, and handed him over to **Pilate**.
Pilate questioned him,
   "Are **you** the **king** of the **Jews**?"
He said to him in reply, "You **say** so."
The chief priests accused him of **many** things.
Again **Pilate** questioned him,
   "Have you **no** answer?
See how many **things** they **accuse** you of."
Jesus gave him **no** further **answer**, so that Pilate was **amazed**.

Now on the **occasion** of the feast he used to **release** to them
   one prisoner whom they **requested**.
A man called **Barabbas** was then in **prison**
   along with the **rebels** who had committed **murder**
      in a rebellion.
The crowd came **forward** and began to **ask** him
   to **do** for them as he was **accustomed**.
Pilate answered,
   "Do you want me to **release** to you the **king** of the **Jews**?"
For he knew that it was out of **envy**
   that the **chief priests** had handed him **over**.
But the **chief priests** stirred up the **crowd**
   to have him release **Barabbas** for them **instead**. »

procurator of occupied Jerusalem was to keep the peace, the mob that appears before him is undoubtedly troubling. Nevertheless, Pilate displays a certain sense of calm as he interrogates Jesus. Jesus, too, seems unmoved by the situation as he responds with silence to Pilate's questions.

At first it seems to be building to an impasse, with Pilate not pushing Jesus too far, and Jesus merely refusing to speak. Then the introduction of Barabbas changes the nature of the scene. Pilate offers the people a choice: they may call for the release either of Jesus or of Barabbas, a

known murderer. "The chief priests stirred up the crowd" (15:11) to demand that Pilate release Barabbas to them. When Pilate asks the crowd what he should do with Jesus, they shout, "Crucify him!" Given that Mark is writing for a Roman audience, it is not surprising that he places the call for Jesus' execution on the Jews rather than on the Romans. In the end, Pilate has no choice and "handed him over to be crucified."

Jesus is once again placed into the hands of the guards, who abuse him greatly. The mockery Jesus endures—being dressed in purple and crowned with thorns

as he hears the people chanting "Hail, King of the Jews"—has to be deeply insulting. He is, in truth, a powerful king, and yet no one understands how. He has spent his ministry opening up the ways of God's kingdom, and yet hearts continue to remain closed to God's offer of love. Like Peter's denial, this corporate rejection on the part of the Jewish people hurts worse than any mortal blow.

Suddenly stripped of his purple cloak and dressed in his own clothes, Jesus is then led away to be crucified. Along the way, Mark introduces us to "a passer-by"

Even emphases on the words in this line.

Avoid the temptation to shout these words.
A subtler delivery intensifies their import.

praetorium = prih-TOHR-ee-uhm

Shifting into the crucifixion, the story
intensifies. The details, of the soldiers,
of Simon the Cyrenian, the wine drugged
with myrrh, for instance, give the scene
its texture. Allow these details their due
in your proclamation.

Avoid the temptation to shout these words.

Cyrenian = sī-REE-nee-uhn
Rufus = ROO-fuhs

Golgotha = GAWL-guh-thuh
myrrh = mer

This line concludes with an iambic rhythm:
to SEE what EACH should TAKE.

Pilate again said to them in reply,
    "Then **what** do you want me to **do**
    with the man you call the **king** of the **Jews**?"
They shouted again, "**Crucify** him."
Pilate said to them, "**Why**? What **evil** has he **done**?"
They only shouted the louder, "**Crucify** him."
So **Pilate**, wishing to **satisfy** the crowd,
    released **Barabbas** to them and, after he had Jesus **scourged**,
    handed him **over** to be **crucified**.

The soldiers led him **away** inside the **palace**,
    that is, the **praetorium**, and assembled the whole **cohort**.
They clothed him in purple and,
    weaving a crown of **thorns**, placed it **on** him.
They began to salute him with, "**Hail**, **King** of the **Jews**!"
    and kept **striking** his head with a **reed** and **spitting** upon him.
They **knelt** before him in **homage**.
And when they had **mocked** him,
    they **stripped him** of the purple **cloak**,
    dressed him in his **own clothes**,
    and led him **out** to **crucify him**.

They **pressed** into service a passer-by, **Simon**,
    a **Cyrenian**, who was coming **in** from the **country**,
    the **father** of Alexander and Rufus,
    to **carry** his cross.

They brought him to the place of **Golgotha**
    —which is translated **Place** of the **Skull**—.
They gave him **wine** drugged with **myrrh**,
    but he did not **take** it.
Then they **crucified** him and divided his **garments**
    by casting **lots** for them to **see** what **each** should **take**.
It was **nine o'clock** in the morning when they **crucified** him.

named Simon of Cyrene. There is no indication that Simon wanted to get involved, but his act of assisting Jesus in carrying the cross has been recalled over the generations as an instance of great discipleship. Simon disappears as quickly from the story as he mysteriously enters it.

They finally arrive at Golgotha, where Jesus is to be crucified, which Mark tells us took place at nine in the morning. But first, the scene of the guardsmen refusing to divide Jesus' garments, but instead casting lots for them, demonstrates Jesus being likened to the victorious man of hope in

Psalm 22: "They divide my garments among them; for my clothing they cast lots" (22:19). Although Jesus will die, he will die a righteous and victorious man. This righteousness is meant to be seen in direct contrast to the two "revolutionaries" who hang one on his left and one on his right. Meanwhile, the insults and mockery issued by those passing by grows all the more intense as they tempt Jesus to exercise divine power that would overturn his suffering.

Then, beginning at noon and lasting until three, "darkness came over the whole land." Once again, in keeping with the righ-

teous man who lives with hope, as found in Psalm 22, Jesus cries out in a loud voice: "My God, my God, why have you forsaken me?" These words have often been used to suggest that Jesus abandoned hope on the cross. However, such is not the case. These words, which open Psalm 22, proceed in a dialogue with God in which the ending is filled with a great profession of faith: "And my soul will live for him." Jesus' cry, while indeed coming from a place of deep agony, expresses ultimate trust and dependence upon the only One who is capable of saving him. Because Jesus' cry was in Aramaic

The **inscription** of the charge against him **read**,
  "The **King** of the **Jews**."
With him they crucified **two revolutionaries**,
  one on his **right** and one on his **left**.
Those passing by **reviled** him,
  shaking their heads and saying,
  "**Aha**! **You** who would **destroy** the **temple**
  and **rebuild** it in three days,
  save yourself by coming **down** from the **cross**."
Likewise the **chief priests**, with the **scribes**,
  mocked him among themselves and **said**,
  "He **saved** others; he **cannot** save **himself**.
Let the **Christ**, the **King** of Israel,
  come down now from the **cross**
  that we may **see** and **believe**."
Those who were **crucified** with him also kept **abusing** him.

At **noon** darkness came over the **whole** land
  until **three** in the **afternoon**.
And at **three o'clock** Jesus cried **out** in a loud voice,
  "Eloi, Eloi, lema sabachthani?"
  which is **translated**,
  "My **God**, my **God**, **why** have you **forsaken** me?"
Some of the bystanders who heard it said,
  "**Look**, he is calling **Elijah**."
One of them **ran**, soaked a **sponge** with wine, put it on a **reed**
  and **gave** it to him to **drink** saying,
  "**Wait**, let us see if **Elijah** comes to take him **down**."
Jesus gave a **loud cry** and **breathed** his last.

  [Here all kneel and pause for a short time.]

The **veil** of the sanctuary was **torn** in two from **top** to **bottom**.
When the **centurion** who stood facing him
  saw how he **breathed** his last he said,
  "**Truly** this man was the **Son** of God!"
There were also **women** looking on from a **distance**. »

Almost even emphases on these words.

Eloi, Eloi, lema sabachthani = el-oh-ee, el-oh-ee, luh-MAH sah-bahk-tah-nee

Even stresses here. Avoid the temptation to shout these words. This is Jesus' direct plea to God in his own tongue.

Elijah = ee-LĪ-juh

centurion = sen-TOOR-ee-uhn

("*Eloi, Eloi, lema sabachthani!*") and not in Hebrew, people failed to understand him and presume that he is calling upon the Prophet Elijah for help.

When Jesus breathes his last, Mark reports that the sanctuary veil was torn in two. This powerful image suggests that the death of Jesus upon the cross has removed the veil that prevents us from seeing the presence of God. All throughout Mark's Gospel, Jesus' identity has been kept a secret, but here at the cross the mystery has been revealed. And who is it that understands? Not one of the disciples or even one

of the Jews among whom Jesus ministered. Instead the one who reveals Jesus' identity is the Roman centurion who makes the profound profession of faith: "Truly this man was the Son of God!" It takes an outsider and a Gentile to be able to pierce the veil. Interestingly, Mark's very next statement notes that there were women watching from a distance. Could Mark be making a commentary regarding the faith of Jesus' female disciples as opposed to the Twelve? They are certainly portrayed as remaining by his side through the bitter end and beyond.

The very last character we are introduced to in Mark's account of the Passion is Joseph of Arimathea. Mark tells us that he is a "distinguished member of the council, who was himself awaiting the kingdom of God." Like Simon of Cyrene, who provided ministry to Jesus along his way to the place of crucifixion, Joseph of Arimathea provides ministry to Jesus as he asks Pilate for possession of the body. Mark does not elaborate on the care or reverence Joseph pays to Jesus' body other than to say that he wrapped it in linen cloth, laid it in a tomb, and completed the burial by rolling a

Give Mary Magdalene and Mary their due by indicating their presence clearly.

Magdalene = MAG-duh-leen
Joses = JOH-seez; JOH-sez
Salome = suh-LOH-mee

Arimathea = ayr-ih-muh-THEE-uh
The focus in this final passage of the reading shifts to Joseph of Arimathea. It is filled with curious and nuanced details. Allow them to unfurl. Even though you are close to the end of this long reading, don't rush. The details are important for the congregation to hear.

Among them were **Mary Magdalene**,
    Mary the **mother** of the younger James and of **Joses**,
        and **Salome**.
These women had followed him when he was in **Galilee**
    and **ministered** to him.
There were also **many other women**
    who had **come up** with him to **Jerusalem**.

When it was **already** evening,
    since it was the **day** of preparation,
    the day before the **sabbath**, Joseph of Arimathea,
    a distinguished member of the **council**,
    who was himself awaiting the **kingdom** of God,
    came and courageously went to **Pilate**
    and **asked** for the body of **Jesus**.
Pilate was **amazed** that he was already **dead**.
He **summoned** the centurion
    and asked him if **Jesus** had already **died**.
And when he **learned** of it from the **centurion**,
    he gave the body to **Joseph**.
Having bought a **linen cloth**, he took him down,
    wrapped him in the linen **cloth**,
    and laid him in a **tomb** that had been **hewn** out of the **rock**.
Then he **rolled** a stone against the **entrance** to the tomb.
Mary **Magdalene** and **Mary** the mother of **Joses**
    watched where **he** was **laid**.

[Shorter: Mark 15:1–39 (see brackets)]

stone against the entrance. The Passion comes to a rather abrupt end, as Mark reports that Mary Magdalene and Mary the mother of Jesus "watched where he was laid." The scene is set for Mary Magdalene to return very early in the morning "on the first day of the week." S. W.

HOLY THURSDAY: MASS OF THE LORD'S SUPPER

LECTIONARY #39

READING I   Exodus 12:1–8, 11–14

A reading from the Book of Exodus

The LORD said to **Moses** and **Aaron** in the land of **Egypt**,
  "This month shall **stand** at the head of your **calendar;**
  you shall **reckon** it the first month of the **year.**
Tell the **whole** community of **Israel:**
  On the **tenth** of this month every **one** of your families
  must **procure** for itself a **lamb,** one apiece for each **household.**
If a family is too **small** for a **whole lamb,**
  it shall **join** the nearest household in **procuring** one
  and shall **share** in the **lamb**
  in **proportion** to the number of **persons** who **partake** of it.
The lamb must be a **year-old male** and without **blemish.**
You may **take** it from either the **sheep** or the **goats.**
You shall **keep it** until the fourteenth day of this **month,**
  and **then,** with the whole assembly of Israel present,
  it shall be **slaughtered** during the evening **twilight.**
They shall take **some** of its blood
  and apply it to the **two doorposts** and the **lintel**
  of **every house** in which they **partake** of the **lamb.**
That **same night** they shall **eat** its roasted **flesh**
  with **unleavened bread** and bitter **herbs.** »

Exodus = EK-suh-duhs

A narrative reading that includes detailed instructions from God to Moses and Aaron to convey to the Israelites so that they will be prepared for the events now commemorated as Passover. The instructions have ritual power anticipating one of the most spectacular narratives in the Old Testament. Read these instructions with some reverence.

These details are part of the appeal of this reading. Don't rush through them.

Emphasis on "slaughtered."

Again, important details.

READING I The first section of Exodus 12 is rightly designated as "The Passover Ritual Prescribed" and is followed by a section entitled "Promulgation of the Passover." While the first is meant to be a thorough explanation of the instruction that will govern the celebration of Passover annually for generations to come, the second reiterates some of these instructions that the Lord gave to Moses and Aaron immediately prior to the execution of the tenth plague upon Egypt, the extinction of the firstborn throughout the land.

God has been preparing the Israelites for quite some time to be ready for their liberation from Egypt. Exodus suggests that shortly before God encountered Moses in the burning bush he heard the cry of his people and knew full well their plight (Exodus 2:24). But God does not simply rush to their rescue. Instead, the Lord calls Moses, the former prince of Egypt who fled the territory after killing an Egyptian and became a shepherd in the land of Midian, to deliver his people from bondage. However, Moses, as well as the people he would eventually set free, would need a

great deal of convincing that God's power could be victorious over Pharaoh and his armies. By the signs that God performs in the ten plagues, which undoubtedly took place over a long period of time, Moses and the Israelites would grow together in their faith that God truly desires to choose them as his people. Even though Moses failed to understand why God would harden Pharaoh's heart, thereby preventing him from letting the Israelites leave Egypt, it later becomes clear that true freedom to worship God with an unfettered heart takes a great deal of time and effort.

girt = gert = belted

This line announces the purpose of this reading; it is followed by the grim details of God's judgment. Give them the emphasis they deserve.

"This is how you are to **eat** it:
> with your loins **girt**, **sandals** on your **feet** and your **staff**
> > in hand,
> you shall **eat** like those who are in **flight**.
It is the **Passover** of the **LORD**.
For on this **same night** I will go through **Egypt**,
> striking down **every firstborn** of the land, both **man** and **beast**,
> and **executing judgment** on all the **gods** of Egypt—I, the **LORD**!
But the **blood** will mark the **houses** where you **are**.
Seeing the blood, I will **pass over** you;
> **thus**, when I strike the land of **Egypt**,
> **no destructive blow** will come **upon** you.

"This **day** shall be a **memorial feast** for **you**,
> which **all** your generations shall **celebrate**
> with **pilgrimage** to the LORD, as a **perpetual** institution."

For meditation and context:

RESPONSORIAL PSALM   Psalm 116:12–13, 15–16bc, 17–18
(1 Corinthians 10:16)

R. Our blessing-cup is a communion with the Blood of Christ.

How shall I make a return to the LORD
> for all the good he has done for me?
The cup of salvation I will take up,
> and I will call upon the name of the LORD.

Precious in the eyes of the LORD
> is the death of his faithful ones.

I am your servant, the son of your
> handmaid;
> you have loosed my bonds.

To you will I offer sacrifice of thanksgiving,
> and I will call upon the name of the LORD.
My vows to the LORD I will pay
> in the presence of all his people.

Such a lengthy period of preparation is to be seen in contrast to the tenor of the events that take place on the night of Passover. Four days after each family has taken an unblemished lamb for itself or together with another household, they are to slaughter the lamb during the "evening twilight" of the Passover. They are instructed to mark the doorways of their homes with the blood of the lamb and to eat the meat. However, the posture of this meal is critical. The Israelites are commanded to eat "like those who are in flight." While the blood on the doorposts will signal to the angel of death that the inhabitants

are to be passed over, they are not to grow complacent. Instead, the Israelites are to be ready to leave at a moment's notice.

Each year in the springtime, the Jewish community celebrates the great feast of the Passover. During the Passover Seder, the celebratory meal of the feast, the account of the Israelites' liberation is proclaimed around the family table in a way that presents it as a present reality. Just as freedom comes each year to the Jewish people, so do Christians see in the Passover the pattern of Christ's own passage from death to life. In the context of the Holy Thursday liturgy, the Exodus story and the prescriptions for

celebrating Passover call the Christian community to be alert and vigilant for the Lord's invitation to the Church into a new liberation and holiness of life.

READING II Paul's reminder to the Christians at Corinth regarding the Lord's actions and words at the Last Supper are set in the context of his condemnation of the Corinthians' practice when celebrating the Lord's Supper. The more affluent members were failing to wait for poorer members of the community, who often arrived later because of work, in order to participate together in the sharing

READING II 1 Corinthians 11:23–26

A reading from the first Letter of Saint Paul to the Corinthians

Brothers and sisters:
I **received** from the Lord what I also **handed** on to you,
　　that the **Lord** Jesus, on the **night** he was handed over,
　　took **bread**, and, after he had given **thanks**,
　　broke it and said, "**This** is my **body** that is for **you**.
Do this in remembrance of **me**."
In the **same way** also the **cup**, after **supper**, saying,
　　"**This cup** is the **new covenant** in my **blood**.
Do this, as **often** as you **drink it**, in **remembrance** of me."
For as **often** as you eat this **bread** and drink the **cup**,
　　you **proclaim** the **death** of the **Lord** until he **comes**.

GOSPEL John 13:1–15

A reading from the holy Gospel according to John

Before the feast of **Passover**, Jesus **knew** that his **hour** had **come**
　　to **pass** from this **world** to the **Father**.
He **loved** his own in the **world** and he **loved** them to the **end**.
The **devil** had already induced **Judas**, son of **Simon** the **Iscariot**,
　　to hand him **over**.
So, during supper,
　　fully aware that the **Father** had put **everything** into his **power**
　　and that he had **come** from God and was **returning** to God,
　　he **rose** from supper and took **off** his outer **garments**.
He took a **towel** and tied it around his **waist**.
Then he **poured water** into a **basin**
　　and **began** to wash the disciples' **feet**
　　and **dry them** with the **towel** around his **waist**.

Corinthians = kohr-IN-thee-uhnz

A narrative commemoration of the words at the heart of the Mass. These words of Paul's to the Corinthians echo the words in the reading from Exodus.

Here begin the words of institution, always spoken by a priest, but here, most likely, spoken by a lector. These words can take on a freshness in your proclamation.

In a slow, commemorative rhythm.

Iscariot = ih-SKAYR-ee-uht
A narrative reading that provides the basis for one of the most powerful of Christian rituals, the washing of feet. Its power resides in the directness of its depiction of the ritual itself but also in the ways the act anticipates Christ's passion.

The details here are important.

---

of the meal (1 Corinthians 11:17–22). Paul chastises them: "For in eating, each one goes ahead with his own supper, and one goes hungry while another gets drunk." Thus, the "words of institution," the liturgical formula to be spoken over the bread and the wine, are found in this letter as the earliest testimony to what Jesus might actually have said at the Last Supper. Scripture scholars are quite certain that by the time of Paul's writing his letter in the mid-50s, the Christian Church would have known this formula.

Liturgical scholars generally employ the four action words found in this recalling of the Last Supper—*take, bless, break,* and *give*—as the important structural components of the eucharistic rite. These words themselves serve as a corrective to the inappropriate behavior of the Christians. The food and the drink that they have been given are to be blessed and given for the sake of others. There is meant to be no suggestion of hoarding in the celebration of the Lord's Supper. Further, eating and drinking are important ways of remembering the Lord. It matters to Paul how the

Corinthians engage in these actions: "For as often as you eat this bread and drink the cup, you proclaim the death of the Lord until he comes." Our assemblies would do well to ask themselves how the manner in which we eat and drink at the Lord's Supper testifies to our true faith in his future coming.

GOSPEL John opens his account of the Last Supper with the theological statement that Jesus knew when "his hour" would come. He is aware and in control: "fully aware that the Father

Peter's inability to understand what Jesus is doing reflects the congregation's. Though Peter is a bit thick, Jesus is gentle but authoritative in his responses.

He **came** to Simon **Peter**, who **said** to him,
    "**Master**, are you going to **wash** my **feet**?"
Jesus answered and said to him,
    "What I am **doing**, you **do not** understand **now**,
    but you will **understand later**."
Peter said to him, "You will **never** wash my **feet**."
Jesus answered him,
    "Unless I **wash** you, you will have no **inheritance** with **me**."
Simon Peter said to him,
    "**Master**, then not only my **feet**, but my **hands** and **head**
        as well."
Jesus said to him,

Emphasis on "feet washed."

    "**Whoever** has bathed has no **need** except to have his
        feet washed,
    for he is **clean** all over;
    so you are **clean**, but not **all**."
For he **knew** who would **betray** him;
    for this **reason**, he said, "Not **all** of you are **clean**."

So when he had **washed** their feet
    and put his **garments** back on and **reclined** at table again,
    he said to them, "Do you **realize** what I have **done** for you?

These lines to the end of the reading are firm and mysterious.

You call me '**teacher**' and '**master**,' and rightly so, for **indeed** I **am**.
If I, therefore, the **master** and **teacher**, have **washed** your feet,
    you ought to wash one another's feet.
I have **given** you a model to **follow**,
    so that as I have done for **you**, **you** should also **do**."

TO KEEP IN MIND
Recognize how important your proclamation of the Word of God is. Prepare well and take joy in your ministry.

---

had put everything into his power and that he had come from God and was returning to God." Even knowing all that he does, Jesus continues to love his disciples to the very end, and he wants to leave them with a clear understanding of what this love means.

John is the only one of the four Gospels not to contain the institution narrative. Instead of leaving his disciples with the commandment to remember him after his death by sharing a cup and breaking bread, Jesus wants them to make him present through the enactment of charity. The self-lessness of the Lord's washing his disciples'

feet, known by tradition as the *mandatum* (commandment), is vividly portrayed in the Gospel by the image of Jesus removing his garments, in he *himself* tying a towel around his waist, in the pouring of water, and in the washing and drying of feet. Jesus performs all of these selfless actions without any assistance. Jesus gives his entire self in this expression of service.

The opposite stance, and perhaps the one that most clearly represents the typical human response to other people's acts of kindness, is Peter's simple statement, "You will never wash my feet." So quick are we

to respond to people's charity and generosity towards us with the words, "No thank you. I am OK. I do not need your help." We are usually suspicious when others approach us with unsolicited compassion. Yet this is precisely what Jesus is attempting to communicate in this newly established ritual. Wash the feet of others without being asked. "I have given you a model to follow, so that as I have done for you, you should also do." Holy Thursday establishes that the emptying of self for the sake of others is the entry point to contemplating the Paschal Mystery of Christ. S. W.

GOOD FRIDAY: CELEBRATION OF THE LORD'S PASSION

LECTIONARY #40

READING I   Isaiah 52:13—53:12

A reading from the Book of the Prophet Isaiah

Isaiah = ī-ZAY-uh

An exhortatory reading whose power arises from bold claims and compelling rhythms. Allow these elements to ring out in your proclamation. Isaiah's prophecy speaks directly to the congregation and the mystery into which it is immersed.

Even emphasis on the words in this line.

The questions Isaiah asks set the tone for the lines to follow.

See, my servant shall **prosper**,
    he shall be **raised high** and greatly **exalted**.
Even as **many** were **amazed** at him—
    so **marred** was his look beyond **human semblance**
    and his **appearance** beyond that of the **sons of man**—
so shall he startle many nations,
    because of **him kings** shall stand **speechless**;
for **those** who have not been **told** shall see,
    those who have not **heard** shall **ponder** it.

Who would **believe** what we have **heard**?
    To **whom** has the **arm** of the LORD been **revealed**?
He grew **up** like a sapling **before** him,
    like a **shoot** from the parched **earth**;
there was **in him** no stately bearing to make us **look** at him,
    nor **appearance** that would **attract** us to him.
He was **spurned** and **avoided** by **people**,
    a man of **suffering**, accustomed to **infirmity**,
one of **those** from whom people hide their **faces**,
    spurned, and we **held him** in no **esteem**. »

READING I This section from the prophet Isaiah constitutes the fourth and final Suffering Servant song, which accentuates God's fidelity to an unidentified servant, one who is the victim of great torture and pain. Scholars have long debated whether the four servant songs in Isaiah were written as a personification of Israel as God's servant subjected to suffering. However, most agree that this last song is composed with a messianic context. It foretells the coming of God's chosen servant, who will undergo much oppression and hardship in announcing God's reign. As the Christian community

contemplates the redemptive value of Christ's suffering on the cross, and thus the redemptive value of suffering endured in the context of self-sacrifice, the Suffering Servant song places before the heart many vivid images of the one who serves God through a willingness to embrace hardship for the sake of others.

The song begins with God claiming the unnamed figure as "my servant." The relationship between God and this servant is clear. Although he has endured horrific suffering, this servant "shall prosper," will "be raised high," and will be "greatly exalted."

While in God's view, this individual will prosper, everything about his condition suggests the opposite. Isaiah states that his appearance is "marred . . . beyond human semblance." However, in the next line we are left to wonder precisely how the servant will "startle many nations" and leave kings standing "speechless." Is it because the servant's physical appearance is so ghastly, or is it because he will overturn the ways of the world by planting the foundation of a kingdom not grounded in power but based on service and compassion?

Isaiah wishes to accentuate that this person was one rejected from the very

Note the rhythms in the lines in this section, many of which place an emphasis on two of the words in the line, "infirmities" and "bore"; "sufferings" and "endured"; and so forth. Let these rhythms carry your proclamation.

The story of the Suffering Servant is of course anticipatory of the Passion in John's Gospel.

The rhythms that prevail in the previous section continue in this one, often with an emphasis on two words in the line. Once again, let these rhythms carry your proclamation.

Words like "slaughter," "condemned," "wicked," and "evildoers" are loaded with significance. Recite them clearly and that significance will be evident to the assembly. No need to over-dramatize the words when you proclaim them.

As the reading concludes, the mood lifts. There is a sense of promise and redemption. Don't, however, overdo it. The hope will come through when you proclaim these words straightforwardly.

Yet it was our **infirmities** that he **bore**,
  our **sufferings** that he **endured**,
while we **thought** of him as **stricken**,
  as one **smitten** by God and **afflicted**.
But he was **pierced** for our offenses,
  crushed for our sins;
upon him was the **chastisement** that makes us **whole**,
  by his **stripes** we were **healed**.
We had all gone **astray** like **sheep**,
  each following his **own** way;
but the LORD laid upon him
  the **guilt** of us **all**.

Though he was **harshly treated**, he **submitted**
  and **opened not** his mouth;
like a **lamb** led to the **slaughter**
  or a **sheep** before the **shearers**,
  he was **silent** and opened not his **mouth**.
Oppressed and **condemned**, he was taken **away**,
  and who would have thought any **more** of his **destiny**?
When he was cut **off** from the land of the **living**,
  and **smitten** for the sin of his **people**,
a **grave** was **assigned** him among the **wicked**
  and a **burial** place with **evildoers**,
though he had **done** no **wrong**
  nor **spoken** any **falsehood**.
But the LORD was pleased
  to **crush him** in **infirmity**.

If he **gives** his life as an **offering** for sin,
  he shall **see** his descendants in a **long life**,
  and the **will** of the LORD shall be **accomplished**
    through him.

Because of his **affliction**
  he shall **see** the light in **fullness** of days;

beginning. People refused to look at him and to face the challenge he posed. Isaiah labels him as "a man of suffering," and suggests that he had been accustomed to this suffering throughout his entire life. Suffering simply became a part of his identity.

However, the next line introduces a crucial qualification regarding the nature of his suffering. "Yet it was our infirmities that he bore, our sufferings that he endured." While the people looked at this man and thought that he was being punished by God, Isaiah makes it clear that he was taking the sins of the people upon himself. By

not struggling for acceptance in the face of rejection and not hiding from those who would mock and deride him, this servant willingly took upon himself all that evildoers would inflict.

Isaiah likens the attitude of this servant to "a lamb led to the slaughter or a sheep before the shearers." He does not resist and does not even open his mouth to protest. Instead, this servant is one who suffers in silence, soon to be forgotten. But no! Fulfilling the opening words of the song, "my servant shall prosper," Isaiah, again speaking in God's voice, promises that if

this servant fulfills his mission and suffers greatly for the sins of others, he will have accomplished the Lord's will and will see a long line of descendants after him flourishing due to the freedom he brought them. God promises to reward this servant with a place among those who have been counted "great." Certainly, the "great" in God's eyes are those men and women who have sacrificed themselves for others, just as this servant has done. God promises that this servant "will take away the sins of many." How appropriate it is for the Christian assembly to contemplate the Suffering

through his **suffering**, my servant shall **justify many**,
    and their **guilt** he shall **bear**.
Therefore I will give him his **portion** among the **great**,
    and he shall **divide** the spoils with the **mighty**,
because he **surrendered** himself to **death**
    and was **counted** among the **wicked**;
and he shall **take away** the sins of **many**,
    and win **pardon** for their **offenses**.

For meditation and context:

RESPONSORIAL PSALM   Psalm 31:2, 6, 12–13, 15–16, 17, 25 (Luke 23:46)

R. Father, into your hands I commend my spirit.

In you, O LORD, I take refuge;
    let me never be put to shame.
In your justice rescue me.
Into your hands I commend my spirit;
    you will redeem me, O LORD,
        O faithful God.

For all my foes I am an object of reproach,
    a laughingstock to my neighbors, and a
        dread to my friends;
    they who see me abroad flee from me.
I am forgotten like the unremembered dead;
    I am like a dish that is broken.

But my trust is in you, O LORD;
    I say, "You are my God.
In your hands is my destiny; rescue me
    from the clutches of my enemies and my
        persecutors."

Let your face shine upon your servant;
    save me in your kindness.
Take courage and be stouthearted,
    all you who hope in the LORD.

READING II   Hebrews 4:14–16; 5:7–9

A reading from the Letter to the Hebrews

Brothers and sisters:
Since we have a **great high priest** who has passed **through**
    the heavens,
    Jesus, the Son of **God**,
    let us **hold fast** to our **confession**.
For we do not have a **high priest**
    who is unable to **sympathize** with our **weaknesses**,
    but one who has similarly been tested in **every** way,
    yet **without** sin. **»**

An exhortatory reading that prepares the assembly to understand the sacrifice of Jesus portrayed in the Passion to follow. The theology suggested in this reading is as mysterious as it is natural. Christ is our model, our exemplar. As a man, he felt things just as we feel them. And yet his suffering, as God, is inconceivable.

Though framed in a negative construction ("We do not have . . ."), this statement expresses the crucial sympathy Christ has for us and that we should have for him. Proclaim this sentence with care.

Servant on Good Friday, when we venerate the wood of the cross. We approach the symbol of suffering not with fear, bitterness, or anger, but rather with loving gratitude: "by his stripes we were healed."

READING II | A priest, by definition, is one who makes an offering on behalf of others. The term "high priest," which we encounter at the outset of this reading from the Letter to the Hebrews, was used for the chief religious leader in Jerusalem during the time of the Second Temple era (450 BC to AD 70). The introduc-

tion of the term *high priest* after the Babylonian Exile brought with it an exaggerated sense of ritual and political power. The high priest essentially ruled as king, and was certainly venerated as such in the Temple precincts.

It is against the backdrop of a powerful political figure that the author of the Letter to the Hebrews designates Jesus as "a great high priest who has passed through the heavens." The high priests known to the people would not have exhibited compassion or empathy, too absorbed with their own status to be concerned about

others. But Jesus, "the Son of God," is not any ordinary high priest. His priesthood, is not like those high priests who are "unable to sympathize with our weaknesses." Jesus knows thoroughly the sufferings of the people, because he has been tested by the sufferings of humanity. Jesus is in communion with the suffering of this world.

This is precisely why the author suggests that we may "confidently approach the throne of grace," and from that throne receive the gifts of God's mercy and grace. Without saying so explicitly, the letter suggests that the offering of this high priest is

So let us **confidently** approach the **throne** of grace
    to receive **mercy** and to find **grace** for timely **help**.

In the **days** when Christ was in the **flesh**,
    he offered **prayers** and **supplications** with loud **cries** and **tears**
    to the **one** who was able to **save** him from **death**,
    and he was **heard** because of his **reverence**.
Son though he was, he learned **obedience** from what he **suffered**;
    and when he was made **perfect**,
    he became the **source** of eternal **salvation** for all who
        obey him.

GOSPEL   John 18:1—19:42

The Passion of our Lord Jesus Christ according to John

Jesus went out with his **disciples** across the Kidron **valley**
    to where there was a **garden**,
    into which he and his disciples **entered**.
Judas his betrayer also **knew** the place,
    because **Jesus** had often **met** there with his **disciples**.
So **Judas** got a band of **soldiers** and guards
    from the **chief priests** and the **Pharisees**
    and **went** there with **lanterns**, **torches**, and **weapons**.
Jesus, knowing **everything** that was going to **happen** to him,
    went out and said to them, "**Whom** are you **looking** for?"
They answered him, "**Jesus** the **Nazorean**."
He said to them, "**I AM**."
Judas his betrayer was also **with** them.
When he said to them, "**I AM**,"
    they turned **away** and fell to the **ground**.
So he again **asked** them,
    "**Whom** are you looking for?"
They said, "**Jesus** the **Nazorean**."

Margin notes (left column):

To intensify the sympathy, "In the days when Christ was in the flesh..."

Even stresses on "source," "salvation," and "obey."

Kidron = KID-ruhn
The Passion narrative in John's Gospel depicts Jesus foreknowing all that will happen to him, giving him an appearance of calm in a storm. John's Passion, like those in the synoptic Gospels, is full of drama, with scenes as vivid as those in any novel or film, but whose focus, Jesus, is defined by quiet intensity. Let that guide your recitation and let the drama inherent in the narrative express itself through you.
Don't overdo these expressions of "I AM." It is not uncommon, because of the length of this reading, for it to be shared among a group of lectors as well as a deacon and priest. While there are several characters in this narrative, including different speakers, avoid the tendency to do voices or to add drama by raising your voice unnecessarily. Let this narrative speak for itself through you.

Bottom notes (three columns):

all that Jesus encountered in humanity. Human illness and disease, war and violence, tragedy and loss are all offered as sacrifice because of this man's willingness to become one with the weaknesses of humanity. The image of the Suffering Servant encountered in the first reading should come into view here in the midst of hearing Hebrews as well. This is a high priest who denounced pride and power so that he could be "pierced for our offenses, crushed for our sins" (Isaiah 53:5).

The author of the letter ends this portion of his discourse by underscoring the

humanity of Jesus. "In the days when Christ was in the flesh," he experienced complete union with humanity. He did not observe the messiness of human flesh from afar, but instead mingled with it. Like all humans, Jesus prayed to God "with loud cries and tears." He recognized the agony that was inflicted upon him, he felt it to the very depths of his being, and he asked God to defend him in his suffering. What Jesus did not do was to shirk any aspect of his suffering. He sought to learn from it, and thus, God recognized both his "reverence" and his complete "obedience." On this Good

Friday, Christians are challenged to make these attitudes of Christ's their own once again. The perfection of Jesus, his willingness to sacrifice himself utterly and completely, is indeed our salvation. But it must be the pattern for a way of life that is practiced every day.

PASSION   The four Gospels contain similar stories of the Passion of Jesus Christ but with very different nuances. As we saw in Mark's Gospel, read this year on Palm Sunday, the evangelist is very much concerned with keeping the

Even stresses on "let these men go."

Even stresses on "struck the high priest's slave."
Malchus = MAL-kuhs

Annas = AN-uhs
Caiaphas = Kī-uh fuhs

John's Gospel tends to heap scorn upon the Jews, which has contributed to an ugly tendency toward anti-Semitism in Christianity. Mindfulness of this history can empower your proclamation.

The story of Peter's denial provides a sympathetic note in an often harsh narrative. Peter's weakness is the assembly's; his denials ("I am not") speak directly to our spiritual struggles.

Even emphasis on the words in this line.

Jesus **answered**,
  "I **told** you that **I AM**.
So if you are **looking** for me, **let these men go**."
This was to fulfill what he had **said**,
  "I have not **lost** any of those you **gave** me."
Then Simon **Peter**, who had a **sword**, **drew it**,
  struck the high priest's slave, and cut off his right **ear**.
The slave's name was **Malchus**.
Jesus said to Peter,
  "Put your **sword** into its **scabbard**.
Shall I not **drink** the **cup** that the **Father** gave me?"

So the band of **soldiers**, the **tribune**, and the Jewish **guards**
    seized **Jesus**,
  bound him, and brought him to **Annas** first.
He was the **father-in-law** of Caiaphas,
  who was **high priest** that year.
It was **Caiaphas** who had counseled the **Jews**
    that it was **better** that one man should die rather than
      the **people**.

Simon **Peter** and another disciple followed **Jesus**.
Now the **other** disciple was known to the high **priest**,
  and he **entered** the courtyard of the high priest with **Jesus**.
But **Peter** stood at the gate **outside**.
So the **other disciple**, the **acquaintance** of the high priest,
  went out and **spoke** to the gatekeeper and brought Peter in.
Then the maid who was the gatekeeper said to Peter,
  "You are **not** one of this man's **disciples**, **are you**?"
He said, "I am **not**."
Now the **slaves** and the **guards** were standing around
    a **charcoal** fire
  that they had **made**, because it was **cold**,
  and were **warming** themselves.
Peter was also **standing** there keeping **warm**. »

messianic identity of Jesus secret until the centurion's revelation made upon Jesus' death: "Truly, this man was the Son of God!" (Mark 15:39). Mark wants his readers to understand that one could be an outsider to Jerusalem and have a better understanding that Jesus is the Son of God than someone who walked with him day by day. Discipleship does not come either from being Jewish or from having followed him during his life.

  The Passion narrative from the Gospel of John portrays Jesus as a divine figure who is completely aware of how and why

the events unfold as they do. John's Jesus knows full well what is demanded of him in order for the Law to be fulfilled, and he has foreknowledge of the outcome itself. For this reason, throughout the Passion narrative, Jesus displays compassion and forgiveness toward his disciples, who are seen making great acts of betrayal in the end.

  One of the details of John's Passion is that it is separated from the Last Supper. Rather than moving directly from the table to the garden where Jesus wishes to pray, John interjects several chapters devoted to Jesus' "farewell discourses" directed to his

disciples. From these discourses come well-known sayings such as "I am the Way, the Truth, and the Life" (14:6), "I am the vine, you are the branches" (15:5), and "A man can have no greater love than to lay down his life for his friends" (15:13). These farewell sermons provide Jesus with the opportunity to speak very clearly of the need for his disciples to maintain faith in him within the context of a hostile world. This is, in fact, the very intent for John's Gospel as a whole—the maintenance of faith in Jesus even though his return seems to be delayed. Thus, when the Passion in

The **high priest** questioned **Jesus**
    about his **disciples** and about his **doctrine**.
Jesus **answered** him,
    "I have spoken **publicly** to the **world**.
I have **always taught** in a **synagogue**
    or in the **temple** area where all the **Jews** gather,
    and in **secret** I have said **nothing**. Why **ask** me?
Ask **those** who **heard me** what I said to **them**.
They **know** what I **said**."
When he had **said** this,
    one of the temple guards standing there struck Jesus and said,
    "Is **this** the way you **answer** the high **priest**?"
Jesus **answered** him,
    "If I have spoken **wrongly**, **testify** to the wrong;
    but if I have spoken **rightly**, why do you strike **me**?"
Then **Annas** sent him bound to **Caiaphas** the high **priest**.

Now **Simon Peter** was standing there keeping **warm**.
And they **said** to him,
    "You are not one of his **disciples**, **are you**?"
He **denied** it and said,
    "I am **not**."
One of the **slaves** of the high **priest**,
    a **relative** of the one whose **ear Peter** had cut **off**, said,
    "Didn't I **see** you in the **garden** with him?"
Again Peter **denied** it.
And **immediately** the cock **crowed**.

Then they **brought Jesus** from Caiaphas to the **praetorium**.
It was **morning**.
And they themselves did not enter the praetorium,
    in order **not** to be **defiled** so that they could **eat** the **Passover**.
So **Pilate** came out to them and said,
    "**What charge** do you bring **against** this **man**?"

Even emphasis on the words in this line.

Jesus' response suggests the core of his resolve to face the suffering to come.

Again, a return to the story of Peter. Don't overly dramatize the denial. Peter's shame will come through clearly when you proclaim this passage deliberately and clearly.

praetorium = prih-TOHR-ee-uhm

Here begins a long passage of exceptional vividness and power. It contrasts the conversation between Pilate and Jesus in the praetorium with the more aggressive exchanges between Pilate and the crowd. It is told from Pilate's point of view, which allows us to sympathize with Pilate. It's a truly remarkable passage whose drama need not be exaggerated. Pace your reading to allow its potent drama to come through on its own.

John begins immediately with Jesus' arrest, we see that it is only after he has commissioned his disciples in the arduous task of remaining in him.

As Jesus enters the garden with his disciples, we discover that Judas, who "also knew the place" has arrived ahead of them. Instead of suggesting that Judas hands Jesus over to hostile authorities, John portrays Judas as the organizer of a sort of posse, complete with "lanterns, torches, and weapons." There is no kiss given by Judas to Jesus to signal that he is the one to be arrested; instead Jesus steps forward

to make himself more visible and accessible. John tells us that Jesus begins the dialogue with the mob precisely because he knows "everything that was going to happen to him." In the synoptic Gospels, Jesus is described as suffering great agony as he spends time in prayer, but here in John, there is no display of emotions, only his calm reply to the crowd's question: he is the one they are looking for.

When Jesus identifies himself as "I AM"—the name by which God instructs Moses to reveal the divine nature to the Israelites and Pharaoh in the Book of

Exodus (3:14)—the crowd accompanying Judas turns away from him and falls to the ground. From this display of humility, it is clear that deep down they recognize the divine presence in their midst. Even as Jesus repeats the question: "Whom are you looking for?" his persecutors respond with the same response: "Jesus of Nazareth." Jesus again applies the divine name to himself, and the crowd continues to act in a passive way, almost as if they are in a trance. The first to act with aggression is Simon Peter, who draws his sword and cuts off the ear of the high priest's slave. Jesus rep-

Pilate is dismissive here, but don't exaggerate his dismissiveness.

The crucial question. Again, don't exaggerate it. Pilate, a government official, is asking an earnest question.

Even emphasis on the words in this question.

Jesus' answer is completely mysterious but supercharged with confidence. Read these words clearly and plainly.

Again, mysterious and confident.

They **answered** and **said** to him,
"If he were **not** a criminal,
we would **not** have handed him **over** to you."
At this, Pilate said to them,
"**Take him yourselves**, and **judge** him according to your **law**."
The Jews answered him,
"We do **not** have the right to execute **anyone**,"
in **order** that the word of **Jesus** might be **fulfilled**
that he said **indicating** the kind of **death** he would **die**.
So Pilate went back into the **praetorium**
and **summoned Jesus** and **said** to him,
"**Are you** the **King** of the **Jews**?"
Jesus answered,
"Do you **say this** on your **own**
or have others **told** you **about** me?"
Pilate answered,
"I am not a **Jew**, am I?
Your own **nation** and the chief **priests** handed you **over** to me.
What have you done?"
Jesus answered,
"My kingdom does not belong to this **world**.
If my kingdom **did** belong to this world,
my **attendants** would be **fighting**
to **keep** me from being handed **over** to the **Jews**.
But as it **is**, my **kingdom** is not **here**."
So Pilate said to him,
"Then you **are** a king?"
Jesus answered,
"You **say** I am a king.
For **this** I was born and for **this** I came into the world,
to **testify** to the **truth**.
Everyone who **belongs** to the truth **listens** to my **voice**."
Pilate said to him, "What is **truth**?" »

rimands Peter and proceeds to offer a teaching on the necessity of his impending death: "Shall I not drink the cup that the Father gave me?" (18:11). Such a statement is much different from the request Jesus makes in prayer in the Synoptic Gospels: "Take this cup away from me" (Mark 14:36).

Without further questioning or altercation, the soldiers and Jewish guards bind Jesus and escort him to Annas, the father-in-law of the high priest. Unlike the synoptic Gospels, in which Peter is said to have been present when Jesus arrived, John states that Peter and another disciple fol-

lowed Jesus. While the unnamed disciple is allowed entrance into the courtyard of the high priest, Peter remains at the gate. This gate clearly marks a separation between those in proximity to Jesus and those distant from him. Just as Peter is about to be brought inside and therefore brought closer to Jesus, he begins his denial of the Lord. The gatekeeper allows Jesus entrance, and Peter moves to a fire to keep himself warm. He continues to remain at a physical distance from Jesus.

Meanwhile Annas begins his interrogation of Jesus, first inquiring about his dis-

ciples and then about his doctrine. Jesus' reply may seem caustic as he tells Annas to find out about these things from those who heard him teaching. His reply carries the bold tone of a prophet. One of the guards strikes Jesus and reproves him for his speech. Jesus' reaction, like his demeanor in the garden, is calm; he simply suggests that he is merely speaking words of truth—the people he taught ought to be able to answer all the questions about Jesus' orthodoxy. John then turns our attention back to Peter, who should have been one of those capable of testifying to Jesus' right teaching.

Almost even emphasis on the words in this line, with extra added to "guilt."

When he had **said** this,
he **again** went out to the Jews and **said** to them,
"I find no **guilt** in him.
But you have a **custom** that I release one **prisoner** to you
at **Passover**.
Do you want me to **release** to you the **King** of the **Jews**?"
They cried out again,
"Not **this** one but **Barabbas**!"
Now **Barabbas** was a **revolutionary**.

Barabbas = buh-RAB-uhs
Avoid the tendency to shout this line.

"Scourged" is a wicked word. Read it slowly, one elongated syllable.

Then **Pilate** took Jesus and had him **scourged**.
And the **soldiers** wove a **crown** out of **thorns** and **placed** it
on his **head**,
and **clothed him** in a purple **cloak**,
and they **came** to him and said,
"**Hail**, **King** of the **Jews**!"
And they **struck** him **repeatedly**.
Once more Pilate went out and said to them,
"**Look**, I am **bringing** him out to you,
so that you may **know** that I find no **guilt** in him."
So **Jesus** came out,
wearing the **crown** of **thorns** and the **purple cloak**.
And he **said** to them, "**Behold**, the **man**!"
When the **chief priests** and the **guards** saw him they cried **out**,
"**Crucify** him, **crucify** him!"
Pilate **said** to them,
"**Take** him **yourselves** and crucify him.
I **find** no **guilt** in him."
The Jews answered,
"We have a **law**, and according to that **law** he ought to **die**,
because he **made** himself the Son of **God**."
Now when Pilate **heard** this statement,
he became even more **afraid**,
and went **back** into the **praetorium** and said to Jesus,
"**Where** are you **from**?"

No need to shout this line. It's all too clear what is happening.
Even stresses on the words in this line.

Pilate is at a loss, but he's also a dutiful Roman bureaucrat.

Lower your voice here. Don't exclaim.

Don't shout.

This question has a note of astonishment.

Such is not the case. Rather, Peter denies him two more times before John tells us "the cock crowed," as Jesus had predicted.

Although John tells us that Annas had Jesus bound and sent to Caiaphas, we are not told anything regarding the interchange between Caiaphas and Jesus. We next encounter Jesus at the Roman praetorium, the seat of Roman authority in occupied Jerusalem. Because entering the praetorium would mean automatic defilement for the Jews, it was necessary that Pilate come to the entrance to meet them. When Pilate, the leading Roman official, asks the crowd

outside regarding the charges against Jesus, they are suddenly vague with their response, suggesting that the act of handing him over to a Roman official ought to make the severity of the charge clear enough. Thus, Pilate must return inside to question Jesus. Pilate discovers that Jesus will not be much help in providing an answer to the simple question "What have you done?"

Jesus chooses not to address this question but instead to return to one posed moments earlier by Pilate: "Are you the King of the Jews?" Jesus does not deny

being a king, but instead, he defines the nature of his kingdom as one not belonging to this world. Nevertheless, Jesus does not directly utter the words "I am a king," which would have been a sufficient threat against Rome to put him to death as an insurrectionist. He continues by suggesting that the title "king" comes from the lips of Pilate. In contrast to the political understanding of being a king, Jesus tells Pilate that he was born into this world to testify to the truth. So, tying the logic of Jesus together, this means that Jesus' kingdom is based on truth, where "everyone who

Jesus did not **answer** him.
So Pilate **said** to him,
  "Do you not **speak** to me?
Do you not **know** that I have **power** to **release** you
  and I have **power** to **crucify** you?"
Jesus **answered** him,
  "You would have **no power** over **me**
  if it had not been **given** to you from **above**.
For this **reason** the one who handed me over to you
  has the greater **sin**."
Consequently, Pilate tried to **release** him;
    but the Jews cried out,
  "If you **release** him, you are not a **Friend** of **Caesar**.
Everyone who makes himself a **king** opposes **Caesar**."

When Pilate **heard these words** he brought Jesus **out**
  and **seated** him on the judge's **bench**
  in the **place** called Stone **Pavement**, in Hebrew, **Gabbatha**.
It was **preparation** day for **Passover**, and it was about **noon**.
And he **said** to the Jews,
  "**Behold**, your **king!**"
They cried out,
  "**Take him away, take him away! Crucify** him!"
Pilate **said** to them,
  "Shall I **crucify** your **king?**"
The chief priests answered,
  "We have **no king** but **Caesar**."
Then he handed him **over** to them to be **crucified**.

So they took **Jesus**, and, carrying the **cross** himself,
  he went out to what is called the **Place** of the **Skull**,
  in Hebrew, **Golgotha**.
There they **crucified** him, and **with** him two **others**,
  one on either **side**, with **Jesus** in the **middle**. »

Jesus' answer to Pilate's question once again is mysterious and confident.

Gabbatha = GAB-uh-thuh

Don't shout.

This line of the chief priests is dismissive; don't overdo the dismissiveness.

Golgotha = GAWL-guh-thuh

In two short lines the act of Jesus' crucifixion, to which this whole Passion has been building, is expressed. Read these lines plainly and slowly.

---

belongs to the truth listens to my voice." Pilate's question, "What is truth?" suggests that he has neither listened to Jesus' voice, nor does he belong to his kingdom.

Undoubtedly, Pilate wishes to bring this controversy to a resolution, but it could be the case that he has begun to listen to what Jesus is communicating about himself. Pilate once again moves outside and tells the crowd that he finds "no guilt in him." He gives the people the opportunity to release Jesus, but the people call instead for the release of Barabbas.

If Pilate wants to prevent an uprising among the people, he has no choice but to bow to their request to put Jesus to death. The Roman soldiers scourge Jesus, dress him in the clothes of a king, place a crown of thorns on his head, and mock him with the words "Hail, King of the Jews!" Pilate goes outside the praetorium once more and presents a bruised and beaten Jesus to the crowd with the introduction "Behold, the man!" Undoubtedly, Pilate is underscoring the weakness of Jesus, as if to say to the people: "Does he look like he could pose any threat?" After Pilate tells the mob that he

finds Jesus to be innocent, they remind him of their law that demands death for the one who claims to be the Son of God. John tells us that Pilate "became even more afraid" (19:9) and retreated back into the praetorium to confront Jesus once again.

Now the confrontation between Pilate and Jesus grows more contentious, primarily because of Pilate's fear of an uprising, but also because Jesus answers his question with silence. Nevertheless, Pilate persists in not discovering a real reason for putting Jesus to death. John tells us that Pilate wanted to release Jesus (19:12), but the

Pilate also had an **inscription** written and put on the **cross**.
It read,
> "**Jesus** the **Nazorean**, the **King** of the **Jews**."

Now **many** of the Jews **read** this inscription,
> because the **place** where Jesus was crucified was near the **city**;
> and it was **written** in **Hebrew**, **Latin**, and **Greek**.

So the **chief priests** of the Jews said to **Pilate**,
> "Do not write 'The **King** of the **Jews**,'
> but that he said, 'I **am** the King of the **Jews**.'"

Pilate answered,
> "What I have **written**, I have **written**."

Pilate's are his final, ominous words in this Passion. Pause slightly after proclaiming them.

When the **soldiers** had crucified **Jesus**,
> they took his **clothes** and divided them into **four shares**,
> a **share** for each **soldier**.

They also took his **tunic**, but the tunic was **seamless**,
> **woven** in one piece from the **top down**.

So they said to one **another**,
> "Let's not **tear** it, but cast **lots** for it to see whose it will **be**,"
> in order that the passage of Scripture might be fulfilled
>> that says:
>> *They **divided** my garments among them,*
>>> *and for my **vesture** they cast **lots**.*

This is what the soldiers **did**.
Standing by the cross of **Jesus** were his **mother**
> and his mother's **sister**, **Mary** the wife of **Clopas**,
> and Mary of **Magdala**.

When Jesus saw his **mother** and the disciple there whom
> he **loved**
> he said to his **mother**, "**Woman**, **behold**, your **son**."

Then he said to the **disciple**,
> "**Behold**, your **mother**."

And from **that hour** the **disciple** took her into his **home**.

Be sure to read the names of these women clearly.

Almost even stresses on the words in this line.

crowd would not have it. They persuade Pilate that he would be seen as disloyal to Caesar if he allowed this supposed king to live. Consequently, Pilate brings Jesus out of the praetorium once more, takes his seat at the judgment bench, and introduces Jesus to the people with the words "Behold, your king!" Pilate is surely mocking the Jews by declaring the weak and battered Jesus their king. As they shout out that he be taken away and crucified, John tells us that the time is about noon, the time when the lambs were beginning to be slaughtered in the Temple. That the begin-

ning of the death process for Jesus coincides with the killing of the Passover lambs is important for John.

The carrying of the cross between the praetorium and Golgotha is omitted in John. We are simply told that Jesus "went out to" the place of his crucifixion, where he is crucified between "two others." John does not identify these two as criminals or engage them in dialogue with Jesus. Instead, John wants the reader to focus on the identity of Jesus alone, as seen in Pilate's ordering the inscription "Jesus the Nazorean, the King of the Jews" to be placed above his head.

Meanwhile, the soldiers are busy dividing Jesus' clothes and gambling for his tunic. The seamlessness of the garment allows for John to demonstrate how Scripture is being fulfilled.

As Jesus hangs upon the cross, John turns our attention to Jesus' mother and the other disciples who remain with him at the foot of the cross. John is unique in including Jesus' mother and the "beloved disciple." Jesus speaks to his mother using language reminiscent of the wedding at Cana, when he addressed her as "Woman" (John 2:4). The scene of Jesus presenting

"I thirst," concentrates the agony of the crucifixion. Say it simply and clearly.

hyssop = HIS-uhp

These words, "It is finished," culminate the drama of the Passion. Give each word even stress, pausing ever so slightly between them, almost: "It. Is. Finished."

The details in the passage that concludes John's Passion are of interest because they speak to the awful economy of torture and execution (on the part of the Roman soldiers) as well as the requirements of the burial of a corpse according to Jewish custom. It's effective to read these words with scrutiny and openness.

John is speaking directly to his audience in these words; through you, directly to the assembly.

After **this**, aware that everything was now **finished**,
in order that the **Scripture** might be **fulfilled**,
Jesus said, "**I thirst**."
There was a **vessel** filled with **common wine**.
So they put a **sponge** soaked in wine on a sprig of **hyssop**
and put it up to his **mouth**.
When **Jesus** had taken the wine, he said,
"**It is finished**."
And **bowing** his head, he **handed** over the **spirit**.

[Here all kneel and pause for a short time.]

Now since it was **preparation** day,
in **order** that the bodies might not remain
on the **cross** on the **sabbath**,
for the **sabbath** day of that **week** was a **solemn** one,
the **Jews** asked Pilate that their **legs** be broken
and that they be taken **down**.
So the **soldiers** came and broke the **legs** of the first
and then of the other one who was **crucified** with **Jesus**.
But when they came to **Jesus** and saw that he was already **dead**,
they did **not** break his **legs**,
but one **soldier** thrust his **lance** into his **side**,
and immediately blood and **water** flowed **out**.
An **eyewitness** has testified, and his **testimony** is true;
he **knows** that he is speaking the **truth**,
so that **you also** may come to **believe**.
For this **happened** so that the **Scripture** passage might
be **fulfilled**:
*Not a **bone** of it will be **broken**.*
And again another passage says:
*They will look **upon him** whom they have **pierced**.* »

his mother to the beloved disciple and presenting the beloved disciple to his mother with the word "behold" has long been interpreted as Jesus instituting the new familial relationship that is to take place in the Church. Great care for this relationship is suggested with the words, "And from that hour the disciple took her into his home."

All Jesus must yet do is fulfill the words of Psalm 69:4: "I am weary with crying out; my throat is parched." Thus, Jesus says the simple words "I thirst" joined with the words "It is finished." It is very clear that John's Jesus is not only aware of how

events will unfold, but he is presented as being in complete control. He is the one to determine when all has been fulfilled and when his mission is finished.

Pilate orders the soldiers to break the legs of those who had been crucified to hasten their deaths before the beginning of the Sabbath. Breaking the last bit of support for the upper body would cause instant suffocation. However, the guards discover that Jesus is already dead. Because his death takes place simultaneously with the killing of the lambs in the Temple, John wishes us to see that Jesus'

legs must be unbroken for him to be likened to an unblemished lamb. Another important symbol for John here is the blood and water that flow from Jesus' side. Both blood and water are primary symbols of the Exodus story, as the Israelites marked their doorposts with the blood of the lamb before they were set free to cross through the waters of the Red Sea. The cross stands as a sign of Paschal liberation in the Gospel of John.

The final element of the Passion of John is the abundance of ritual connected with the burial of Jesus. We are told that

Arimathea = ayr-ih-muh-THEE-uh

Nicodemus = nik-uh-DEE-muhs
Don't hurry over these details.
myrrh = mer
aloes = AL-ohz

Read this concluding phrase, "for the tomb
was close by," slowly.

After **this**, Joseph of **Arimathea**,
    secretly a disciple of **Jesus** for **fear** of the **Jews**,
    asked **Pilate** if he could **remove** the body of **Jesus**.
And Pilate **permitted** it.
So he came and took his **body**.
Nicodemus, the one who had **first come** to him at **night**,
    also came bringing a mixture of **myrrh** and **aloes**
    weighing about one **hundred** pounds.
They took the body of **Jesus**
    and bound it with **burial cloths** along with the **spices**,
    according to the **Jewish burial custom**.
Now in the **place** where he had been **crucified** there was
        a **garden**,
    and in the **garden** a new **tomb**, in which **no one** had yet
        been **buried**.
So they laid **Jesus** there because of the Jewish **preparation** day;
    for the **tomb** was close **by**.

Joseph of Arimathea is assisted by Nicodemus, "the one who had first come to him at night" (19:19). Nicodemus first appeared in the third chapter of John and recognized Jesus as "a teacher who comes from God" (3:2), and he is the first disciple whom Jesus instructs on the kingdom of God. Clearly, John wants us to see that, unlike the disciples that accompanied Jesus along the way during his earthly ministry, Nicodemus has come out of the shadows as a figure of light who takes great care in attending to Jesus' body. John tells us that the spices Nicodemus brings with him to anoint Jesus' body weigh almost one hundred pounds. Joseph and Nicodemus proceed to bind Jesus' body in burial clothes, placing it in a new tomb in the garden. Even in the midst of death, there seems to be here the reverent care for life. S. W.

HOLY SATURDAY: EASTER VIGIL

LECTIONARY #41

READING I   Genesis 1:1—2:2

A reading from the Book of Genesis

[In the **beginning**, when God created the **heavens** and the **earth**,]
     the **earth** was a formless **wasteland**, and **darkness** covered
          the **abyss**,
     while a **mighty wind** swept **over** the **waters**.

Then God said,
     "Let there be **light**," and there was **light**.
God saw how **good** the light was.
God then **separated** the **light** from the **darkness**.
God called the light "**day**," and the darkness he called "**night**."
Thus **evening** came, and **morning** followed—the **first** day.

Then God said,
     "Let there be a **dome** in the **middle** of the **waters**,
     to separate one **body** of water from the **other**."
And so it **happened**:
     God **made** the dome,
     and it separated the water **above** the dome from the water
          below it.
God called the dome "the **sky**."
Evening came, and **morning** followed—the **second** day.

Then God said,
     "Let the **water** under the **sky** be gathered into a **single basin**,
     so that the **dry land** may appear." »

Genesis = JEN-uh-sihs

A narrative reading of one of the most familiar passages in all of Scripture. Because the language in this reading is so grand, you maybe tempted to dramatize your proclamation. No need. The language is so finely wrought that if you read at a measured pace, its glories will come through.

The word "and" appears repeatedly in this reading. It's one of the main sources of its power. It functions almost like a verb. Let the word do the work for you as you proclaim.

Pause ever so slightly after "first day." You will repeat this slight pause five more times.

Pause slightly after "second day."

There are options for today's readings. Contact your parish staff to learn which readings will be used.

READING I   The seven Old Testament readings that precede the two New Testament readings in the Liturgy of the Word for the Easter Vigil constitute the broad brush strokes of salvation history. After the creation of the world, in which God calls everything "good," sin enters the world and calls for redemption. The readings we hear this night recall the many voices and events leading Israel, and in fact the entire created world, back to the fullness of relationship with God. At the Vigil, we hear these stories as the context for participating in the Baptism of new Christians, renewing our own baptismal promises, and celebrating the Eucharist. This whole event is an act of *anamnesis*, in which these tales of salvation remain not simply historical fact, but constitute the "living present" of the community today. They call us to ponder the way in which God continues to be active in the world, saving all things and drawing creation unto himself.

The very first words of the Old Testament, Genesis 1:1—2:2, present the primordial creation story, in which everything that exists was brought into being in the course of six days, with the seventh day of the week being designated as a day for God to rest from all his labors. Although science convinces us today to believe that the world came into being through something like the big bang theory, which suggests that the expansion of the cosmos began 13.8 billion years ago through the chaotic combination of dense gases and high temperatures, this ancient story is still worth

Almost even stresses on the words in this line, with "good" receiving a little extra emphasis.

And so it **happened**:
  the **water** under the **sky** was gathered into its **basin**,
  and the **dry land** appeared.
God called the dry land "the **earth**,"
  and the basin of the water he called "the **sea**."
God saw how **good** it was.
Then God said,
  "Let the **earth** bring **forth** vegetation:
  every **kind** of plant that bears **seed**
  and every **kind** of fruit tree on **earth**
  that bears **fruit** with its seed **in** it."
And so it **happened**:
  the **earth** brought forth every **kind** of plant that bears **seed**
  and every **kind** of fruit tree on **earth**
  that bears **fruit** with its **seed** in it.
God saw how **good** it was.
Evening came, and **morning** followed—the **third** day.

Pause slightly after "third day."

The passage that follows, describing the fourth day of creation, includes a series of oppositions to emphasize the separation of night from day. Stress the words that indicate these oppositions.

Then God said:
  "Let there be **lights** in the **dome** of the **sky**,
  to separate **day** from **night**.
Let them mark the **fixed times**, the **days** and the **years**,
  and serve as **luminaries** in the **dome** of the **sky**,
  to shed **light** upon the **earth**."
And so it **happened**:
  God **made** the two great **lights**,
  the **greater** one to govern the **day**,
  and the **lesser** one to govern the **night**;
  and he made the **stars**.
God set them in the **dome** of the **sky**,
  to shed **light** upon the **earth**,
  to govern the **day** and the **night**,
  and to separate the **light** from the **darkness**.
God saw how **good** it was.
Evening came, and **morning** followed—the **fourth** day.

Pause slightly after "fourth day."

taking seriously, albeit not literally. The creation story in Genesis reveals the love of God, who meticulously cares for each detail of that which comes forth from the utterance of his Word. From this foundational account of creation, we can say that all things are meant to exist in perfect harmony; chaos is not meant to be a part of the pieces of the world's puzzle fitting together. All that is works together.

Genesis opens with a description of what was before God showed his desire to create: Genesis describes this as a "formless wasteland," filled with darkness. Thus it is meant to be viewed as rather chaotic—there is simply no point to it. But then God speaks, and from his voice comes light, which changes everything. Light serves to balance darkness. The two are not meant to be seen as waging some sort of cosmic war against each other; rather, they complement each other and serve as the foundation of time. Light is called the time of "day," and darkness is called the time of "night."

Over the course of days, God creates a highly coordinated and patterned material world. On the second day, God distinguishes the waters by the dome of the sky. This separation makes way for God's work on the third day in which he creates the earth and the vegetation upon it. This moment in the creation story suggests that God takes great care for the endurance of life, as all the plants and trees are to be bear seed in order to regenerate life. After focusing his attention upon the earth, God centers the work of the fourth day on the skies and creates the sun and the moon—"the greater one to govern the day, and the lesser one to govern the night"—and the stars. Once again, Genesis depicts God creating distinc-

Then God said,
  "Let the **water teem** with an abundance of **living creatures**,
  and on the **earth** let birds fly **beneath** the dome of the sky."
And so it **happened**:
  God created the great **sea monsters**
  and all kinds of **swimming creatures** with which the
    water **teems**,
  and all kinds of **winged birds**.
God saw how **good** it was, and God **blessed** them, saying,
  "Be **fertile**, **multiply**, and **fill** the water of the **seas**;
  and let the **birds** multiply on the **earth**."
Evening came, and **morning** followed—the **fifth** day.

Then God said,
  "Let the **earth** bring **forth** all kinds of **living creatures**:
  cattle, **creeping things**, and wild **animals** of all **kinds**."
And so it **happened**:
  God made **all kinds** of wild **animals**, all **kinds** of **cattle**,
  and all **kinds** of **creeping things** of the earth.
God saw how **good** it was.

Then [God said:
  "Let us make **man** in our image, **after** our **likeness**.
Let them have **dominion** over the **fish** of the **sea**,
  the **birds** of the **air**, and the **cattle**,
  and over **all** the wild **animals**
  and **all** the creatures that **crawl** on the **ground**."
God created **man** in his **image**;
  in the **image** of **God** he created **him**;
  male and **female** he created **them**.
God **blessed** them, saying:
  "Be **fertile** and **multiply**;
  fill the earth and **subdue** it.
Have **dominion** over the **fish** of the **sea**, the **birds** of the **air**,
  and **all** the living things that **move** on the earth." **»**

Pause slightly after "fifth day."

Keep an even pace through this line.

This passage repeats the word "kinds" four times. These "kinds" anticipate the image of "humankind" shortly to come.

Don't treat the appearance of humankind at this point as a break, as something separate; rather, treat it as part of a continuum. The tone and pitch of your proclamation does not need to change here.

tion and separation as a means of governing all things in harmony.

On the fifth day, God continues his focus on the sky, but he also looks at the waters and brings forth "living creatures" to inhabit the seas. The sixth day's work turns to providing inhabitants for the dry land. It is significant that God commands: "Let the earth bring forth all kinds of living creatures." The earth itself has a role to play in providing for the life that is to dwell upon its surface. Then comes the crown of creation, God's final mark of care for creation: God creates humanity. The human creature is distinguished from the other

aspects of creation in two primary ways. First, male and female are created in the divine image. Rather than thinking of this as a similarity in physical form, it is better to understand that the divine image is able to understand the significance of generative love. To multiply is meant to be a means of expressing divine love. Second, God creates human beings to "have dominion" over all the living creatures of the world. Instead of conceiving of "dominion" as some type of rule, it is better to understand it in terms of stewardship. In all that they do, men and women are to care for God's good creation.

Finally, on the seventh day, God rests. Jewish Law will come to understand the Sabbath rest as a command for all of creation. Genesis suggests that God did not create the world to have its various components labor against one another in order to survive. Darwin's theory of the survival of the fittest, while a recognizable characteristic of the cosmos, really has no place in this primeval story of creation. Here, God takes a rest from his labors, and all creation is called to do the same in order to restore the original intention of God's creation—all things existing together in perfect harmony. This is really the ultimate hope of our salvation.

God also said:
   "**See**, I give you every **seed-bearing** plant all over the **earth**
      and every **tree** that has seed-bearing **fruit** on it to be
         your **food**;
   and to all the **animals** of the land, all the **birds** of the air,
      and all the **living creatures** that crawl on the **ground**,
   I give all the green plants for **food**."
And so it **happened**.
God looked at **everything** he had made, and he found it
      very good.]
Evening came, and **morning** followed—the **sixth** day.

Thus the **heavens** and the **earth** and all their **array**
      were **completed**.
Since on the **seventh** day God was **finished**
   with the **work** he had been **doing**,
      he **rested** on the seventh day from **all** the work he
         had **undertaken**.

[Shorter: Genesis 1:1, 26–31a (see brackets)]

Pause slightly after "sixth day."

For these concluding lines of this reading, which describe the sabbath, you can allow your proclamation to relax a little without overdoing it.

For meditation and context:

RESPONSORIAL PSALM   Psalm 104:1–2, 5–6, 10, 12, 13–14, 24, 35 (30)

R. Lord, send out your Spirit, and renew the face of the earth.

Bless the LORD, O my soul!
   O LORD, my God, you are great indeed!
You are clothed with majesty and glory,
   robed in light as with a cloak.

You fixed the earth upon its foundation,
   not to be moved forever;
with the ocean, as with a garment, you
      covered it;
   above the mountains the waters stood.

You send forth springs into the watercourses
   that wind among the mountains.
Beside them the birds of heaven dwell;
   from among the branches they send forth
      their song.

You water the mountains from your palace;
   the earth is replete with the fruit
      of your works.
You raise grass for the cattle,
   and vegetation for man's use,
producing bread from the earth.

How manifold are your works, O LORD!
   In wisdom you have wrought them all—
the earth is full of your creatures.
   Bless the LORD, O my soul!

Or:

READING II   Moving away from the creation of the world at the outset of Genesis, the story continues to unfold with the introduction of sin into the world and the subsequent outcome of repeated chaos. Quite quickly we see how jealousy between brothers leads to death (Cain and Abel in Genesis 4:1–16), how the corruption of humanity can move God to destroy it (Noah and the flood in Genesis 6:5—9:29), and how the desire to be like God produces confusion among the peoples of the earth (Tower of Babel in Genesis 11:1–9). After these various episodes dem-onstrating how far humanity moves itself away from God's original designs and exploits creation for its own success, we are introduced to Abraham in Genesis 12. He will be called by God to be the father of a great nation, with descendants as numerous as the stars of heaven and the sands on the shore of the sea (Genesis 22:17). What God intended to accomplish with the goodness of his original creation, he hopes to restore in the people established through the lineage of Abraham.

Although Abraham's story of departing from his homeland to take possession of the land God would bestow upon him would include many hardships, there is no harsher test for him than the story we read in Genesis 22, the binding of Isaac. It is important to remember that when Abraham receives God's covenant assuring him that he will be the father of a great nation, he was already an old man and his wife Sarah was well beyond childbearing years. The two of them wrestled long and hard with the question of how they would ever have offspring. Taking matters into their own hands, Abraham sleeps with Sarah's maid-servant, Hagar, who bears a child named

For meditation and context:

RESPONSORIAL PSALM   Psalm 33:4–5, 6–7, 12–13, 20 and 22 (5b)

R. The earth is full of the goodness of the Lord.

Upright is the word of the LORD,
   and all his works are trustworthy.
He loves justice and right;
   of the kindness of the LORD the earth
      is full.

By the word of the LORD the heavens
      were made;
   by the breath of his mouth all their host.
He gathers the waters of the sea as in a flask;
   in cellars he confines the deep.

Blessed the nation whose God is the LORD,
   the people he has chosen for his own
      inheritance.
From heaven the LORD looks down;
   he sees all mankind.

Our soul waits for the LORD,
   who is our help and our shield.
May your kindness, O LORD, be upon us
   who have put our hope in you.

READING II   Genesis 22:1–18

A reading from the Book of Genesis

[God put **Abraham** to the **test**.
He called to him, "**Abraham**!"
"**Here** I am," he replied.
Then God said:
   "Take your son **Isaac**, your **only** one, whom you **love**,
      and **go** to the land of **Moriah**.
There you shall offer him up as a **holocaust**
   on a **height** that I will point **out** to you."]
Early the next morning Abraham saddled his **donkey**,
   took with him his son **Isaac** and two of his **servants** as well,
   and with the **wood** that he had cut for the **holocaust**,
   set **out** for the place of which **God** had told him.

On the third day **Abraham** got sight of the place from **afar**.
Then he **said** to his servants:
   "**Both** of you stay here with the **donkey**,
      while the **boy** and I go on over **yonder**.
We will **worship** and then come **back** to you." »

Genesis = JEN-uh-sihs
Moriah = moh-RĪ-uh
A narrative reading of another very familiar story from Scripture. The reading is mythic: its elements, including its conclusion, are known, but that does not diminish its power. A passage such as this is already so dramatic, your task is to proclaim as clearly as you can. Even though there are several exclamations in this passage, you will not need to raise your voice any more than you normally do when proclaiming.

Case in point: the first acclamation. There is an aura of otherworldly silence around Abraham's name. No need to shout.

The great literary critic Erich Auerbach describes this passage as "fraught with background." a delicious phrase. He means that while the action is spare, the scene itself is filling with tension. When you proclaim "On the third day," you are skipping over two full days of traveling.

Ishmael. God is greatly displeased with Abraham's (and Sarah's) lack of faith and therefore declares to Hagar that her descendants will be too numerous to be counted (Genesis 16:10). Even though God will return to Abraham, restore the covenant with him, and make it possible for Sarah to give birth to Isaac, the great nation descending from his name will forever be at odds with the great nation descending from Hagar and her son Ishmael. (Note that Muslims believe themselves to be descendants of Ishmael.)

All of this is background to understanding the weighty significance of Abraham's test in being willing to sacrifice his son. At stake here is not only the death of a precious child, but the potential end to the future of the nation as a whole. The future of Abraham's great nation relies upon the flourishing of his son Isaac. The story begins with God's call, "Abraham," and he replies with the conventional words of a servant: "Here I am." Then God instructs Abraham to take his son Isaac up the mountain where Abraham is to offer him as a holocaust. In its original sense, a holocaust

is a specific type of offering, one that is to be burned. Thus, not only is Abraham to kill his son, but the sacrifice will obliterate Isaac entirely from the world.

While we might wonder what kind of thoughts were running through Abraham's head as he prepared his son and the wood for the fire and made the journey up the mountain, we are given no evidence of Abraham's interior disposition. Instead, what we see is his obedience put into action. To add to the mystery of Abraham's thoughts, it is significant to note that he and his son are up on the mountain alone

Thereupon Abraham took the **wood** for the **holocaust**
   and laid it on his son Isaac's **shoulders**,
   while he himself carried the **fire** and the **knife**.
As the two walked on together, Isaac **spoke** to his
   father Abraham:
   "**Father**!" Isaac said.
"Yes, son," he replied.
Isaac continued, "**Here** are the **fire** and the **wood**,
   but **where** is the **sheep** for the **holocaust**?"
"Son," Abraham answered,
   "God **himself** will provide the **sheep** for the **holocaust**."
Then the two **continued** going forward.

[When they **came** to the place of which **God** had told him,
   Abraham built an **altar** there and arranged the **wood** on it.]
Next he tied up his son **Isaac**,
   and put him on **top** of the **wood** on the **altar**.
[Then he **reached out** and took the **knife** to **slaughter** his son.
But the LORD's messenger **called** to him from **heaven**,
   "**Abraham, Abraham**!"
"**Here** I am," he answered.
"Do **not** lay your **hand** on the **boy**," said the messenger.
"Do **not** do the **least thing** to him.
I know **now** how devoted you are to **God**,
   since you did not **withhold** from me your **own beloved** son."
As Abraham looked about,
   he spied a **ram** caught by its **horns** in the **thicket**.
So he **went** and took the **ram**
   and offered it up as a **holocaust** in place of his **son**.]
Abraham named the site **Yahweh-yireh**;
   hence people now say, "On the **mountain** the Lord will **see**."

Second exclamation: Don't shout.

"Continued": This word is "fraught with background."

Take note of the details. Abraham is preparing an altar for sacrifice.

Third exclamation: Don't shout.

Yahweh-yireh = YAH-way-YEER-ay

together, along with two of Abraham's servants, before the site for the sacrifice becomes apparent to Abraham. Certainly, waiting for three days had to increase the horror and dread of what Abraham would be called to do.

When Abraham finally detects the place that would be suitable for the sacrifice, he and Isaac depart from the two servants and proceed along to the site, with Isaac carrying the wood for the fire on his shoulders. In a metaphorical sense, it is the future of all of Israel that is laid upon his shoulders. When Isaac asks his father about the missing sheep for the holocaust, Abraham is given the opportunity to make a great profession of faith: "God himself will provide the sheep for the holocaust." This statement will have lasting significance for salvation history, as only God can provide the means for a sacrifice that is truly worthy of his reception. Christians will understand that Jesus must be given by God in order to be a sacrifice for all of creation. We can only be mystified by Abraham's stoic faith in the midst of this horrific scene.

The gruesomeness of the event builds as Abraham prepares the altar for sacrifice, ties up his beloved son, and places him upon the wood on the altar. But then comes the call of God once again: "Abraham! Abraham!" Abraham's reply changes not at all: "Here I am." With this loving exchange between God and Abraham, the test is over. God has no doubt that Abraham is filled with faith, since he was willing even to sacrifice his beloved son. Abraham expresses his gratitude to God by making the sacrifice of a ram caught in the thicket, an animal placed there no doubt by God himself. Seeing the beauty of Abraham's faith, God blesses him and restores the

Though an angel of God is relaying these words, it's God himself who speaks here. Set off the phrase "declares the Lord" in such a way to make it clear that God is speaking.

[Again the LORD's **messenger** called to Abraham from **heaven** and said:
"I **swear** by myself, **declares** the Lord,
that **because** you acted as you **did**
in not **withholding** from me your beloved **son**,
I will **bless you** abundantly
and make your **descendants** as **countless**
as the **stars** of the **sky** and the **sands** of the **seashore**;
your **descendants** shall take **possession**
of the **gates** of their **enemies**,
and in your **descendants** all the **nations** of the earth shall
find **blessing**—
all **this** because you **obeyed** my command."]

[Shorter: Genesis 22:1–2, 9a, 10–13, 15–18 (see brackets)]

For meditation and context:

RESPONSORIAL PSALM   Psalm 16:5, 8, 9–10, 11 (1)

R. You are my inheritance, O Lord.

O LORD, my allotted portion and my cup,
  you it is who hold fast my lot.
I set the LORD ever before me;
  with him at my right hand I shall not
  be disturbed.

Therefore my heart is glad and my
  soul rejoices,
  my body, too, abides in confidence;

because you will not abandon my soul
  to the netherworld,
  nor will you suffer your faithful one
  to undergo corruption.

You will show me the path to life,
  fullness of joys in your presence,
  the delights at your right hand forever.

covenant with him: "I will bless you abundantly and make your descendants as countless as the stars of the sky and the sands of the seashore."

READING III   The third reading for the Easter Vigil continues the story of salvation history with the account of Moses leading the Israelites out of the land of the Egyptians by passing through the sea. This story, which is told in the context of the annual Passover Seder in the Jewish community, has great importance for Christians as the natural element of

water becomes a primary symbol in the story of salvation. Remember that water is created by God in the Book of Genesis for the purpose of providing life for the creatures of the sea. In the Book of Exodus, the water is not only a symbol of new life for the Israelites, as they pass through to safety on dry land, but is also a symbol of death, as the Egyptians are completely destroyed as the waters flow in upon them. The Christian "Passover," the celebration of Christ's Resurrection, is the celebration of God's infinite love that is capable of producing new life at the hour of death.

This passage from Exodus opens with Moses and Aaron having just led the Israelites south of the land of Goshen in Egypt only to be given the instructions to circle around to the north again to set up camp at the shore of the sea (Exodus 14:1–4). Seeing the Israelites wandering with no direct escape route, Pharaoh recognizes his mistake in letting them go, and once again, his heart is hardened so that he orders his armies to chase after the Israelites. This will provide God with the opportunity to defeat the powers (i.e., to be read "gods") of Egypt once and for all. By defeating the Egyptians

Exodus = EK-suh-duhs

Another very familiar story, this reading is full of action, with occasional instruction by God himself. But mostly action. Its drama will come through your proclamation if you allow the details of the action to be voiced. Let the words of the reading speak for themselves.

Here, God instructs Moses on how to perform a miraculous act. He's a little impatient, but he's also providing the details of a carefully considered plan.

The passage that follows includes many vivid details.

READING III   Exodus 14:15—15:1

A reading from the Book of Exodus

The Lord said to Moses, "**Why** are you crying **out** to me?
Tell the **Israelites** to go **forward**.
And **you**, lift up your **staff** and, with **hand** outstretched
    over the **sea**,
  split the sea in **two**,
  that the **Israelites** may pass through it on **dry land**.
But I will make the **Egyptians** so **obstinate**
  that they will go in **after** them.
Then I will **receive glory** through **Pharaoh** and all his **army**,
  his **chariots** and **charioteers**.
The **Egyptians** shall know that I am the Lord,
  when I receive **glory** through **Pharaoh**
  and his **chariots** and **charioteers**."

The **angel** of God, who had been leading Israel's **camp**,
  now **moved** and went around **behind** them.
The column of cloud **also**, leaving the front,
  took up its place **behind** them,
  so that it came **between** the camp of the **Egyptians**
  and that of **Israel**.
But the cloud now became **dark**, and thus the night **passed**
  without the rival camps coming any **closer together** all
    night long.
Then **Moses** stretched out his **hand** over the **sea**,
  and the LORD swept the **sea**
  with a **strong east wind** throughout the night
  and so **turned** it into **dry** land.
When the **water** was thus **divided**,
  the Israelites **marched** into the **midst** of the sea on dry **land**,
  with the **water** like a **wall** to their **right** and to their **left**.

in the neutral territory of the Red Sea, the whole world will be able to see God's great power. Thus, the exodus of the Hebrews is as an opportunity to lead those beyond the Israelite community to faith in God.

At the outset of the reading, Moses echoes to God the cry of the Israelites who see the Egyptians pursuing them and recognize that remaining as slaves in Egypt may well have been better than to have been led out to their death. As he has done all along with Pharaoh, God promises that he will make the Egyptians "obstinate" and therefore incapable of recognizing that

moving into the waters will result in their being swallowed up to death. God makes it clear that the death of these Egyptians will bring him glory.

The work of the angel of God, beginning in verse 19, is particularly important. Throughout their journey from Egypt, the angel had taken a position in front of the Israelites, leading them along the way. At the Red Sea, the angel moves around behind the Israelites to come in between the Israelites and the Egyptians. This move represents a marking out of sacred space through a process known as the "pivoting

of the sacred." The angel "pivots" positions, and as a result, the power of the sacred moves forward with the Israelites and is removed from the grasp of the Egyptians. In a sense, this pivoting becomes a marker of the passage. Here at the sea, the Israelites say goodbye once and for all to the life they knew so well, and are invited to take possession of a new and exciting reality. Theirs is the movement into a territory of the unknown, in which they will have to come to understand the authority of God in a developmental sort of way.

Again, vivid details. Give your voice to them.

The **Egyptians** followed in **pursuit**;
    all Pharaoh's **horses** and **chariots** and **charioteers** went
        after them
    right into the **midst** of the **sea**.
In the **night watch** just before **dawn**
    the Lord cast through the **column** of the fiery **cloud**
    upon the Egyptian force a **glance** that **threw** it into a **panic**;
    and he so **clogged** their chariot wheels
    that they could hardly **drive**.
With that the **Egyptians** sounded the **retreat** before **Israel**,
    because the Lord was fighting for them against the **Egyptians**.

God speaks, once again instructing Moses on how to perform another miraculous act, one that parallels the earlier act.

Then the Lord told Moses, "**Stretch** out your hand over the **sea**,
    that the **water** may flow **back** upon the **Egyptians**,
    upon their **chariots** and their **charioteers**."
So Moses stretched **out** his hand over the **sea**,
    and at dawn the **sea** flowed **back** to its normal **depth**.
The Egyptians were fleeing head **on** toward the **sea**,
    when the Lord **hurled** them into its **midst**.
As the **water** flowed back,
    it covered the **chariots** and the **charioteers** of Pharaoh's
        whole army
    which had followed the **Israelites** into the **sea**.
Not a single **one** of them **escaped**.

Don't overly dramatize the doom that comes to Pharaoh and his army. Let the grim details speak for themselves.

But the **Israelites** had masrched on **dry land**
    through the **midst** of the **sea**,
    with the **water** like a **wall** to their right and to their **left**.
Thus the Lord saved **Israel** on that day
    from the **power** of the **Egyptians**. »

The Lord parts the sea, through the intercession of Moses stretching his staff out over the mighty waters. After the Israelites had marched through on dry land, and after the waters receded back upon the Egyptians, swallowing them up in defeat, the Book of Exodus reports that the Israelites feared and believed in the Lord and in his servant Moses. This stands as a statement of being a newly constructed people. Having passed through the waters, the Israelites are now committing themselves to the new way of life that God has in store for them. The song that the Israelites sing with joy, "I will sing to the Lord, for he is gloriously triumphant; horse and chariot he has cast into the sea," is the verbal recognition that the Israelites want to be God's people. Although we know that the story of Exodus proceeds with many failures on the part of the people to remain faithful to God, here at the Red Sea we have the establishment of a new nation. What remains to be discovered by the Israelites is that freedom from slavery in Egypt is not simply liberation from oppression; it is to discover that true freedom is found in loving and serving God.

READING IV The next stop in our hearing of salvation history comes from the context of the Babylonian Exile, which can be dated to 586 BC, and the destruction of Solomon's Temple in the city of Jerusalem. After the northern tribes of Israel fell to the Assyrians earlier in the previous century, the two stronger tribes in the southern part of the nation (Judah and Israel) fell into the hands of the Babylonians, who forced the people from their land and deported them as slaves to Babylon to the east. Just as was the situation for many of the Israelites during their captivity in Egypt,

"Power": Its manifestation defines this reading.

When Israel saw the **Egyptians** lying dead on the **seashore**
and beheld the great **power** that the LORD
had **shown** against the **Egyptians**,
they **feared** the LORD and **believed** in him and in his
servant **Moses**.

The reading concludes with the words of a song. The song is triumphant, but its contents are a little grim. The entire song is sung as the responsorial psalm.

Then **Moses** and the Israelites sang this song to the LORD:
I will **sing** to the Lord, for he is **gloriously** triumphant;
horse and **chariot** he has **cast** into the **sea**.

For meditation and context:

RESPONSORIAL PSALM   Exodus 15:1–2, 3–4, 5–6, 17–18 (1b)

R. Let us sing to the Lord; he has covered himself in glory.

I will sing to the LORD, for he is gloriously
triumphant;
horse and chariot he has cast into the sea.
My strength and my courage is the LORD,
and he has been my savior.
He is my God, I praise him;
the God of my father, I extol him.

The LORD is a warrior,
LORD is his name!
Pharaoh's chariots and army he hurled
into the sea;
the elite of his officers were submerged in
the Red Sea.

The flood waters covered them,
they sank into the depths like a stone.
Your right hand, O LORD, magnificent
in power,
your right hand, O LORD, has
shattered the enemy.

You brought in the people you redeemed
and planted them on the mountain
of your inheritance—
the place where you made your seat,
O LORD,
the sanctuary, LORD, which your
hands established.
The LORD shall reign forever and ever.

READING IV   Isaiah 54:5–14

Isaiah = ī-ZAY-uh

An exhortatory reading in which the prophet speaks on behalf of God to the people, seeking to intensify the intimacy between them.

A reading from the Book of the Prophet Isaiah

The **One** who has become your **husband** is your **Maker**;
his **name** is the Lord of hosts;
your **redeemer** is the **Holy One** of Israel,
called **God** of all the **earth**.

---

many of the Hebrews during the Babylonian captivity found it easy to assimilate into the surrounding culture and were therefore able to take advantage of the situation. Many found their new life to be much more rewarding than they had previously experienced in Jerusalem. And for those Hebrews born in Babylon, this was the only life they knew.

Thus, the reading from Isaiah, which is considered the work of Deutero-Isaiah, and was almost certainly constructed in the final days of the Babylonian captivity, is written as part of a sweeping call to the exiles to return home to their land. Because the peo-

ple have long been surrounded by the gods of the Babylonians, it is necessary to remind the people just who their God is. Isaiah reminds the people that God is their "husband," their "Maker," "your redeemer," the "God of all the earth." First and foremost, Isaiah wants to restore the people's faith in God's fidelity. Like a wife who has been cast off and abandoned, yet wants nothing more than her husband to return, so too does God yearn for his people's restoration.

Isaiah continues to describe God's invitation to Israel to come home with powerful relational language in which God

admits to having allowed Israel to fall from his grace. Thus, speaking in the Lord's name, Isaiah writes: "For a brief moment I abandoned you, but with great tenderness I will take you back." God recognizes that his wrath may have gotten the better of him when he likens the exile to Noah and the flood. There he promised that he would never again destroy creation. Certainly, the exiles believed that the destruction of their Temple and all of Jerusalem signaled that God, in his wrath, was once again punishing them for some grave sin. But God does not wish them to see their situation in this light

The core of the reading is this simile comparing the people ("you") to a forsaken wife whom God, as the husband, wants back. The conflict described and the strife implied in this passage should be familiar to many in the assembly. Don't get too dramatic with your proclamation, but don't shy away from its implications.

God promises peace, despite previously turbulent times.

Many jewels. The names of jewels are appealing to say and hear.

carnelians = kahr-NEEL-yuhnz = red semiprecious stones

carbuncles = KAHR-bung-k*lz = bright red gems

The peace God promises is like the jewels: enduring, precious, and consoling.

The LORD calls you **back**,
    like a **wife** forsaken and **grieved** in spirit,
    a wife **married** in youth and then **cast off**,
    says your God.
For a **brief moment** I **abandoned** you,
    but with **great tenderness** I will take you **back**.
In an **outburst** of wrath, for a **moment**
    I hid my **face** from you;
but with enduring **love** I take **pity** on you,
    says the LORD, your **redeemer**.
This is for me like the **days** of Noah,
    when I **swore** that the waters of Noah
    should **never again** deluge the **earth**;
so I have **sworn** not to be **angry** with you,
    or to **rebuke** you.
Though the **mountains** leave their **place**
    and the **hills** be shaken,
my **love** shall never **leave** you
    nor my **covenant** of peace be **shaken**,
    says the LORD, who has **mercy** on you.
O **afflicted** one, storm-battered and **unconsoled**,
    I lay your **pavements** in **carnelians**,
    and your **foundations** in **sapphires**;
I will make your **battlements** of **rubies**,
    your **gates** of **carbuncles**,
    and all your **walls** of precious **stones**.
All your **children** shall be **taught** by the LORD,
    and **great** shall be the **peace** of your **children**.
In **justice** shall you be **established**,
    far from the **fear** of **oppression**,
    where **destruction** cannot come **near** you.

---

anymore: "so I have sworn not to be angry with you, or to rebuke you."

The final portion of this reading dwells not on the afflictions of the past but with great hope for the future. The Lord promises his people the gift of his mercy and the assurance that his love will never abandon them again. The Lord will provide the strength for the founding of a restored nation. He will lay the stones of the foundation and will provide for the building of its walls. Perhaps the greatest gift of all is that the Lord promises that the children of the new Israel will be taught by the Lord himself, so great is the personal relationship he wishes to establish with them: "and great shall be the peace of your children." The words and the tone of Isaiah's prophecy make the invitation to return one that would be foolish to ignore; no matter what fortune has been discovered in Babylon, nothing can match the promises the Lord makes to the people in his desire to make them his own possession once again.

READING V Each year in the context of the Easter Vigil, we hear Isaiah calling the thirsty and the poor to "come to the water!" We hear these words knowing that in a matter of moments the Church will immerse men and women into the life-giving waters of Baptism. These are waters that do not discriminate and do not distinguish male from female, rich from poor, young from old. These waters equalize and make all people members of Christ. Whether one comes to Baptism a millionaire or a pauper, one comes out of the

For meditation and context:

RESPONSORIAL PSALM   Psalm 30:2, 4, 5–6, 11–12, 13 (2a)

R. I will praise you, Lord, for you have rescued me.

I will extol you, O LORD, for you drew
　　me clear
　　and did not let my enemies rejoice
　　　　over me.
O LORD, you brought me up from the
　　netherworld;
　　you preserved me from among those
　　　　going down into the pit.

Sing praise to the LORD, you his
　　faithful ones,
　　and give thanks to his holy name.
For his anger lasts but a moment;
　　a lifetime, his good will.
At nightfall, weeping enters in,
　　but with the dawn, rejoicing.

Hear, O LORD, and have pity on me;
　　O LORD, be my helper.
You changed my mourning into dancing;
　　O LORD, my God, forever will I give
　　　　you thanks.

READING V   Isaiah 55:1–11

Isaiah = ī-ZAY-uh

An exhortatory reading in which God through the voice of the prophet Isaiah promises forgiveness. The message of this reading is direct and should be relatable to many in your assembly.

"You who have no money": Even in affluent parishes, there are people who have felt this pinch. God is speaking directly to these people.

A reading from the Book of the Prophet Isaiah

Thus says the LORD:
All **you** who are **thirsty**,
　　come to the **water**!
You who have no **money**,
　　come, receive **grain** and **eat**;
come, without **paying** and without **cost**,
　　drink **wine** and **milk**!
Why spend your **money** for what is not **bread**,
　　your **wages** for what fails to **satisfy**?
Heed me, and you shall **eat** well,
　　you shall **delight** in rich **fare**.
Come to me **heedfully**,
　　listen, that you may have **life**.
I will **renew** with you the everlasting **covenant**,
　　the **benefits** assured to **David**.

water a disciple of Christ. Thus, the waters of Baptism are ultimately about God's justice, a justice that does not condemn but instead desires right relationship. In God's Kingdom, where right relationship prevails, all will delight in rich foods and will come to know what truly satisfies.

Following upon the prophecy just heard from the previous chapter of the Book of Isaiah, the prophecy uttered here continues to be one of great hope. Whereas the previous reading made the invitation for the people to return to Jerusalem one that would be hard to refuse, now Isaiah's words are meant to embrace a wider audience. The people's return to the Land will serve as a witness to all the nations of God's great abundance. The nations of the world will stand in awe of all that God has done, and Israel will act as missionaries to attract people to God, who says to those still in exile: "so shall you summon a nation you knew not; and nations that knew you not shall run to you." Not only is the return of the people about the establishment of peace in their homeland, it is meant to serve as the means by which the whole world will come to be at peace. The invitation to come to the water goes out to all the inhabitants of the earth.

Toward the middle of the passage, we hear yet another invitation that is meant to go out to the whole world: "Seek the Lord while he may be found, call him while he is near." The prophet's words continue to elaborate on the theme of developing a relationship with the One who is always faithful. All one has to do is to abandon former ways, turn to the Lord, and accept his gift of mercy. While the cost of such a relationship is not based upon wealth or material possessions, it does require the desire

As I made him a **witness** to the **peoples**,
   a **leader** and commander of **nations**,
so shall you **summon** a nation you knew **not**,
   and **nations** that knew you not shall **run** to you,
because of the LORD, your **God**,
   the **Holy One** of Israel, who has **glorified** you.

Seek the LORD while he may be **found**,
   call him while he is **near**.
Let the **scoundrel** forsake his **way**,
   and the **wicked man** his **thoughts**;
let him **turn** to the LORD for **mercy**;
   to our **God**, who is generous in **forgiving**.
For my **thoughts** are not **your** thoughts,
   nor are your ways **my** ways, says the LORD.
As **high** as the heavens are above the **earth**,
   so **high** are my **ways** above your **ways**
   and my **thoughts** above your **thoughts**.

For **just** as from the **heavens**
   the rain and snow come **down**
and do not **return** there
   till they have **watered** the earth,
   making it **fertile** and **fruitful**,
giving **seed** to the one who **sows**
   and **bread** to the one who **eats**,
so shall my word be
   that goes **forth** from my **mouth**;
my word shall not **return** to me **void**,
   but shall do my **will**,
   achieving the **end** for which I **sent** it.

Sidebar notes:

"Seek the Lord while he may be found": This command speaks to the hope inherent in this reading. We hope it's true, that God may be found, especially when we call him.

Forgiveness. This is the heart of this reading.

Even stresses on the words in this line.

---

to forsake the past and to try to discern the Lord's ways.

Those who are preparing to be immersed in the waters of Baptism as well as the whole Church, who prepares to renew baptismal promises, hear the words of Isaiah as a call to ongoing conversion. Isaiah suggests that the word of God nurtures the earth, making it "fertile and fruitful." The word of God is meant to be productive, "giving seed to the one who sows and bread to the one who eats." There is nothing unsatisfying about the word of God that is freely given in abundance. All that is necessary is for hearts to attempt to seek such generosity. We look at the men and women who hunger for Baptism this night, and we see evidence of such conversion, seeking the Lord "while he is near."

READING VI | The sixth reading is a rather obscure poem/hymn from Baruch in praise of Wisdom. While the poem opens with the acknowledgement that the Babylonian exile still lingers in the minds and hearts of the Hebrew people, its basic theme centers around an invitation to embrace the Law as a lasting treasure and the source of life. Once again, placing this reading into the overall context of salvation history, too often do people forsake the commands of the Law by being distracted by other concerns of this world. Baruch reminds us of the truth that attuning one's heart to Wisdom, which he says is "the book of the precepts of God, the law that endures forever," will never disappoint.

Baruch establishes the authority of Wisdom in the middle stanza of this poem. Here he suggests that just as God created every aspect of the world to reflect the glory of God, so too has God "probed her

For meditation and context:

RESPONSORIAL PSALM Isaiah 12:2–3, 4, 5–6 (3)

R. You will draw water joyfully from the springs of salvation.

God indeed is my savior;
    I am confident and unafraid.
My strength and my courage is the LORD,
    and he has been my savior.
With joy you will draw water
    at the fountain of salvation.

Give thanks to the LORD, acclaim his name;
    among the nations make known
      his deeds,
    proclaim how exalted is his name.

Sing praise to the LORD for his glorious
    achievement;
    let this be known throughout all
      the earth.
Shout with exultation, O city of Zion,
    for great in your midst
    is the Holy One of Israel!

READING VI Baruch 3:9–15, 32—4:4

Baruch = buh-ROOK

An exhortation on wisdom, personified in this reading in her ancient feminine principle. A powerful reminder.

The reading makes use of rhetorical questions. Use these questions—this first one stretches over several lines—to organize the pace of your proclamation.

Take note of the questions here.

A reading from the Book of the Prophet Baruch

Hear, O Israel, the **commandments** of life:
    listen, and know **prudence**!
How **is it**, Israel,
    that you are in the **land** of your **foes**,
    grown **old** in a foreign **land**,
defiled with the **dead**,
    accounted with those **destined** for the **netherworld**?
You have **forsaken** the fountain of **wisdom**!
    Had you **walked** in the way of **God**,
    you would have **dwelt** in enduring **peace**.
Learn where prudence is,
    where **strength**, where **understanding**;
that you may know **also**
    where are length of **days**, and **life**,
    where **light** of the eyes, and **peace**.
Who has found the place of **wisdom**,
    who has entered into her **treasuries**?

(Wisdom) by his knowledge." Similarly, just as every part of creation responds to the voice of God with the words "Here we are!" so is the Wisdom of God contained in the law meant to help all creation respond to God with joy. Baruch states that God "has traced out the whole way of understanding, and has given her to Jacob, his servant, to Israel, his beloved Son." If human beings are meant to be good stewards over all the things of the world, then human beings also must cherish the gift that is the Law.

Baruch ends the poem by suggesting that Wisdom has been with creation from the foundation of the world. To all those who know of her, a choice is to be made: "All who cling to her will live, but those will die who forsake her." The people God has chosen as his own is indeed richly blessed because they have been given the knowledge of the Law. This is their prized possession, the treasure they should cherish above all things. The challenge is quite clear for Israel as of old as it is for us today: "Give not your glory to another." Follow the commandments of God as the source of unfailing light, and the way of darkness will never prevail.

READING VII We have heard this night from the prophet Isaiah and from Baruch concerning the crushing blow dealt to Israel as a result of the Babylonian Exile; the prophet Ezekiel also writes from this perspective. In this reading, the cause of the exile is the misdeeds committed by the people, especially idol worship. Rather than seeing the people of Israel as the victims of the Babylonian conquest, they are responsible for defiling the land and bringing ruin to the nation. Furthermore, according to the word of the Lord spoken to Ezekiel, it is not the

"Her" refers to Wisdom, *Hokhmah* in Hebrew, *Sophia* in Greek, always personified in feminine form in the ancient imagination.

The One who knows all things **knows** her;
    he has **probed** her by his **knowledge**—
the One who established the **earth** for all time,
    and **filled** it with four-footed **beasts**;
he who **dismisses** the light, and it **departs**,
    calls it, and it obeys him **trembling**;
before whom the **stars** at their posts
    shine and **rejoice**;
when he **calls** them, they **answer**, "**Here** we are!"
    shining with joy for their **Maker**.
Such is our **God**;
    no **other** is to be **compared** to him:
he has **traced out** the whole way of understanding,
    and has **given** her to Jacob, his **servant**,
    to **Israel**, his beloved **son**.

Wisdom's divinity—the part she plays in God's creative imagination—is implied in this closing passage.

Since then she has **appeared** on **earth**,
    and **moved** among people.
She is the **book** of the precepts of **God**,
    the **law** that endures **forever**;
all who **cling** to her will **live**,
    but those will **die** who **forsake** her.
Turn, O Jacob, and **receive** her:
    walk by her light toward **splendor**.
Give not your **glory** to another,
    your **privileges** to an alien **race**.
Blessed are **we**, O Israel;
    for what **pleases** God is **known** to us!

Babylonians that expel the people from the Land. Rather, it is the Lord himself who "scattered" the people to captivity, "dispersing them over foreign lands."

In the covenantal relationship between God and his Chosen People, the bond between them is the gift of the Land that God makes their own. For the people to act in such a way that takes away from the sacredness of the Land is a true act of idolatry; it exhibits a forgetfulness of God. However, the Lord also recognizes that the dispersion of his people also serves as a means for profaning his name. For when

people from other nations see that the Chosen People have been forced from their land, they mock and ridicule the relationship God has with those he has chosen. In this way, nations doubt God's power and authority and question the abundant generosity from which his gifts flow, for what kind of God would abandon his people and disperse them?

Thus, there is only one solution to such a dilemma, only one way to restore the honor of God's holy name: restore the people to the Land. The Lord makes it clear: his desire to return Israel back to their

home is not out of concern for them, but rather "for the sake of my holy name," spoken throughout the world. What the prophecy of Ezekiel suggests here is that the restoration of Israel serves to universalize God's desire to draw the entire world to himself. No longer will he simply show concern for his people, but now God will see to it that all nations seek to rid themselves of idolatry and strive to speak his holy name.

God will perform a sign for all to see that will make certain that his name be profaned no more. This sign will be the gathering together again of all the people

For meditation and context:

RESPONSORIAL PSALM   Psalm 19:8, 9, 10, 11 (John 6:68c)

R. Lord, you have the words of everlasting life.

The law of the LORD is perfect,
  refreshing the soul;
the decree of the LORD is trustworthy,
  giving wisdom to the simple.

The precepts of the LORD are right,
  rejoicing the heart;
the command of the LORD is clear,
  enlightening the eye.

The fear of the LORD is pure,
  enduring forever;
the ordinances of the LORD are true,
  all of them just.

They are more precious than gold,
  than a heap of purest gold;
sweeter also than syrup
  or honey from the comb.

READING VII   Ezekiel 36:16–17a, 18–28

A reading from the Book of the Prophet Ezekiel

Ezekiel = ee-ZEE-kee-uhl

A challenging exhortatory reading. Challenging because the tone of this passage is largely wrathful and accusatory. The language in this reading is so charged, the wrath will come through. It consists almost entirely of the words of God spoken to Ezekiel.

Here the tone is clear: the words *fury*, *defiled*, and *profane* set that tone.

The **word** of the LORD **came** to me, saying:
  Son of man, when the **house** of Israel lived in their **land**,
  they **defiled** it by their **conduct** and **deeds**.
Therefore I poured **out** my fury **upon** them
  because of the **blood** that they poured **out** on the **ground**,
  and because they **defiled** it with idols.
I **scattered** them among the **nations**,
  dispersing them over foreign **lands**;
  according to their **conduct** and **deeds** I **judged** them.
But when they **came** among the nations wherever they **came**,
  they served to **profane** my holy **name**,
  because it was **said** of them: "**These** are the **people** of
    the **LORD**,
  yet they had to **leave** their land."
So I have **relented** because of my holy **name**
  which the **house** of Israel **profaned**
  among the **nations** where they **came**.
Therefore say to the house of Israel: **Thus** says the Lord GOD:
  Not for **your sakes** do I act, house of Israel,
  but for the **sake** of my holy **name**,
  which you **profaned** among the **nations** to which you **came**.

God is so worked up, he begins quoting himself!

dispersed from the Land. God tells the people that he will "sprinkle clean water" upon them, cleansing them from their past sins. In this symbolic act of purification, the Lord makes a new creation. Making the people a new nation is seen further in God giving the people a "new heart" and a "new spirit." And it is not just any spirit that God will place in them, it is his very own. This is so that the people will abide by God's commandments and decrees. Thus, the sign of salvation for the world in this prophecy of

Ezekiel is found in the words of the very last sentence: "You shall live in the land I gave your fathers; you shall be my people, and I will be your God." When all the world sees the relationship between God and his people flourishing, they too will profess his holy name.

EPISTLE   It is important to take note of a liturgical shift that takes place in the Liturgy of the Word at the Easter Vigil after the final reading from the Old Testament: the candles at the altar are lit, the bells sound, and the assembly joins together in singing the Gloria. In our hearing of the various readings from the Old Testament, we have been invited to contemplate the mystery of salvation history. Ours is a God intimately involved with the goodness of his creation, who leads people

Note the shift into the future tense. The tone doesn't change significantly, but from here to the conclusion of the reading, God is speaking about the future.

I will **prove** the holiness of my great **name**, profaned among
 the **nations**,
 in whose **midst** you have **profaned** it.
Thus the **nations** shall know that **I** am the LORD, says the
 Lord GOD,
 when in their **sight** I prove my **holiness** through **you**.
For I will take you **away** from among the **nations**,
 gather you from **all** the foreign lands,
 and bring you **back** to your own land.

God wants to cleanse the future of its impurities.

I will **sprinkle** clean water upon you
 to **cleanse** you from all your **impurities**,
 and from **all** your idols I will **cleanse** you.

And give people a new heart.

I will give you a new **heart** and place a new spirit **within** you,
 taking from your bodies your **stony hearts**
 and **giving** you **natural** hearts.
I will put my **spirit** within you and make you **live** by my
 statutes,
 careful to observe my **decrees**.

God's hope: this is his covenant.

You shall **live** in the land I **gave** your fathers;
 you shall be my **people**, and I will be your **God**.

For meditation and context:

RESPONSORIAL PSALM   Psalm 42:3, 5; 43:3, 4 (2)

R. Like a deer that longs for running streams, my soul longs for you, my God.

Athirst is my soul for God, the living God.
 When shall I go and behold the face
  of God?

I went with the throng
 and led them in procession to the house
  of God,
amid loud cries of joy and thanksgiving,
 with the multitude keeping festival.

Or:

Send forth your light and your fidelity;
 they shall lead me on
and bring me to your holy mountain,
 to your dwelling-place.

Then will I go in to the altar of God,
 the God of my gladness and joy;
then will I give you thanks upon the harp,
 O God, my God!

---

out of bondage into freedom, who asks only that we love him in return for his many expressions of care and kindness. But now, our telling of salvation history approaches the pinnacle in our preparation for hearing from the New Testament, for we Christians believe that salvation history comes to a definitive resolution through the Incarnation of Jesus, his life and ministry on earth, and the ultimate gift of his Paschal Mystery (his suffering, death, and Resurrection). Our joy is not to be contained, because we are not simply waiting for some future savior. Our

Savior has already appeared and is among us still; he will not abandon us until the day when all things will be gathered together as one in God's great love. We live in a new age.

Paul's address to the Christians at Rome could very well be used as a piece of final catechesis for the elect as they prepare to be immersed in the waters of Baptism. The question that opens Paul's address could be asked directly to them: "Brothers and sisters: are you unaware that we who were baptized into Christ Jesus were baptized into his death?" How good it

is for not only the elect, but for the entire Church as well, to be reminded that Baptism entails a fundamental death. And it is not a death that occurs only once, but takes place again and again as a Christian learns over a lifetime the art of self-sacrifice.

To add to the notion of Baptism as death, Paul employs the image of being "buried" with Christ. In our contemporary culture, in which burial practices are rapidly changing, with many people preferring cremation over burying the body, the notion of burial here suggests another level of

For meditation and context:

RESPONSORIAL PSALM   Isaiah 12:2–3, 4bcd, 5–6 (3)

R. You will draw water joyfully from the springs of salvation.

God indeed is my savior;
  I am confident and unafraid.
My strength and my courage is the LORD,
  and he has been my savior.
With joy you will draw water
  at the fountain of salvation.

Give thanks to the LORD, acclaim his name;
  among the nations make known his deeds,
  proclaim how exalted is his name.

Sing praise to the LORD for his glorious
    achievement;
  let this be known throughout all the earth.
Shout with exultation, O city of Zion,
  for great in your midst
  is the Holy One of Israel!

Or:

For meditation and context:

RESPONSORIAL PSALM   Psalm 51:12–13, 14–15, 18–19 (12a)

R. Create a clean heart in me, O God.

A clean heart create for me, O God,
  and a steadfast spirit renew within me.
Cast me not out from your presence,
  and your Holy Spirit take not from me.

Give me back the joy of your salvation,
  and a willing spirit sustain in me.
I will teach transgressors your ways,
  and sinners shall return to you.

For you are not pleased with sacrifices;
  should I offer a holocaust, you would not
    accept it.
My sacrifice, O God, is a contrite spirit;
  a heart contrite and humbled, O God, you
    will not spurn.

EPISTLE   Romans 6:3–11

A reading from the Letter of Saint Paul to the Romans

Brothers and **sisters**:
Are you **unaware** that **we** who were **baptized** into Christ **Jesus**
  were **baptized** into his **death**?
We were **indeed** buried with him through **baptism** into **death**,
  so that, **just** as Christ was **raised** from the dead
  by the **glory** of the Father,
  we **too** might live in **newness** of life.

A didactic reading focused on Baptism. Because the Easter Vigil often includes the Baptism of the elect, you should imagine you are speaking directly to those about to be baptized.

Paul begins by making a connection between Baptism, life and death, and resurrection. These are the terms that define this passage from his letter to the Romans.

responsibility. Not only does one have to die to self when immersed in the waters of Baptism, one must also be ready to bury the past. It is precisely in burial that God can perform the mighty task of raising to new life.

Paul continues his address by linking death to self with the abandonment of sin. This is very important for Paul; he believes that membership in Christ necessitates ridding oneself of attractions and allurements that might distract from living fully the new

life of Christ. When Paul writes "We know that our old self was crucified with him, so that our sinful body might be done away with, that we might no longer be in slavery to sin," we might very well hear in the background the prophecy of Ezekiel, who told the people that the Lord would place in them a "new heart" and his very own spirit. The bottom line for Paul is that Baptism entails becoming a new creation in Christ— a "living for God in Christ Jesus"—which

means that nothing in life can be the same as it was before Baptism.

GOSPEL   Having gathered around the Easter fire, having been led into the church by light of the Paschal Candle, and having heard the ancient Scriptures that paint the broad themes of salvation history, we are now flooded with the word of the New Covenant. Moments prior, the assembly heard the address of Paul on the topic of Baptism, and now the

> For if we have **grown** into union with him through a **death**
>   like his,
>   we shall also be **united** with him in the **resurrection**.
> We know that our **old self** was **crucified** with him,
>   so that our sinful **body** might be done **away** with,
>   that we might no longer be in **slavery** to **sin**.
> For a **dead** person has been **absolved** from sin.
> If, then, we have **died** with Christ,
>   we **believe** that we shall also **live** with him.
> We know that **Christ**, **raised** from the **dead**, **dies** no more;
>   death no longer has **power** over him.
> As to his **death**, he **died** to **sin once** and for **all**;
>   as to his **life**, he lives for **God**.
> Consequently, **you too** must think of yourselves as being **dead**
>   to sin
>   and **living** for God in Christ **Jesus**.

To die with Christ is also to live with him, to be resurrected with him. Baptism is rebirth.

Paul reemphasizes this point about resurrection in these concluding words.

For meditation and context:

RESPONSORIAL PSALM Psalm 118:1–2, 16–17, 22–23

R. Alleluia, alleluia, alleluia.

Give thanks to the LORD, for he is good,
  for his mercy endures forever.
Let the house of Israel say,
  "His mercy endures forever."

The right hand of the LORD has struck
  with power;
  the right hand of the LORD is exalted.

I shall not die, but live,
  and declare the works of the LORD.

The stone which the builders rejected
  has become the cornerstone.
By the LORD has this been done;
  it is wonderful in our eyes.

---

faithful participate in the beautiful scene of a new day depicted in Mark's Gospel. "The Sabbath was now over" are the words that open this passage, in which Mary Magdalene and the other women come to the tomb for the purpose of anointing Jesus' body. Mark is very specific about the timing of this event: "Very early when the sun had risen, on the first day of the week." We, the Church, gathered to vigil and wait prayerfully for the break of dawn and the joy of Easter morn, are meant to recognize that we have begun a new day.

Yet there is great anxiety expressed among the women as they make their way to the grave. They are concerned that they will lack the strength to roll the stone away from the entrance to the tomb. This fear, along with Mark deliberately describing the stone as "very large," suggests to the reader that something spectacular has taken place here. No ordinary person could possibly have rolled the stone away.

Although the women see that the stone had been moved, they express no reaction; instead they quickly run inside,

where they were "utterly amazed" at seeing a young man wearing a white robe sitting inside the tomb. What did the women think initially when they saw this him? Did they suppose that he was responsible for removing the stone from the entrance and hiding the body somewhere? As he begins to speak to them, they undoubtedly recognize him as an angelic messenger. He tells them, "Do not be amazed!" Since the women remain silent throughout, we can surmise that they were filled with fear. Mark affirms this in the last verse of the

Magdalene = MAG-duh-leen
Salome = suh-LOH-mee

A narrative reading from the conclusion of Mark's Gospel. The perspective is important: We are seeing the scene through the eyes of three women.

Read the names of these women with care.

Note with your voice the strangeness of the young man in the white robe.

Here is the message of the young man in the white robe. "Do not be amazed!"

GOSPEL   Mark 16:1–7

A reading from the holy Gospel according to Mark

When the **sabbath** was over,
    Mary **Magdalene**, **Mary**, the mother of **James**, and **Salome**
    bought **spices** so that they might go and **anoint** him.
Very **early** when the sun had **risen**,
    on the first **day** of the **week**, they came to the **tomb**.
They were **saying** to one another,
    "**Who** will roll back the **stone** for us
    from the **entrance** to the **tomb**?"
When they looked **up**,
    they **saw** that the **stone** had been rolled **back**;
    it was **very large**.
On entering the tomb they saw a young **man**
    sitting on the right **side**, clothed in a **white robe**,
    and they were **utterly amazed**.
He said to them, "Do **not** be amazed!
You seek **Jesus** of Nazareth, the **crucified**.
He has been **raised**; he **is not here**.
Behold the place where they **laid** him.
But go and tell his **disciples** and **Peter**,
    'He is going **before** you to **Galilee**;
    there you will **see** him, as he **told** you.'"

passage that has been omitted for proclamation in the liturgical assembly: "Then they went out and fled from the tomb, seized with trembling and bewilderment. They said nothing to anyone, for they were afraid" (16:8).

The angel's instructions to the women are both brief and very clear. First, he reassures them that "he has been raised." Next, he invites the women to inspect the tomb and to see for themselves that "he is not here." Finally, the young man clad in white tells the women to "go and tell" Peter and the other disciples that they are to meet

him in Galilee where he will appear to them. Because Mark's Gospel was written for a Roman community, with the Roman centurion being the first to announce Jesus' true identity, it is fitting that this Gospel would place the appearance of the Risen Lord at the location where his ministry began rather than at the tomb. This serves as a sort of universalizing of the Resurrection appearances. Just as the ministry of Jesus testifies to his willingness to journey into the world to meet people along the way rather than demanding that people come to him, so will his Resurrection appear-

ances have this missionary bent. The Risen Lord goes out to meet his disciples; they do not come to him. S. W.

EASTER SUNDAY

LECTIONARY #42

READING I   Acts of the Apostles 10:34a, 37–43

A reading from the Acts of the Apostles

Peter **proceeded** to speak and said:
   "You **know** what has **happened** all over **Judea**,
   beginning in **Galilee** after the **baptism**
   that **John** preached,
   how **God** anointed **Jesus** of **Nazareth**
   with the Holy **Spirit** and **power**.
He went **about** doing **good**
   and healing all those **oppressed** by the **devil**,
   for **God** was **with** him.
We are **witnesses** of all that he **did**
   both in the country of the **Jews** and in **Jerusalem**.
They put him to **death** by hanging him on a **tree**.
This man God raised on the third day and **granted** that he
      be **visible**,
   not to all the people, but to **us**,
   the **witnesses** chosen by **God** in advance,
   who **ate** and drank with him after he **rose** from the dead.
He **commissioned** us to preach to the **people**
   and **testify** that he is the one **appointed** by God
   as **judge** of the **living** and the **dead**.
To him all the **prophets** bear **witness**,
   that everyone who **believes** in him
   will receive **forgiveness** of sins through his **name**."

Judea = joo-DEE-uh

A didactic reading in the form of a narrative. Peter is telling an assembled crowd the story of Jesus' life and the important lessons learned from his instructions.

Here is the first point: Jesus went about doing good.

Here is the second point: He was crucified.

Here is the third point: He was resurrected. Mostly even stresses on the words in this line.

Here is the fourth point: He commissioned Peter and the other disciples to preach.

And finally, the fifth point: If you believe in Jesus, your sins will be forgiven. This point speaks directly to the assembly.

There are options for today's readings. Contact your parish staff to learn which readings will be used.

READING I   Peter's speech concerning "what has happened all over Judea" most certainly stems from catechetical preaching in the early Church and has been accommodated by Luke to fit Peter's address in the house of Cornelius. This house represents a Gentile audience, therefore Peter attempts to be all-encompassing in summarizing the events surrounding the life and ministry of Jesus. Peter's speech is crafted to be evangelizing; his words suggest that it would be foolish not to give oneself over to a life of discipleship.

This discourse underscores the credibility of the Apostles: "We are witness of all that he did both in the country of the Jews and in Jerusalem." This is particularly important for the effectiveness of Peter's speech. Because they witnessed the ministry of the Lord, his death on the cross, and numerous encounters with his resurrected body, these witnesses make present the deeds of the Lord. Peter suggests that Jesus commissioned his followers to preach, to witness, to judge, and to herald the "forgiveness of sins through his name." There is no denying the great responsibility handed on to those who have been called to testify to the Lord's Resurrection.

Another form of witness that Peter provides in this address is his highlighting the actions of eating and drinking with Jesus after his Resurrection. The theme of sharing a meal is seen throughout Luke's Gospel and occurs in Acts as a means of demonstrating the particular people that God has carved out in calling forth witnesses.

For meditation and context:

RESPONSORIAL PSALM   Psalm 118:1–2, 16–17, 22–23 (24)

R. This is the day the Lord has made; let us rejoice and be glad.
or
R. Alleluia.

Give thanks to the LORD, for he is good,
   for his mercy endures forever.
Let the house of Israel say,
   "His mercy endures forever."

"The right hand of the LORD has struck
   with power;
   the right hand of the LORD is exalted.

I shall not die, but live,
   and declare the works of the LORD.

The stone which the builders rejected
   has become the cornerstone.
By the LORD has this been done;
   it is wonderful in our eyes.

READING II   Colossians 3:1–4

Colossians = kuh-LOSH-uhnz
An exhortatory reading, compressed in its length but powerful in its message.
The focal word in this reading is "above."

A reading from the Letter of Saint Paul to the Colossians

Brothers and **sisters**:
If then you were raised with **Christ**, seek what is **above**,
   where **Christ** is seated at the **right hand** of God.
Think of what is **above**, not of what is on **earth**.
For you have **died**, and your **life** is hidden with **Christ** in God.
When Christ your life **appears**,
   then **you too** will appear with him in **glory**.

Or:

The syntax here is strange. Be sure to practice.

This was granted "not to all the people, but to us." Luke substantiates his catechesis on the mystery of the Lord with the authority of Peter and the Apostles.

As Peter concludes his preaching, he leaves those assembled in Cornelius' household with an unspoken choice that they must make: to believe in this man raised up by God on the third day or not. In some ways, Peter makes the choice a simple one. Since the prophets have foretold of his coming for many ages, and because belief brings with it the forgiveness of sins, it would be foolish not to believe.

READING II | **Colossians.** As Paul so often does in his letters, he lists moral imperatives as the outcome of a theological truth. In the case of these four sentences from his letter to the Colossians, being raised with Christ entails striving for things that are above. The things of this world are no longer to hold the attention of those refashioned into Christ. Instead, those who are grafted onto Christ are meant to see life from the perspective of being "seated at the right hand of God."

Nevertheless, Paul hints at the reality that living a life focused on "what is above"

is no easy task, as it will not be possible to make sense of a life "hidden with Christ" until the glory of his return. Baptismal life is best understood as a life of vigilance. Those baptized into Christ are meant to ask themselves how their lives manifest the presence of Christ. Although we do not hear of them in this liturgical proclamation of Colossians, Paul follows his reminder that Christianity entails a new worldview with a list of vices that the baptized must avoid at all cost (Colossians 3:5–8). By leading a life that is so contrary to the ways of the world,

Corinthians = kohr-IN-thee-uhnz

An exhortatory reading, compressed in its length but powerful in its message.

Yeast is Paul's metaphor for Christ's sacrifice. Just as there would be no feast without bread, so there is no spiritual life without leaven.

For meditation and context:

TO KEEP IN MIND

Sequences originated as extensions of the sung Alleluia before the proclamation of the Gospel, although they precede the Alleluia now. The Easter Sequence is an ancient liturgical hymn that praises Christ, the Paschal victim, for his victory over death. Mary Magdalene recounts her experience at Christ's tomb, proclaiming, "Christ my hope is arisen."

READING II   1 Corinthians 5:6b–8

A reading from the first Letter of Saint Paul to the Corinthians

Brothers and **sisters**:
Do you not **know** that a little **yeast** leavens all the **dough**?
Clear **out** the old **yeast**,
 so that you may become a fresh **batch** of **dough**,
 inasmuch as you are **unleavened**.
For our **paschal lamb**, Christ, has been **sacrificed**.
Therefore, let us **celebrate** the **feast**,
 not with the **old yeast**, the yeast of **malice** and **wickedness**,
 but with the **unleavened bread** of **sincerity** and **truth**.

SEQUENCE   Victimae paschali laudes

Christians, to the Paschal Victim
 Offer your thankful praises!
A Lamb the sheep redeems;
 Christ, who only is sinless,
 Reconciles sinners to the Father.
Death and life have contended in that
  combat stupendous:
 The Prince of life, who died,
  reigns immortal.
Speak, Mary, declaring
 What you saw, wayfaring.

"The tomb of Christ, who is living,
 The glory of Jesus' resurrection;
Bright angels attesting,
 The shroud and napkin resting.
Yes, Christ my hope is arisen;
 to Galilee he goes before you."
Christ indeed from death is risen, our new
  life obtaining.
 Have mercy, victor King, ever reigning!
 Amen. Alleluia.

Christians help to reveal the Lord's glory in a gradual way.

What is most fundamental in this reading is the present effect of Baptism. Death and Resurrection have actually taken place for those baptized into Christ. If these actions have already taken place, then it simply squeezes out behavior that is at odds with life in Christ. Salvation is not something to be waited for in the end, it is something to be lived out every day.

1 Corinthians. Paul's exhortation concerning the need to "clear out the old yeast" in order to "become a fresh batch of dough"

takes place in his condemning the Corinthians for apparent sexual immorality. Paul makes no attempt to withhold his contempt: "I have been told as an undoubted fact that one of you is living with his father's wife" (1 Corinthians 5:1). Not only is this act of incest shameful for the individual accused, but the entire community is judged culpable by Paul. This community of Christians has been noted for being prideful, when in fact, they have reason to fear the Lord's judgment for actions so contrary to the Body of Christ.

The sin of this particular individual constitutes the "old yeast" that has the ability to

leaven all the dough in a manner that betrays the community's participation in Christ's sacrifice. The old yeast has the potential for them to "rise" in a way that nurtures immorality. Nevertheless, Paul's instructions are clear: "Clear out the old yeast, so that you may become a fresh batch of dough."

Paul situates this teaching within the context of celebrating the feast. Just as the Jews keep the annual celebration of Passover, which commemorates their freedom from slavery in Egypt, so Christians celebrate the passage from sin to freedom in the sacrifice of the Lord. Similarly, just as

A narrative reading relating a scene of enduring power.

Magdala = MAG-duh-luh

The detail of the burial cloths is important. When Peter recognizes that the head cloth has been folded up, he understands that the body of Jesus was not stolen (since thieves wouldn't take the time to fold up the linens).

Seeing is believing: belief dawns on them here.

Believing and understanding are two separate things. Understanding can take more time than belief.

GOSPEL   John 20:1–9

A reading from the holy Gospel according to John

On the **first day** of the week,
 Mary of **Magdala** came to the tomb **early** in the morning,
 while it was still **dark**,
 and saw the **stone removed** from the **tomb**.
So she ran and went to Simon **Peter**
 and to the other **disciple** whom Jesus **loved**, and told them,
 "They have **taken** the Lord from the **tomb**,
 and we don't **know** where they **put** him."
So **Peter** and the other **disciple** went out and came to the **tomb**.
They both **ran**, but the other **disciple** ran faster than **Peter**
 and **arrived** at the tomb **first**;
 he bent **down** and saw the **burial cloths** there, but did **not**
  go in.
When Simon **Peter** arrived **after** him,
 he went into the **tomb** and saw the **burial cloths** there,
 and the **cloth** that had covered his **head**,
 not **with** the burial cloths but rolled **up** in a separate **place**.
Then the **other** disciple also went **in**,
 the one who had arrived at the tomb **first**,
 and he **saw** and **believed**.
For they did not yet **understand** the Scripture
 that he had to **rise** from the **dead**.

---

the Jewish community marks the enduring nature of their liberation by eating unleavened bread for seven days after the Passover, so too do Christians mark their freedom in Christ with the unleavened bread of sincerity and truth." Paul's point is that the purification of life that comes with Baptism is meant to be lived out daily by keeping the post-Passover spirit alive by their moral conduct.

 GOSPEL   John is the only evangelist to report Mary Magdalene as the sole visitor to the tomb of Jesus,

"early in the morning," "on the first day of the week." John's simplification of Mary's visit—she neither encounters an angel nor is she invited to peer into the empty tomb—downplays Mary as a primary witness to the Lord's Resurrection. Instead, John places the emphasis on Peter "and the other disciple" who come to see and believe because of what they see at the empty tomb.

There is great urgency in the way Peter and his companion run to the tomb. The unnamed disciple runs faster than Peter and is the first to see the burial cloths. Nevertheless, he refrains from entering the

tomb. This honor belongs to Simon Peter alone. He is to be seen as the first of the Apostles who witness to the Resurrection of the Lord. Peter enters by himself and sees the burial cloths. Only after this does the other disciple enter. John reports that "he saw and believed." It has long been understood that John intended this unnamed disciple to symbolize the believing Christian in general. Therefore, while Peter is the first to "see," it is every faithful and loving Christian who is called to "believe." Because this mysterious disciple is the "beloved disciple," the one who stood by the cross of Christ,

AFTERNOON GOSPEL   Luke 24:13–35

A reading from the holy Gospel according to Luke

That very day, the first **day** of the week,
    two of Jesus' **disciples** were going
    to a **village** seven miles from Jerusalem called **Emmaus**,
    and they were **conversing** about all the things that
        had occurred.
And it **happened** that while they were **conversing** and debating,
    Jesus **himself** drew **near** and walked **with** them,
    but their **eyes** were prevented from **recognizing** him.
He asked them,
    "What are you **discussing** as you walk **along?**"
They **stopped**, looking downcast.
One of them, named **Cleopas**, said to him in **reply**,
    "Are you the **only visitor** to Jerusalem
    who does not **know** of the things
    that have taken **place there** in these days?"
And he **replied** to them, "What **sort** of things?"
They said to him,
    "The **things** that happened to **Jesus** the Nazarene,
    who was a **prophet** mighty in **deed** and **word**
    before **God** and all the **people**,
    how our **chief priests** and rulers both **handed** him **over**
    to a **sentence** of **death** and **crucified** him.
But we were **hoping** that he would be the **one** to redeem Israel;
    and **besides** all this,
    it is now the **third day** since this took **place**.
Some women from our group, however, have **astounded** us:
    they were at the tomb **early** in the morning
    and did not find his **body;**
    they came **back** and reported
    that they had **indeed seen** a vision of **angels**
    who **announced** that he was **alive.** »

A narrative reading with great drama built into it. The focus of the reading is recognition, specifically the time it takes Jesus' two disciples to recognize that he has been raised from the dead. The build-up of the narrative intensifies the excitement and joy of their recognition.

This phrase introduces the motif of recognition that guides the passage. Recognition is connected initially to seeing.

It's interesting that only one of these two disciples are named.

Note that "they" are speaking, both of them, even though it's one unified speech. The purpose of this description of Jesus' deeds and words is to build toward recognition.

Note "a vision of angels." Recognition and seeing are still urgently connected.

---

we are also meant to see the connection between faith and love.

Although the beloved disciple believes, John makes it clear that such is not the universal experience of all of Jesus' followers. Mary Magdalene stands outside the tomb and weeps. However, her agony provides John the opportunity to include an angelic intervention like those found in the synoptic accounts. Interestingly enough, Mary has no reaction to seeing two angels clad in white sitting in the tomb, asking why she is weeping. In fact, she seems quite calm as she explains: "They have taken away my

Lord, and I do not know where they have laid him." In response to this statement, another takes over questioning Mary, who presumes he is the gardener. "Whom are you looking for?" For John, this is the primary evangelical invitation. Mary fails to hear this invitation coming from the lips of the resurrected Lord. Instead, it takes the mention of her name to make her turn to face Jesus and to recognize him at last. With this first sighting of the resurrected Lord, Mary is sent with the mission to tell her good news to the other disciples: "I

have seen the Lord." Mary becomes the first to truly "see and believe."

AFTERNOON GOSPEL | Surely there must have been tears shed and cries of anger uttered on that dusty road. How could something so beautiful as the mission they had been called to crumble so very quickly? Amid their grief and anxiety, the resurrected Lord appears to them and enquires about the nature of their conversation. They are given the opportunity to profess the first post-Resurrection creed. They proclaim Jesus as

Then some of those with us went to the **tomb**
and found things **just as** the women had **described**,
but him they did not **see**."
And he said to them, "**Oh**, how **foolish** you are!
How slow of heart to believe **all** that the prophets **spoke**!
Was it not **necessary** that the Christ should **suffer** these things
and **enter** into his **glory**?"
Then beginning with **Moses** and all the **prophets**,
he **interpreted** to them what referred to him
in all the **Scriptures**.
As they **approached** the village to which they were **going**,
he gave the **impression** that he was going on **farther**.
But they **urged** him, "**Stay** with us,
for it is **nearly evening** and the day is almost **over**."
So he went in to **stay** with them.
And it happened that, while he was **with** them at table,
he took bread, said the **blessing**,
broke it, and **gave** it to them.
With **that** their eyes were **opened** and they **recognized** him,
but he **vanished** from their **sight**.
Then they **said** to each other,
"Were not our **hearts** burning **within** us
while he **spoke** to us on the **way** and opened the **Scriptures**
to us?"
So they set out at once and **returned** to Jerusalem
where they found **gathered together**
the eleven and those with them who were **saying**,
"The **Lord** has truly been **raised** and has **appeared** to Simon!"
Then the two recounted
what had taken **place** on the **way**
and how he was made **known** to them in the **breaking**
of **bread**.

After spending time with Jesus (whom they still don't recognize), these disciples have a desire for further fellowship with him. They are beginning to sense something different than seeing something.

In the breaking of the bread—the ritual that repeats the Passover when they last were in Jesus' company—there is recognition. Ritual reveals presence.

Confirmation of their recognition, repeated in the phrase "the breaking of bread," the message of this reading.

a mighty prophet; they witness to the charges lodged at Jesus and his subsequent death; they reveal their hope that he was the Messiah; and they attest that Jesus has been discovered to be alive. These are the developing strains of the faith that would be professed by the early Church.

Telling the story is precisely what the Risen Lord seeks to do when he takes over and interprets for them "what referred to him in all the Scriptures." Although we are given no indication that the preaching opens their eyes, we can detect that it is indeed opening their hearts. Even in their confused state, they make the invitation to the stranger to remain with them for the evening and to share a meal with them. In Luke's Gospel, it is precisely meal sharing that opens eyes to the wonders of Jesus' presence, and indeed, this is the case at Emmaus. Three things happen simultaneously: "their eyes were opened and they recognized him but he vanished from their sight."

If fear and a sense of failure filled their hearts when they left the city earlier that day, now it is joy and zeal that fill them as they return to tell the other disciples of their good news. Upon their reunion with the other disciples, we see a grand collision of stories of the Lord's appearances, all of which must have produced a sense of overwhelming peace. It is the testimony to the growth of Easter faith, as Luke leaves us with the words: "Then the two recounted what had taken place on the way and how he was made known to them in the breaking of bread." S. W.

SECOND SUNDAY OF EASTER

LECTIONARY #44

READING I   Acts of the Apostles 4:32–35

A reading from the Acts of the Apostles

A narrative description of the early Christian community, suggesting both an ideal and a pattern for current Christian communities to follow. The word "no" is repeated two times, in each case to negate possession or claim.

The **community** of believers was of one **heart** and **mind**,
  and no one **claimed** that any of his **possessions** was his **own**,
  but they had **everything** in common.
With great **power** the apostles bore **witness**
  to the **resurrection** of the Lord **Jesus**,
  and great **favor** was **accorded** them all.
There was no **needy person** among them,
  for those who owned **property** or **houses** would **sell** them,
  bring the **proceeds** of the sale,
  and put them at the **feet** of the **apostles**,
  and they were **distributed** to each according to **need**.

Because this reading concludes with a description of the equitable distribution of wealth, it feels more relevant than ever. Let the phrase "each according to need" resonate in the sanctuary.

For meditation and context:

RESPONSORIAL PSALM   Psalm 118:2–4, 13–15, 22–24 (1)

R. Give thanks to the Lord, for he is good; his love is everlasting.
or
R. Alleluia.

Let the house of Israel say,
  "His mercy endures forever."
Let the house of Aaron say,
  "His mercy endures forever."
Let those who fear the LORD say,
  "His mercy endures forever."

I was hard pressed and was falling,
  but the LORD helped me.
My strength and my courage is the LORD,
  and he has been my savior.

The joyful shout of victory
  in the tents of the just.

The stone which the builders rejected
  has become the cornerstone.
By the LORD has this been done;
  it is wonderful in our eyes.
This is the day the LORD has made;
  let us be glad and rejoice in it.

READING I In today's first reading, we are invited to reflect upon the activities of Christian communities soon after Jesus' Resurrection. The Acts of the Apostles describes this as a time of great boldness for those filled with the Holy Spirit. Peter and some of the other disciples of Jesus were performing miracles in Jesus' name and preaching the good news of his Resurrection in spite of threats from the religious authorities to keep quiet. This is the context for Luke's description of how early Christians shared (or should share) their Spirit-filled lives. Luke may have been patterning his description of the community's common life after the Greek vision of a utopian society where everything is perfectly arranged and where nothing harmful exists. He also may have been thinking of a Greek proverb about friends having all things in common (Plato, *Republic* 4.424). But giving away whatever they had sounds quite extreme. Yet, Luke describes a similar challenge from Jesus to those who would follow him: "Every one of you who does not renounce all his possessions cannot be my disciple" (Luke 14:33). In what ways might we realize this model of the Christian community today?

READING II The First Letter of John beautifully underscores many of the themes of the Gospel of John with some small modifications. For example, in this reading, the Christian community's calling is to love God and obey God's commandment, which is to love the children of God. However, in John's Gospel, the commandment is attributed to Jesus, and it is a command to love one another. Also embedded in this reading is a message of

A didactic reading full of passion and conviction. It almost reads like a poem in the force of its language.

READING II   1 John 5:1–6

A reading from the first Letter of Saint John

Beloved:
Everyone who **believes** that **Jesus** is the **Christ** is **begotten**
      by God,
   and everyone who **loves** the Father
   loves **also** the one **begotten** by him.
In this way we **know** that we love the children of God
   when we **love** God and obey his **commandments**.
For the **love** of God is **this**,
   that we keep his commandments.
And his **commandments** are not **burdensome**,
   for **whoever** is begotten by God **conquers** the world.
And the **victory** that conquers the **world** is our **faith**.
Who indeed is the victor over the **world**
   but the one who **believes** that **Jesus** is the Son of **God**?

This is the one who came through **water** and **blood**,
      Jesus Christ,
   not by water **alone**, but by **water** and blood.
The **Spirit** is the one that **testifies**,
   and the **Spirit** is **truth**.

"For the love of God is this": the key phrase in the reading.

Followed by a statement of conviction: keeping these commandments is not a burden. Give "commandments" and "burdensome" equal weight.

Slow your pace slightly for this concluding line.

GOSPEL   John 20:19–31

A reading from the holy Gospel according to John

On the **evening** of that first day of the **week**,
   when the **doors** were locked, where the **disciples** were,
   for **fear** of the **Jews**,
   Jesus came and stood in their **midst**
   and said to them, "**Peace** be with you."

A narrative reading of a passage containing a great deal of inherent and relatable mystery. Thomas not only stands for the person who needs to see in order to believe; he is also a stand-in for the reluctant believer or for anyone struggling with belief, giving his recognition of Jesus and his expression of faith even greater resonance.

Jesus announces his presence with the word "peace" in this passage. The word is focal.

---

consolation; God's commandment is not burdensome, because those who are begotten of God will conquer the world. Biblical scholars are not of one mind about exactly how to translate and interpret the final verse of this reading, but the general consensus is that "water and blood" refers to the incarnate Son of God who shed his blood for us.

GOSPEL   Today's Gospel highlights the source of energy for the post-Resurrection Christian community: the presence of the crucified and risen

Christ and his message of peace. There is no disconnect. The crucified Jesus, whom the disciples knew as their master, is the risen Christ. He has triumphed over death, even as the evidence of his wounds remain. Moreover, his ability to be present with them has no barriers, neither locked doors nor debilitating fear. This is cause for great joy, as is demonstrated by the disciples' reaction to his appearance.

   The risen Christ's message—"peace to you"—recalls the teaching that Jesus gave to his disciples in his Farewell Discourse (John 14:1–31). Jesus told them that he would be

leaving soon but that they should not let their hearts (i.e., their inner selves) be troubled, because he would not leave them orphaned. Instead, he would ask the Father to send the Holy Spirit as their Paraclete (Gk. *parakletos*, meaning "helper or court-appointed advocate") to be with them. All they needed to do is to obey his commandment and believe in him. The commandment is to love one another as Jesus has loved them. In John's Gospel, to believe in Jesus is to trust in him and align oneself with him and with the Father. The greeting of peace (Gk. *eirenen*; Heb. *shalom*) is a wish that the

Repetition of "peace."

When he had **said** this, he **showed** them his hands and his **side**.
The disciples **rejoiced** when they saw the **Lord**.
Jesus said to them again, "**Peace** be with you.
As the **Father** has sent me, so I send **you**."
And when he had **said** this, he **breathed** on them and **said**
    to them,
    "**Receive** the Holy Spirit.
Whose sins you **forgive** are **forgiven** them,
    and whose **sins** you **retain** are **retained**."

Thomas' expressions of doubt in this passage should be treated with care.

Thomas, called **Didymus**, one of the **Twelve**,
    was not **with** them when Jesus **came**.
So the other disciples said to him, "We have **seen** the Lord."
But he said to them,
    "Unless I see the **mark** of the nails in his **hands**
    and put my **finger** into the nailmarks
    and put my **hand** into his side, I will **not** believe."

Now a **week later** his disciples were **again** inside
    and **Thomas** was with them.
Jesus came, although the doors were **locked**,
    and stood in their **midst** and said, "**Peace** be with you."
Then he said to Thomas, "Put your finger **here** and see
        my **hands**,
    and bring your **hand** and put it into my **side**,
    and do not be **unbelieving**, but **believe**."

Another repetition of "peace."
Jesus' words to Thomas are spoken with gentleness.

Thomas answered and said to him, "My **Lord** and my **God**!"
Jesus said to him, "Have you come to **believe** because you have
        seen me?
Blessed are those who **have not seen** and have **believed**."

Thomas' recognition is joyful—its expression conveys the joy. No need to overemphasize it.

Now Jesus did many other signs in the presence of his **disciples**
    that are not **written** in this **book**.
But these are **written** that you may come to **believe**
    that **Jesus** is the **Christ**, the Son of **God**,
    and that **through this belief** you may have **life** in his name.

The conclusion of this Gospel reading speaks directly to the assembly, using the second person pronoun. Even though the word isn't rhythmically emphasized, it is thematically focal.

disciples experience a sense of security and safety, because of the saving power of God and Jesus Christ, who is God's agent in the world. Those last words of the soon-to-be-crucified Jesus are now realized in the message of the risen Christ to his fearful disciples.

Like other appearance narratives in the Gospels, this story of the appearance of the risen Christ contains a commissioning: "As the Father has sent me, so I send you" (John 20:21). In the ancient world, kings and other powerful figures would send out their representatives to accomplish their work among their subjects. In this capacity, the king's representative took on the role of the king and for all intents and purposes became the king in their midst. In the same way, we are called to join in Christ's ministry, a ministry characterized by peace and reconciliation in a hostile and unreceptive world.

As part of the commissioning, we are told that Jesus "breathed on" (Gk. *enephysesen*) the disciples. This word appears only once in the entire New Testament, but it suggests the second creation story, in which God breathes on Adam and gives him a life-giving spirit (Genesis 2:7). It also recalls the vision in which Ezekiel calls the wind to breathe into the dry bones to bring to life those who had once been exiled (Ezekiel 37).

Reflect for yourself. Are you willing to respond to the breath of the Holy Spirit and share in Christ's ministry of peace and reconciliation in a broken world? C. C.

THIRD SUNDAY OF EASTER

LECTIONARY #47

READING I   Acts of the Apostles 3:13–15, 17–19

A reading from the Acts of the Apostles

Peter said to the **people**:
"The God of **Abraham**,
   the God of **Isaac**, and the God of **Jacob**,
   the God of our **fathers**, has glorified his **servant** Jesus,
   whom you handed over and denied in Pilate's **presence**
   when he had **decided** to **release** him.
You denied the Holy and **Righteous** One
   and asked that a **murderer** be **released** to you.
The author of life you put to **death**,
   but God raised him from the dead; of **this** we are **witnesses**.
Now I **know**, brothers,
   that you **acted** out of ignorance, just as your **leaders** did;
   but **God** has thus **brought** to **fulfillment**
   what he had **announced** beforehand
   through the **mouth** of all the **prophets**,
   that his **Christ** would **suffer**.
Repent, therefore, and be **converted**, that your **sins** may be
   wiped **away**."

Abraham = AY-bruh-ham
Isaac = Ī-zik

An exhortatory reading whose contents are harsh but whose message edges into hope.

These repetitions—"the God of . . ."—place Jesus in a prophetic context and establish the rhythm of this passage.

Give subtle stress to "life" and "death," the core of this reading.

These lines have the foreordained quality of prophecy.

Stress, without undue emphasis, the imperative of this final line. Let the last word, "away," linger for a moment.

> **TO KEEP IN MIND**
> The words in bold are suggestions for ways to express the meaning of the reading. Consider using them as you practice the reading, then choose to stress them or to find your own way of proclaiming.

READING I   How does one preach and give witness to the horrible paradox of a crucified messiah? This is the question that is addressed in today's readings.

The first reading, from the Acts of the Apostles, is part of a much longer speech attributed to Peter and delivered after he had cured a crippled man at the Beautiful Gate of the Temple in Jerusalem. Luke describes Peter taking advantage of the opportunity to speak to a large group of Jewish people gathered in Solomon's Portico about how, in their ignorance, they denied God's Holy and Righteous One, Jesus, and put him to death. Peter then testifies to Christ's Resurrection and calls for his audience to repent of their sin.

Some readers have wrongly interpreted biblical texts like this one to suggest that Jews who do not convert to Christianity are forever to blame for the crucifixion of Jesus. But, actually, this scene is simply one part of Luke's book-length explanation of how the Jesus movement extended beyond the Jewish people to the Gentile world. This was necessary in Luke's mind because he understood that the Jewish people were God's chosen ones. If the Christian movement, which he calls "the Way," were to spread to the Gentiles, he needed to provide a narrative explanation for that expansion. Also, we should note that Luke counters this seemingly anti-Semitic rant by reminding his readers that it had long been part of the divine plan that Christ would suffer. Although Luke does not identify his scriptural source, he was likely referring to the Suffering Servant Song (Isaiah 52:13—53:12) to make this point.

For meditation and context:

RESPONSORIAL PSALM   Psalm 4:2, 4, 7–8, 9 (7a)

R. Lord, let your face shine on us.
or
R. Alleluia.

When I call, answer me, O my just God,
　you who relieve me when I am in distress;
　have pity on me, and hear my prayer!

Know that the LORD does wonders for his
　faithful one;
　the LORD will hear me when I call
　upon him.

O LORD, let the light of your countenance
　shine upon us!
　You put gladness into my heart.

As soon as I lie down, I fall peacefully asleep,
　for you alone, O LORD,
　bring security to my dwelling.

READING II   1 John 2:1–5a

A didactic reading in which John stresses that following the commandments of God is a way to know God.

A reading from the first Letter of Saint John

My **children**, I am writing this to you
　so that you may **not** commit **sin**.
But if anyone **does** sin, we have an **Advocate** with the **Father**,
　Jesus Christ the **righteous** one.
He is **expiation** for our **sins**,
　and not for our sins **only** but for **those** of the whole **world**.
The way we may be **sure** that we **know** him
　is to **keep** his **commandments**.
Those who say, "I **know** him," but do not keep
　his **commandments**
　are liars, and the **truth** is not in them.
But whoever **keeps** his word,
　the love of God is truly **perfected** in him.

The sentiment of this line is universal. Stress "only" and "world."

"Commandments" appears twice. Give the word a little extra emphasis.

GOSPEL   Luke 24:35–48

A reading from the holy Gospel according to Luke

The two **disciples** recounted what had taken **place** on the way,
　and how **Jesus** was made known to them
　in the **breaking** of **bread**. »

Emmaus = eh-MAY-uhs

A narrative reading from the passage directly following the tale from the road to Emmaus. The mystery and energy of the previous passage carry through into this passage.

READING II The tone of the First Letter of John suggests a Christian community that had recently experienced a schism over doctrine and practice, and feelings within the community, or at least in the mind of the author, are still raw. Apparently, some who once belonged to the community —opponents of the author of this letter— were saying that they know God, they have union with God, and they have no sin. The author is fierce in his refutation of these claims, charging them with being liars and walking in darkness.

In today's reading from this letter, the author directs his words to the remaining community members, cautioning them about not committing sin but also consoling them by reminding them that they have an Advocate (Gk. *parakletos*, meaning "helper" or "counselor") in Jesus Christ, because he is expiation for humanity's sin. Historically, *expiation* referred to a type of blood sacrifice that was offered in the Jerusalem Temple to blot out the people's sin. For Christians, then, Jesus' crucifixion is the most perfect expiation, because his death was for the atonement of sin. Notice that

this identification of the Advocate with Jesus Christ is different from the Gospel of John, which identifies the Advocate with the Holy Spirit. Finally, the author addresses his opponents' claim to know God by advising his community that the true test of knowledge of God is that he or she obeys God's commandment, which is to love one another. Obviously, the author's opponents do not! Otherwise, they would not have abandoned the community.

"Peace" is the word that introduces Jesus' presence.

"It is I myself" is an awkward phrase in English; don't trip over it.

Jesus' question whether there is something to eat immediately humanizes the scene. This question is crucial, about hunger and hospitality.

This line expresses what the whole passage itself demonstrates, an opening of the mind.

Witnessing is the subject of this passage. Give the word "witnesses" a little extra emphasis.

While they were still **speaking** about this,
   he **stood** in their midst and said to them,
    "**Peace** be with you."
But they were **startled** and **terrified**
   and thought that they were seeing a **ghost**.
Then he said to them, "**Why** are you **troubled**?
And **why** do questions **arise** in your **hearts**?
Look at my **hands** and my **feet**, that it is I myself.
Touch me and **see**, because a ghost does not have **flesh** and **bones**
   as you can **see** I have."
And as he **said** this,
   he **showed** them his hands and his **feet**.
While they were still **incredulous** for joy and were **amazed**,
   he asked them, "Have you **anything** here to **eat**?"
They gave him a piece of **baked fish**;
   he **took** it and **ate** it in **front** of them.

He said to them,
   "**These** are my words that I **spoke** to you while I was still
    with you,
   that **everything** written about me in the **law** of Moses
   and in the **prophets** and **psalms** must be **fulfilled**."
Then he opened their **minds** to understand the **Scriptures**.
And he **said** to them,
   "**Thus** it is written that the **Christ** would suffer
   and **rise** from the dead on the **third** day
   and that **repentance**, for the forgiveness of **sins**,
   would be **preached** in his name
   to all the **nations**, **beginning** from Jerusalem.
You are **witnesses** of these things."

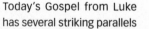

GOSPEL Today's Gospel from Luke has several striking parallels with last week's reading from the Gospel of John. Both tell the story of the risen Jesus' appearance to the disciples very soon after his Resurrection. Both stories mention the disciples' fright at seeing Christ in their midst and the message of peace that he delivered to them. In both stories, the risen Jesus gives the disciples physical evidence of his bodily Resurrection: "Look at my hands and my feet . . . touch me and see, because a ghost does not have flesh and bones as you can see I have" (cf. John 20:19).

But there are important differences, as well. For example, the source of the disciples' fright is different in each. In Luke's Gospel, the disciples fear they are seeing a ghost. However, in John's Gospel, the disciples are afraid that the Jewish religious authorities will seek them out and kill them as they did Jesus. However, a very important difference in Luke's account is the assertion that the risen Jesus will be known and fully experienced in the breaking of the bread, that is, in the community's sharing of the Eucharist (Luke 24:13–35).

Another important difference is Luke's explanation of why it was that the messiah had to suffer and die. We should not discount or diminish the crisis of faith that came with realizing that the long-awaited messiah of early Judaism was not what they expected. Luke describes Jesus as reminding the disciples that he had told them beforehand that he would be killed—Jesus is trustworthy—and that their sacred Scriptures testified to all that would happen. Now they are called to testify about the good news to all the nations. C. C.

FOURTH SUNDAY OF EASTER

LECTIONARY #50

READING I Acts of the Apostles 4:8–12

A reading from the Acts of the Apostles

Peter, filled with the Holy **Spirit**, said:
    "**Leaders** of the people and **elders**:
    If we are being **examined** today
    about a **good deed** done to a **cripple**,
    namely, by what **means** he was **saved**,
    then **all of you** and all the **people** of Israel should know
    that it was in the **name** of Jesus Christ the **Nazorean**
    whom you **crucified**, whom God **raised** from the **dead**;
    in his **name** this man stands before you **healed**.
He is the **stone rejected** by you, the **builders**,
    which has **become** the **cornerstone**.
There is no **salvation** through anyone **else**,
    nor is there any other **name** under **heaven**
    given to the human race by which we are to be **saved**."

An exhortatory reading in which Peter makes insistent claims in an emphatic manner. Your proclamation can be similarly emphatic.

"Cripple" is a harsh word that sets the tone of this reading.

Nazorean = naz-uh-REE-uhn

The use of "you" in these lines, carrying into the quotation, is accusatory.

The reading concludes insistently, ending on a hopeful note with "saved."

READING I Today's reading from the Acts of the Apostles is the first part of Peter's speech before the Sanhedrin. According to Luke's chronology, Peter had just finished his speech to the people who had gathered in Solomon's Portico of the Jerusalem Temple to ogle his healing of a crippled man (Acts 3:11–26). Almost immediately, Peter and John were confronted by a group of religious leaders associated with the Temple—priests, the captain of the Temple guard, which consisted of Levites, and some Sadducees— who were upset with them for preaching

about the resurrected Jesus and healing in his name. Sadducees did not believe in resurrection of the dead. They arrested the two and made them appear before the Sanhedrin to answer for their crimes. Luke makes it clear that it is by the power of the Holy Spirit that Peter witnesses to the risen Jesus. Peter is described as giving a speech much like the one he gave earlier in Solomon's Portico—beginning with a charge against the religious authorities for putting to death Jesus Christ, whom God raised from the dead, followed by a call to repentance and a proclamation of the salvific

power of Christ. The image of the stone rejected that becomes a cornerstone comes from Psalm 118:22 and is intended to convey the notion of victory over one's enemies.

READING II This reading from the First Letter of John is part of a larger section devoted to what it means to be children of God. The form of the verb "to see" has the sense of a command, "Behold!" or "Hey, everyone, look!" Also, in its context, the phrase "what love" is intended to focus the reader's attention on the character or nature of God's love. It is the kind of fatherly

For meditation and context:

RESPONSORIAL PSALM   Psalm 118:1, 8–9, 21–23, 26, 28, 29 (22)

R. The stone rejected by the builders has become the cornerstone.
or
R. Alleluia.

Give thanks to the LORD, for he is good,
  for his mercy endures forever.
It is better to take refuge in the LORD
  than to trust in man.
It is better to take refuge in the LORD
  than to trust in princes.

I will give thanks to you, for you have
  answered me
  and have been my savior.
The stone which the builders rejected
  has become the cornerstone.

By the LORD has this been done;
  it is wonderful in our eyes.

Blessed is he who comes in the name
  of the LORD;
  we bless you from the house of the LORD.
I will give thanks to you, for you have
  answered me
  and have been my savior.
Give thanks to the LORD, for he is good;
  for his kindness endures forever.

READING II   1 John 3:1–2

A reading from the first Letter of Saint John

A short, exhortatory reading bursting with passion.

Beloved:
See what love the **Father** has **bestowed** on us
  that we may be **called** the children of **God**.
Yet so we **are**.
The **reason** the world does not **know** us
  is that it did not know **him**.
Beloved, we are **God's** children now;
  what we shall **be** has not yet been **revealed**.
We do **know** that when it is **revealed** we shall be **like him**,
  for we shall **see** him as he **is**.

Contrast "know" with "him" in the next line.

"Be" yields "revealed." You can link these by emphasizing the words.

---

love that makes it possible for us to be called children of God. Moreover, the author uses the diminutive form of "children," which might be translated as "kiddos" or "chiquitos / chiquitas," suggesting an intimate familial relationship. As evidence that we are part of the family of God, the author says, the world (i.e., those who are not allied with God) does not know us, just as they did not know Jesus. But children of God can be confident that they will enjoy a marvelous reward—at the end time, we will be like God and see God as God is! Who can imagine such a gift? Biblical schol-

ars think this idea is derived from the Hellenistic principle of "like will know like."

GOSPEL Today's reading is part of a lengthy section of John's Gospel, called the Good Shepherd discourse (John 10:1–42), which follows immediately after the story of the healing of a man born blind and his encounters with people who do not accept that he was once blind and is now healed. The extended story is generally understood to be an example of how the Christian believer should be willing to witness to Jesus in a hostile world. It ends

with Jesus' pronouncement that he came "so that those who do not see might see, and those who do see might become blind" (John 9:39).

The Good Shepherd discourse is addressed to these same people, specifically the Jewish religious authorities, who are divided over what they think about Jesus' identity. Using metaphorical language, Jesus identifies himself as the good (Gk. *kalos*, meaning "noble" or "ideal") shepherd who lays down his life for the sheep. The sheep symbolize the Jewish people. The wolf represents threats that

GOSPEL John 10:11–18

A reading from the holy Gospel according to John

An exhortatory reading that provides one of the basic metaphorical understandings of Jesus.
Emphasize "I" and "shepherd."

Jesus said:
"I am the good **shepherd**.
A good **shepherd** lays down his **life** for the **sheep**.
A **hired** man, who is not a **shepherd**
and whose **sheep** are not his **own**,
sees a **wolf** coming and leaves the **sheep** and runs **away**,
and the wolf **catches** and **scatters** them.
This is because he works for **pay** and has no **concern** for
the **sheep**.

Shift the emphasis to "good."

I am the **good** shepherd,
and I know **mine** and mine know **me**,

"Just as" is a formula John commonly uses when Jesus speaks in his Gospel. He uses it to create an analogy between God the Father and Jesus the Son.

just as the Father knows **me** and I know the **Father**;
and I will **lay down** my life for the **sheep**.
I have other **sheep** that do not **belong** to this **fold**.
These **also** I must lead, and they will **hear** my voice,
and there will be one **flock**, one **shepherd**.
This is why the **Father** loves me,

Contrast "down" with "up."

because I **lay down** my life in order to **take** it **up** again.
No one takes it **from** me, but I lay it down on my **own**.

And here, contrast "power to lay it down" with "power to take it up."

I have **power** to lay it **down**, and **power** to take it **up** again.
This command I have **received** from my Father."

come in the form of false messiahs and others who claim to provide people with a path to salvation. The hired man represents ineffective efforts to protect the community, because he has no commitment to the community and only works for pay. But the noble or ideal shepherd is so committed that he will freely give his life to protect the community.

Anyone who has worked with farm animals knows that they recognize your voice and will come when you call them, especially if it involves food. Jesus, the Good Shepherd, says something similar, but with symbolic meaning, of course. Knowledge of another suggests an intimate relationship: Jesus knows his sheep as the Father knows him. The other sheep that Jesus wants to lead are probably the Samaritans and the Greeks who are represented elsewhere in the Gospel.

Jesus' words likely infuriated the Jewish religious authorities, because, being well-versed in sacred Scripture, they likely would have understood them as an attack on their leadership. They would have remembered the words of the prophet of Ezekiel, who said "Woe to the shepherds of Israel who have been pasturing themselves! Should not shepherds pasture the flock?" (Ezekiel 34:2b–3). Later, he said, "Look! I am coming against these shepherds. I will take my sheep out of their hand and put a stop to their shepherding my flock, so that these shepherds will no longer pasture them." (Ezekiel 34:10). And again there was division among these religious leaders, some saying Jesus was possessed and others saying he was deranged. The tension is palpable! C. C.

FIFTH SUNDAY
OF EASTER

LECTIONARY #53

READING I   Acts of the Apostles 9:26–31

A reading from the Acts of the Apostles

When Saul **arrived** in Jerusalem he tried to **join** the disciples,
 but they were all **afraid** of him,
 not **believing** that he was a **disciple**.
Then **Barnabas** took charge of him and brought him
   to the **apostles**,
 and he **reported** to them how he had seen the **Lord**,
 and that he had **spoken** to him,
 and how in **Damascus** he had spoken out **boldly** in the name
   of **Jesus**.
He moved about **freely** with them in **Jerusalem**,
 and spoke out **boldly** in the name of the **Lord**.
He also spoke and **debated** with the **Hellenists**,
 but they tried to **kill** him.
And when the brothers **learned** of this,
 they took him down to **Caesarea**
 and sent him on his **way** to **Tarsus**.

The church throughout all **Judea**, **Galilee**, and **Samaria** was
   at **peace**.
It was being built **up** and walked in the **fear** of the **Lord**,
 and with the consolation of the Holy **Spirit** it grew
   in **numbers**.

Saul = sawl
Barnabas = BAHR-nuh-buhs

A narrative reading that tells something of the origin of Paul, when he was still known by his Jewish name, Saul, including some of the tensions he encountered in joining the early Christian community. It's useful to know that everything didn't always run smoothly in the past, just as is true in the present.

Damascus = duh-MAS-kuhs
Hellenists = HEL-uh-nist

This rehearsal of Paul's experiences uses the word "boldly" twice. Give the word extra emphasis both times.

This fact is crucial, "they tried to kill him." Speak it clearly.

Caesarea = sez-uh-REE-uh
Tarsus = TAHR-suhs
Judea = joo-DEE-uh
Galilee = GAL-ih-lee
Samaria = suh-MAYR-ee-uh

The reading concludes with a sense of the formation of the early Church.

READING I   The readings for the Fifth Sunday of Easter focus on what God can do through those who believe in the Risen Christ. In the scene that precedes today's first reading, we learn about Saul's encounter with the Risen Christ on the road to Damascus. This encounter resulted in him being identified as the evangelist to the Gentiles. He stayed in Damascus for a while and preached about Jesus the messiah in the local synagogues, until he had to flee the city to avoid being killed. This is where we pick up the story.

Saul, who would later be known by his Greek name, Paul, made his way to Jerusalem with the intention of joining the disciples of Jesus, but they were afraid to trust him because of his reputation of harassing and arresting Jewish followers of Jesus. All that changed when Barnabas, a Cypriot Jew, a Levite, and a follower of Jesus (Acts 4:36), took Saul under his wing and gave him a proper introduction to the Jewish Christian community in Jerusalem. Saul continued his passionate preaching about Jesus as the messiah, and again he had to be rescued because of threats against

his life. The Hellenists who perpetrated violence against Saul were Greek-speaking Jews who lived in Jerusalem. They probably thought that Saul's teaching was much too innovative for them to tolerate. To save his life, the disciples sent Saul to Tarsus, which, by the way, was his hometown.

Today's First Reading ends with a comment about the Jewish Christian communities of Palestine living in peace. Could the reason be that Saul is gone and no longer a problem? Perhaps, but more likely this is Luke's way of transitioning to the next set of stories in Acts of the Apostles.

For meditation and context:

RESPONSORIAL PSALM   Psalm 22:26–27, 28, 30, 31–32 (26a)

R. I will praise you, Lord, in the assembly of your people.
or
R. Alleluia.

I will fulfill my vows before those who fear
    the LORD.
    The lowly shall eat their fill;
they who seek the LORD shall praise him:
    "May your hearts live forever!"

All the ends of the earth
    shall remember and turn to the LORD;
all the families of the nations
    shall bow down before him.

To him alone shall bow down
    all who sleep in the earth;
before him shall bend
    all who go down into the dust.

And to him my soul shall live;
    my descendants shall serve him.
Let the coming generation be told of
    the LORD
    that they may proclaim to a people
    yet to be born
    the justice he has shown.

READING II   1 John 3:18–24

A reading from the first Letter of Saint John

Children, let us love not in **word** or **speech**
    but in **deed** and **truth**.

Now this is how we shall **know** that we belong to the **truth**
    and **reassure** our hearts **before** him
    in whatever our hearts **condemn**,
    for **God** is greater than our **hearts** and knows **everything**.
Beloved, if our **hearts** do not **condemn** us,
    we have **confidence** in God
    and **receive** from him whatever we **ask**,
    because we **keep** his commandments and **do** what
        pleases him.
And his **commandment** is this:
    we should **believe** in the name of his **Son**, Jesus Christ,
    and **love** one another **just** as he **commanded** us.
Those who **keep** his commandments **remain** in him,
        and **he** in them,
    and the way we **know** that he **remains** in us
    is from the **Spirit** he **gave** us.

A didactic reading that continues the themes from the previous two weeks from John's first epistle, specifically the theme of love and the theme of keeping God's commandment.

Stress "Beloved," as well as "hearts" and "condemn."

John shifts his emphasis to "commandment," which includes the command to "love one another." This command simply cannot be overstressed.

READING II   In the section that precedes today's Second Reading, the author of the First Letter of John has already established that we are children of God because of God's precious act of love in giving us his Son, and that we ought to love one another, even in troubled times, so that God's love can abide in us. Using the story of Cain and Abel (Genesis 4:1–16), he also warns his readers that the world will hate them. However, just as Christ laid down his life as an act of love for us, we must do the same for others.

With this background in mind, we can better understand today's lectionary reading. The author addresses his audience as "children" and urges them to love one another not with empty words but "in deed and truth." But what does it mean to love "in truth"? As humans we will not always do what is right, and, if "our hearts condemn us," meaning that we experience shame or guilt, we can be confident that God is so much greater—more understanding and more loving—than our self-condemnation. Thus, we can stand in confidence before God. All God asks is that we keep God's

commandments—believe in the name of Jesus and love one another—thus doing what God asks. Then we will remain or abide in God and God in us. Can we ask for more?

GOSPEL   Today's Gospel offers us a compelling metaphor for what it means to abide in the risen Christ and let God's good work be done through us. Imagine, if you can, a farmer who carefully tends his grape vines from day to day and year to year in order to harvest their fruit one beautiful fall day. Farming is risky business even today, and much more so in

An exhortatory reading involving another extensive metaphor: Jesus the true vine and God the Father the vine grower. The metaphor includes a sense of natural growth as well as care and tending.

This parallel phrase characterizes this reading completely: I to you, vine to branches.

Another parallel: remain in me, remain in you.

GOSPEL   John 15:1–8

A reading from the holy Gospel according to John

Jesus said to his disciples:
   "1 am the **true vine**, and my **Father** is the **vine grower**.
He takes away every **branch** in me that does not bear **fruit**,
   and every one that **does** he **prunes** so that it bears **more** fruit.
You are **already** pruned because of the **word** that I **spoke** to you.
Remain in me, as I **remain** in you.
Just as a **branch** cannot bear **fruit** on its **own**
   unless it **remains** on the **vine**,
   so neither can you unless you **remain** in me.
I am the **vine**, **you** are the **branches**.
Whoever **remains** in me and **I** in him will bear **much fruit**,
   because **without** me you can do **nothing**.
Anyone who does **not** remain in me
   will be **thrown** out like a **branch** and **wither**;
   people will **gather** them and **throw** them into a **fire**
   and they will be **burned**.
If you **remain** in **me** and my words **remain** in **you**,
   ask for whatever you **want** and it will be **done** for you.
By this is my Father **glorified**,
   that you bear **much fruit** and become my **disciples**."

the ancient world. We know that ancient vineyards were built with a fence, often made of stones and topped with brambles, to keep animals from helping themselves to the tender fruit. In addition, these vineyards often had a wine press and a tower where someone could keep watch over the harvest and keep it safe from two-legged thieves. Even so, other disasters, like storms or drought or even poor rootstock, could dash one's hope of a good crop.

   In this section of the Gospel of John, Jesus is presented as giving an extended farewell talk to his disciples after he shared

a last meal with them and before he is arrested in a garden across the Kidron valley from the Jerusalem Temple. He has already told his disciples that he is going to leave them, but they should not be troubled or afraid, because the Father will send the Holy Spirit to be their advocate—as in a court of law—in times of trouble. The Johannine Jesus uses the metaphor of a vineyard to tell them that they must remain in his love and act as his disciples: God the Father is the vine grower, Jesus is the vine that was grown from God's specially chosen rootstock, and we are the branches.

The Johannine Jesus expands the metaphor by talking about how a good vine grower needs to cut off the unproductive branches and prune the good branches to make them produce even more. The central message of the metaphor: we need to remain with the vine if we want to bear fruit as disciples of Jesus. C. C.

SIXTH SUNDAY OF EASTER

LECTIONARY #56

READING I Acts of the Apostles 10:25–26, 34–35, 44–48

A reading from the Acts of the Apostles

When Peter **entered**, Cornelius **met** him
 and, **falling** at his feet, paid him **homage**.
Peter, however, **raised** him **up**, saying,
 "Get **up**. I myself am **also** a human **being**."

Then Peter proceeded to **speak** and said,
 "In **truth**, I see that God shows **no** partiality.
Rather, in every nation whoever **fears** him and acts **uprightly**
 is **acceptable** to him."

While Peter was still **speaking** these things,
 the Holy **Spirit** fell upon all who were **listening** to the word.
The **circumcised believers** who had accompanied **Peter**
 were **astounded** that the gift of the Holy **Spirit**
 should have been **poured out** on the **Gentiles also**,
 for they could **hear** them speaking in tongues and
  glorifying **God**.
Then Peter responded,
 "Can anyone withhold the **water** for baptizing these **people**,
 who have **received** the Holy Spirit even as **we** have?"
He ordered them to be **baptized** in the name of Jesus **Christ**.

A narrative reading with a few exhortatory passages. Peter is the focal character but the Holy Spirit is the consecrating power at work in this reading.

Peter's claim here democratizes apostolic work. Emphasis on "also."

The contrast between the "circumcised" and the "Gentiles" is important. Under the influence of the Holy Spirit, these two groups of people are unified.

The reading concludes with an order for Baptism. Emphasize "water," "received," and "baptized."

READING I The Acts of the Apostles contains the stories of the Holy Spirit's activity in the lives of early church leaders and their communities. Today's lectionary reading is a small part of a much longer story in which a centurion named Cornelius had a vision that prompted him to ask Peter to visit him. Centurions were Roman military leaders who were stationed throughout the Roman provinces and were in charge of a hundred military personnel. However, Cornelius was no ordinary centurion. Luke describes him as a Gentile who was interested in Judaism and was a generous contributor to the needs of the Jewish community in Caesarea. On the day after Cornelius received his vision, Peter also received a vision in which a heavenly voice told him to eat ritually unclean animals. Peter responded by saying "Certainly not!" This would have been a violation of Jewish dietary regulations. Nevertheless, the heavenly voice said, "What God has made clean, you are not to call profane" (Acts 10:15).

Even though Peter was unsure of the meaning of his vision, when the Holy Spirit told him to go with the soldiers to meet Cornelius at his home, he went. Upon entering Cornelius' house, he encountered a large group of family and colleagues waiting for him. When they had completed all of the niceties of introduction and welcome, Cornelius asked Peter to speak to them about Jesus' message. Peter had not yet finished speaking, when he saw the Holy Spirit descend on the gathering. Peter's companions, all circumcised followers of Jesus, were astounded—literally, out of their minds—at the thought that Gentiles could receive the Holy Spirit, because it was reserved for Jews alone, or so they thought.

For meditation and context:

RESPONSORIAL PSALM   Psalm 98:1, 2–3, 3–4 (2b)

R. The Lord has revealed to the nations his saving power.
or
R. Alleluia.

Sing to the LORD a new song,
    for he has done wondrous deeds;
His right hand has won victory for him,
    his holy arm.

The LORD has made his salvation known:
    in the sight of the nations he has revealed
        his justice.

He has remembered his kindness and his
    faithfulness
    toward the house of Israel.

All the ends of the earth have seen
    the salvation by our God.
Sing joyfully to the LORD, all you lands;
    break into song; sing praise.

READING II   1 John 4:7–10

Cornelius = kohr-NEEL-yuhs

A short but intense exhortatory reading in which the focus is love. "Love" is used nine times, each time expanding the meaning of the word.

This whole line, especially its concluding four words, "for God is love," expresses one of the core tenets of our faith. Practice this line a couple of times.

A reading from the first Letter of Saint John

Beloved, let us **love** one another,
    because **love** is of **God**;
    everyone who **loves** is begotten by **God** and **knows** God.
Whoever is **without** love does **not** know **God**, for **God** is **love**.
In this way the love of **God** was **revealed** to us:
    God sent his **only** Son into the **world**
    so that we might have life through him.
In **this** is **love**:
    not that we have loved God, but that he loved **us**
    and sent his **Son** as **expiation** for our **sins**.

TO KEEP IN MIND

Pause to break up separate thoughts, set apart significant statements, or indicate major shifts. Never pause in the middle of a thought. Your primary guide for pauses is punctuation.

But "God shows no partiality." Peter needed no further confirmation, and therefore called for the Baptism of Cornelius and his household. As Paul says elsewhere, "There is neither Jew nor Greek, there is neither slave nor free person, there is not male and female; for you are all one in Christ Jesus" (Galatians 3:28).

READING II   Today's Second Reading does not appear to have an obvious connection to the First Reading unless we consider how an inclusive community of faith is formed and sustained.

Love is the answer, but not the kind of love that shows favorites or seeks a "feel-good" experience from the other. Biblical scholars recognize that the writers of the Gospel of John and the Letters of John are not entirely consistent in the way they talk about love, but the Greek word which is translated here as "love" is *agape.* It is a self-giving love that expects no return.

Using the word *agape* and related words, the author of this letter admonishes the beloved members of the community, saying that they ought to love one another, because God is love and love is of God.

How do we know the love of God? The author says that we know it not in what we do for God but what God does for us, in particular, in the sending of his Son. The Greek word *hilasmos,* which is here translated as "expiation," appears only twice in the entire New Testament—here and in 1 John 2:2—and it could also be translated as "appeasement," "expiation," or "sin offering." However, we should not think of expiation in terms of an angry God who demands his "pound of flesh" for humanity's sin through the death of his Son. No! The love of God consists in God loving us first and always!

GOSPEL   John 15:9–17

A reading from the holy Gospel according to John

Jesus said to his **disciples**:
"As the Father loves **me**, so I also love **you**.
Remain in my **love**.
If you keep my **commandments**, you will remain in my **love**,
   just as **I** have kept my Father's **commandments**
   and **remain** in his **love**.

"I have told you this so that my **joy** may be in **you**
   and your **joy** might be **complete**.
This is my commandment: **love** one another as I love **you**.
No one has greater love than **this**,
   to lay down one's **life** for one's **friends**.
You are my **friends** if you do what I **command** you.
I no **longer** call you **slaves**,
   because a **slave** does not **know** what his master is **doing**.
I have called you **friends**,
   because I have told you **everything** I have heard from
    my **Father**.
It was not **you** who chose **me**, but **I** who chose **you**
   and appointed you to **go** and bear **fruit** that will **remain**,
   so that whatever you **ask** the Father in my **name** he may
    give you.
This I command you: **love** one another."

An exhortatory reading in which Jesus expresses his commandment to love one another. The reading exudes a kind of rational passion.

One of several parallels in this reading: "Father" to "me," "I" to "you."

In John's Gospel, when Jesus speaks and uses the phrase "just as," he is typically making an analogy between God the Father and himself the Son; or, as here, he is suggesting that as he relates to God the Father, so we the people relate to him.

This commandment could not be stated more clearly.

Another parallel, another contrast: from slaves to friends.

And another: not you to me, but me to you.

The commandment is so important, Jesus repeats it. Consider that your assembly still needs to hear this, over and over.

GOSPEL   Today's Gospel is a continuation of last Sunday's reading from the Gospel of John. It is part of the "vine and the branches" section of the farewell discourse that Jesus delivers to his disciples before his arrest and crucifixion. Imagine Jesus trying to prepare his disciples for what will happen in the chaotic and violent days ahead. In the section of the discourse that follows today's reading, he warns them about the world's hate, and he tells them that they should not be surprised that they will be persecuted just as he was persecuted, because "no slave is greater than his master" (John 15:20).

And what is the antidote to the world's hate? Amazingly, it is love. Again, imagine Jesus trying to raise his disciples out of deep despair by telling them to love one another as he loves them, but this is no casual or superficial love. Rather, it is rooted in the love that the Father and Son have for each other. It is the kind of love that prompts someone to give their life for another. It is the kind of love that changes the disciples' status from slaves to friends; it brings them into an intimacy with Christ such that only his dearest friends know what the Father shares with him. What have the disciples done to earn this special status? Nothing! They did not choose Jesus. Rather, Jesus chose them, and now they must go out and bear fruit by loving one another. C. C.

THE ASCENSION OF THE LORD

LECTIONARY #58

READING I   Acts of the Apostles 1:1–11

A reading from the Acts of the Apostles

In the **first** book, Theophilus,
  I dealt with **all** that Jesus **did** and **taught**
  until the **day** he was taken **up**,
  after giving **instructions** through the Holy **Spirit**
  to the **apostles** whom he had **chosen**.
He presented himself **alive** to them
  by many **proofs** after he had **suffered**,
  appearing to them during forty **days**
  and **speaking** about the **kingdom** of God.
While **meeting** with them,
  he **enjoined** them not to **depart** from **Jerusalem**,
  but to **wait** for "the **promise** of the **Father**
  about which you have **heard** me **speak**;
  for John baptized with **water**,
  but in a few days you will be **baptized** with the Holy **Spirit**."

When they had gathered **together** they asked him,
  "**Lord**, are you at this time going to **restore**
  the **kingdom** to Israel?"
He answered them, "It is not for you to know the **times**
    or **seasons**
  that the **Father** has established by his own **authority**.

Theophilus = thee-AWF-uh-luhs

A narrative reading that recounts the Ascension of Jesus, along with some of last words. The reading is dramatic and visionary. You will only need to proclaim it with care for its power to come through.

"The day he was taken up": the Ascension. The vertical direction is important.

This question allows Jesus to provide the disciples specific details of their task as well as advice before he departs.

There are options for today's readings. Contact your parish staff to learn which readings will be used.

READING I Christians celebrate the Ascension of the Lord forty days after Easter. The number forty is symbolic, often representing a period of transition from one state to another. Luke recounts the event briefly in his Gospel (Luke 24:50–53), but the more detailed account is found in the Acts of the Apostles, also written by Luke. In today's reading, Luke begins by recalling what he wrote to Theophilus ("lover of God") in the prologue of his Gospel (Luke 1:1–4) about what Jesus said and did until the time he was taken up (Gk. *analambano*, meaning "to take up, to raise, or to take to oneself"). The passive form of the verb suggests that God is the source or cause of the "taking up." Luke adds that the Apostles and others were witnesses to Jesus' Resurrection insofar as they were privy to his appearances, but he singles out the Apostles as the ones who received Jesus' instructions through

Emphasize "witnesses." Witnessing is
essential to discipleship.

Judea = joo-DEE-uh

Samaria = suh-MAYR-ee-uh

But you will **receive** power when the Holy **Spirit** comes
>   **upon** you,
>   and you will be my **witnesses** in Jerusalem,
>   throughout **Judea** and **Samaria**,
>   and to the **ends** of the **earth**."
When he had **said** this, as they were looking **on**,
>   he was lifted **up**, and a **cloud** took him from their **sight**.
While they were looking **intently** at the sky as he was **going**,
>   suddenly two men **dressed** in white **garments** stood
>   **beside** them.
They said, "Men of **Galilee**,
>   why are you **standing** there looking at the **sky**?
This Jesus who has been taken **up** from you into **heaven**
>   will **return** in the same way as you have **seen** him going
>   into **heaven**."

The reading concludes with a vision of two
angelic beings. Give their speech that
follows emphasis by slowing your pace ever
so slightly.

For meditation and context:

RESPONSORIAL PSALM   Psalm 47:2–3, 6–7, 8–9 (6)

R. God mounts his throne to shouts of joy: a blare of trumpets for the Lord.
or
R. Alleluia.

All you peoples, clap your hands,
>   shout to God with cries of gladness.
For the LORD, the Most High, the awesome,
>   is the great king over all the earth.

God mounts his throne amid shouts of joy;
>   the LORD, amid trumpet blasts.

Sing praise to God, sing praise;
>   sing praise to our king, sing praise.

For king of all the earth is God;
>   sing hymns of praise.
God reigns over the nations,
>   God sits upon his holy throne.

READING II   Ephesians 1:17–23

A reading from the Letter of Saint Paul to the Ephesians

Brothers and **sisters**:
May the **God** of our Lord Jeus **Christ**, the Father of **glory**,
>   give you a Spirit of **wisdom** and **revelation**
>   resulting in **knowledge** of him. »

Ephesians = ee-FEE-zhuhnz

An exhortatory reading, filled with high-
hearted blessings.

The first blessing comes from God to the
people of Ephesus.

the Holy Spirit. The "promise of the Father" recalls the ending of the Gospel (Luke 24:49) and refers to the sending of the Holy Spirit.

Luke uses language of the coming kingdom of God and the return of Christ at the end time to talk about what will happen in this new age of the Spirit. We hear that the Apostles will be commissioned to be

his witnesses in Jerusalem and even to the ends of the earth. Then suddenly Jesus is lifted up (Gk. *eperthe*, meaning "taken up or exalted") and received or hidden by a cloud, as the Apostles looked on. The two men dressed in white are a reminder of the Resurrection story (cf. Luke 24:4–9). Their message, that Jesus will return in the same way that he was taken up—on a cloud—is

an allusion to the end-time return of Christ (see Luke 21:27). Thus, the Ascension of Jesus becomes a precursor and promise of the Parousia, whenever it may come.

READING II **Ephesians 4.** Our second reading indirectly addresses a question somewhat similar to the one the Apostles of Jesus ask in the first reading:

The second blessing comes from Paul to the people of Ephesus, including knowledge, hope, and the riches of glory. Give each aspect of this blessing its due by emphasizing it slightly.

These are the traditional names of some of the angelic powers.

Paul concludes by invoking the power of Jesus himself.

May the **eyes** of your hearts be **enlightened**,
    that you may **know** what is the **hope** that belongs to his **call**,
    what are the **riches** of glory
    in his **inheritance** among the holy **ones**,
    and what is the surpassing **greatness** of his **power**
    for **us** who **believe**,
    in **accord** with the exercise of his **great might**,
    which he **worked** in **Christ**,
    raising him from the **dead**
    and **seating** him at his right **hand** in the **heavens**,
    far above every **principality**, **authority**, **power**, and **dominion**,
    and every **name** that is **named**
    not only in this **age** but also in the one to **come**.
And he put **all things** beneath his **feet**
    and gave him as **head** over all things to the church,
    which is his **body**,
    the **fullness** of the one who fills **all things** in every **way**.

Or:

READING II   Ephesians 4:1–13

A reading from the Letter of Saint Paul to the Ephesians

[**Brothers** and **sisters**,
I, a prisoner for the **Lord**,
    urge you to live in a **manner** worthy of the **call** you
        have **received**,
    with all **humility** and **gentleness**, with **patience**,
    bearing with one another through **love**,
    striving to preserve the **unity** of the **spirit**
    through the **bond** of peace:
    one **body** and one **Spirit**,
    as you were also **called** to the one **hope** of your **call**;

Ephesians = ee-FEE-zhuhnz

An exhortatory reading in which Paul attempts to convince the members of the early Church at Ephesus to unify despite what seem to be significant differences, perhaps even strife. Paul's message in this reading can feel particularly resonant today.

"Lord, are you at this time going to restore the kingdom?" (Acts 1:6). At least the response is similar. Inspired by the Spirit, Christians are told to take up the call to be witnesses to the crucified and resurrected Christ. How best do we witness to Christ? In our behavior, which the author of the Letter to the Ephesians describes as humility, gentleness, patience, and restraint motivated by love. It is manifest in the believers' commitment to a sevenfold unity of the

spirit. Seven is a symbolic number, representing fullness and perfection. But unity of spirit does not mean conformity or collapsing of roles within the Christian community. This author identifies five as necessary for "building up the Body of Christ" and for completing its "work of ministry." To contextualize and add validity to the giving of these gifts, this author cites a version of Psalm 68:19 and gives it a Christological interpretation. Now, the ascended one is

Jesus Christ, and, if he ascended, the author argues, he must have first descended to the earth.

Ephesians 1. Our alternate reading for the feast of the Ascension comes from the Letter to the Ephesians. In this reading, the author offers a prayer of intercession that focuses on the exaltation of the risen Christ and on the Church as Christ's body. It is preceded by a brief statement of thanksgiving for the faith and love of the Ephesian

Note the rhythms created by the use of "one," stressing unity.

one **Lord**, one **faith**, one **baptism**;
one **God** and Father of **all**,
who is **over all** and **through all** and in **all**.

But grace was given to each of us
according to the **measure** of Christ's **gift**.]
Therefore, it says:
*He **ascended** on high and took **prisoners** captive;*
*he gave **gifts** to men.*
What does "he ascended" **mean** except that he also **descended**
into the **lower regions** of the **earth**?
The one who **descended** is also the one who **ascended**
far above all the **heavens**,
that he might fill all **things**.

Read slowly here to allow for the assembly to follow Paul's unusual logic.

[And he gave **some** as **apostles**, others as **prophets**,
others as **evangelists**, others as **pastors** and **teachers**,
to equip the **holy ones** for the **work** of ministry,
for **building** up the body of **Christ**,
until we **all** attain to the **unity** of faith
and **knowledge** of the Son of **God**, to mature manhood,
to the **extent** of the full **stature** of Christ.]

Emphasize each of these different roles as part of the unity of the early Church.

[Shorter: Ephesians 4:1–7, 11–13 (see brackets)]

GOSPEL   Mark 16:15–20

A reading from the holy Gospel according to Mark

A narrative reading with exhortations from the longer ending to Mark's Gospel, offering a more optimistic ending than Mark 16:8.

Jesus said to his disciples:
"**Go** into the whole **world**
and proclaim the **gospel** to every **creature**.
Whoever **believes** and is **baptized** will be **saved**;
whoever does not believe will be **condemned**. ≫

Emphasize these three words "believes," "baptized," and "saved." Contrast them to "condemned" in the next line.

community (Ephesians 1:15–16). The author of this letter first asks for a spirit of wisdom and revelation (Gk. *apocalypseos*, also meaning "a laying bare or manifestation") in knowledge of "the Father of glory" for this community of faith. He also prays that the eyes of their heart might be enlightened so they can realize the power of their calling in Christ. In the ancient world, eyes were about insight, and the heart was the seat of the emotions. Note also the author's

many uses of words such as "glory" and "power" in this reading, as well as allusions to Psalm 110:1 and Psalm 8:7 to make this point. This same power, the author says, was used to exalt Christ to his place at the right hand of God's throne, to establish his authority over all things, and to make him head of the Church, which is his body. Thus, he makes the Church a recipient of Christ's authority over all things.

GOSPEL Today's reading belongs to the longer ending of Mark's Gospel (Mark 16:9–20). It is generally thought to be a second-century addition to the original Gospel, which concludes at 16:8 with the women running from the empty tomb and telling no one what they saw, because they were afraid. This longer ending compensates for the absence of appearance narratives like those in the other Gospels. It also includes a commissioning

Note each of the signs Jesus names.

These signs will accompany those who **believe**:
    in my **name** they will drive out **demons**,
    they will **speak** new languages.
They will pick up **serpents** with their **hands**,
    and if they drink any deadly **thing**, it will not **harm** them.
They will lay **hands** on the sick, and they will **recover**."

The passage—and Mark's Gospel in the longer ending—concludes with Jesus' Ascension. Emphasize "confirmed" and "accompanying" in the last line.

So then the Lord Jesus, after he **spoke** to them,
    was taken **up** into **heaven**
    and took his seat at the **right hand** of **God**.
But they went **forth** and preached **everywhere**,
    while the Lord worked **with** them
    and **confirmed** the word through **accompanying** signs.

PRAYERFUL READING, OR *LECTIO DIVINA*

1. *Lectio:* Read a Scripture passage aloud slowly. Notice what phrase captures your attention and be attentive to its meaning. Silent pause.

2. *Meditatio:* Read the passage aloud slowly again, reflecting on the passage, allowing God to speak to you through it. Silent pause.

3. *Oratio:* Read it aloud slowly a third time, allowing it to be your prayer or response to God's gift of insight to you. Silent pause.

4. *Contemplatio:* Read it aloud slowly a fourth time, now resting in God's Word.

---

of the Apostles to go out to preach and baptize in Jesus' name that sounds very much like that in Matthew 28:18–20 and in Luke 24:47. Likewise, the risen Jesus gives authority to his followers to perform signs to accompany their preaching. It ends with a brief mention of Jesus being taken up to heaven to assume his seat at the right hand of God. C. C.

SEVENTH SUNDAY OF EASTER

LECTIONARY #60

READING I   Acts of the Apostles 1:15–17, 20a, 20c–26

A reading from the Acts of the Apostles

Peter stood up in the **midst** of the brothers
—there was a **group** of about one hundred and twenty persons
in the one place—.
He said, "My **brothers**,
the **Scripture** had to be **fulfilled**
which the Holy **Spirit** spoke **beforehand**
through the **mouth** of David, concerning **Judas**,
who was the **guide** for those who arrested **Jesus**.
He was **numbered** among us
and was **allotted** a share in this ministry.

"For it is **written** in the Book of Psalms:
May another take his **office***.*

"**Therefore**, it is **necessary** that one of the men
who **accompanied** us the whole time
the Lord Jesus came and went **among** us,
beginning from the baptism of **John**
until the **day** on which he was taken **up** from us,
become with us a **witness** to his **resurrection**."
So they proposed **two**, **Judas** called **Barsabbas**,
who was also known as **Justus**, and **Matthias**. »

A narrative reading that emphasizes the effectiveness of Peter's leadership of the early Church, as well as demonstrating some of the process of its inner workings. "My brothers," as a statement, is an example of Peter's leadership.

"Therefore" initiates a description of the process of selecting a new disciple to replace Judas.

Barsabbas = bahr-SAH-buhs
Justus = JUS-tuhs
Matthias = muh-THĪ-uhs

READING I   Today's first reading, which is taken from the Acts of the Apostles, addresses another of the first tasks of the post-Easter Church: restoring the number of Jesus' Apostles to twelve by replacing the one who betrayed him. In Luke's chronology, this story appears between the Ascension of Jesus and Pentecost. The story begins in Jerusalem. Peter is surrounded by a group of 120 brothers (Gk. *adelphos*, also meaning "kinfolk or fellow believer"), suggesting a group of closely connected disciples of Jesus that encompasses more than the twelve

Apostles. The number is significant because it is a multiple of twelve, a perfect number, and a recollection of the twelve tribes that inhabited the land of Israel.

Peter rises, signaling that he is about to give a speech. His opening phrase, "the Scripture had to be fulfilled," contains the Greek word *dei*, which means "it is necessary that" or "God ordained it that." Quoting Psalm 109:8—"May another take his office"—Peter indicates that Judas' replacement should be someone who had been part of the group that was with Jesus from his baptism in Galilee to his death and resurrection

in Jerusalem. Of the two names that were put forward, Matthias was chosen by lot. Judas Barsabbas is mentioned again in Acts 15:22 as a participant in the Jerusalem Conference, where Paul and the leaders of the Jerusalem church agreed that Gentiles could become Jesus' followers without first becoming Jews. Matthias is mentioned nowhere else in the New Testament. In some parts of the ancient world, selection by lottery was considered part of a democratic form of governance. Here, it is a way of turning the decision over to God of who should take on the Apostle's task to be a

Ultimately, Matthias is chosen.

Then they prayed,
  "You, Lord, who **know** the hearts of **all**,
    show which one of these **two** you have **chosen**
    to **take** the place in this apostolic **ministry**
    from which **Judas** turned away to **go** to his own **place**."
Then they gave **lots** to them, and the lot fell upon **Matthias**,
    and he was **counted** with the eleven **apostles**.

For meditation and context:

RESPONSORIAL PSALM   Psalm 103:1–2, 11–12, 19–20 (19a)

R. The Lord has set his throne in heaven.
or
R. Alleluia.

Bless the LORD, O my soul;
  and all my being, bless his holy name.
Bless the LORD, O my soul,
  and forget not all his benefits.

For as the heavens are high above the earth,
  so surpassing is his kindness toward
    those who fear him.

As far as the east is from the west,
  so far has he put our transgressions
    from us.

The LORD has established his throne
    in heaven,
  and his kingdom rules over all.
Bless the LORD, all you his angels,
  you mighty in strength, who do
    his bidding.

READING II   1 John 4:11–16

An exhortatory reading from John's first epistle, insisting that God is love.
This is at the core of John's message: We must love one another.

A reading from the first Letter of Saint John

Beloved, if God so **loved** us,
  we also must **love** one **another**.
No one has ever **seen** God.
Yet, if we **love** one another, God **remains** in us,
  and his **love** is brought to perfection in **us**.

This is how we know that we **remain** in him and he in **us**,
  that he has **given** us of his **Spirit**.
Moreover, we have **seen** and **testify**
  that the **Father** sent his Son as **savior** of the world.

Emphasize "seen" and "testify."

---

witness to Christ's Resurrection and to share in the apostolic ministry.

READING II This reading from the First Letter of John focuses on two interrelated themes that appear frequently in the Gospel and Letters of John: the command to love one another and the invitation to remain or abide with God or abide with Jesus, who abides with the Father. Concerning the first theme, this is no ordinary love. No, this command to love (Gk. *agapao*, meaning "to love, to be full of good will and act on it") is predicated on

knowing and experiencing God's love. We are commanded to love as God loves and because God first loved us. It is this divine love that we should manifest to others. And the evidence of God's love is that God sent his Son to be our savior. Related to this theme, the author of this letter calls to mind a central theme of the Gospel of John, "No one has ever seen God," that is, except Jesus who reveals God to us (John 1:18).

The second interrelated theme of this reading is abiding (Gk. *menein*, meaning "to sojourn, to tarry, to continue to be, to remain"). The concept is a difficult one

to grasp, but we might think of it as being in such an intimate relationship with the other —in this case, God—that for all intents and purposes we dwell in God and God dwells in us. The author of this letter tells us that we know we abide in God, because God has given us of his Spirit. But he also asserts that God is love, so whoever abides in love abides in God and God in him. This is what it means to have God's love perfected in us.

GOSPEL Today's Gospel belongs to what is sometimes called

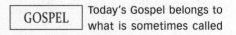

Whoever **acknowledges** that Jesus is the **Son** of God,
God **remains** in him and **he** in God.
We have come to **know** and to **believe** in the love God **has** for us.

God is **love**, and whoever **remains** in love
remains in **God** and **God** in **him**.

The message in this line simply cannot be overstated. Express it clearly to acknowledge its breadth and importance.

GOSPEL   John 17:11b–19

A reading from the holy Gospel according to John

Lifting up his eyes to **heaven**, Jesus prayed, saying:
"Holy Father, **keep** them in your name that you have
given me,
so that they may be **one** just as **we** are one.
When I was **with** them I **protected** them in your name that you
gave me,
and I **guarded** them, and **none of them** was lost
except the **son** of destruction,
in order that the **Scripture** might be **fulfilled**.
But **now** I am coming to **you**.
I **speak** this in the **world**
so that they may **share** my joy **completely**.
I gave them your **word**, and the world **hated** them,
because they do not **belong** to the world
any more than **I** belong to the world.
I do not **ask** that you take them **out** of the world
but that you **keep** them from the **evil** one.
They do not **belong** to the world
any more than I belong to the world.
Consecrate them in the **truth**. Your **word** is **truth**.
As you **sent** me into the **world**,
so **I** sent them into the world.
And I **consecrate** myself **for** them,
so that they **also** may be consecrated in **truth**."

An exhortatory reading. It's actually a prayer Jesus offers to his disciples. By extension, through this Gospel reading, it's offered to the Church.

The opening of the prayer is particularly sincere.

"But now I am coming to you." This phrase is keen with anticipation. Jesus wants God to take care of his followers.

He expresses his care in a wish for their consecration in the truth. "Truth" occurs three times at the end of this passage. Give the word a little extra emphasis each time you speak it.

---

the Priestly Prayer of Jesus (John 17:1–26). It begins with details that evoke a setting of formal prayer, especially the mention of Jesus' eyes directed toward heaven. Although the Johannine Jesus regularly identifies God as Father, this is the only time God is addressed as "Holy Father." His petition that the Father keep the disciples in his name, as Jesus had done, suggests a time when Jesus will no longer be with them in the flesh. The notion of Jesus "keeping" the disciples might be an allusion to the image of Jesus as the Good Shepherd who keeps his sheep (John 10:11–18).

Guarding the disciples so that "none of them was lost" anticipates the arrest of Jesus, in which he tells his captors to release the others. "This was to fulfill what he had said, 'I have not lost any of those you gave me'" (John 18:9). The phrase "son of destruction" refers to Judas, who betrayed Jesus. Further, the phrase "in order that the Scripture might be fulfilled" might be a reference to John 13:1–11, the story of Jesus washing the disciples' feet, in which John's Jesus says, "Whoever has bathed has no need except to have his feet washed, for he is clean all over; so you are clean, but not all" (John 13:10).

Finally, Jesus asks that the disciples might experience joy at the news that Jesus is returning to the Father. He also asks that God keep them from the evil one. Because they accepted Jesus and abide with him, they should expect to experience the world's hate, just as Jesus did. But unlike Jesus, they remain in the world and therefore are vulnerable to its challenges. In John's Gospel, the "world" is a symbol for the forces that are not aligned with Jesus. C. C.

PENTECOST SUNDAY: VIGIL

LECTIONARY #62

READING I   Genesis 11:1–9

A reading from the Book of Genesis

The whole **world** spoke the same **language**, using the same **words**.
While the **people** were migrating in the east,
    they came upon a **valley** in the land of **Shinar** and settled there.
They said to one another,
    "**Come**, let us mold **bricks** and harden them with **fire**."
They used **bricks** for stone, and **bitumen** for mortar.
Then they said, "**Come**, let us **build** ourselves a **city**
    and a **tower** with its **top** in the **sky**,
    and so make a **name** for ourselves;
    otherwise we shall be **scattered** all over the **earth**."

The **LORD** came down to see the **city** and the **tower**
    that the **people** had built.
Then the LORD said: "If **now**, while they are one **people**,
    all **speaking** the same **language**,
    they have **started** to do this,
    nothing will later stop them from doing **whatever** they
        presume to do.
Let us then go **down** there and **confuse** their language,
    so that **one** will not **understand** what another **says**."
Thus the LORD **scattered** them from **there** all over the **earth**,
    and they **stopped** building the city.
That is why it was called **Babel**,
    because **there** the LORD **confused** the speech of **all** the world.
It was from **that** place that he **scattered** them all over the **earth**.

Genesis = JEN-uh-sihs
Shinar = SHĪ-nahr
bitumen = bih-TYOO-m*n

A narrative reading of a story absorbed in mysterious power. As much a parable as it is a demonstration of the incomprehensible mind of God, it can seem almost like science fiction. It's probably best to treat it that way in terms of proclaiming it: Read what's in the text, straightforwardly and clearly.

The two repetitions of "Come" stand for the aspirations—or arrogance—of the people. Give a little edge to the word when you speak it.

God's use of "let us" repeats the use of the builders of the tower. Here, God's intention is unhelpful, destructive even. "Confuse" is the loaded word.

Babel = BAB-*l

Note the repetition of "confuse" in "confused." The word suggests something of the power of God.

There are options for today's readings. Contact your parish staff to learn which readings will be used.

READING I   The Tower of Babel is the last in a series of stories contained in Genesis 1—11 that are about human sin and its consequences. One of the central themes of these stories is humanity's desire to be great or wise like God. Another is God's wish to respect humans' ability to choose, while also trying to limit the negative effects of humanity's sin on the created order. It is a bit like a patient but determined parent trying to corral a difficult and disobedient child! In the chapters that precede the Tower of Babel story, we learn that God wanted the people who survived the flood to migrate and repopulate the earth. But as they wandered, they came to a place called Shinar (today, southern Iraq), and they decided to settle down and build a great city and a tower so as to appear very powerful in order not to be scattered across the land.

The tower that the people wanted to build was intended to penetrate the heavens where God dwelt, which, of course, could not be permitted, because it went against the relationship of creator and creature. If humans were able to bridge the gap between the human and divine world, they might even impinge on the sovereignty of God and there would be no end to the evil they might do. Thus, God decided to limit their ability to harm themselves by confusing their language so that one could not speak to the other. The Hebrew word

For meditation and context:

RESPONSORIAL PSALM   Psalm 33:10–11, 12–13, 14–15

R. Blessed the people the Lord has chosen to be his own.

The Lord brings to nought the plans
    of nations;
  he foils the designs of peoples.
But the plan of the Lord stands forever;
  the design of his heart, through all
    generations.

Blessed the nation whose God is the Lord,
  the people he has chosen for his own
    inheritance.

From heaven the Lord looks down;
  he sees all mankind.
From his fixed throne he beholds
  all who dwell on the earth,
He who fashioned the heart of each,
  he who knows all their works.

READING II   Exodus 19:3–8a, 16–20b

Exodus = EK-suh-duhs

A narrative reading of the sealing of the covenant between God and humankind, attended by powerful natural phenomena. The scene of this reading is especially vivid.

A reading from the Book of Exodus

Moses went up the **mountain** to God.
Then the Lord **called** to him and said,
  "**Thus** shall you **say** to the house of **Jacob**;
  tell the **Israelites**:
  You have **seen** for yourselves how I **treated** the Egyptians
  and how I **bore** you up on **eagle wings**
  and **brought** you here to **myself**.

"Therefore" initiates the terms of the covenant. Say it with authority.

Therefore, if you **hearken** to my voice and **keep** my covenant,
  you shall be my **special** possession,
  dearer to me than **all** other people,
  though **all** the earth is **mine**.
You shall be to me a **Kingdom** of priests, a **holy** nation.
That is what you must **tell** the Israelites."
So **Moses** went and summoned the **elders** of the people.
When he set **before** them
  all that the Lord had **ordered** him to tell them,
  the people all answered together,
  "**Everything** the Lord has **said**, we will **do**." »

"Everything the Lord has said, we will do": With these words, the covenant is sealed. Emphasis on "do."

---

for "confused" is *balal*, a play on the word *babel*, which is the Hebrew form of the name of the city Babylon. To the Babylonians it meant "gate of god." The tower imagery is reminiscent of the Babylonian high holy places, the ziggurats.

READING II This reading recalls the Jewish feast after which the Christian Pentecost is named. Also called Shavuot or the Feast of Weeks, the Jewish Pentecost occurs fifty days, or seven weeks, after Passover. Likewise, the

Christian Pentecost occurs fifty days, or seven weeks, after Easter. Shavuot is celebrated in thanksgiving for the giving of the Law on Mount Sinai. Exodus 19 provides an account of this important event. It begins with Moses going up the mountain and God calling down to him (Exodus 19:3–8a). A brief liturgical poem follows: God reminds the people that he has been keeping covenant with them, protecting them and making them into God's sacred people (Exodus 19:4–6). Notice that God is compared to an eagle caring for its young and keeping them

safe from harm. This image of God as an eagle appears again in Deuteronomy 32:10–14 and with greater detail.

After the poem, the narrator of the story explains that Moses did what God directed him to do—and how the people gave their assent to obey all that God told them (Exodus 19:7–8). The lectionary omits the next section of the reading from Exodus, the consecration of the people in preparation for their encounter with God (Exodus 19:9–15).

Natural forces express themselves vividly in response.

Even stresses on the words in this line.

On the **morning** of the third **day**
  there were **peals** of thunder and lightning,
  and a heavy **cloud** over the mountain,
  and a very loud trumpet blast,
  so that all the **people** in the camp **trembled**.
But **Moses** led the people **out** of the camp to meet **God**,
  and they **stationed** themselves at the foot of the **mountain**.
Mount **Sinai** was all wrapped in **smoke**,
  for the LORD came down **upon** it in **fire**.
The smoke **rose** from it as though from a **furnace**,
  and the whole **mountain** trembled **violently**.
The trumpet blast grew **louder** and **louder**, while Moses
      was speaking,
  and God **answering** him with **thunder**.

When the LORD came **down** to the top of Mount **Sinai**,
  he summoned **Moses** to the top of the **mountain**.

The vision of smoke and fire signals the power of God. These words paint a potent picture. No need, however, to raise your voice. Keep it steady.

For meditation and context:

RESPONSORIAL PSALM   Daniel 3:52, 53, 54, 55, 56

R. Glory and praise for ever!

"Blessed are you, O Lord, the God of
    our fathers,
  praiseworthy and exalted above
    all forever;
And blessed is your holy and glorious name,
  praiseworthy and exalted above
    all for all ages."

"Blessed are you in the temple of your
    holy glory,
  praiseworthy and glorious above
    all forever."

Or:

"Blessed are you on the throne of
    your Kingdom,
  praiseworthy and exalted above
    all forever."

"Blessed are you who look into the depths
    from your throne upon the cherubim,
  praiseworthy and exalted above
    all forever."

"Blessed are you in the firmament of heaven,
  praiseworthy and glorious forever."

TO KEEP IN MIND
The responsorial psalm "has great liturgical and pastoral importance, since it fosters meditation on the Word of God," the *General Instruction on the Roman Missal* says. Pray it as you prepare.

Today's reading picks up the story again with a description of God's descent to the mountaintop (Exodus 19:16–20b). What a marvelous theophany—manifestation of the divine—complete with thunder, lightning, smoke, and fire! The trumpet, whose sound gets louder and louder, is the shofar, a religious instrument made from a ram's horn. The mountain is now God's holy mountain for all time, because God has come down to visit God's people on this mountain.

READING III   The prophet Ezekiel was a priest of the Jerusalem Temple in the early decades of the sixth century BC, during the time that Babylon was amassing power in the region. Judah's king Jehoiakim attempted to break from Babylon's rule, and in 598 the Babylonian army plundered Jerusalem and deported its skilled and elite to Babylon. Ezekiel was among them, and there he began his ministry. Back in Judah, the Babylonian

king Nebuchadnezzar installed a "puppet" king named Zedekiah, but he too tried to rebel against the Babylonians, and the Babylonian armies returned in vengeance to utterly destroy the kingdom of Judah. In a little more than a decade, the Temple in Jerusalem was destroyed, and the cities of Judah were decimated. Zedekiah, too, was deported to Babylon, where he eventually died. The scope of the devastation was enormous. Having lost king, land, and

For meditation and context:

RESPONSORIAL PSALM   Psalm 19:8, 9, 10, 11

R. Lord, you have the words of everlasting life.

The law of the Lord is perfect,
refreshing the soul;
The decree of the Lord is trustworthy,
giving wisdom to the simple.

The precepts of the Lord are right,
rejoicing the heart;
The command of the Lord is clear,
enlightening the eye.

The fear of the Lord is pure,
enduring forever;
The ordinances of the Lord are true,
all of them just.

They are more precious than gold,
than a heap of purest gold;
Sweeter also than syrup
or honey from the comb.

READING III   Ezekiel 37:1–14

A reading from the Book of the Prophet Ezekiel

The **hand** of the Lord came **upon** me,
and he led me **out** in the **spirit** of the Lord
and set me in the **center** of the **plain**,
which was now **filled** with **bones**.
He made me **walk** among the **bones** in every **direction**
so that I saw how **many** they were on the **surface** of the plain.
How **dry** they were!
He asked me:
Son of **man**, can these **bones** come to **life**?
I answered, "Lord God, you **alone know** that."
Then he said to me:
Prophesy over these **bones**, and **say** to them:
Dry bones, **hear** the **word** of the Lord!
Thus **says** the Lord God to these **bones**:
See! I will bring spirit into you, that you may come to **life**.
I will put **sinews** upon you, make flesh grow **over** you,
cover you with **skin**, and put spirit **in** you
so that you may come to **life** and **know** that I am the Lord.

Sidebar notes (left margin):

Ezekiel = ee-ZEE-kee-uhl

A narrative reading with visionary passages of exquisite strangeness and power. God speaks to and through Ezekiel throughout this reading. Because the punctuation isn't entirely clear, it's useful to have markers for when God is speaking and when Ezekiel is speaking for himself.

This reading makes use of the verb "prophesy" as well as its past tense, "prophesied." Pronunciation is important. Prophesy = PROPH-eh-sigh (not PROPH-eh-see); prophesied = PROPH-eh-side (not PROPH-eh-seed). Be sure to practice!

The vision, which is frightening, begins here with the valley of dry bones. The life of this vision relies on these dry bones coming to life.
God begins to speak here.
sinews = sin-yooz

Emphasis on "know."

---

holy place, the exiles were grief-stricken, because they believed that God had completely abandoned the chosen people.

This is the historical context for Ezekiel's vision of the valley of dry bones and the interpretation that follows it. The text suggests that the vision is a response to the people's lament, "Our bones are dried up, our hope is lost, and we are cut off." The plain to which Ezekiel is led appears to be the same one where he encountered the glory of the Lord earlier in his career and was told to restrain himself and not speak, except when the Lord tells him, and then only to say, "They are truly a rebellious house." Now, Ezekiel is made to see the full extent of the devastation brought on by the Babylonians against Judah—dry bones everywhere!

After acknowledging that only God can bring dead Israel back to life, Ezekiel is told to prophesy to the bones, and tell them that, if they hear God's word, God will bring spirit into them and they will return to life. Ezekiel does as he is told, and, before his eyes, the bones come together and flesh grows on them. Ezekiel is also told to prophesy to the spirit and tell it to breathe life into the bodies lying on the plain. The Hebrew word for "spirit" is *ruah*, meaning also "wind" and "breath." God's *ruah* will bring Israel back to life and make it into a mighty army! The reference to graves in the next couple

Ezekiel himself is speaking here.

I, **Ezekiel**, **prophesied** as I had been **told**,
    and even as I was **prophesying** I heard a **noise**;
    it was a **rattling** as the bones came together, **bone** joining **bone**.
I saw the **sinews** and the **flesh** come **upon** them,
    and the skin **cover** them, but there was no spirit in them.
Then the LORD said to me:

God begins to speak again here.

    Prophesy to the **spirit**, **prophesy**, son of man,
    and **say** to the spirit: **Thus** says the Lord GOD:
    From the **four winds come**, O spirit,
    and **breathe** into these **slain** that they may **come** to life.

Ezekiel himself is speaking again here.

I **prophesied** as he told me, and the spirit came **into** them;
    they came **alive** and stood **upright**, a vast **army**.
Then he said to me:
    Son of **man**, these **bones** are the **whole house** of Israel.

From here to the end of the reading, God is speaking, even as he quotes the house of Israel.

They have been **saying**,
    "Our **bones** are dried up,
    our **hope** is lost, and we are cut **off**."
Therefore, **prophesy** and say to them: **Thus** says the Lord GOD:
    O my **people**, I will open your **graves**
    and have you **rise** from them,
    and bring you **back** to the land of **Israel**.
Then you shall **know** that I am the LORD,
    when I open your **graves** and have you **rise** from them,
    O my **people**!
I will put my **spirit** in you that you may **live**,
    and I will **settle** you upon your **land**;
    thus you shall **know** that I am the LORD.
I have **promised**, and I will **do** it, says the LORD.

of verses seems out of place, and some biblical scholars think they are a later addition to the text, but the point is clear: only God can bring Israel back to life and, because of the covenant promise, God will do it!

READING IV In earlier Old Testament writings, the Spirit is bestowed only on people who are called to perform a special divine task, for example,

kings and Prophets. Joel makes the astonishing announcement that at some future time the Lord will pour out the Spirit on "all flesh." To emphasize the inclusiveness of those whom God will call, Joel names specifically the young, the old, and servants, those who were undervalued in the biblical world and would be the least likely to be chosen for important missions. Nevertheless, when the Lord pours out the Spirit, they too will proph-

esy. They will take up the tasks of seeing and communicating where God is acting in the human realm.

Joel associates the universal ability to prophesy with the long-expected "day of the Lord," the time when all the invisible divine attention to and working within human affairs through the ages will be recognized by all peoples and nations. This "day" is the Old Testament version of the

For meditation and context:

RESPONSORIAL PSALM Psalm 107:2–3, 4–5, 6–7, 8–9

R. Give thanks to the Lord; his love is everlasting. or
R. Alleluia.

Let the redeemed of the LORD say,
   those whom he has redeemed from the
      hand of the foe
And gathered from the lands,
   from the east and the west, from the north
      and the south.

They went astray in the desert wilderness;
   the way to an inhabited city they did
      not find.
Hungry and thirsty,
   their life was wasting away within them.

They cried to the LORD in their distress;
   from their straits he rescued them.
And he led them by a direct way
   to reach an inhabited city.

Let them give thanks to the LORD for
   his mercy
   and his wondrous deeds to the children
      of men,
Because he satisfied the longing soul
   and filled the hungry soul with
      good things.

READING IV Joel 3:1–5

prophesy = PROF-uh-sī

An exhortatory reading, with a prophetic vision of a cataclysmic event. Scripture often shifts into this visionary mode, which can be exciting to proclaim because the language is so vivid.

A reading from the Book of the Prophet Joel

Thus says the LORD:
I will **pour out** my spirit upon all **flesh**.
   Your **sons** and **daughters** shall **prophesy**,
      your old men shall dream **dreams**,
      your young men shall see **visions**;
   even upon the **servants** and the **handmaids**,
      in those days, I will pour out my **spirit**.
   And I will work **wonders** in the **heavens** and on the **earth**,
      blood, **fire**, and columns of **smoke**;
   the **sun** will be turned to **darkness**,
      and the **moon** to **blood**,
   at the **coming** of the day of the LORD,
      the **great** and terrible **day**. »

"The great and terrible day": with these words, Joel concludes his vision.

Parousia, the return of the risen Christ at the end of time. Both testaments employ apocalyptic language—like the darkened sun, the bloodied moon—to convey the Lord's unrivaled power and reach.

| EPISTLE | The theme of rebirth and new life pervades all of the readings for the Vigil of Pentecost, and this is no less true of today's second reading from Paul's Letter to the Romans. This lec-

tionary reading appears at the end of a long section of text that began at Romans 5:1. The overarching theme of this section is the benefits that come to those who are justified by faith in Jesus Christ. Very briefly, Paul teaches that, through God's love and as a free gift, all who open themselves to receive it are acquitted of wrongdoing by the death and Resurrection of Jesus. Justification is a legal term that means "acquittal," as in a court of law. Acquittal

does not mean that humanity has not sinned, only that God dismissed the charges to usher in new life for the Christian believer. Of course, new life is accompanied by suffering, whether it be the labor pains of a mother about to give birth to a child or the struggles of creation as it emerges out of winter and moves into spring. Paul uses both images in this text as he writes about the destiny of Christian believers who hope, that is, practice steadfast endurance, as

The vision is immediately followed by the promise of rescue from God, which continues to the end of the reading. Don't overdo your reading, but you can shift to a slightly more optimistic tone.

Then **everyone** shall be **rescued**
who **calls** on the name of the LORD;
for on Mount **Zion** there shall be a **remnant**,
as the LORD has said,
and in **Jerusalem** survivors
whom the LORD shall **call**.

For meditation and context:

RESPONSORIAL PSALM   Psalm 104:1–2, 24 and 35c, 27–28, 29bc–30 (SEE 30)

R. **Lord, send out your Spirit, and renew the face of the earth.**
or
R. **Alleluia.**

Bless the LORD, O my soul!
    O LORD, my God, you are great indeed!
You are clothed with majesty and glory,
    robed in light as with a cloak.

How manifold are your works, O LORD!
    In wisdom you have wrought them all—
the earth is full of your creatures;
    bless the LORD, O my soul! Alleluia.

Creatures all look to you

to give them food in due time.
When you give it to them, they gather it;
    when you open your hand, they are filled
    with good things.

If you take away their breath, they perish
    and return to their dust.
When you send forth your spirit, they are
    created,
    and you renew the face of the earth.

EPISTLE   Romans 8:22–27

A reading from the Letter of Saint Paul to the Romans

An exhortatory reading that contains a potent and not easily digested message: that life is challenging—Paul compares it to childbirth —and its pain does not abate, even as we hope for its end. Nevertheless, we hope.

The first line after the greeting contains the core of Paul's message. Emphasize "know," "groaning," and "now."

Brothers and **sisters**:
We **know** that all creation is **groaning** in labor pains even
    until **now**;
    and not only **that**, but we **ourselves**,
    who have the **firstfruits** of the **Spirit**,
    we also groan within **ourselves**
    as we wait for **adoption**, the **redemption** of our **bodies**.
For in **hope** we were **saved**.
Now hope that **sees** is not **hope**.

they await the glory that will be theirs as children of God.

Paul earlier asserted that Christian believers are in the spirit and the Holy Spirit dwells in them (Romans 8:9). Here he writes that the believer already possesses the first fruits of the Spirit. In early Judaism, the first fruits of the harvest were offered to God to represent the consecration of the whole harvest to God. However, in this context, Paul probably means that their experience of the Holy Spirit now is a pledge of the glory that is to come. And what is their experience of the Holy Spirit? Paul reminds

them that the Spirit is their helper and that the Spirit intercedes for us in prayer. The Greek word that is translated here as "intercedes" has the sense of "bending over" or "going above and beyond" to intercede. The phrase "who searches hearts" refers to God. Paul is saying that God knows and understands Spirit-assisted prayer, because the Spirit is doing God's will (and only God's will) by interceding for us.

GOSPEL   The feast to which today's Gospel refers is *Sukkot*, also called the Feast of Tabernacles or

Booths. It began as a one-day fall harvest festival, but over time it became linked with a celebration of the dedication of Solomon's Temple. Also, because it was a pilgrimage festival and the massive crowds of visitors to Jerusalem were housed in tents, it became a reminder of the Exodus when the Israelites dwelt in tents. By the first century AD, the feast lasted seven or possibly eight days. It was a time of great celebration, including thanksgiving for the harvest and prayers for God's blessing of rain for the coming year. Every morning during *Sukkot*, priests and Levites of the Temple would go

For who **hopes** for what one **sees**?
But if we **hope** for what we do not **see**, we wait with **endurance**.

In the **same way**, the Spirit too comes to the **aid** of
    our **weakness**;
  for we do not **know** how to pray as we **ought**,
  but the Spirit himself **intercedes** with inexpressible **groanings**.
And the one who searches **hearts**
  knows what is the **intention** of the Spirit,
  because he **intercedes** for the **holy** ones
  according to God's **will**.

Slight extra emphasis on "endurance."

"In the same way": Paul intends to compare our life to the work of the Holy Spirit, who comes to our aid. In the Spirit lies our hope.

GOSPEL   John 7:37–39

A reading from the holy Gospel according to John

On the **last** and greatest **day** of the **feast**,
  Jesus stood up and **exclaimed**,
  "Let anyone who **thirsts** come to me and **drink**.
As Scripture says:
  *Rivers of living water will **flow** from within him* who
    believes *in me*."

He said this in reference to the **Spirit**
  that **those** who came to **believe** in him were to **receive**.
There was, of course, no **Spirit** yet,
  because **Jesus** had not yet been **glorified**.

A brief narrative reading with an extraordinary exhortation embedded in it.

"Rivers of living water" is an especially evocative phrase, especially as a sign of belief.

The reading concludes with an anticipatory claim about Jesus' eventual glorification.

---

to the Pool of Shiloah (or Siloam), just south of the Temple mount, to draw water, which was then poured on the altar of the Temple as a libation, accompanied by trumpets and singing crowds. It was a time of great joy! *Sukkot* and its water-drawing ceremony provide the backdrop for today's Gospel. But this is the last day, described as "the great day." Perhaps it is Sabbath or at least a Sabbath-like day, when no work was allowed, so on this day there was no water-drawing ceremony. This is when Jesus stands and proclaims himself to be the giver of water. Most likely, his audience

would have been shocked by this announcement, after all the excitement of the feast. Is Jesus competing to be the joy of *Sukkot*? Biblical scholars are not sure how to translate verses 37–38, due to the absence of punctuation in early manuscripts. Where does the phrase "who believes in me" belong? Should the text read "As Scripture says: Rivers of living water will flow from within him who believes in me," or should it read "If anyone thirst, let him come to me, and let him who believes in me drink. As the scripture has said . . ." The translation used for our lectionary reading has the believer

overflowing with living water, whereas the other translation has Jesus overflowing with living water. Regardless, the main point is that living water is a metaphor for the Holy Spirit and that Jesus promises the sending of the Holy Spirit, when he is crucified and exalted. C. C.

PENTECOST SUNDAY: DAY

LECTIONARY #63

READING I   Acts of the Apostles 2:1–11

A reading from the Acts of the Apostles

When the **time** for Pentecost was **fulfilled**,
   they were all in one place **together**.
And suddenly there came from the **sky**
   a **noise** like a strong driving **wind**,
   and it filled the entire **house** in which they **were**.
Then there appeared to them **tongues** as of fire,
   which **parted** and came to **rest** on each **one** of them.
And they were all **filled** with the Holy **Spirit**
   and began to **speak** in different **tongues**,
   as the Spirit **enabled** them to **proclaim**.

Now there were devout **Jews** from every **nation** under **heaven**
   staying in **Jerusalem**.
At this **sound**, they gathered in a large **crowd**,
   but they were **confused**
   because each one heard them **speaking** in his own **language**.
They were **astounded**, and in amazement they **asked**,
   "Are not all these **people** who are speaking **Galileans**?
Then how does each of us **hear** them in his native **language**?
We are **Parthians**, **Medes**, and **Elamites**,
   inhabitants of **Mesopotamia**, **Judea** and **Cappadocia**,
   Pontus and **Asia**, **Phrygia** and **Pamphylia**,

A narrative reading that directly inverts the Tower of Babel passage from Genesis. (See the first reading for the Pentecost Vigil.) This kind of inverted symmetry is one of the enduring pleasures of reading Scripture. Babel doesn't need to be mentioned in order for your assembly to sense its presence.

Air and fire are the two elements associated with the Holy Spirit. Here, it's air in the form of wind.

And here in the form of tongues of fire.

And here, the Holy Spirit becomes language.

Read all of these names with care.
Be sure to practice their pronunciation:
Parthians = PAHR-thee-uhnz
Medes = meedz
Elamites = EE-luh-mīts
Mesopotamia = mes-uh-poh-TAY-mee-uh
Judea = joo-DEE-uh
Cappadocia = cap-uh-DOH-shee-uh
Pontus = PON-tuhs
Phrygia = FRIJ-ee-uh
Pamphylia = Pam-FIL-ee-uh

There are options for today's readings. Contact your parish staff to learn which readings will be used.

READING I   Acts of the Apostles is the only New Testament book to tell the story of the first Christian Pentecost. Its author, Luke, indicates that this event took place on the Jewish Pentecost, *Sukkot*, also known as the Feast of Tabernacles or Booths. Because it was a pilgrimage feast, the city of Jerusalem would have been filled with visitors from near and far. The Apostles and some women, including Mary, the mother of Jesus, and some of Jesus' kinfolk were gathered in the place where they were staying. Suddenly, a noise like a driving wind comes from the sky and fills the entire building. The Greek word *pnoé* means "wind," but it can also mean "a gust" or "breath." The adjective, translated here as "driving," also means "violent," or "rushing." Such is the power of the Holy Spirit—strong enough to knock everyone off their feet!

Sukkot was a joyous harvest festival, but it was also a time for Jews to remember the years their ancestors dwelt in tents during their Exodus sojourn. The Exodus story of God's appearance on Mount Sinai describes God coming down from the heavens in fire (Exodus 19:18). Perhaps Luke had this story in mind when he described the appearance of tongues of fire coming down and resting upon the people gathered in the house. In any case, Luke clearly wants to highlight the Holy Spirit's heavenly origin and its power to unite peoples of all nations through confident and intelligible preaching of "the mighty acts of God." In some respects, we might think of this Pentecost scene as a return to the begin-

Libya = LIB-ee-uh
Cyrene = sī-REE-nee
Cretans = KREE-tuhnz

Egypt and the districts of **Libya** near **Cyrene**,
as well as **travelers** from **Rome**,
both **Jews** and converts to **Judaism**, **Cretans** and **Arabs**,
yet we **hear them** speaking in our own **tongues**
of the **mighty acts** of **God**."

For meditation and context:

RESPONSORIAL PSALM   Psalm 104:1, 24, 29–30, 31, 34 (30)

R. **Lord, send out your Spirit, and renew the face of the earth.**
or
R. **Alleluia.**

Bless the LORD, O my soul!
  O LORD, my God, you are great indeed!
How manifold are your works, O LORD!
  The earth is full of your creatures.

If you take away their breath, they perish
  and return to their dust.

When you send forth your spirit,
  they are created,
  and you renew the face of the earth.

May the glory of the LORD endure forever;
  may the LORD be glad in his works!
Pleasing to him be my theme;
  I will be glad in the LORD.

READING II   1 Corinthians 12:3b–7, 12–13

Corinthians = kohr-IN-thee-uhnz

A didactic reading with claims of enduring force.
The invocation of the Holy Spirit is meant to echo the same in the first reading at Pentecost. Here the Holy Spirit is understood in terms of spiritual gifts.

A reading from the first Letter of Saint Paul to the Corinthians

Brothers and **sisters**:
No one can say, "**Jesus** is Lord," **except** by the Holy Spirit.

There are different **kinds** of spiritual gifts but the same **Spirit**;
  there are different **forms** of service but the same **Lord**;
  there are different **workings** but the same **God**
  who produces **all** of them in **everyone**.
To each individual the **manifestation** of the Spirit
  is **given** for some **benefit**.

Even stress on these three words: "so also Christ."

As a **body** is one though it has many **parts**,
  and all the **parts** of the body, though **many**, are one **body**,
  so also Christ. »

---

ning, before the dispersal of peoples and confusion of language that transpired in the Tower of Babel story (Genesis 11:1–9). What marvelous grace!

READING II   **1 Corinthians.** One of the concerns that Paul raises with the Corinthian community is their fascination with the gift of speaking in tongues. The technical term is "glossolalia." This is what Peter and the rest of Jesus' disciples experienced on the first Christian Pentecost. Paul criticizes these so-called spirit-people and calls them spiritual

babies, because of their quarreling and the divisions that exist in their community (1 Corinthians 3:1). Paul tries to correct their thinking by saying that it is all about the Holy Spirit. A person cannot speak even the most basic statement of belief in Jesus except by the Holy Spirit! He likens the community of believers to a human body. In Baptism, they drank of the one Spirit. Therefore, just as a body has many parts and these parts cannot exist except as one body, the community is the one body of Christ. Whatever spiritual gifts individuals possess, whatever ministries they perform,

they are the one body of Christ animated by the Holy Spirit.

Galatians. Today's reading is part of Paul's *paraenesis,* or moral exhortation to the churches of Galatia. As with most of the communities to which he writes, Paul founded the churches in Galatia (in modern Turkey), so we can surmise that he was personally invested in their well-being, sometimes relating to them as a doting father and at other times as a strict disciplinarian.

This letter begins with Paul giving the churches a good scolding, because they had taken up "another gospel" in his

The vision of radical equality that Paul stresses in these lines is something the Church continues to aspire to.

For in one **Spirit** we were all **baptized** into one **body**,
    whether **Jews** or **Greeks**, **slaves** or **free persons**,
    and we were all **given** to drink of one **Spirit**.

Or:

READING II   Galatians 5:16–25

A reading from the Letter of Saint Paul to the Galatians

An exhortatory reading in which Paul condemns the flesh to exalt the spirit.

Brothers and **sisters**, **live** by the Spirit
    and you will certainly not **gratify** the desire of the **flesh**.
For the **flesh** has desires **against** the Spirit,
    and the **Spirit** against the **flesh**;
    these are **opposed** to each other,
    so that you may not **do** what you **want**.
But if you are **guided** by the Spirit, you are not **under** the law.
Now the **works** of the flesh are **obvious**:

In this reading, the Spirit is understood in terms of what it is not or the ways desire impedes the Spirit. As with other such passages in Paul's letters, it's best to proclaim neutrally and straightforwardly.

    immorality, impurity, lust, idolatry,
    sorcery, hatreds, rivalry, jealousy,
    outbursts of fury, acts of selfishness,
    dissensions, factions, occasions of envy,
    drinking bouts, orgies, and the like.
I **warn** you, as I **warned** you before,
    that those who do such things will not **inherit** the kingdom
        of **God**.
In contrast, the **fruit** of the Spirit is love, joy, peace,
    patience, kindness, generosity,
    faithfulness, gentleness, self-control.
Against such there is no **law**.

Read this list of the fruits of the Spirit similarly to the previous list, giving the items equal emphasis.

Now those who belong to Christ Jesus have **crucified** their flesh
    with its **passions** and **desires**.
If we **live** in the Spirit, let us also **follow** the Spirit.

---

absence (Galatians 1:6–10). Pauline scholars believe that this other gospel came from Jewish-Christian missionaries who told these Gentile Christians that they had to become circumcised and follow Jewish law in order to be followers of Jesus. Although Paul himself was a Jew and observed Jewish law, he was very much opposed to the idea that Gentiles needed to do so. He reminds them that they first experienced the Spirit through faith in the preaching that they received, the good news of Jesus Christ, not from the Law (Galatians 3:1–3). They are already liberated from the

power of sin and death, he says, so abandoning that grace to take up circumcision and all that entails is, in a sense, to return to the flesh (Galatians 3:3). Thus, Paul uses "spirit" and "flesh" as shorthand for the communities' new life in Christ and their former lives without Christ.

In this reading, Paul follows his initial exhortation to live by the Spirit and not pursue the desires of the flesh with a catalog of vices and a catalog of virtues. These were popular among philosophers and teachers in the ancient world to outline the right and wrong ways to live. Paul's catalog

of vices is not intended to suggest that the churches were actually doing all these terrible things. Rather, he is illustrating what becomes of people who live according to the flesh. By contrast, his catalog of virtues illustrates how people who live by the Spirit manifest themselves in the world. These virtues are not bound by law. Many of us know this catalog of virtues as the Fruits of the Holy Spirit.

GOSPEL | **John 20.** Today's Gospel tells the story of the risen Jesus' appearance to his disciples on the

TO KEEP IN MIND

Sequences originated as extensions of the sung Alleluia before the proclamation of the gospel, although they precede the Alleluia now. The Pentecost Sequence, also called the Golden Sequence, is an ancient liturgical hymn praising the Holy Spirit. It is source of the hymn "Come, Holy Ghost."

SEQUENCE   Veni, Sancte Spiritus

Come, Holy Spirit, come!
And from your celestial home
   Shed a ray of light divine!
Come, Father of the poor!
Come, source of all our store!
   Come, within our bosoms shine.
You, of comforters the best;
You, the soul's most welcome guest;
   Sweet refreshment here below;
In our labor, rest most sweet;
Grateful coolness in the heat;
   Solace in the midst of woe.
O most blessed Light divine,
Shine within these hearts of yours,
   And our inmost being fill!

Where you are not, we have naught,
Nothing good in deed or thought,
   Nothing free from taint of ill.
Heal our wounds, our strength renew;
On our dryness pour your dew;
   Wash the stains of guilt away:
Bend the stubborn heart and will;
Melt the frozen, warm the chill;
   Guide the steps that go astray.
On the faithful, who adore
And confess you, evermore
   In your sevenfold gift descend;
Give them virtue's sure reward;
Give them your salvation, Lord;
   Give them joys that never end. Amen.
   Alleluia.

GOSPEL   John 20:19–23

A reading from the holy Gospel according to John

On the **evening** of that first day of the **week**,
   when the **doors** were locked, where the **disciples** were,
   for **fear** of the Jews,
   Jesus came and **stood** in their midst
   and **said** to them, "**Peace** be with you."
When he had **said** this, he **showed** them his hands and his side.
The disciples **rejoiced** when they saw the Lord.
Jesus said to them again, "**Peace** be with you.
As the **Father** has sent me, so I send **you**."
And when he had **said** this, he **breathed** on them and **said**
   to them,
   "**Receive** the Holy Spirit.
Whose **sins** you **forgive** are **forgiven** them,
and whose **sins** you **retain** are **retained**."

Or:

A narrative reading that depicts the transmission of the Holy Spirit through Jesus himself to his disciples.

Jesus enters the scene with the word "Peace."

Breath is the most ancient sign of life in scripture. Here, Jesus' powers are transmitted directly through his breath.

Note the parallel construction: forgive/forgiven; retain/retained.

night of the Resurrection. The disciples had hidden themselves away in a locked room. But locked doors could not deter the risen Jesus. Jesus shows his wounded body to the disciples, demonstrating that he is alive, and offers them a greeting of peace. Appearance narratives were designed to witness to the Resurrection, but this one is special in the sense that it fulfills the promises made in the Farewell Discourse. He told them that he would come back to them (John 14:18; 16:22) and he did! On the night he was arrested, he wished them peace (John 14:27) in the same way he does here. He

promised that they would rejoice once again (John 16:23), as they do here. In his prayer to the Father on the night he was arrested, he announces that he is sending his disciples in the same way that the Father sent him (John 17:18). And now he breathes on them and sends the Holy Spirit upon them, just as he promised (John 16:7b). The Greek word *emphusaó* can also mean "to blow into." With a little imagination, we might relate this action to the second creation story in Genesis; God breathed into a lump of clay and gave Adam a life-giving spirit (Genesis 2:7).

Biblical scholars have long debated the precise meaning of the saying about forgiving and retaining sins and why it appears in this appearance narrative. The most likely explanation is that, in the Farewell Discourse, the Spirit is described as the Spirit of truth (John 15:26; 16:13), who will recall everything Jesus said and teach them everything (John 14:26). Moreover, the Spirit will expose the world concerning sin, righteousness, and judgment (John 16:8). Thus, the disciples' ability to forgive and retain sins is closely tied to the promised activity of the Holy Spirit.

GOSPEL　John 15:26–27; 16:12–15

A reading from the holy Gospel according to John

A didactic reading. Jesus is speaking to his disciples in an anticipatory manner to help them plan for the future.

Jesus said to his disciples:
　"When the **Advocate** comes whom I will **send** you
　　from the **Father**,
　the Spirit of truth that **proceeds** from the Father,
　he will **testify** to me.
And you also testify,
　because you have **been** with me from the **beginning**.

"But when he comes . . ." This expresses Jesus' anticipation. He is alluding to the Holy Spirit. The tone of the reading shifts at "But."

Contrast the use of "speak" and "hears." The future that Jesus anticipates is audible to the Spirit.

Give emphasis to "you."

"I have much **more** to tell you, but you cannot **bear** it now.
But when he **comes**, the Spirit of **truth**,
　he will **guide** you to all truth.
He will not **speak** on his own,
　but he will **speak** what he **hears**,
　and will **declare** to you the things that are **coming**.
He will **glorify** me,
　because he will **take** from what is **mine** and **declare** it to you.
Everything that the Father has is **mine**;
　for this **reason** I told you that he will **take** from what is **mine**
　and **declare** it to **you**."

John 15. Today's Gospel reading is part of Jesus' Farewell Discourse to his disciples (John 14—17). This literary device, also called a testament, was frequently employed in early Jewish literature as a way to communicate the sum of a great and holy person's teaching to his disciples (for example, *Testament of the Twelve Patriarchs, Testament of Moses*). A noteworthy figure knows he is about to die and therefore gathers his disciples to deliver his last words. His disciples react with grief or dismay, requiring some kind of reassurance from the teacher. The teacher's words also include a predic-tion of the future, because of the belief in Mediterranean cultures of the time that those who were about to die possessed prophetic powers, because they had already begun to pass over into the divine realm.

In the two brief excerpts from Jesus' Farewell Discourse that make up today's Gospel reading, we learn how Jesus will give reassurance to his grief-stricken disci-ples, namely, the Holy Spirit. The Spirit bears the title Advocate or Paraclete. The Greek word *paraklētos* means "intercessor, con-soler or comforter." However, it was also used to describe a legal assistant or some-one who pleads another person's case in a court of law. This is the meaning preferred here, because Jesus said the Advocate, which is the Spirit of truth, would stand beside them and convey to them all that the Father had given him. C. C.

THE MOST HOLY TRINITY

LECTIONARY #165

READING I Deuteronomy 4:32–34, 39–40

Deuteronomy = doo-ter-AH-nuh-mee

A reading from the Book of Deuteronomy

An exhortatory reading in which Moses characterizes the nature of the God whom the Israelites wandering in the desert serve. Moses is trying to fill his people with hope.

Moses said to the people:
  "Ask **now** of the days of **old**, before your **time**,
    ever since **God** created **man** upon the **earth**;
  ask from **one end** of the sky to the **other**:
    Did **anything** so **great** ever **happen** before?
Was it ever **heard** of?
Did a **people** ever hear the voice of **God**
    speaking from the midst of **fire**, as you did, and **live**?
Or did any **god** venture to go and take a **nation** for himself
    from the **midst** of another **nation**,
  by **testings**, by **signs** and **wonders**, by **war**,
  with **strong hand** and outstretched **arm**, and by great **terrors**,
  all of which the LORD, your God,
    did for you in **Egypt before** your very **eyes**?
This is why you must now **know**,
    and **fix** in your heart, that the LORD is God
  in the **heavens above** and on **earth below**,
    and that there **is** no other.
You must **keep** his statutes and **commandments** that I **enjoin**
      on you **today**,
    that **you** and your children **after** you may **prosper**,
    and that you may have **long life** on the land
    which the LORD, your God, is **giving** you **forever**."

Each of these elements is stressed: "testings," "signs and wonders," "wars."

Pause slightly between "Egypt" and "before."

Note the contrast between "heaven above" and "earth below."

READING I Although prayers to God as Trinity existed earlier, the feast of the Most Holy Trinity was not included in the liturgical calendar until the fourteenth century, when it was designated for the Sunday after Pentecost. In fact, Christians did not have a universally agreed upon doctrine of the Trinitarian God until the Council of Constantinople in AD 381. This is the creed we now know as the Nicene Creed. Therefore, we should not expect a fully formed doctrine of the Trinity in the Bible. Yet, we find allusions to the Trinitarian God, even in the Old Testament, as is evident in today's first reading.

The Book of Deuteronomy, which was written over an extended period of time between the eighth and sixth centuries BC, is presented as the words of Moses to the Israelites before their entry into the Promised Land. In this brief excerpt, we are reminded of God's amazing deeds on behalf of humanity from the time of creation and of God's special care of God's chosen ones, demonstrated in presence and power. In Moses' words, this is why God's people must know in their hearts that God is their only God. Two details of this reading allude to the Holy Spirit—the mention of creation and the image of fire. You may recall the detail of the wind sweeping over the waters in the first creation story (Genesis 1:2) and, in the second, the reference to God breathing into Adam to make the human a living being (Genesis 2:7). Fire is an image associated with God's presence in the Exodus (Exodus 19:18), but it also reminds us of the Christian Pentecost story, when the Holy Spirit descended on the disciples in tongues of fire (Acts 2:3).

For meditation and context:

RESPONSORIAL PSALM   Psalm 33:4–5, 6, 9, 18–19, 20, 22 (12b)

R. Blessed the people the Lord has chosen to be his own.

Upright is the word of the LORD,
    and all his works are trustworthy.
He loves justice and right;
    of the kindness of the LORD the earth
        is full.

By the word of the LORD the heavens
        were made;
    by the breath of his mouth all their host.
For he spoke, and it was made;
    he commanded, and it stood forth.

See, the eyes of the LORD are upon those
        who fear him,
    upon those who hope for his kindness,
to deliver them from death
    and preserve them in spite of famine.

Our soul waits for the LORD,
    who is our help and our shield.
May your kindness, O LORD, be upon us
    who have put our hope in you.

READING II   Romans 8:14–17

A reading from the Letter of Saint Paul to the Romans

An exhortatory reading, rousing and passionate and complex, despite its short length.

Brothers and **sisters**:
Those who are led by the **Spirit** of God are **sons** of God.
For you did not **receive** a spirit of **slavery** to fall **back** into **fear**,
    but you **received** a Spirit of **adoption**,
        through whom we cry, "**Abba, Father!**"
The Spirit **himself** bears **witness** with our **spirit**
        that we are **children** of God,
        and if **children**, then **heirs**,
        heirs of God and joint **heirs** with Christ,
        if only we **suffer** with him
        so that we may also be **glorified** with him.

Paul declares we are children of God; the word "heirs" appears three times subsequently. Emphasize the word.

"Suffer" is contrasted with "glorified." But give "suffer" its due; don't underemphasize it.

TO KEEP IN MIND
Use the pitch and volume of your voice to gain the attention of the assembly.

READING II Today's second reading is part of a long section of the Letter to the Romans, Romans 5:1—8:39. In this section, Paul highlights the benefits that come to those who are justified by faith in Jesus Christ as a free gift from God. Paul has already asserted that Christian believers are in the spirit and that the Holy Spirit dwells in them (Romans 8:9). Here he writes that, through the Holy Spirit, the Christian believer has received a spirit of adoption that makes them children of God and that allows them to cry, "Abba, Father." Perhaps you have heard someone say that

abba is an affectionate form of "father," like "daddy." In fact, it is the vocative form (used to address a person) of the Hebrew word *ab*, which means "father." It is used three times in the New Testament, always paired with the Greek word *patēr*, which means "father." When used in this way, it is an intimate address to God in prayer, as a child might address a parent.

Our Eastern Orthodox brothers and sisters have a fitting term to talk about the triune God, namely, *perichoresis*. This Greek term suggests the intimacy and perfect balance of relationships among the Father,

Son, and Holy Spirit, centered in love and harmony. Some modern theologians have likened this relationship to a divine dance. Thus, when we cry, "Abba, Father," through the power of the Holy Spirit and with knowledge that we are children of God and heirs with Christ, we are invited to participate in the divine dance of love and harmony!

GOSPEL Participation in the life of God necessarily means taking up our mission as God's agents in the world. Today's Gospel reading is known as the "Great Commission," which is often

GOSPEL Matthew 28:16–20

A reading from the holy Gospel according to Matthew

A narrative reading from the conclusion of the Gospel of Matthew, which includes a well-known exhortation.

Emphasis on "Go."

You can linger usefully on "until the end of the age."

The eleven disciples went to **Galilee**,
    to the **mountain** to which Jesus had **ordered** them.
When they all **saw** him, they **worshiped**, but they **doubted**.
Then Jesus **approached** and **said** to them,
    "All **power** in heaven and on **earth** has been **given** to me.
Go, therefore, and make **disciples** of all nations,
    baptizing them in the name of the **Father**,
    and of the **Son**, and of the **Holy Spirit**,
    teaching them to observe **all** that I have **commanded** you.
And **behold**, I am with you **always**, until the **end** of the **age**."

used as a biblical warrant for missionary activity. There are other commissioning stories in the Gospels, but this is the only account of the risen Christ's commissioning of the eleven to go out and make disciples of all nations, baptizing them and teaching all that Jesus had taught them. The Greek verb that is translated here as "make disciples" requires action. Moreover, it bears the authority of the risen Christ, which was conferred on him by God. And how are they to "make disciples"? By baptizing and teaching. The threefold formula for Baptism "in the name of the Father, and of the Son, and of the Holy Spirit" was probably already in use by the time Matthew's Gospel was written. The *Didache*, an early church order written sometime around the end of the first century or beginning of the second century, says, "And concerning baptism, baptize this way: Having first said all these things [teachings about the moral life], baptize into the name of the Father, and of the Son, and of the Holy Spirit in living water" (*Didache* 7.1).

And what about Jesus' assurance that he will be with them always? This ending of the Gospel takes us back to the beginning where God's angel tells Joseph that the child with whom Mary is pregnant will fulfill the prophecy of Isaiah, "and they shall name him Emmanuel" (Matthew 1:23; cf. Isaiah 7:14). Emmanuel means "God with us." C. C.

THE MOST HOLY BODY AND BLOOD OF CHRIST

LECTIONARY #168

READING I Exodus 24:3–8

Exodus = EK-suh-duhs

A narrative reading with vivid, even visceral images and a compelling rhythm.

A reading from the Book of Exodus

When **Moses** came to the **people**
    and related all the **words** and **ordinances** of the LORD,
    they all **answered** with one **voice**,
    "We will do **everything** that the LORD has **told us**."
Moses then wrote **down** all the **words** of the LORD and,
    rising **early** the next day,
    he **erected** at the foot of the **mountain** an **altar**
    and **twelve pillars** for the **twelve tribes** of Israel.
Then, having sent certain young **men** of the Israelites
    to offer **holocausts** and **sacrifice** young **bulls**
    as **peace offerings** to the LORD,
    Moses took **half** of the blood and put it in large **bowls**;
    the **other half** he **splashed** on the **altar**.
Taking the book of the **covenant**, he read it **aloud** to the people,
    who answered, "**All** that the LORD has **said**, we will **heed**
        and **do**."
Then he took the **blood** and **sprinkled** it on the people, saying,
    "**This** is the blood of the **covenant**
    that the LORD has made with **you**
    in **accordance** with all these **words** of his."

The details are particular, especially in describing Moses' role as priest and the obligations he performs with the blood of the sacrificed animals. Emphasize the word "splashed."

The sprinkling of the blood seals the covenant between the people and God. Emphasis on "sprinkled."

READING I The Solemnity of the Most Holy Body and Blood of Christ, also known as Corpus Christi, is celebrated on the Sunday after Trinity Sunday in the United States. This feast was first observed in the thirteenth century, but it was not officially mandated in the Church's liturgical calendar until the fourteenth century. It commemorates the Real Presence of the Body and Blood of Jesus Christ in the appearance of bread and wine in the Eucharist. Today's first reading from the book of Exodus is one of several that prefigure the new covenant effected in the Eucharist. In the sections that precede today's reading, the book lists a set of ordinances—the Covenant Code—that the Israelites were obligated to keep (Exodus 20—23) and a promise of rewards for serving God faithfully (Exodus 23:20–33).

Now Moses is invited to come up the mountain close to God and to ratify the covenant in a blood ritual. First Moses writes down the words God had given him, and he builds an altar for the sacrifice. Part of the blood of the sacrifice is sprinkled on the altar, which symbolizes God. Moses reads from the book of the covenant, and the people formally assent to it. Later, the rest of the blood will be sprinkled on the people as Moses says, "This is the blood of the covenant which the Lord has made with you according to all these words." Sharing blood symbolizes the unity of God and the people; they are joined as one family by blood. Additionally, the reference to the blood of the covenant ought to remind us of the phrase "the blood of the new and everlasting covenant" that we proclaim in our Eucharistic prayer.

For meditation and context:

RESPONSORIAL PSALM   Psalm 116:12–13, 15–16, 17–18 (13)

R. I will take the cup of salvation, and call on the name of the Lord.
or
R. Alleluia.

How shall I make a return to the Lord
   for all the good he has done for me?
The cup of salvation I will take up,
   and I will call upon the name of the Lord.

Precious in the eyes of the Lord
   is the death of his faithful ones.

I am your servant, the son of your
   handmaid;
   you have loosed my bonds.

To you will I offer sacrifice of thanksgiving,
   and I will call upon the name of the Lord.
My vows to the Lord I will pay
   in the presence of all his people.

READING II   Hebrews 9:11–15

A reading from the Letter to the Hebrews

Brothers and **sisters**:
When **Christ** came as high **priest**
   of the **good things** that have come to **be**,
   passing through the **greater** and more perfect **tabernacle**
   not **made** by hands, that is, not **belonging** to this creation,
   he entered **once** for all into the **sanctuary**,
   not with the blood of **goats** and **calves**
   but with his **own blood**, thus obtaining **eternal** redemption.
For if the blood of **goats** and **bulls**
   and the **sprinkling** of a heifer's **ashes**
   can **sanctify** those who are **defiled**
   so that their flesh is **cleansed**,
   how much **more** will the blood of **Christ**,
   who **through** the eternal **Spirit** offered himself **unblemished**
     to God,
   cleanse our **consciences** from dead **works**
   to **worship** the living **God**. »

A didactic reading about the nature and meaning of the covenant Jesus represents as high priest.

"The greater and more perfect tabernacle" suggests something mystical, something beyond comprehension. Allow the phrase to resonate.

Jesus is both priest of the sacrifice and the sacrifice itself.

READING II The second reading comes from the Letter to the Hebrews. Although we call it a letter, it is better categorized as a sermon that consists of alternating units of exhortation and exposition. The expositions follow a form of argument used by rabbis of early Judaism called "from the lesser to the greater." It works like this: if something can be demonstrated to be true or good in a small matter, then we can say that it is even more true or good when it concerns a greater matter that is analogous to the first.

In the section of Hebrews that precedes today's reading, the author describes the worship of the first covenant, in which only the high priest was allowed to enter the Holy of Holies to offer sin sacrifices for himself and for the people. The feast to which this scene refers is probably Yom Kippur or the Day of Atonement. While this was considered one of the most important holy days of early Judaism, the author of Hebrews makes the argument that Jesus' sacrifice was so much greater and more perfect. Why? Because the author of Hebrews

understood that Christ is the perfect high priest who passed into the heavenly tabernacle. He is also the most perfect sacrifice, who, with his own blood, obtained redemption and deliverance from sin. If the sacrificial activity of the high priest in the Holy of Holies each year on Yom Kippur was great, how much greater was the activity of Christ, who is both perfect high priest and perfect sacrifice offered once and for all time?

Here are the terms of the covenant.
Stress the final three words of the reading.

For **this reason** he is **mediator** of a new **covenant**:
    since a **death** has taken place for **deliverance**
    from **transgressions** under the first **covenant**,
    those who are **called** may receive the **promised**
        eternal inheritance.

A narrative reading from Mark's Passion, focusing on the covenantal qualities of the body and blood as shared at the Passover meal. This passage has truly compelling narrative elements, especially the details.

GOSPEL   Mark 14:12–16, 22–26

A reading from the holy Gospel according to Mark

On the **first** day of the **Feast** of Unleavened **Bread**,
    when they **sacrificed** the **Passover** lamb,
    Jesus' **disciples** said to him,
    "**Where** do you want us to **go**
    and **prepare** for you to eat the **Passover**?"

Proclaim "when they sacrificed the Passover lamb" with almost even emphasis on all the words.

He sent **two** of his disciples and said to them,
    "**Go** into the city and a **man** will **meet** you,
    carrying a **jar** of water.

Emphasis on "follow."

Follow him.
Wherever he **enters**, say to the **master** of the house,
    'The **Teacher** says, "Where is my **guest room**
    where I may **eat** the Passover with my **disciples**?"'
Then he will **show you** a **large upper room furnished** and ready.
Make the **preparations** for us **there**."
The disciples then went **off**, entered the **city**,
    and found it **just** as he had **told** them;
    and they **prepared** the Passover.

These are the words of the institution of the Eucharist proclaimed by the priest at every Mass. Read them with the same reverence.

While they were **eating**,
    he took **bread**, said the **blessing**,
    broke it, **gave** it to them, and **said**,
    "**Take** it; this is my **body**."

GOSPEL   The account of Jesus' last supper with his disciples as they celebrated the Passover meal comes from Mark's Gospel. The lambs of the Passover would have been slaughtered in the Temple on the afternoon of the fourteenth of Nisan, before the first day of the Feast of Unleavened Bread began at sunset. Jerusalem would have been filled with visitors for Passover. Did Jesus possess foreknowledge such that he just knew that a man with a water jar would walk by as his disciples were looking for a place to celebrate Passover? Or had Jesus prearranged

a place for them to gather for Passover? While we may never know the answer to this question, the point is clear. Jesus' disciples went off and found everything exactly as Jesus said. Thus, Mark emphasizes the intentionality of having Jesus' last supper before his death coincide with the Passover meal, the great feast of liberation from slavery.

The lectionary omits Mark 14:17–22 from this reading. The principle behind the omission of certain verses from the lectionary is to present to the congregation what is most helpful from a pastoral perspective.

Sometimes the full reading might be too long, or it might contain verses that are problematic or that otherwise distract from the key message of the text. The General Introduction to the Lectionary emphasizes that the decision to omit problematic verses is not taken lightly and never in a way that distorts the meaning of the text (n. 77).

In this case, however, the lector might appreciate knowing that Mark 14:17–22 and Mark 14:27–31 are positioned in the narrative to provide a "sandwich" for the story of Jesus' last supper with his disciples. The former is Jesus' prediction that one of his

Then he took a **cup**, gave thanks, and **gave** it to them,
and they all **drank** from it.
He **said** to them,
"**This** is my **blood** of the **covenant**,
which will be **shed** for **many**.
Amen, I **say** to you,
I shall not **drink** again the **fruit** of the vine
until the **day** when I drink it **new** in the kingdom of **God**."
Then, after singing a **hymn**,
they went **out** to the Mount of **Olives**.

own—Judas—would betray him to the authorities. The latter is Jesus' prediction that another of his own—Peter—would deny him three times before the night was over. Recognizing the "sandwich" that Mark has created adds great poignancy to this meal setting and to the citation of Zechariah 13:7, "I will strike the shepherd, and the sheep will be dispersed." Mark likely imagined a deep sadness enveloping Jesus at this moment of his life, when even his closest associates were about to turn on him.

In the ancient world, to share a meal was to invite your guests into the hospitality and protection that makes them family. At this Passover meal, meant to be a reminder of God's graciousness and protection of the Israelites as they were about to be released from captivity in Egypt, Jesus is surrounded by a broken "family," one that will suffer greatly when their shepherd is struck down. Knowing this, Jesus breaks bread as any other host of a Passover meal might have been doing in homes and guest rooms across Jerusalem, but he adds a new level of meaning to the feast by saying, "Take it; this is my body." Likewise, with the Passover cup of wine, he passed it to his disciples and added, "This is my blood of the covenant, which will be shed for many." Thus, the celebration of the Passover of the Jews is expanded and extended in hospitality to everyone in God's "broken" family. Moreover, it is not a Passover that ends in death but in newness of life in God's coming kingdom. This is what we celebrate when we gather for Eucharist. It is cause for great joy! C. C.

ELEVENTH SUNDAY IN ORDINARY TIME

LECTIONARY #92

READING I   Ezekiel 17:22–24

·Ezekiel = ee-ZEE-kee-uhl

A reading from the Book of the Prophet Ezekiel

Thus says the Lord GOD:
> I, too, will **take** from the crest of the **cedar**,
>> from its **topmost branches** tear **off** a tender **shoot**,
> and plant it on a **high** and lofty **mountain**;
>> on the mountain heights of **Israel** I will **plant** it.
> It shall put forth **branches** and bear **fruit**,
>> and become a majestic **cedar**.
> **Birds** of every kind shall dwell **beneath** it,
>> every **winged thing** in the **shade** of its **boughs**.
> And all the **trees** of the field shall **know**
>> that **I**, the LORD,
> bring **low** the high **tree**,
>> lift **high** the lowly **tree**,
> wither up the **green** tree,
>> and make the **withered tree** bloom.
> As I, the LORD, have **spoken**, so will I **do**.

An exhortatory reading in which God speaks through the prophet Ezekiel. The reading is short, highly charged and poetic, and it sustains a single image through its course. Treat your proclamation as though you are reading a poem.

This line provides an especially poetic image. Consider saying "wing-ed" as opposed to "wingd."

Note the contrasts between "high" and "low" in these two lines.

TO KEEP IN MIND
Pay attention to the pace of your reading. Varying the pace gives listeners clues to the meaning of the text. The most common error for proclaimers new to the ministry is speaking too fast.

READING I   As we return to the Sundays of Ordinary Time, our first reading comes to us from the prophet Ezekiel, whose ministry centered on the Judean exiles in Babylon in the sixth century BC, when it appeared that all hope was lost and that God had finally abandoned the covenant with the Israelite people. The book attributed to him is dramatic and occasionally bizarre, as it incorporates oracles of doom and oracles of hope mixed with visions, symbolic actions, poetry, and historical narratives.

Today's reading follows an oracle of doom in the form of an allegory (Ezekiel 17:1–10) and an interpretation (vv. 11–21). The allegory, we are told, is a riddle. A great eagle plucks a twig from the top of a cedar of Lebanon and brought it to a city of merchants. It takes a native seed and plants it in fertile soil near lots of water, and the seed grows quickly. Then another great eagle comes, and the plant bends its roots to him and presents its branches for the eagle to water. But will the plant survive in this place? It will surely be torn out of the ground and it will wither in the east wind!

The interpretation makes it clear that the first eagle is Nebuchadnezzar, king of Babylon. The twig is Jehoiachin, who was taken from Jerusalem ("Lebanon") to the city of merchants (Babylon). The native seed is Zedekiah, who was set up as king in Judea in place of his uncle, but who broke covenant with Nebuchadnezzar by making a treaty with Psammetichus II of Egypt against the Babylonians. Nebuchadnezzar retaliated with great force and destroyed Jerusalem and Judea.

But there is hope! The prophet continues the allegory of the two eagles by

For meditation and context:

RESPONSORIAL PSALM   Psalm 92:2–3, 13–14, 15–16 (2a)

R. Lord, it is good to give thanks to you.

It is good to give thanks to the LORD,
    to sing praise to your name, Most High,
to proclaim your kindness at dawn
    and your faithfulness throughout
        the night.

The just one shall flourish like the
        palm tree,
    like a cedar of Lebanon shall he grow.

They that are planted in the house of
        the LORD
    shall flourish in the courts of our God.

They shall bear fruit even in old age;
    vigorous and sturdy shall they be,
declaring how just is the LORD,
    my rock, in whom there is no wrong.

READING II   2 Corinthians 5:6–10

A reading from the second Letter of Saint Paul to the Corinthians

An exhortatory reading in which Paul places the courage he attributes to the members of the early Church in Corinth in the context of judgment.

The words "home" and "away" define the tone of the reading. Paul uses these words repeatedly.

Brothers and **sisters:**
We are **always** courageous,
    although we know that while we are at **home** in the **body**
    we are **away** from the **Lord**,
    for we walk by **faith**, not by **sight**.
Yet we are **courageous**,
    and we would rather **leave** the body and go **home** to the Lord.
Therefore, we aspire to **please** him,
    whether we are at **home** or **away**.
For we must **all appear** before the **judgment** seat of **Christ**,
    so that **each** may receive **recompense**,
    according to what he **did** in the body, whether **good** or **evil**.

The conclusion, which alludes to judgment, is striking. Allow the words "good" and "evil" to linger.

declaring God's intention to intervene on Israel's behalf. Now God will pluck a twig from the top of the cedar of Lebanon and plant it on the highest mountain of Israel. This twig represents a new messianic king from the line of David. His reign will become so great that all the tiny living things will be protected under its branches. Moreover, every other tree (the kings of other nations) will know that God is Lord, capable of determining the destiny of all nations, but especially God's chosen ones.

READING II   In the second reading, Paul is writing to the Corinthian community about the future destiny of the believer in a section of his letter that focuses on the trials and tribulations of his ministry of evangelization. Suffering is to be welcomed, he says, because it joins us with the suffering Christ, but he also welcomes death, because he would then be able to join with Christ in the resurrection. But Paul reminds the Corinthian church (and perhaps himself) that what matters at that moment is preaching "Jesus Christ as Lord" (2 Corinthians 4:5). This is the context for Paul's exhortation to courage in today's reading. He reminds his audience that we always "walk by faith, not by sight" (2 Corinthians 5:7) and that our desire should always be to please Christ as we await our judgment and reward.

GOSPEL   Today's Gospel brings us back to the agrarian imagery of the first reading, as we witness the

GOSPEL   Mark 4:26–34

A reading from the holy Gospel according to Mark

Jesus **said** to the crowds:
  "**This** is how it is with the kingdom of **God**;
  it is as if a **man** were to scatter **seed** on the **land**
  and would **sleep** and rise **night** and **day**
  and **through it all** the seed would **sprout** and **grow**,
  he **knows** not how.
Of its own **accord** the land yields **fruit**,
  first the **blade**, then the **ear**, then the full **grain** in the ear.
And when the grain is **ripe**, he wields the sickle at **once**,
  for the **harvest** has come."

He said,
  "To **what** shall we compare the kingdom of God,
  or what **parable** can we **use** for it?
It is like a **mustard seed** that, when it is **sown** in the **ground**,
  is the **smallest** of all the **seeds** on the **earth**.
But once it is **sown**, it springs up and becomes the **largest**
    of plants
  and puts forth **large branches**,
  so that the **birds** of the sky can **dwell** in its shade."
With **many** such parables
  he spoke the **word** to them as they were able to **understand** it.
Without **parables** he did not **speak** to them,
  but to his own **disciples** he explained **everything** in private.

A narrative reading consisting of a parable in two linked parts. Jesus mastered the form of the parable, which this one amply demonstrates.

With his first line, Jesus introduces his parable. You can read in an instructive tone.

Here, Jesus begins to scrutinize his own parable, adding in more detail.

The reading concludes with the tantalizing claim that Jesus explained everything in private to his disciples. Worth thinking about.

---

retelling of two parables from Mark's Gospel. To better interpret these stories, it is important to understand the literary genre called "parable." First, the word itself means "a comparison" of one thing to another, an analogy. Second, parables are fictional stories derived from everyday life experiences but often with a surprising twist that prompts the hearer to dig deeply into their meaning. Third, in most cases, gospel parables are presented without interpretation, but the literary context—what comes before and after the parable—often can help us know how to interpret them.

The parables under consideration in this Gospel reading are the parable of the seed that grows secretly and the parable of the mustard seed. In both cases, the comparison is to the kingdom of God. The kingdom of God is not to be equated with heaven and, in general, it is not a place. For this reason, some people prefer to use "reign of God" instead, because it better conveys the idea that the kingdom of God is about a time when God's power for good is fully manifest in the world and evil is defeated. Thus, the first of these parables tells us that the reign of God grows often without our knowing how, until at some point we start to see signs of its growth and even its fruits. And in the fullness of time, the crop will be ready for harvesting. Harvest imagery is usually used to refer to the end time, which in Mark's Gospel would be accompanied by the Second Coming of Christ. The second of these parables is a metaphor of hope. Like the reign of God, the smallest of seeds will grow into the greatest of shrubs such that the birds may nest under its branches. Such is the magnificent reign of God coming to fullness in our midst! C. C.

TWELFTH SUNDAY IN ORDINARY TIME

LECTIONARY #95

READING I   Job 38:1, 8–11

An enormously poetic and powerful exhortation from the Book of Job. God is speaking. The reading should be treated like a visionary poem, one of great expressive power. The rhetorical question of the opening two lines, "Who shut within doors the sea, / when it burst forth from the womb," is undiminished in its force more than twenty-five hundred years since it was first uttered.

Emphasis on "thus far" and "farther."

A reading from the Book of Job

The **Lord** addressed **Job** out of the **storm** and said:
Who shut within **doors** the **sea**,
when it **burst forth** from the **womb**;
when I made the **clouds** its garment
and thick **darkness** its **swaddling bands**?
When I set **limits** for it
and **fastened** the **bar** of its **door**,
and said: **Thus** far shall you come but **no farther**,
and **here** shall your **proud waves** be **stilled**!

For meditation and context:

RESPONSORIAL PSALM   Psalm 107:23–24, 25–26, 28–29, 30–31 (1b)

R. Give thanks to the Lord, his love is everlasting.
or
R. Alleluia.

They who sailed the sea in ships,
trading on the deep waters,
these saw the works of the LORD
and his wonders in the abyss.

His command raised up a storm wind
which tossed its waves on high.
They mounted up to heaven; they sank to
the depths;
their hearts melted away in their plight.

They cried to the LORD in their distress;
from their straits he rescued them.
He hushed the storm to a gentle breeze,
and the billows of the sea were stilled.

They rejoiced that they were calmed,
and he brought them to their
desired haven.
Let them give thanks to the LORD for
his kindness
and his wondrous deeds to the children
of men.

TO KEEP IN MIND

Read the Scripture passage and its commentary in *Workbook*. Then read it from your Bible, including what comes before and after it, so that you understand the context.

READING I To better understand the Book of Job and today's reading, it is helpful to know its genre. The story that frames the book is a folk tale about a holy man named Job who is tormented by a series of terrible personal losses (Job 1:1—2:13) but who is mercifully restored to well-being in the end (Job 42:7–17). In between, the main character, Job, is described as carrying on a series of conversations—perhaps "debates" is a better term—with his friends over the cause for his suffering. His friends recite all of the standard explanations for why bad things happen to people, while Job fiercely defends his innocence. Finally, God appears on the scene and confronts Job in two speeches (Job 38:2—39:25 and 40:6—41:26). Today's reading is taken from the first part of the first speech, in which God questions Job about whether he understands God's "counsel."

The reading begins with God confronting Job from within a mighty storm (Hebrew *ca'ar*, meaning "whirlwind" or "tempest"), suggesting a theophany or manifestation of the divine. Although not included in this lectionary reading, the author then describes God as calling on Job to stand up, as for battle, and answer why he is clouding God's counsel (Hebrew *etsah*, meaning "strategy, designs, or advice") with his ignorance. How dare Job do such a thing! Who does he think he is? God goes on to ask Job where he was when God founded the earth and laid its foundations. Can you sense the sarcasm and derision in God's voice? But remember that these are the words of the author of this book who is trying to capture what he thinks God would say to this man who dares to challenge God.

Returning to the lectionary reading, notice how the author of Job describes the

---

READING II　2 Corinthians 5:14–17

Corinthians = kohr-IN-thee-uhnz

An exhortatory reading in which Paul uses the death of Jesus to make bold claims about creation itself.

Note the repetition of "live" in this line.

The syntax is a little tricky in this line. Practice it a few times.

Emphasize the contrast between "old things" and "new things."

A reading from the second Letter of Saint Paul to the Corinthians

Brothers and **sisters**:
The **love** of Christ **impels** us,
　once we have **come** to the conviction that one **died** for all;
　therefore, **all** have died.
He **indeed** died for all,
　so that those who **live** might no longer **live** for **themselves**
　but for **him** who for their sake **died** and was **raised**.

Consequently, from now on we regard **no one** according to
　　the flesh;
　even if we once knew **Christ** according to the **flesh**,
　yet now we **know** him so no **longer**.
So whoever is in **Christ** is a new **creation**:
　the **old things** have passed **away**;
　behold, **new things** have **come**.

GOSPEL　Mark 4:35–41

A narrative reading of a vivid scene in the early ministry of Jesus involving violent natural forces that suggest something of the supernatural power Jesus commands.

The detail of Jesus asleep makes this scene somehow cinematic. Emphasize "asleep."

A reading from the holy Gospel according to Mark

On that day, as **evening** drew **on**, Jesus said to his disciples:
　"Let us cross to the other **side**."
Leaving the crowd, they took **Jesus** with them in the boat **just**
　　as he was.
And other boats were **with** him.
A **violent squall** came up and waves were breaking over
　　the **boat**,
　so that it was **already** filling **up**.
Jesus was in the **stern**, **asleep** on a **cushion**.

---

sea. In the ancient world, the sea was considered to be mysterious, difficult to control and even dangerous. But here it is described as a baby that issued from the womb (Hebrew *rechem*; a derivative of *racham*, which means "to love or to have compassion") and that God wrapped in swaddling clothes, covered with a blanket of darkness, and set boundaries for protection and safety, much as a parent might do. The metaphor is beautiful and evocative of the parental attributes of God toward the created world.

READING II　Our second reading is a continuation of last week's reading from 2 Corinthians, in which Paul talks about the trials and tribulations of his ministry of evangelization and exhorts his audience to courage as they "walk by faith, not by sight" (2 Corinthians 5:7). Here he talks about the source of this courage, namely, the love of Christ or the love that Christ shows us. The lectionary translation reads "the love of Christ impels us." The Greek word is *sunechó*, meaning "to hold together, to hold fast, or to press together." And "us" refers to those who have embraced

the conviction that one—that is, Christ—died for all humanity. Imagine! This is the fullest extent of Christ's love. Nothing more is possible. It requires of us, then, to die to our old way of life and to embrace a new way of life that is centered on the other, just as Jesus' death was centered on the other. Are you up for the challenge?

GOSPEL　The story of the stilling of the storm, which is taken from Mark's Gospel, follows a collection of parables that address the proper response to the word of God planted in the soil that

No need to shout these words. Jesus can calm the sea with an unshouted command.

Ask these questions in a gentle tone.

Even emphasis on all the words in "Who then is this."

They **woke** him and said to him,
    "**Teacher**, do you not care that we are **perishing**?"
He woke **up**,
    rebuked the wind, and said to the sea, "**Quiet! Be still!**"
The wind **ceased** and there was great **calm**.
Then he **asked** them, "Why are you **terrified**?
Do you not yet have **faith**?"
They were filled with **great awe** and said to one another,
    "**Who then is this** whom even **wind** and **sea obey**?"

is humanity (the Parable of the Sower) and the coming kingdom of God (the Parables of the Lamp, the Seed Growing Secretly, and the Mustard Seed.) The meaning of these parables, we are told, is hidden from outsiders, but is revealed to the disciples in private.

In light of the privileged place given to the disciples, today's Gospel reading is especially striking. The setting is the Sea of Galilee. Located at seven hundred feet below sea level and nestled among the hills of northern Israel, the sea measures nearly eight miles wide and twelve miles long and

is two hundred feet deep in some places. Its geography makes it subject to frequent and violent storms. The disciples are portrayed as wrestling with a violent windstorm on the sea, about to be swamped by the waves, while Jesus is asleep on a pillow in the back of the boat. When the disciples can no longer contain their fright, they awaken him and indirectly scold him for his apparent lack of concern.

Without responding to them, Jesus firmly orders the wind to be silent. What Mark does not explicitly say, but what is evident in the first reading, is that only God

can control the wind and the water. Hence the disciples' response. They are witnessing a theophany, a manifestation of the divine, and despite all that Jesus has been teaching them, they respond poorly. Yet, despite their ignorance, Jesus does not abandon his disciples, nor will he abandon us. C. C.

THIRTEENTH SUNDAY IN ORDINARY TIME

LECTIONARY #98

READING I   Wisdom 1:13–15; 2:23–24

A reading from the Book of Wisdom

God did **not** make death,
  nor does he **rejoice** in the **destruction** of the **living**.
For he **fashioned** all things that they might have **being**;
  and the **creatures** of the world are **wholesome**,
and there is **not** a destructive **drug** among them
  nor any **domain** of the **netherworld** on **earth**,
  for **justice** is undying.
For **God** formed **man** to be **imperishable**;
  the **image** of his own **nature** he **made** him.
But by the **envy** of the **devil**, **death** entered the **world**,
  and **they** who belong to his **company experience** it.

An exhortatory reading that begins with a claim about death—that God did not make death—and that concludes with a claim about how death entered the world—by the envy of the devil. Though the reading is mostly high-hearted, it concludes on a note of condemnation.

Emphasize the note of condemnation by emphasizing the words "envy," "devil," "death," and "world."

For meditation and context:

RESPONSORIAL PSALM   Psalm 30:2, 4, 5–6, 11, 12, 13 (2a)

R. I will praise you, Lord, for you have rescued me.

I will extol you, O LORD, for you drew
    me clear
  and did not let my enemies rejoice
    over me.
O LORD, you brought me up from the
    netherworld;
  you preserved me from among those
    going down into the pit.

Sing praise to the LORD, you his
    faithful ones,
  and give thanks to his holy name.

For his anger lasts but a moment;
    a lifetime, his good will.
At nightfall, weeping enters in,
    but with the dawn, rejoicing.

Hear, O LORD, and have pity on me;
    O LORD, be my helper.
You changed my mourning into dancing;
    O LORD, my God, forever will I give
    you thanks.

TO KEEP IN MIND

Pause after you announce the book of the Bible at the beginning of the reading. Pause again after the reading, before you proclaim the concluding statement ("The Word of the Lord" or "The Gospel of the Lord").

READING I The Book of Wisdom is a first-century AD Jewish work written in Greek, which begins with an exhortation to justice or righteousness. Our lectionary reading is taken from the last few verses of the first two units of the book: Wisdom 1:1–15 and 1:16—2:24. We know these are two discrete units because of the author's use of the *inclusio*, a literary device used to mark the beginning and end of a segment of literature by repeating the same words or phrases. For example, note the *inclusio* in Wisdom 1:1 ("Love righteousness") and 1:15 ("For righteousness is undying") that ties this unit together. Also, notice the *inclusio* in Wisdom 1:16 ("Because they deserve to be allied with it [death]" and 2:24 ("and they who are allied with him [the devil] experience it [death]").

As edited for the lectionary, this reading makes a profound response to a pair of questions that theologians and spiritual writers have wrestled with over the centuries: If God is all goodness, how do we account for suffering and death? If God is all powerful, how is evil allowed to exist in the created world? It asserts that God created all things wholesome and good and that humans are made in the image of God, imperishable. Sin, suffering, and death, then, are the consequence of human choice.

If you wish to dig more deeply into the literary context for this reading, consider looking at the story of the vindication of the righteous one in Wisdom 1:16—2:22. Pessimistic about their own lives, the wicked scorned the righteous one and his reliance on God. To test his faith and try his patience, they tortured and killed him. But they did not understand the hidden mysteries of God or the reward for the innocent, and they did not know that God had formed

Corinthians = kohr-IN-thee-uhnz

An exhortatory reading. Paul begins with praise in order to urge the members of the early Church at Corinth to be more generous in sharing their wealth.

"This gracious act" to which Paul is referring in the first paragraph is the more equitable sharing of wealth.

READING II   2 Corinthians 8:7, 9, 13–15

A reading from the second Letter of Saint Paul to the Corinthians

Brothers and **sisters**:
As you **excel** in every respect, in **faith**, **discourse**,
    knowledge, all **earnestness**, and in the **love** we have for you,
    may you **excel** in this **gracious act** also.

For you know the **gracious act** of our Lord Jesus **Christ**,
    that though he was **rich**, for your sake he became **poor**,
    so that by his **poverty** you might become **rich**.
Not that others should have **relief** while you are **burdened**,
    but that as a **matter** of **equality**
    your **abundance** at the present time should supply their **needs**,
    so that their abundance may **also** supply your **needs**,
    that there may be **equality**.
As it is **written**:
    *Whoever had **much** did not have **more**,*
        *and whoever had **little** did not have **less**.*

A narrative reading that depicts two scenes of healing, both different demonstrations of Jesus' power.

Jairus = JĪ-ruhs
Talitha koum = tah-lee-thah KOOM

GOSPEL   Mark 5:21–43

A reading from the holy Gospel according to Mark

[When **Jesus** had crossed **again** in the boat
    to the other **side**,
    a large **crowd** gathered around him, and he stayed **close**
        to the sea.
One of the synagogue officials, named **Jairus**, came forward.
Seeing him he **fell** at his feet and **pleaded** earnestly
    with him, saying,
    "My **daughter** is at the point of **death**. »

humanity to be imperishable (Wisdom 2:22–23). Thus, in the foolishness of their thinking, and through the envy of the devil, death entered the world (Wisdom 2:21, 24). But in the end, the righteous one triumphs through the grace of God. Although clearly a Jewish work, this story sounds a lot like the story of Jesus.

READING II Often, in the lectionary the first reading and the Gospel have close thematic connections, but not the second reading, which is chosen to expose us to larger parts of the New

Testament than we might read on our own. However, this reading is very much related to the first reading as theory is to practice. In this section of the Second Letter to the Corinthians, Paul is appealing to the community to support his collection for the Christian church in Jerusalem, which was undergoing severe persecution.

Paul is extremely clever in his appeal, first giving the example of the churches in Macedonia, who gave generously despite their own struggles and even begged to be able to contribute to Paul's mission (2 Corinthians 8:1–5). Then he says that he

wants Titus to come to Corinth and help them complete the work that they began earlier. They were supposed to be taking up a collection every Sunday and setting it aside so that it would be ready for Paul to pick up when he returned to their city (1 Corinthians 16:1–4), but apparently they were all talk and little action (2 Corinthians 8:10–11).

Thus, Paul appeals to their sense of self-importance, praising them for the many gifts they have received—notice he says little about their actions—and his love for them to convince them to excel in their

The first healing story concerns this unnamed woman. The nature of her illness is disturbing because it's clearly as social as it is physical, as it involves menstruation. This woman would have been completely isolated. And because of her condition (which involved social shunning), it would have been a punishable transgression for her to touch another person, especially a man. This orients us to her act as well as Jesus' forgiveness.

Upon touching Jesus' cloak, she is healed immediately.
Emphasize "power" and "out." One of the few depictions of what Jesus' powers felt like to him.

Here, the reading shifts to the other story of miraculous healing.

Don't rush over these names.

Please, come lay your **hands** on her
    that she may get **well** and **live**."
He went **off** with him,
    and a large crowd **followed** him and pressed **upon** him.]

There was a **woman** afflicted with **hemorrhages** for twelve years.
She had suffered **greatly** at the hands of many **doctors**
    and had spent **all** that she **had**.
Yet she was not **helped** but only grew **worse**.
She had **heard** about Jesus and came up **behind** him in the crowd
    and **touched** his cloak.
She said, "If I but **touch** his clothes, I shall be **cured**."
Immediately her **flow** of blood dried **up**.
She felt in her **body** that she was **healed** of her **affliction**.
Jesus, aware at once that **power** had gone **out** from him,
    turned around in the crowd and asked, "**Who** has **touched** my **clothes**?"
But his disciples said to Jesus,
    "You **see** how the crowd is **pressing upon** you,
    and yet you **ask**, 'Who **touched** me?'"
And he looked **around** to see who had **done** it.
The **woman**, realizing what had **happened** to her,
    approached in **fear** and **trembling**.
She fell **down** before Jesus and told him the **whole** truth.
He said to her, "**Daughter**, your **faith** has **saved** you.
Go in **peace** and be **cured** of your **affliction**."

[While he was **still speaking**,
    people from the synagogue official's house **arrived** and **said**,
    "Your daughter has **died**; why trouble the teacher any **longer**?"
Disregarding the message that was **reported**,
    Jesus said to the **synagogue** official,
    "Do not be **afraid**; just have **faith**."
He did not allow **anyone** to accompany him **inside**
    except **Peter**, **James**, and **John**, the brother of **James**.

giving. Finally, he appeals to the example of Jesus Christ, because he wants the community not only to give but to give willingly. He also not so subtly reminds them that he is not asking much of them. He is only asking for equity for those who have little. To make this point, he cites Exodus 16:18, which refers to the manna that was given to the Israelites during the Exodus. Some were able to gather only a little and others a lot, but all had enough in the end.

This reading reminds us that sin and death, for which humans are responsible, are not confined to violent acts against others. It includes sins of omission. Our failures to act are also death dealing because they mean that we are not acknowledging and acting upon the realization that all humanity is made in the image of God's own nature (cf. Wisdom 2:23).

GOSPEL   In its long form, today's Gospel is presented to us as an intercalation, a story within a story. Because these intercalations appear rather frequently in Mark's Gospel, biblical scholars have coined the term "Markan sandwich" to describe them. To understand the

main message of these intercalated stories, you need to look to the middle story. As in a sandwich, the "good stuff" is in the middle, whereas the outside story is like the bread that holds everything together. Also, to better understand what is going on in the intercalated stories of today's Gospel, we need to understand the formal structure of a miracle story. At its most basic, it has three parts: (a) description of a problem, (b) the miracle worker's word or deed that effects the miracle, and (c) evidence that the miracle took place.

Jesus' healing is conducted through his words "The child is not dead but asleep." For this he is "ridiculed." Give that word some emphasis.

When they **arrived** at the house of the **synagogue** official,
  he caught **sight** of a **commotion**,
  people **weeping** and wailing **loudly**.
So he went **in** and said to them,
  "Why this **commotion** and **weeping**?
The child is not **dead** but **asleep**."
And they **ridiculed** him.
Then he put them all **out**.
He took along the child's **father** and **mother**
  and those who were **with** him
  and entered the **room** where the child **was**.
He took the **child** by the hand and said to her, *"Talitha koum,"*
  which means, "Little **girl**, I say to you, **arise**!"
The **girl**, a child of twelve, arose **immediately** and
    walked **around**.
At **that** they were utterly **astounded**.
He gave strict **orders** that no one should **know** this
  and said that she should be **given** something to **eat**.]

[Shorter: Mark 5:21–24, 35b–43 (see brackets)]

Talitha koum = tah-lee-thah KOOM

This Aramaic phrase survives from Jesus' time to the present. (Only a few other such phrases similarly survive.) It offers a rare instance to hear Jesus' speech. The following phrase, "I say to you, arise!" need not be exclaimed, but said in an even tone.

The outer story, the healing of Jairus' daughter, encompasses verses 21–24 and 35–43. It's a fairly straightforward miracle story: (a) Jairus' daughter is at the point of death; (b) Jesus takes her by the hand and says, "Little girl, I say to you arise!"); (c) the girl awakes immediately, and the people are astounded. What is surprising is the fact that Jesus could raise the dead, because people believed in folk healers to cure illnesses, but only God could raise the dead! Also notable is the statement that Jesus makes to Jairus: "Do not be afraid; just have faith."

The inner story is most interesting. The description of the woman's situation is exhausting. In Greek, Mark 5:26–28 is written as one sentence. Her hemorrhage, which she had for twelve years, is described as a scourge, and her flow of blood like a fountain. Twelve is the number of fullness. In other words, for the full amount of her adult years she is considered ritually unclean and she cannot conceive. She is like the walking dead! But overcoming her fear, she touches Jesus, probably knowing that her touch makes him ritually unclean, and he responds by saying, "Daughter, your faith has saved you." Amazing! The woman effected the miracle, not Jesus! The message of these intercalated stories is that, despite one's fear, faith (trust in Jesus) can save you and make you whole. C. C.

FOURTEENTH SUNDAY IN ORDINARY TIME

LECTIONARY #101

Ezekiel = ee-ZEE-kee-uhl

A powerful and brief exhortatory reading about the vocation of prophecy.

From this point forward, to the end of the reading, God is speaking.

Emphasize the words "know," "prophet," and "among." These words provide a sense of the vocation to which Ezekiel has been called by God.

For meditation and context:

READING I Ezekiel 2:2–5

A reading from the Book of the Prophet Ezekiel

As the LORD spoke to me, the **spirit** entered **into** me
    and set me on my **feet**,
    and I heard the one who was speaking **say** to me:
    Son of **man**, I am sending you to the **Israelites**,
    rebels who have rebelled **against** me;
    they and their **ancestors** have revolted **against** me
        to this very **day**.
Hard of **face** and obstinate of **heart**
    are **they** to whom I am **sending** you.
But you shall **say** to them: **Thus** says the LORD **God**!
And whether they **heed** or **resist**—for they are a
        rebellious house—
    they shall **know** that a **prophet** has been **among** them.

RESPONSORIAL PSALM Psalm 123:1–2, 2, 3–4 (2cd)

R. Our eyes are fixed on the Lord, pleading for his mercy.

To you I lift up my eyes
    who are enthroned in heaven—
as the eyes of servants
    are on the hands of their masters.

As the eyes of a maid
    are on the hands of her mistress,
so are our eyes on the LORD, our God,
    till he have pity on us.

Have pity on us, O LORD, have pity on us,
    for we are more than sated with
        contempt;
our souls are more than sated
    with the mockery of the arrogant,
    with the contempt of the proud.

READING I All three of today's readings focus on the challenges of being a prophet in the world. This first reading also highlights one of the primary roles of the biblical prophet. Unlike our modern stereotypes of wild-eyed fortune-tellers of the desert, the biblical prophet was deemed to be a spokesperson for God who called God's people to return to the covenant and advocated justice for the poor and marginalized.

Our lectionary reading is an excerpt from a much longer call narrative of the prophet Ezekiel (1:28b—3:11). It is preceded by an elaborate vision of God's throne and the one seated on the throne full of fire and light. When Ezekiel witnesses this amazing sight, we are told, he fell on his face. Ancients believed that one could not see the face of God and live. This is when he heard the heavenly voice, which addressed him as "son of man." While our thoughts might go to the Gospels' multifaceted descriptions of Jesus as Son of Man, in Ezekiel it is God's way of addressing the prophet as a human representing the human community; Ezekiel is a creature and not God. The words he speaks are God's word, not his, and the judgment he announces is God's judgment.

Thus, we hear how Ezekiel is called to deliver a message of condemnation against his fellow Israelites for refusing to abide by God's covenant. Notice the intensity of the language used against this rebellious people. God is definitely not pleased! Yet, even in this most appalling situation, the heavenly voice sends the prophet to the people with an invitation to repentance. But Ezekiel will suffer much for the sake of his calling. In what follows this lectionary reading, the heavenly voice tells him that his task will be

READING II   2 Corinthians 12:7–10

A reading from the second Letter of Saint Paul to the Corinthians

Brothers and **sisters**:
That **I**, Paul, might not become **too** elated,
    because of the **abundance** of the **revelations**,
    a thorn in the flesh was **given** to me, an **angel** of **Satan**,
    to **beat** me, to **keep** me from being too **elated**.
Three **times** I begged the Lord about this, that it might **leave** me,
    but he **said** to me, "My **grace** is **sufficient** for you,
    for **power** is made perfect in **weakness**."
I will rather **boast** most gladly of my **weaknesses**,
    in order that the **power** of Christ may dwell with **me**.
Therefore, I am **content** with weaknesses, insults,
    hardships, persecutions and constraints,
    for the **sake** of Christ;
    for when I am **weak**, then I am **strong**.

GOSPEL   Mark 6:1–6

A reading from the holy Gospel according to Mark

Jesus **departed** from there and came to his native **place**,
    accompanied by his **disciples**.
When the **sabbath** came he began to **teach** in the synagogue,
    and many who **heard** him were **astonished**.
They said, "Where did this man **get** all this?
What kind of **wisdom** has been **given** him?
What mighty **deeds** are wrought by his **hands**!
Is he not the **carpenter**, the son of **Mary**,
    and the brother of **James** and **Joses** and **Judas** and **Simon**?
And are not his sisters here **with** us?"
And they took **offense** at him. **»**

Corinthians = kohr-IN-thee-uhnz

An exhortatory reading in which Paul describes some of the challenging features of his own vocation as an apostle of Jesus'.

God's words set a limit on Paul's misery. Emphasize "grace" and "sufficient" especially.

Even emphasis on all five of these challenges.

Contrast "weak" with "strong."

A narrative reading that leads towards an expression of discouragement, which makes this reading notable.

All these questions, which seem to ask praiseworthy things, pile up as evidence against Jesus.

Joses = JOH-seez or JOH-sez

"Offense" is the key word in this reading.

---

like sitting among scorpions (Ezekiel 2:6) and that the word he has been given to speak, symbolized by a scroll, will make him sick to his stomach.

READING II In today's second reading, Paul asserts his credentials to be called an apostle who is in no way inferior to those so-called "superapostles" (2 Corinthians 11:5 and 12:11) who have come to preach a different message than the one Paul first preached. Clearly, all is not well in the Christian community in Corinth, and Paul is not shy about saying

so! Perhaps in a mocking tone, he goes on to boast of the many sufferings he endured for the sake of preaching the message of Jesus Christ (2 Corinthians 11:21b–33). He goes on to boast—foolishly he says—of the visions and revelations he has experienced. It is in this context that Paul talks about "a thorn in the flesh" (2 Corinthians 12:7), which has traditionally been interpreted to be a physical disability or a psychological disorder. However, it could also refer to his opponents who are like a thorn in his side because of their persistent attacks. Paul describes it as coming from Satan. Yes, his

sufferings are great, but notice how Paul makes sense of this never-ending suffering for the sake of God's work. In his weakness, Paul says, the power of Christ is able to dwell in him. Such is the mystery of the cross!

GOSPEL Today's Gospel reading from Mark tells of Jesus' rejection at the hands of his own people. In the chronology of the Gospel, Jesus has already called disciples, taught with authority, and performed many miracles. Faith or trust in God is an important theme of the

"Amazed at their lack of faith" expresses Jesus' discouragement as clearly as anything can.

Jesus said to them,
  "A **prophet** is not without honor **except** in his native **place**
  and among his own **kin** and in his own **house**."
So he was not able to **perform** any mighty **deed** there,
  apart from curing a few **sick** people by laying his **hands**
    on them.
He was **amazed** at their lack of **faith**.

PRAYERFUL READING, OR *LECTIO DIVINA*

1. *Lectio:* Read a Scripture passage aloud slowly. Notice what phrase captures your attention and be attentive to its meaning. Silent pause.

2. *Meditatio:* Read the passage aloud slowly again, reflecting on the passage, allowing God to speak to you through it. Silent pause.

3. *Oratio:* Read it aloud slowly a third time, allowing it to be your prayer or response to God's gift of insight to you. Silent pause.

4. *Contemplatio:* Read it aloud slowly a fourth time, now resting in God's Word.

Gospel thus far. However, the Jewish religious authorities have already joined with the Herodians in a plot to get rid of Jesus (Mark 3:1–6). In this emerging tension between the people's perception of Jesus as teacher and miracle worker and the religious authorities' view of him as a threat to their power, we are told that Jesus returned to his *patris*, his native place or native land, presumably Nazareth.

This story is dripping with irony, but of course irony only works when the reader recognizes it. The witnesses to Jesus' teaching in the synagogue ask where he got his knowledge and power, meaning, who was his teacher. What they do not understand is that God is his teacher and the source of his power. If you read carefully, you can almost imagine Mark's believing community snickering at the ignorance of the characters in the story. The Greek word used to describe the crowd's amazement is *ekplésso*, essentially a positive expression of astonishment. But the mood quickly turns dark when the crowd starts to belittle Jesus, calling him a carpenter and son of a woman. Again, Mark's readers know the truth of Jesus' identity. But not understanding, the crowd took offense at him. The Greek word is *skandalizó*, meaning, "to put out a stumbling block." You can hear our English word "to scandalize" here. In response, Jesus recites a proverb that we still hear today. Further, we are told that Jesus could do no miracles there, not because his power was diminished, but because of the crowd's lack of faith. C. C.

FIFTEENTH SUNDAY IN ORDINARY TIME

LECTIONARY #104

READING I   Amos 7:12–15

A reading from the Book of the Prophet Amos

Amaziah, priest of Bethel, said to Amos,
   "**Off** with you, visionary, **flee** to the land of **Judah**!
There earn your bread by **prophesying**,
   but never again prophesy in **Bethel**;
   for it is the **king's** sanctuary and a royal **temple**."
Amos answered Amaziah, "I was no **prophet**,
   nor have I belonged to a **company** of prophets;
   I was a **shepherd** and a **dresser** of **sycamores**.
The LORD **took** me from following the flock, and said to me,
   Go, **prophesy** to my people **Israel**."

RESPONSORIAL PSALM   Psalm 85:9–10, 11–12, 13–14 (8)

R. Lord, let us see your kindness, and grant us your salvation.

I will hear what God proclaims;
   the LORD—for he proclaims peace.
Near indeed is his salvation to those
      who fear him,
   glory dwelling in our land.

Kindness and truth shall meet;
   justice and peace shall kiss.

Truth shall spring out of the earth,
   and justice shall look down from heaven.

The LORD himself will give his benefits;
   our land shall yield its increase.
Justice shall walk before him,
   and prepare the way of his steps.

Amos = AY-m*s
Amaziah = am-uh-ZĪ-uh; Bethel = BETH-*l
Judah = joo-duh

A narrative reading that describes the challenges of the vocation of prophecy and by extension any vocation to serve God. This reading uses the verb "prophesy" and its participle "prophesying." The proper pronunciation of these words is: prophesy = PROPH-eh-sigh and prophesying = PROPH-eh-sighing. Practice these.

There is no irony when Amos says, "I was no prophet." He's speaking the truth. He's also speaking to the difficulty of his vocation.

The call to prophecy comes from God. Emphasis on "Go," "prophesy," and "Israel."

TO KEEP IN MIND

As you prepare your proclamation, make choices about what emotions need to be expressed. Some choices are evident from the text, but some are harder to discern. Understanding the context of the Scripture passage will help you decide.

READING I In this week's first reading we hear from another prophet, Amos, who has a fierce message of condemnation for Israel because of the hard-heartedness of God's people. Amos comes on the scene during a time of considerable prosperity for Israel. However, Israel's prestige soon began to diminish, until its capital, Samaria, fell to the Assyrians in 721 BC.

The brief snippet of autobiography in today's lectionary reading interrupts a series of five visions (Amos 7:1—9:10). The theme of each of these visions is the impending punishment of the Northern Kingdom of Israel because of its unfaithfulness to God's covenant. Amos is considered so great a threat to the status quo that Amaziah, the priest of the Israelite temple in Bethel, orders him to flee the city and return to the land of Judah, from which he came.

Pay attention to the contempt with which Amaziah treats Amos. He accuses him of conspiring against King Jeroboam and calls him a seer (Hebrew *chozeh*, sometimes translated "visionary"), which is a very early term for prophets, but in this case it is most likely intended to insult Amos. He adds to the insult when he suggests that Amos is a prophet for hire and a foreigner besides. Amos counters by saying that he was never a professional prophet, meaning he is not beholden to the temple or the king. Rather, he was a shepherd and an orchard keeper, and he came to Bethel to deliver his prophetic message only because God commissioned him to do so.

READING II Today's second reading continues the theme of chosenness. Unlike other New Testament

Ephesians = ee-FEE-zhuhnz

An exhortatory reading of high energy, consisting of a blessing of God followed by five descriptions of praise. Your proclamation will be energetic by simply reading the words.

Almost even emphasis on the words in this line.

Here begin the praises initiated by the word "in." As a preposition, "in" is always followed by the noun that the preposition points to. Give that noun—whether "love," "him," or "wisdom and insight"— its due emphasis.

READING II   Ephesians 1:3–14

A reading from the Letter of Saint Paul to the Ephesians

[**Blessed** be the God and Father of our Lord Jesus **Christ**,
  who has **blessed** us in **Christ**
  with **every spiritual blessing** in the **heavens**,
  as he **chose** us in him, before the **foundation** of the world,
  to be **holy** and without blemish **before** him.
In **love** he destined us for adoption to **himself** through
    Jesus Christ,
  in **accord** with the **favor** of his **will**,
  for the **praise** of the **glory** of his **grace**
  that he granted us in the **beloved**.
In **him** we have **redemption** by his **blood**,
  the **forgiveness** of transgressions,
  in **accord** with the **riches** of his **grace** that he lavished
    upon us.
In all **wisdom** and **insight**, he has made **known** to us
  the **mystery** of his will in **accord** with his favor
  that he set **forth** in him as a **plan** for the fullness of **times**,
  to sum up **all** things in Christ, in **heaven** and on **earth**.]

In **him** we were also **chosen**,
  destined in accord with the **purpose** of the **One**
  who accomplishes **all things** according to the **intention**
    of his will,
  so that we might **exist** for the praise of his **glory**,
  we who first **hoped** in Christ.

letters attributed to Paul, the Letter to the Ephesians incorporates a blessing between the opening of the letter (Ephesians 1:1–2) and the thanksgiving (vv. 15–23). The blessing begins with the "blessed be" that is found both in the Old Testament and in many prayers of the early Church. The author of the Letter to the Ephesians uses the phrase "in Christ" in the sense that Christ is the instrument or agent of this blessing (see Ephesians 1:1, 10, 12, 20). And why are the recipients of this letter "blessed"? Not through their own merit, but because God chose them from the

beginning of time to be "holy and without blemish." This is consistent with the author's belief that the church resides with the heavenly powers (Ephesians 3:10) and that we will one day reign with Christ seated on his heavenly throne (Ephesians 2:6).

Much of the remainder of this blessing is dedicated to an explanation of why we are blessed. Notice, in particular, the preponderance of references to Baptism traditions: the description of Christ as God's beloved (Ephesians 1:6; cf. Mark 1:11, Matt 3:17; Luke 3:22), our destiny as adopted children of God, the recognition that we

have been redeemed (literally, "bought back") from sin through Christ's death, and finally, the mention of being sealed with the Holy Spirit. Many of these allusions still can be found today in the prayers of the Baptism ritual. But notice, too, that this blessing is not due to our merit. It comes to us only because a loving God chose us and brought us into existence so that we might be God's beloved possession and praise his glory.

Some of the phrases of this blessing are also found in the Letter to the Colossians (cf. Colossians 1:13–14, 19, 20, 22, 25). These similarities—along with differences in style,

In **him** you also, who have **heard** the word of **truth**,
  the **gospel** of your salvation, and have **believed** in him,
  were **sealed** with the **promised Holy Spirit**,
  which is the **first installment** of our **inheritance**
  toward **redemption** as God's **possession**, to the **praise**
  of his **glory**.

[Shorter: Ephesians 1:3–10 (see brackets)]

GOSPEL   Mark 6:7–13

A reading from the holy Gospel according to Mark

Jesus summoned the **Twelve** and began to send them out
  two by **two**
and gave them **authority** over unclean **spirits**.
He **instructed** them to take **nothing** for the journey
  but a **walking** stick—
  no **food**, no **sack**, no **money** in their belts.
They were, however, to wear **sandals**
  but **not** a second tunic.
He said to them,
  "**Wherever** you enter a **house**, stay there until you **leave**.
Whatever **place** does not **welcome** you or **listen** to you,
  leave there and shake the **dust** off your **feet**
  in **testimony** against them."
So they went **off** and preached **repentance**.
The **Twelve** drove out many **demons**,
  and they **anointed** with oil many who were **sick** and
  cured them.

Again, almost even emphasis on the words in this line.

A narrative reading describing some of the challenging features of the vocation to serve as a disciple of Jesus in the early days of his ministry.

The details are vivid, in particular the sandals they are told to wear.

Now the meaning of the sandals comes clear: so they can kick the dust from them.

These specific descriptions of the disciples' powers continue to resonate.

---

vocabulary, and theology from other letters clearly identified with Paul—have prompted biblical scholars to conclude that both Colossians and Ephesians were written by later pseudonymous authors to preserve the memory of Paul beyond his death in AD 62–64.

GOSPEL   Today's Gospel focuses on what it means to be chosen, in this case, chosen by Jesus. Immediately prior to this lectionary reading, we learn that Jesus was rejected in his native Nazareth (Mark 6:1–6a), but he continues to teach in the surrounding villages (Mark 6:6b). Instead of shrinking from his mission of proclaiming the coming reign of God in words and deeds, he extended it by sending out the Twelve (see Mark 3:13–19) to do what he was doing: teaching and healing. In the first-century world, many people believed that illnesses were the result of demonic possession. Hence, the reference to the Twelve being given power over unclean spirits. Moreover, they were told not to take lots of clothes or financial resources. This fits with the overall urgency of the Markan Jesus' ministry. Don't even bother with a second undergarment. "This is the time of fulfillment. The kingdom of God is at hand!" (Mark 1:15). For us, too, the reign of God is at hand. What will you do today to extend Jesus' ministry in the world? And don't be surprised if your ministry is rejected at times. We are called to be with Jesus and do what he did to bring about the kingdom, but that means also suffering as he suffered. C. C.

SIXTEENTH SUNDAY IN ORDINARY TIME

LECTIONARY #107

READING I Jeremiah 23:1–6

A reading from the Book of the Prophet Jeremiah

Woe to the shepherds
  who **mislead** and **scatter** the flock of my **pasture**,
  says the LORD.
Therefore, thus says the LORD, the God of **Israel**,
  against the **shepherds** who shepherd my **people**:
  You have **scattered** my sheep and **driven** them away.
You have not **cared** for them,
  but I will take **care** to punish your evil **deeds**.
I **myself** will gather the **remnant** of my **flock**
  from all the **lands** to which I have **driven** them
  and bring them **back** to their meadow;
  there they shall **increase** and **multiply**.
I will appoint **shepherds** for them who will **shepherd** them
  so that they need no **longer** fear and tremble;
  and **none** shall be missing, says the LORD.

  Behold, the days are coming, says the LORD,
    when I will **raise up** a righteous **shoot** to David;
  as **king** he shall reign and govern **wisely**,
    he shall **do** what is just and **right** in the land.
  In his days **Judah** shall be **saved**,
    Israel shall dwell in **security**.
  This is the name they **give** him:
    "The LORD our justice."

Jeremiah = jayr-uh-MĪ-uh

An exhortatory reading in which God speaks through Jeremiah. It involves three parts: A condemnation of bad shepherds; an offer of protection for the sheep; and a vision of coming justice.

Contrast "you" with "I" here as well as emphasizing "myself" in the following line.

The syntax in this line is a little tricky because "shepherd" is used twice, but once as a noun and again as a verb.

From "Behold," we have a vision of the days of justice that are coming. The tone shifts slightly here to something more anticipatory.

READING I Today's first reading follows a section of oracles presumably delivered by Jeremiah against the kings of Judah during the reign of King Zedekiah, when Judah and Jerusalem were destroyed by the Babylonians (597–586 BC). It is followed by another series of messages against false prophets who were associated with the priests of Jerusalem. This is the context for Jeremiah's oracle of consolation about God as the shepherd who will gather the remnant of those who had been taken into exile and bring them back to the land. This God, we are told, will also appoint other shepherds who will guide God's chosen to safety. The metaphor of shepherding was widely used in the ancient world to describe the responsibility of kings and leaders toward their people; Jeremiah 34 is another such example.

Jeremiah goes on to write about the restoration of David's kingly dynasty (cf. 2 Samuel 7). In contrast to the kings with whom Jeremiah had been dealing, this future king will be a righteous branch from David's line. He will be just, or right in conduct and in character, and his name will be "the Lord our justice." The Hebrew word is *tsaddiq*. We can reasonably consider this prophecy to be a critique against Zedekiah, who was a puppet king set up by the Babylonian authorities. Consider the irony that his name, *Tsidqiyyah* in Hebrew, means "God is righteous." Later, Christians understand this messianic prophecy to refer to Jesus.

RESPONSORIAL PSALM   Psalm 23:1–3, 3–4, 5, 6 (1)

R. The Lord is my shepherd; there is nothing I shall want.

The LORD is my shepherd; I shall not want.
  In verdant pastures he gives me repose;
beside restful waters he leads me;
  he refreshes my soul.

He guides me in right paths
  for his name's sake.
Even though I walk in the dark valley
  I fear no evil; for you are at my side
with your rod and your staff
  that give me courage.

You spread the table before me
  in the sight of my foes;
you anoint my head with oil;
  my cup overflows.

Only goodness and kindness follow me
  all the days of my life;
and I shall dwell in the house of the LORD
  for years to come.

READING II   Ephesians 2:13–18

A reading from the Letter of Saint Paul to the Ephesians

Brothers and **sisters**:
In Christ **Jesus** you who once were **far off**
  have become **near** by the blood of **Christ**.

For he is our **peace**, he who made both **one**
  and broke down the **dividing** wall of enmity, through
    his **flesh**,
  abolishing the law with its **commandments** and legal claims,
  that he might **create** in himself **one new person** in place
    of the **two**,
  thus **establishing** peace,
  and might **reconcile** both with **God**,
  in one **body**, through the **cross**,
  putting that **enmity** to death **by** it.
He came and preached **peace** to you who were **far** off
  and **peace** to those who were **near**,
  for **through** him we both have **access** in one **Spirit**
    to the **Father**. »

Ephesians = ee-FEE-zhuhnz

An exhortatory reading. Paul wants to demonstrate to the Church at Ephesus the ways Jesus brings them closer, both to God and to each other.

The contrast between "far off" and "near" sets the tone of the reading.

TO KEEP IN MIND

If you are assigned to proclaim the second reading, take a look at the previous week's second reading, as well as the following week's, to see where the second reading is coming from and where it is going.

Repetition of "far off" and "near," but this time in the context of the peace that Jesus has brought.

READING II   The second reading, from the Letter to the Ephesians, touches on a similar theme of messianic expectation. Prior to the excerpt chosen for the lectionary reading, the author writes about a time when the uncircumcised were separated from the community of Israel and the covenants of the promise. Although the vocabulary is different, this topic of whether Gentiles could be included among the Jesus followers is common in Paul's authentic writings (for example, Romans 1:16; Galatians 3:12). Therefore, it is not sur-

prising to see the same topic appearing in the Letter to the Ephesians.

Where we see the pronouns "you" and "we" in the Letter to the Ephesians, biblical scholars have questioned to whom the author is referring, but we can be fairly certain that "you who once were far off" refers to the recipients of the letter who were Gentile (non-Jewish) Christians. Here, too, we see many allusions to Pauline theology, though using different vocabulary. Christ is described as the one who reconciles Jews and Gentiles in his one body, an allusion to Paul's notion of the Church as

the body of Christ (cf. 1 Corinthians 12:12–27; Romans 12:3–8). Likewise, Christ is the new Adam, who reversed the state of humanity's alienation from God due to sin and who made humanity a new creation (cf. Romans 5:12–17). Paul also talks about Jesus as the one who effects reconciliation (2 Corinthians 5:11–21). However, the beautiful imagery of Christ as our peace is not found in Paul's authentic letters. The Greek word is *eiréné*, meaning "peace, harmony or tranquility" but also "safety and security" in the sense of a promise of salvation that will indeed be fulfilled.

GOSPEL   Mark 6:30–34

A reading from the holy Gospel according to Mark

A narrative reading that depicts something of what it was like to participate in Jesus' early ministry.

Jesus wants his disciples to rest. "Deserted place" signals that rest.

The deserted place is contrasted to the activity of the people who want to be in Jesus' presence.

Jesus ends the brief retreat because he pities those who have gathered, needy as they are for some guidance.

The **apostles** gathered **together** with **Jesus**
  and **reported** all they had done and taught.
He said to them,
  "Come away by yourselves to a **deserted place** and **rest**
    a while."
People were **coming** and **going** in great **numbers**,
  and they had **no** opportunity even to **eat**.
So they went **off** in the boat by **themselves** to a **deserted place**.
People saw them leaving and many came to **know** about it.
They **hastened** there on foot from all the **towns**
  and **arrived** at the place **before** them.

When he **disembarked** and saw the vast **crowd**,
  his **heart** was moved with **pity** for them,
  for they were like **sheep** without a **shepherd**;
  and he began to **teach** them many **things**.

GOSPEL   Today's Gospel returns to the theme of shepherding, which we saw in the first reading. This reading is also the second half of the story that we encountered in last week's Gospel, the sending out of the Twelve (Mark 6:6b–13). In several places in Mark's Gospel, the author uses a literary technique, which some biblical scholars call a "Markan sandwich." The technical term is "intercalation." Briefly, an intercalation is when one story is inserted within another, such that the inner story informs the outer story. Here, the outer story is the sending out of the Twelve and their return from missionary activity. The inner story is the murder of John the Baptist by Herod Antipas, who wondered whether Jesus was John raised from the dead (Mark 6:14–29). It is important to note that the story of the murder of John the Baptist contains a number of clues that suggest Mark intends it to be a preview of Jesus' death and burial.

Thus, we hear in today's Gospel that Jesus welcomes the Twelve back from their missionary journey and listens to their reports of all that they had done. But the crowds that gathered around Jesus and the Twelve were overwhelming! Recognizing that they were exhausted from their journey, he takes them away by boat—they are near the Sea of Galilee—to find a deserted place where they can rest. But the crowds follow them and arrive even before they can disembark from the boat. This is when the narrator identifies Jesus as the compassionate shepherd of the lost sheep. But Mark's inner story reminds us that this shepherd's compassion will reach its fullness when he lays down his life for the sheep. C. C.

SEVENTEENTH SUNDAY IN ORDINARY TIME

Baal-shalishah = BAY-uhl SHAHL-ih-shuh or BAH-uhl SHAUL-ih-shuh
Elisha = ee-Lī-shuh

A narrative reading that reinforces the prophetic authority God has endowed Elisha with. It also directly anticipates the Gospel reading from John that initiates the "bread of life" discourse for the next few weeks.

The repetition of "Give it to the people to eat" is an emphatic expression of Elisha's authority.

Emphases on "eat" to "over" and then "eaten" to "over."

For meditation and context:

LECTIONARY #110

READING I   2 Kings 4:42–44

A reading from the second Book of Kings

A man came from **Baal-shalishah** bringing to **Elisha**,
　　the man of **God**,
　twenty barley loaves made from the **firstfruits**,
　　and fresh **grain** in the **ear**.
Elisha said, "**Give** it to the people to **eat**."
But his **servant** objected,
　　"How can I **set this** before a hundred **people**?"
Elisha insisted, "**Give** it to the people to **eat**.
For **thus** says the LORD,
　　'They shall **eat** and there shall be some left **over**.'"
And when they had **eaten**, there was some left **over**,
　　as the LORD had **said**.

RESPONSORIAL PSALM   Psalm 145:10–11, 15–16, 17–18 (16)

R. The hand of the Lord feeds us; he answers all our needs.

Let all your works give you thanks, O LORD,
　　and let your faithful ones bless you.
Let them discourse of the glory of
　　your kingdom
　and speak of your might.

The eyes of all look hopefully to you,
　　and you give them their food in
　　due season;

you open your hand
　　and satisfy the desire of every living thing.

The LORD is just in all his ways
　　and holy in all his works.
The LORD is near to all who call upon him,
　　to all who call upon him in truth.

TO KEEP IN MIND
If you are assigned to proclaim the first reading, read the Gospel for that week as well. They are connected in thematic ways.

READING I Today's first reading is part of a collection of stories about Elisha, a prophet of the Northern Kingdom of Israel in the ninth century BC (2 Kings 2—8). This story opens with a man coming to Elisha, who was known to be a miracle worker, with a generous gift of twenty loaves of bread made from fresh barley, the first fruits of the harvest. Barley bread was a flat bread, the food of the poor. Based on the biblical story, Elisha was located at Gilgal at the time. We do not know the historical location of ancient Gilgal—the term means "circle of stones" so it could have been anywhere—nor do we know the location of Baal-shalishah. However near or far apart, the detail about this man coming to Gilgal to deliver his gift of bread suggests that Elisha was highly regarded by the people. Notice, then, the hostile reaction of Elisha's servant when Elisha commands him to distribute the bread to the people gathered. But, of course, at the end of the story everyone has enough to eat with plenty of leftovers. Sound familiar?

READING II As you reflect on today's second reading, you will likely find it hard to make a thematic connection to the first reading or the Gospel. This is not an error in the design of the lectionary. Rather, the Sundays of Ordinary Time are used to introduce New Testament readings that might not be as familiar to the average Catholic. In this case, the Letter to the Ephesians is assigned to the Fifteenth through Twenty-First Sundays of Ordinary Time during Year B. The goal is for all of us to hear as much of the Word of God as possible in our three-year lectionary cycle.

READING II   Ephesians 4:1–6

A reading from the Letter of Saint Paul to the Ephesians

Brothers and **sisters**:
I, a prisoner for the Lord,
    urge you to live in a manner **worthy** of the call
        you have **received**,
    with all **humility** and **gentleness**, with **patience**,
    bearing with one another through **love**,
    striving to preserve the **unity** of the spirit through the **bond**
        of peace:
    one **body** and one **Spirit**,
    as you were also **called** to the one **hope** of your **call**;
    one **Lord**, one **faith**, one **baptism**;
    one **God** and Father of **all**,
    who is **over** all and **through** all and in all.

Ephesians = ee-FEE-zhuhnz

An exhortatory reading driven by a rhythmic propulsion like a poem.

Note the repetitions in which "one" introduces holy presences.

Emphasis on the prepositions: "over," "through," and "in."

GOSPEL   John 6:1–15

A reading from the holy Gospel according to John

Jesus went across the **Sea** of Galilee.
A large **crowd** followed him,
    because they saw the **signs** he was performing on the **sick**.
Jesus went up on the **mountain**,
    and there he sat **down** with his **disciples**.
The Jewish feast of **Passover** was near.
When Jesus raised his **eyes**
    and saw that a large crowd was **coming** to him,
    he said to **Philip**,
    "**Where** can we buy enough **food** for them to **eat**?"
He said this to **test** him,
    because he himself **knew** what he was going to **do**.

Galilee = GAL-ih-lee

A narrative reading of John's version of one of Jesus' best-known miracles. The narrative is full of dramatic energy and perspective.

This note of foreknowledge is interesting. Emphasis on "knew" and "do."

The theme of this reading is unity in the body of Christ. The author of the letter is evoking the voice of Paul in the opening sentence by exhorting his readers to live moral lives as one body in Christ, a common theme in Paul's own writings. First, the Letter to the Ephesians lists the virtues that we should exercise to make Christian living a reality: humility, gentleness, patience, and forbearance (moderation). Note that there are four. Second, the letter writer describes the nature and extent of the unity we share: one body, one Spirit, one Lord, one faith, one Baptism, one God who is over all, through all, and in all. Consider the profound nature of this statement. This kind of community defines who we are as children of God. Note that there are seven descriptors. In biblical terms, four is a universal, all-encompassing number, and seven is a number of fullness or perfection.

GOSPEL Hopefully, the story of Elisha's miraculous multiplication of bread reminded you of the Gospel stories in which Jesus multiplies loaves and fishes to feed the crowds. The Gospel of John shares only a few stories with the other three Gospels, but this story is in all four (Matthew 14:13–21; Mark 9:32–44; Luke 9:10–17). One detail that makes John's version distinctive from the others is the mention of barley loaves, which ties it to today's first reading.

Today's Gospel opens with a reference to location (the shore of the Sea of Galilee), the motivation of the crowd (they were looking for signs, or miracles), and time period (near the Feast of Passover). Passover is a commemoration of the Israelites' rescue from slavery, and it is celebrated with unleavened bread and other reminders of

Philip answered him,
"Two hundred days' wages worth of **food** would **not** be enough
for each of them to have a **little**."
One of his disciples,
Andrew, the brother of **Simon Peter**, said to him,
"There is a boy here who has **five barley loaves** and two **fish**;
but what **good** are these for so **many**?"
Jesus said, "Have the **people recline**."
Now there was a **great deal** of **grass** in that place.
So the men reclined, about **five thousand** in number.
Then Jesus took the **loaves**, gave **thanks**,
and **distributed** them to those who were **reclining**,
and also as much of the **fish** as they **wanted**.
When they had had their **fill**, he said to his **disciples**,
"**Gather** the fragments left **over**,
so that **nothing** will be **wasted**."
So they **collected** them,
and filled **twelve wicker baskets** with **fragments**
from the **five barley loaves**
that had been **more** than they could **eat**.
When the **people** saw the **sign** he had done, they said,
"This is **truly** the Prophet, the **one** who is to come into
the world."
Since Jesus **knew** that they were going to **come** and carry
him **off**
to make him **king**,
he **withdrew** again to the **mountain alone**.

"Recline": a curious but vivid word.

The message of this line remains relevant.

The recognition of the people that Jesus is holy is contrasted with his need to be alone, connected again to foreknowledge.

their time in Egypt and of promises for the future. While the mountain is unnamed, this detail may have been included to make the reader think of Sinai, where God made covenant with Moses and the Israelites.

John's version of the story features Philip and Andrew, two of the disciples who were among the first to be called to follow Jesus (see John 1:35–51). Also unique to John's version of the story is the mention that Jesus himself distributes the loaves. In the synoptic Gospels, the disciples are given the task of distributing the food. Before distributing the loaves, the narrator says that Jesus gave thanks. The Greek word is *eucharisteó*. It reminds us of the Jewish prayer before meals, but it also points to the Bread of Life discourse that will follow (John 6:32–59).

All four Gospels mention the twelve baskets of leftovers, but John describes Jesus' command to the disciples with these words: "Gather the fragments left over, so that nothing will be wasted." This vocabulary is also found in the *Didache*, a second-century church order that includes the following Eucharistic prayer: "We thank You, our Father, for the life and knowledge which You made known to us through Jesus Your Servant; to You be the glory forever. Even as this broken bread [fragment] was scattered over the hills, and was gathered together and became one, so let Your Church be gathered together from the ends of the earth into Your kingdom" (*Didache* 9:3–4; http://www.newadvent.org/fathers/0714.htm). C. C.

EIGHTEENTH SUNDAY IN ORDINARY TIME

LECTIONARY #113

READING I   Exodus 16:2–4, 12–15

Exodus = EK-suh-duhs

A narrative reading that provides one of the deep metaphors of the culture. Interestingly, the word "manna" does not appear in this inherently dramatic reading.

A reading from the Book of Exodus

The **whole Israelite community** grumbled against **Moses**
    and **Aaron**.
The Israelites said to them,
    "**Would** that we had **died** at the LORD's **hand** in the land
        of **Egypt**,
    as we sat by our **fleshpots** and ate our fill of **bread**!
But you had to **lead** us into this **desert**
    to make the whole **community** die of **famine**!"

Try not to overdo the complaint of the Israelites.

Then the LORD said to **Moses**,
    "I will now rain down **bread** from **heaven** for you.
Each **day** the people are to go out and gather their daily **portion**;
    thus will I **test** them,
    to see whether they follow my **instructions** or not.

"I have **heard** the grumbling of the **Israelites**.
Tell them: In the evening **twilight** you shall eat **flesh**,
    and in the **morning** you shall have your **fill** of **bread**,
    so that you may know that I, the LORD, am your **God**."

Note: flesh in the evening; bread in the morning. Emphasize "flesh" and "fill of bread."

In the **evening quail** came up and **covered** the camp.
In the **morning** a **dew** lay all about the camp,
    and when the dew **evaporated**, **there** on the surface
        of the **desert**
    were **fine flakes** like **hoarfrost** on the ground.

The exact nature of manna is mysterious, especially since it appears as remnant flakes on the ground after the dew has evaporated. Provide these details with care.

READING I   Today's first reading provides the historical backdrop for today's Gospel. It even gives us a hint at the mood of the crowd, as you will see below. At the beginning of the story, the Israelites grumble against Moses and Aaron, because they were hungry, so much so that they regretted having left slavery in Egypt and the pots of meat stew provided by the pharaoh. In fact, they are grumbling against God, because they know well that it was God who rescued them from Egypt. Notice that God does not retaliate but instead simply acquiesces to their demand and tells Moses that he will provide the Israelites with bread and meat. This bread, we are told, will rain down from heaven, so that they will know "I, the Lord, am your God." But this food comes with strings attached. They must precisely follow God's instructions concerning its collection in order to show that they acknowledge God as their God and themselves as God's people.

READING II   Again this week, our second reading comes from the Letter to the Ephesians. The theme is conversion or transformation of heart, mind, and action among those who have "learned Christ." The author contrasts their

On seeing it, the Israelites asked one another, "What **is** this?"
　　for they did not **know** what it **was**.
But Moses told them,
　　"**This** is the bread that the LORD has **given** you to eat."

For meditation and context:

RESPONSORIAL PSALM　Psalm 78:3–4, 23–24, 25, 54 (24b)

R. The Lord gave them bread from heaven.

What we have heard and know,
　and what our fathers have declared to us,
we will declare to the generation to come
　the glorious deeds of the LORD and
　　his strength
and the wonders that he wrought.

He commanded the skies above
　and opened the doors of heaven;
he rained manna upon them for food
　and gave them heavenly bread.

Man ate the bread of angels,
　food he sent them in abundance.
And he brought them to his holy land,
　to the mountains his right hand had won.

Ephesians = ee-FEE-zhuhnz

An exhortatory reading, expressing Paul's frustration with the community in Ephesus while also showing his conviction that in Jesus there is a new self and new life.

"Truth is in Jesus": This is one of Paul's core convictions.

Emphasize "new self."

READING II　Ephesians 4:17, 20–24

A reading from the Letter of Saint Paul to the Ephesians

Brothers and **sisters**:
I **declare** and **testify** in the Lord
　　that you must **no longer** live as the **Gentiles** do,
　　in the **futility** of their **minds**;
　　that is not how you **learned** Christ,
　　assuming that you have **heard** of him and were **taught** in him,
　　as **truth** is in **Jesus**,
　　that you should **put away** the old self of your **former way**
　　　of life,
　　corrupted through deceitful **desires**,
　　and be **renewed** in the spirit of your **minds**,
　　and put on the **new self**,
　　created in God's way in **righteousness** and **holiness** of truth.

new life with their old life as pagan Gentiles, which he says was impacted by "the futility of their minds." The Greek word for "futility" can also be translated as "perverseness, depravation, or vanity." It can also refer to things that are "devoid of truth and appropriateness." The lectionary omits verses 18 and 19, which reflect Jewish stereotypes about Gentiles at that time, but a quick read will give you a sense of the meaning of the phrase "the futility of their minds." The phrases "put away the old self" and "put on the new self" are traditional baptismal language (cf. Galatians 3:27). In essence, then, the author of this letter is telling the community to live into their baptismal calling in a robust and truthful way. He describes this Christian way of life as "created in God's way in righteousness and holiness of truth" insofar as it belongs to God and represents all that is godly for those who have given up the futility of their minds and allowed themselves to be renewed in spirit.

GOSPEL　Today's Gospel is a continuation of last Sunday's story of the miracle of loaves and fishes. In some respects, it reflects the dark side of human nature, much like last Sunday's first reading

GOSPEL   John 6:24–35

A reading from the holy Gospel according to John

When the **crowd** saw that neither **Jesus** nor his **disciples**
    were there,
  they **themselves** got into **boats**
  and came to **Capernaum** looking for **Jesus**.
And when they **found** him across the sea they said to him,
  "**Rabbi**, when did you get **here**?"
Jesus answered them and said,
  "**Amen**, **amen**, I say to you,
  you are looking for me not because you saw **signs**
  but because you **ate** the loaves and were **filled**.
Do not **work** for food that **perishes**
  but for the **food** that **endures** for eternal **life**,
  which the **Son** of **Man** will **give** you.
For on him the Father, God, has **set** his **seal**."
So they said to him,
  "What can we **do** to accomplish the **works** of God?"
Jesus answered and **said** to them,
  "**This** is the work of God, that you **believe** in the one he **sent**."
So they said to him,
  "What **sign** can you do, that we may **see** and **believe** in you?
What can you **do**?
Our **ancestors** ate manna in the desert, as it is written:
  He gave them **bread** *from* **heaven** *to* **eat**."
So Jesus said to them,
  "**Amen**, **amen**, I say to you,
  it was not **Moses** who gave the bread from heaven;
  my **Father** gives you the **true bread** from heaven.
For the **bread** of **God** is that which comes **down** from **heaven**
  and gives **life** to the **world**."

Capernaum = kuh-PER-nee-*m
A narrative reading in which Jesus introduces to the gathered crowd a metaphor of crucial vibrancy to the Christian imagination. In effect, the reading is an argument that concludes with the metaphor itself, that Jesus is the bread of life.

Here Jesus points to the contrast between ordinary bread and the spiritual bread he provides. Emphasize the contrast between "perishes" and "endures."

Emphasis on "this."

The true bread is the new manna. Note that it comes "down" from heaven. Emphasize the preposition.

---

from Exodus shows the faithlessness of the Israelites in the wilderness. It begins with the crowds seeking Jesus, even securing boats with which to cross the Sea of Galilee in order to find him. "Seeking and finding" is one of the central themes of John's Gospel, as it is associated with discipleship. See, for example, John 1:35–51 and John 20:1–18. But when this crowd finds Jesus, they address him only as "rabbi," teacher, and

Jesus knows what is on their minds. Their "seeking" is not for the purpose of discipleship, but only to have their bellies full! Thus, he exhorts them to work for "food that endures for eternal life." Consistent with many dialogues in John's Gospel, the narrator presents the crowd as clueless at best or even somewhat hostile. "What can we do to accomplish the works of God?" they say. Their question opens the door for Jesus

to make a remarkably profound statement: "Believe in the one he [God] sent."

But the crowd persists in their supposed ignorance—"What sign can you do, that we may see and believe in you?"—and they even back up their question with a reference to the manna given to the Israelites in the wilderness (Exodus 16:4–5). "Seeing and believing" is another important theme in John's Gospel. Only those who believe

Equal emphasis on "I," "bread," and "life."

So they said to him,
    "**Sir**, **give us** this bread **always**."
Jesus said to them,
    "**I** am the **bread** of **life**;
    whoever **comes** to me will never **hunger**,
    and whoever **believes** in me will never **thirst**."

can truly see. Obviously, this crowd does not see, because they dare him to perform a sign greater than that of Moses in the desert of the Exodus. Notice how the Johannine Jesus reinterprets the biblical text by changing the verb tenses and the referents of the pronouns in Scripture. The past tense "gave" is changed to the present tense "gives," The referent for the pronoun "he" is changed from Moses to God the Father. Moreover, the bread to which Jesus refers is no longer the manna, which was intended only for the Israelites in the desert, and which would miraculously appear in the morning but become rotten later in the day, so the desert dwellers would have to rely on God for their daily sustenance. No, this bread is eternal, and it gives life to the world! Still missing the point and wanting only for full bellies, the crowd asks for this bread. Finally, Jesus reveals to them that he is "the bread of life." Imagine their shock and awe! Later, they will grumble, asking one another, "How can this man claim that he came down from heaven?" and "How dare he suggest that we should eat his flesh!" C. C.

NINETEENTH SUNDAY IN ORDINARY TIME

LECTIONARY #116

READING I   1 Kings 19:4–8

A reading from the first Book of Kings

Elijah went a day's **journey** into the **desert**,
> until he **came** to a **broom tree** and sat **beneath** it.

He prayed for **death**, saying:
> "This is **enough**, O LORD!

Take my life, for I am no **better** than my **fathers**."

He lay **down** and fell **asleep** under the **broom tree**,
> but then an **angel** touched him and ordered him to get up
>> and **eat**.

Elijah **looked** and there at his head was a **hearth cake**
> and a jug of **water**.

After he **ate** and **drank**, he lay **down** again,
> but the **angel** of the LORD came back a **second** time,
> **touched** him, and **ordered**,
>> "Get **up** and **eat**, else the **journey** will be too **long** for you!"

He got **up**, **ate**, and **drank**;
> then **strengthened** by that food,
> he walked **forty days** and **forty nights** to the mountain
>> of God, **Horeb**.

A narrative reading that relates a harrowing scene in which Elijah, exhausted, lies down to die but is fed by an angel and inspired to journey extensively onward. It reads like a parable.

Even emphasis on "Take my life."

Elijah = ee-LĪ-juh

Emphasize the repetition of "up."

READING I Our first reading is one of a series of stories about the prophet Elijah that are recorded in 1 Kings 17—19. Prior to this lectionary reading, Elijah confronts King Ahab and the people of Israel who were divided in their loyalty between the God of Abraham, Isaac, and Jacob and Baal, a fertility god and lord of rain and dew, on Mount Carmel. During a time of terrible drought in the land, Elijah challenged the prophets of Baal to a test. Each would build an altar and pray to their god to start the fire. Whichever god started the fire would be their God. The people agreed and, of course, the God of Abraham, Isaac, and Jacob won the test. Elijah ordered the people to seize the prophets of Baal, and he slaughtered all four hundred of them in the Wadi Kishon. Shortly after this, he prophesied to King Ahab that a heavy rain was coming toward them, and indeed it did! Ahab drove his chariot the seventeen miles from Mount Carmel to Jezreel, while Elijah, aided by "the hand of God," ran the entire way and arrived in Jezreel before Ahab.

But King Ahab betrayed Elijah and told his wife Jezebel, a Phoenician princess and devotee of Baal, what Elijah had done to the prophets of Baal and she, in turn, vowed to do the same to Elijah before the passing of a day. Elijah was so frightened that he fled to Beersheba, one hundred miles away, and then went another day's journey into the wilderness to get away from Queen Jezebel. Thus, at the start of the lectionary reading, we need not wonder why Elijah prays for death as he sits beneath a solitary bush in the middle of a desert. Elijah does not see the angel who touched him and spoke to him in his sleep. Instead, he finds only a flatbread and some water. After eating, he goes back to sleep,

For meditation and context:

RESPONSORIAL PSALM   Psalm 34:2–3, 4–5, 6–7, 8–9 (9a)

R. Taste and see the goodness of the Lord.

I will bless the Lord at all times;
   his praise shall be ever in my mouth.
Let my soul glory in the Lord;
   the lowly will hear me and be glad.

Glorify the Lord with me,
   let us together extol his name.
I sought the Lord, and he answered me
   and delivered me from all my fears.

Look to him that you may be radiant
   with joy,
   and your faces may not blush with shame.
When the afflicted man called out, the
   Lord heard,
   and from all his distress he saved him.

The angel of the Lord encamps
   around those who fear him and
   delivers them.
Taste and see how good the Lord is;
   blessed the man who takes refuge in him.

READING II   Ephesians 4:30—5:2

A reading from the Letter of Saint Paul to the Ephesians

Ephesians = ee-FEE-zhuhnz

An exhortatory reading with a passionate and appealingly poetic quality.

Even emphasis for all these strong emotions.

Brothers and **sisters**:
Do not **grieve** the Holy Spirit of God,
   with which you were **sealed** for the day of **redemption**.
All bitterness, fury, anger, shouting, and reviling
   must be **removed** from you, along with all **malice**.
And be **kind** to one another, **compassionate**,
   forgiving one another as God has forgiven **you** in **Christ**.

So be **imitators** of God, as beloved children, and **live** in love,
   as Christ **loved** us and handed himself over **for** us
   as a sacrificial **offering** to God for a **fragrant** aroma.

Allow the "fragrant aroma" that concludes the reading to linger as you conclude your proclamation.

> **TO KEEP IN MIND**
> Smile when you share good news. Nonverbal cues like a smile help the assembly understand the reading.

---

but he is again awakened by the angel who tells him to eat, so he has strength for the journey ahead of him, Where is he going? To God's mountain, Horeb, also known as Sinai, where he will encounter God and be renewed in his resolve to serve God (1 Kings 19:12).

 Today's second reading, from the Letter to the Ephesians, is part of the author's teaching about how the Christian community ought to live out their baptismal call in thought, word, and action. In light of the many allusions to communal life in this section of the letter, the command not to grieve God's Holy Spirit should be understood in terms of avoiding offenses against the community. The Greek word translated here as "grieve" can also mean "offend or throw into sorrow." What should the Christian do instead? "Be imitators of God," he says, for we are God's children. And love as Christ loved in giving himself as a sweet-smelling sacrificial offering to his Father. The reference to being sealed by the Holy Spirit is intended to recall the ritual of Baptism. This sealing should be viewed as a promise and foretaste of what we will know in full at the end of our lives, our redemption in Christ.

GOSPEL Today's Gospel is part of what is often called the Bread of Life discourse (John 6:22–71), though, in fact, it is broken up by the narrator's several mentions of "the Jews" and Jesus' disciples who were listening to Jesus' teaching. As readers and interpreters of John's Gospel, we must be careful not to misconstrue his extremely negative comments about the Jews. The author of John's Gospel, himself a Jew, was most

GOSPEL   John 6:41–51

A reading from the holy Gospel according to John

A narrative reading that includes compelling exhortations. It also narrates a challenge to Jesus' authority, in this case over the claim that he had come down from heaven. Jesus is extending the bread of life metaphor in this reading to strengthen his argument.

The Jews **murmured** about Jesus because he said,
  "I am the **bread** that came **down** from **heaven**,"
  and they said,
  "Is this not **Jesus**, the son of **Joseph**?
Do we not **know** his **father** and **mother**?
Then **how** can he say,
  'I have come down from **heaven**'?"
Jesus answered and said to them,
  "Stop **murmuring** among yourselves.

The syntax of this sentence is tricky. (Specifically, the word "draw," which is in the subjunctive mood.)

No one can come to me unless the Father who **sent** me
    draw him,
  and I will **raise** him on the last day.
It is written in the prophets:
  *They shall **all** be **taught** by **God**.*
Everyone who **listens** to my Father and **learns** from him **comes**
    to me.
Not that anyone has **seen** the Father
  except the **one** who is from **God**;
  he has seen the Father.
Amen, amen, I say to you,
  whoever **believes** has eternal **life**.

Equal emphasis on "I," "bread," and "life."

I am the **bread** of **life**.
Your **ancestors** ate the **manna** in the **desert**, but they **died**;
  this is the bread that comes down from **heaven**
  so that one may **eat** it and not **die**.
I am the **living bread** that came **down** from **heaven**;
  whoever **eats** this bread will live **forever**;

Jesus explicitly connects bread to his flesh in this last line of the reading.

  and the **bread** that I will give is my **flesh** for the **life**
    of the **world**."

likely engaged in an intra-family dispute over what it meant to be a Jew who believed Jesus was the messiah. Thus, most Johannine biblical scholars suggest that we substitute "Judeans" or "Jewish religious authorities" for "the Jews," so as not to encourage modern forms of antisemitism, which was not the intention of the biblical text.

The Bread of Life discourse is an example of Jewish midrash, which is an in-depth commentary on a biblical text, in this case, "He gave them bread from heaven to eat" (cf. Exodus 16:4–5). Today's lectionary reading focuses on Jesus' commentary on the phrase "bread *from heaven*." Remember that the temporal setting for this discourse is near Passover. Also, note the mention of the Jews' grumbling and recall what the Israelites did when they found themselves in the wilderness without food. Their unbelief was revealed in their grumbling. So, too, here the people's grumbling reveals their unbelief in God and in Jesus, God's agent in the world. They are offended by Jesus' claim to have come down from heaven, but they are totally clueless about the bigger truth—that everything has its origin in God, even the desire to believe in Jesus, and that one cannot hear the word of God except through Jesus.

This reading concludes with a summary statement of Jesus' midrash on "He gave them bread from heaven." It is followed by an exposition of what it means "to eat" of the bread of life (John 6:51b–58).
C. C.

THE ASSUMPTION OF THE BLESSED VIRGIN MARY: VIGIL

LECTIONARY #621

READING I   1 Chronicles 15:3–4, 15–16; 16:1–2

A reading from the first Book of Chronicles

David assembled **all Israel** in **Jerusalem** to bring the **ark** of
　　the **LORD**
　to the **place** that he had **prepared** for it.
David also called together the **sons** of **Aaron** and the **Levites**.

The **Levites** bore the **ark** of God on their **shoulders** with **poles**,
　as **Moses** had **ordained** according to the **word** of the LORD.

David commanded the **chiefs** of the **Levites**
　to **appoint** their **kinsmen** as **chanters**,
　to play on **musical** instruments, **harps**, **lyres**, and **cymbals**,
　to make a **loud sound** of **rejoicing**.

They brought in the **ark** of **God** and set it **within** the **tent**
　which **David** had **pitched** for it.
Then they offered up **burnt offerings** and **peace offerings** to **God**.
When **David** had finished offering up the **burnt offerings** and
　　peace offerings,
　he **blessed** the people in the **name** of the LORD.

Chronicles = KRAH-nih-k*ls

A narrative reading that describes the preparation and then the activities of a celebration ordained by King David.

Chronicles = KRAH-nih-k*ls
Aaron = AYR-uhn
Levites = LEE-vīts

Don't rush through the details. These—including the musical instruments signify the nature and quality of the celebration.

Note the parallel emphases on "burnt offerings" and "peace offerings."

READING I　"The ark, of the Lord" is a ritual object that reminds the Israelites that their Lord is present with them and involved in everything that happens to them. The ark first appears in the traditions that were collected and passed on by the northern tribes that the Lord brought out of bondage in Egypt. After Moses' encounter with God on Mount Sinai, they build the ark to hold the covenant that details how this new relationship will work.

　　The ark then leads them on their long journey through the wilderness to the Promised Land. In Numbers 10:35–36, the Lord, through the ark, determines when they break camp and move on, and when they stop at a new place. Before each move, Moses prays that the Lord will protect them from their enemies. Upon their arrival at the border of the Promised Land, the priests carry the ark into the Jordan River, stopping its flow so that the tribes can walk across on dry land. Then, as instructed by the Lord, they carry the ark in a liturgical procession that encircles the city of Jericho, whose walls consequently collapse.

　　These traditions about the ark carried less weight for the southern tribes to which Saul, Israel's first king, and David belonged. Though Saul ignored them, David appreciates the ark's significance as a sign of the Lord's protecting presence for the northern tribes, and therefore brings it with great ceremony to Jerusalem. This move is part of his political strategy to make these tribes feel like they belong in the nation that he is forging out of fiercely independent groups. Another piece of his plan is the choice of Jerusalem for his capital. Because it has no historical connection to or significance for any tribe, Jerusalem is

For meditation and context:

RESPONSORIAL PSALM   Psalm 132:6–7, 9–10, 13–14 (8)

R. Lord, go up to the place of your rest, you and the ark of your holiness.

Behold, we heard of it in Ephrathah;
  we found it in the fields of Jaar.
Let us enter into his dwelling,
  let us worship at his footstool.

May your priests be clothed with justice;
  let your faithful ones shout merrily
    for joy.

For the sake of David your servant,
  reject not the plea of your anointed.

For the LORD has chosen Zion;
  he prefers her for his dwelling.
"Zion is my resting place forever;
  in her will I dwell, for I prefer her."

READING II   1 Corinthians 15:54b–57

Corinthians = kohr-IN-thee-uhnz

An exhortatory reading in which Paul insists on the victory over the death that results from the defiance of sin gained through Christ's sacrifice.

In this quotation, emphasize the first and last word in each italicized line.

Note the rhythm of these two lines, each of which has three beats: sting, death, sin, and power, sin, law.

A reading from the first Letter of Saint Paul to the Corinthians

Brothers and **sisters**:
When **that** which is **mortal** clothes **itself** with **immortality**,
  then the **word** that is **written** shall come **about**:

  Death is swallowed up in *victory*.
  Where, O death, is your *victory*?
  Where, O death, is your *sting*?

The **sting** of **death** is **sin**,
  and the **power** of **sin** is the **law**.
But **thanks** be to **God** who gives us the **victory**
  through our **Lord** Jesus **Christ**.

> **TO KEEP IN MIND**
> Make eye contact with the assembly. This helps keep the assembly engaged with the reading.

---

the best place for the new nation's political and religious center.

The Chronicler's version of David bringing the ark to Jerusalem was written down c. 400 BC, roughly eight hundred years after the event. Compared to the version of the same event in 2 Samuel 6, it emphasizes the interest of that later period in liturgical correctness. Accordingly, the ceremony is run by the sons of Aaron (the priests) and the Levites; they appoint the chanters and musicians and offer the appropriate sacrifices.

READING II   Instead of resting in the Jerusalem Temple, however, Israel's Lord came in the flesh to reside among humankind in the person of Jesus of Nazareth and in all who believe in him in every generation.

In this passage, Paul reminds these believers that when Christ was raised by God from the dead, he defeated Death, the arch-enemy of the human race. Paul clarifies that they will not understand or experience Christ's victory completely until they too are raised to eternal life, or as he puts

it, until "that which is mortal clothes itself in immortality."

Paul personifies Death and Sin, raising them to a mythical level. In other words, he presents them as realities which are active within all creation. They work constantly to influence human beings—the images and likenesses of God in the world, the people in whom Christ lives on and who continue his mission to bring Life—to live like they are still in bondage.

The sway of Death and Sin extend beyond that of any individual. Death is the orchestrator of global evils like narcissism,

GOSPEL   Luke 11:27–28

A reading from the holy Gospel according to Luke

While **Jesus** was **speaking**,
   a **woman** from the crowd called **out** and **said** to him,
   "**Blessed** is the **womb** that **carried** you
   and the **breasts** at which you **nursed**."
He replied,
   "**Rather**, blessed are **those**
   who **hear** the **word** of **God** and **observe** it."

A short but intense Gospel reading in which an exhortation is embedded in a brief narrative. This reading can seem like a rebuke or at least a correction on Jesus' part. Instead, consider it an intensification of the excited statement made by the woman in the crowd.

Don't change your tone at "Rather." Instead, treat what Jesus says as an affirmation and furthering of what the woman has said.

prejudice, exclusiveness, abuses of power, dependencies of all kinds, and so much more. Paul insists that the Spirit of the risen Christ empowers believers to resist the manipulative attractions that Death and Sin set before them. He urges Christians to hold their heads up and taunt these ancient foes by confronting them fearlessly and stubbornly when they arise in daily life. In short, he urges Christians to live in such a way that those who see them see the victorious Christ, risen and reigning in their midst.

GOSPEL   *Makarios*, the Greek word used in this reading both for the blessing of Mary and for the one that Jesus pronounces, marks those whom God declares righteous and who, therefore, experience the joy and privilege of sharing divine life. Jesus calls blessed those who hear the word of God and put it into practice—in other words, his disciples who carry on his work in every age.

For Luke, Mary fits the criteria of both blessings. She is worthy of sharing in God's own life because she is Jesus' mother. However, this honor flows from her decision to heed the perplexing word of God that came to her through the angel Gabriel. Without comprehending the divine strategy, she gives her *fiat* and takes up her task.

No fanfare accompanies Mary's quiet consent that paves the way for God to come into the earthly realm. Just as there is seldom fanfare when Jesus' disciples give their *fiat* to his teachings. Such celebratory salutes, however, do take place in the heavenly realm. In today's liturgy, we participate in one of these, namely, the Assumption of the *Blessed* Virgin Mary, body and soul, into heavenly glory. E. N.

THE ASSUMPTION OF THE BLESSED VIRGIN MARY: DAY

LECTIONARY #622

READING I   Revelation 11:19a; 12:1–6a, 10ab

A reading from the Book of Revelation

God's **temple** in **heaven** was **opened**,
   and the **ark** of his **covenant** could be **seen** in the **temple**.

A great **sign appeared** in the **sky**, a **woman clothed** with the **sun**,
   with the **moon** under her **feet**,
   and on her **head** a crown of **twelve stars**.
She was with **child** and **wailed aloud** in **pain** as she **labored**
      to give **birth**.
Then another **sign** appeared in the **sky**;
   it was a **huge red dragon**, with seven **heads** and ten **horns**,
   and on its **heads** were seven **diadems**.
Its **tail** swept away a **third** of the **stars** in the **sky**
   and hurled them **down** to the **earth**.
Then the **dragon** stood before the **woman about** to give **birth**,
   to **devour** her **child** when she gave **birth**.
She gave **birth** to a **son**, a **male child**,
   destined to **rule** all the **nations** with an iron **rod**.
Her **child** was caught up to **God** and his **throne**.
The woman **herself fled** into the **desert**
   where she had a **place prepared** by **God**.

A narrative reading full of vivid depictions and visionary intensity. Avoid the temptation to exaggerate your tone; instead, proclaim this text straightforwardly, allowing its inherent drama to ring out to your assembly. Proclaim at an even pace so that the extraordinary details can be clearly imagined.

Slight pause between woman and clothed.

Note the repeated use of the word birth in this reading. Themes and visualizations of birth dominate the details.

Slight pause between "woman" and "about."

Once again, the theme of birth.

Slight pause between herself and fled.

READING I   The author of the Book of Revelation writes to give hope to the baptized who are suffering for their commitment to Christ. Their belief that Jesus was raised from the dead and rules over the whole world clashes with the claims made by Roman emperors to dominion and, by some of them, to divinity. For example, Domitian (AD 81–96), who likely ruled when Revelation was composed, gives himself the title "Our Lord and our God."

To inspire the baptized to live like *Christ* is their Lord and God (Revelation 4:11), the author sets heavenly visions before them. In these, "heaven" is not a distant ideal place, but rather a realm that exists side by side and intermingles with the earthly realm. The image of Jesus standing at the door and knocking conveys this reality. One has only to open the door to be with him (3:20).

The first verse of this reading concludes the section of Revelation that presents Jesus as the victorious Lamb who reigns from his heavenly throne (4:1—11:19). He won the decisive battle with evil on the cross, and thus his arch-adversary Satan no longer has power in the heavenly realm.

The glimpse of the ark of God's covenant in the celestial temple reminds Christians that God, who protected his people from their enemies in the past, is also with them now. (See Assumption Vigil, Reading I.)

The vision of the woman and the dragon presents Christ's victory from a different angle. Here, the woman represents the twelve tribes of Israel from whom the Messiah (Greek *Christos*) comes, as well as all those who believe that Christ is alive and reigns. She is surrounded by light: the sun envelops her, the moon is beneath her feet, a crown of twelve stars rests on her head.

The loud voice indicates the Anointed One. You don't need to raise your voice any more than you already have. Instead, you can slow your pace just slightly.

Then I heard a **loud voice** in heaven **say**:
"**Now** have **salvation** and **power** come,
    and the **Kingdom** of our **God**
    and the **authority** of his **Anointed One**."

For meditation and context:

RESPONSORIAL PSALM   Psalm 45:10, 11, 12, 16 (10bc)

R. The queen stands at your right hand, arrayed in gold.

The queen takes her place at your right hand
    in gold of Ophir.

Hear, O daughter, and see; turn your ear,
    forget your people and your
    father's house.

So shall the king desire your beauty;
    for he is your lord.

They are borne in with gladness and joy;
    they enter the palace of the king.

READING II   1 Corinthians 15:20–27

Corinthians = kohr-IN-thee-uhnz

A reading from the first Letter of Saint Paul to the Corinthians

A didactic reading in which Paul makes a set of forceful claims he wants the members of the early Church in Corinth to understand.

Brothers and **sisters**:
Christ has been **raised** from the **dead**,
    the **firstfruits** of **those** who have fallen **asleep**.
For since **death** came through **man**,
    the **resurrection** of the **dead** came **also** through **man**.
For just as in **Adam** all **die**,
    so too in **Christ** shall all be **brought** to **life**,
    but each **one** in proper **order**:
    Christ the **firstfruits**;
    then, at his **coming**, **those** who **belong** to **Christ**;
    then comes the **end**,
    when he hands **over** the **Kingdom** to his **God** and **Father**,
    when he has **destroyed** every **sovereignty**
    and every **authority** and **power**.
For he must **reign** until he has put all his **enemies** under
    his **feet**.
The last **enemy** to be **destroyed** is **death**,
    for "he subjected **everything** under his **feet**."

Paul uses analogy here to contrast the original sin of Adam to the redemption from sin of Christ.

Note the repetition of the biblical word "firstfruits."

The conclusion of this reading is quite forceful; note the emphatic connection between "enemies" and "death."

The dragon represents the forces of darkness that exercise power on earth. Seven crowns flaunt its false claims to absolute authority. A sweeping tail demonstrates its horrific and paralyzing proficiency. Red skin symbolizes death, the fate it intends for the woman's child and for those who believe in this child. The dragon, however, fails and the newborn is "caught up to God and his throne," a metaphor for Jesus' Resurrection. Earth and heaven intermingle as Jesus dies on the battlefield of the cross and God rescues him from death—a scene that recurs at every Christian death.

The dragon fails because God intends the child "to rule all the nations with an iron rod." This phrase evokes Psalm 2, which was originally recited at the ascension of an Israelite king to the throne. Its opening verses depict the earthly and heavenly reactions to this event. World leaders protest and plot to remove the Lord's new "messiah" or "anointed one" (Psalm 2:1–3). From heaven, God laughs, mocks their futile efforts, and declares that no one can unseat the one he puts on the throne (Psalm 2:4–6).

Back in Revelation, the woman (the Church) flees to a desert place prepared for her by God. There he watches over her as the dragon continues its assaults—its death-throes—for a limited time. It rages about struggling to unseat God's messiah, trying to persuade earth's inhabitants that it is in charge. Above all, it aims to intimidate Christians, to change them from staunch supporters of their king into spineless herds, into cowards who cringe before its terrors and slink away from the battle. The last thing the dragon wants to see is the baptized joining together and fearlessly

Judah = JOO-duh

Zechariah = zek-uh-RĪ-uh

A narrative reading from Luke's Gospel included in the nativity story. Its familiarity to your assembly will not diminish its power. No need to over-dramatize it; let the words of the reading convey its power.

The focus of this reading is on sound, especially of Mary's voice. Let that voice ring out.

Words at the core of one of our most familiar prayers.

Once again, the emphasis is on the sound of Mary's voice and the joy it brings.

Here, Mary proclaims the words of the Magnificat, one of the most solemn hymns in the Church. We aren't necessarily accustomed to hearing these words nowadays. These are the words of a joyful affirmation the Gospels uniquely possess.

"He has shown," "He has cast down," "He has filled," "He has come": These phrases drive the rhythm of the Magnificat as it is proclaimed in this Gospel reading.

GOSPEL   Luke 1:39–56

A reading from the holy Gospel according to Luke

Mary set out
   and **traveled** to the hill country in **haste**
   to a town of **Judah**,
   where she **entered** the house of **Zechariah**
   and greeted **Elizabeth**.
When Elizabeth heard Mary's **greeting**,
   the infant **leaped** in her **womb**,
   and **Elizabeth**, filled with the **Holy Spirit**,
   cried **out** in a **loud** voice and **said**,
   "**Blessed** are **you** among **women**,
   and **blessed** is the **fruit** of your **womb**.
And **how** does this **happen** to me,
   that the **mother** of my **Lord** should **come** to me?
For at the **moment** the **sound** of your **greeting** reached my **ears**,
   the **infant** in my **womb** leaped for **joy**.
Blessed are **you** who **believed**
   that what was **spoken** to you by the **Lord**
   would be **fulfilled**."

And Mary said:

   "My **soul** proclaims the **greatness** of the **Lord**;
      my **spirit** rejoices in **God** my **Savior**
      for he has with **favor** on his lowly **servant**.
   From **this day** all **generations** will call me **blessed**:
      the **Almighty** has done great **things** for me
      and **holy** is his **Name**.
   He has **mercy** on those who **fear** him
      in every **generation**.
   He has shown the **strength** of his **arm**,
      and has scattered the **proud** in their **conceit**.

fighting it with the courage that their King showed on the cross—fighting because they believe that God delivers them from its evils and that Christ's kingdom will come on earth as it is in heaven.

READING II   Paul assures all those who hope for Jesus' return and their own resurrection from the dead that God's plan is on schedule. The two men, Adam and Christ, divide human existence into two ages. From Adam until Christ, life ended when a person died. But once Christ became a human being and joined himself

to our race, he made it possible for all to be brought to life through him.

Though many first-century Jews believed in resurrection from the dead, they expected this to happen to them as a group at the end of time. To explain Jesus' advance Resurrection, Paul draws on the biblical imagery of the "first fruits" of a crop. These are offered to God, as a sign of one's faith that God will provide a bountiful harvest. Christ, the first fruits, is already with God, and all "who belong to Christ" will join him at the end of time.

GOSPEL   This Gospel recounts what has come to be known as the Visitation and the Magnificat. Of Mary's visit to her cousin, Luke mentions only that Elizabeth's child (John the Baptist) twice leaps in her womb and that she thrice pronounces Mary to be blessed.

The child's joyful leaping is a literary technique called a "child in the womb" type scene. Its function is to foreshadow the roles that significant biblical figures will play in salvation history. John's leaping in response to Jesus in Mary's womb portrays

He has cast down the **mighty** from their **thrones**,
   and has **lifted up** the **lowly**.
He has filled the **hungry** with **good things**,
   and the **rich** he has sent away **empty**.
He has come to the **help** of his servant **Israel**
   for he has **remembered** his promise of **mercy**,
   the **promise** he made to our **fathers**,
   to **Abraham** and his children for **ever**."

Mary **remained** with her about three **months**
   and then **returned** to her **home**.

him as the prophet who will recognize Jesus and point him out to others.

Filled with the Holy Spirit, Elizabeth declares: "Blessed are you among women, and blessed is the fruit of your womb." Here, the Greek *eulogēmenē* ("blessed") expresses thanks to God not only for the blessing of a child—the desire of all biblical women—but also for the child that Mary will bear. He is none other than the Lord (*Kyrios*) whom Elizabeth faithfully served her whole life long.

In Elizabeth's third blessing, the Greek *makaria* (used in the Beatitudes) replaces *eulogēmenē*. *Makaria* marks Mary as righteous before God because she trusts that God fulfills promises. Her faith makes it possible for her, and for all who emulate her, to begin sharing in God's own life on earth.

Jesus is the "help" that God sends to Israel and the "remembrance" of the promise made to Abraham. Jesus' Resurrection reversed the seemingly unchangeable status of the mighty and the lowly, the hungry and the rich. In God's kingdom, the proud and powerful lose their positions and influence. *Divine* power works through the humble who trust that God is in control and defer to his will—like Mary and Elizabeth. All who hunger for good things are filled with *divine* gifts. But those who hunger for what money and machination can procure, God sends away empty-handed. E. N.

TWENTY-FIRST SUNDAY IN ORDINARY TIME

LECTIONARY #122

READING I Joshua 24:1–2a, 15–17, 18b

A reading from the Book of Joshua

Shechem = SHEK-uhm
A narrative reading in which the choice of faith in God is affirmed.

Joshua gathered together **all** the tribes of **Israel** at **Shechem**,
   summoning their **elders**, their **leaders**,
   their **judges**, and their **officers**.
When they **stood** in ranks before **God**,
   Joshua addressed all the **people**:
   "If it does not please you to serve the Lord,
   decide **today** whom you will **serve**,
   the gods your **fathers** served beyond the **River**
   or the gods of the **Amorites** in whose **country** you are
      now **dwelling**.
As for me and my **household**, we will **serve** the Lord."

Amorites = AM-her-ītz

Joshua sets up the choice and then insists on his choice to serve the Lord. Emphasis on "serve" and "Lord."

But the people answered,
   "Far be it from **us** to forsake the Lord
   for the **service** of other **gods**.
For it was the Lord, our God,
   who brought **us** and our **fathers up** out of the **land** of **Egypt**,
   out of a **state** of **slavery**.

Slight pause between "fathers" and "up."

He **performed** those great **miracles** before our very **eyes**
   and **protected** us along our entire **journey**
   and among the **peoples** through whom we **passed**.
Therefore we **also** will serve the Lord, for **he** is our **God**."

After "Therefore," a further affirmation by the people to serve the Lord. Emphasis on "he" and "God."

READING I The inhabitants of the biblical world believed that gods controlled geographical areas. Thus, to survive and thrive in a place, one must respect and serve the regional deities. As primitive as this notion may seem, most live by it today. For example, when people move into a new neighborhood, begin a new job, or resettle in a foreign country, they naturally fall in with the priorities and customs of most of the locals. They adopt and worship the "gods" that their new neighbors and coworkers serve. Most obvious among these are power, money, and

the good opinion of those who have what they want or are idolized by the majority, but there are countless more.

In this reading, Joshua gathers God's people and asks them to choose again whom they will follow. Are they still serving the Lord and living by the covenant teachings, or do they fit in with the people around them? Do their neighbors see them as somehow different (the biblical meaning of "holy"), their lifestyle as at least a bit odd, or are they indistinguishable from those who do not worship the Lord?

Joshua prefaces the choice he sets before Israel with a condition: "*If* it does not please you to serve the Lord." The Hebrew for "not please" and "unwilling" can also convey the ideas that serving the Lord seems like a useless undertaking or one that is not gratifying. If this is the case, Israel needs to decide if they will serve the gods that their ancestors relied upon before the Lord called Abraham, or the gods of the Amorites in whose land they now dwell.

The people respond that they will not leave the Lord. Why? Because he is the God

For meditation and context:

Ephesians = ee-FEE-zhuhnz

A didactic reading whose contents are difficult for many in the modern Church to hear and assent to. The reading focuses on what might be called "household code," especially the hierarchies controlling it. Even if you find its contents disagreeable, you can proclaim the reading in a neutral tone.

Analogies and parallels organize the content of this letter.

Almost even emphasis on the words of this line.

RESPONSORIAL PSALM   Psalm 34:2–3, 16–17, 18–19, 20–21 (9a)

R. Taste and see the goodness of the Lord.

I will bless the LORD at all times;
  his praise shall be ever in my mouth.
Let my soul glory in the LORD;
  the lowly will hear me and be glad.

The LORD has eyes for the just,
  and ears for their cry.
The LORD confronts the evildoers,
  to destroy remembrance of them from
  the earth.

When the just cry out, the LORD hears them,
  and from all their distress he
  rescues them.
The LORD is close to the brokenhearted;
  and those who are crushed in spirit
  he saves.

Many are the troubles of the just one,
  but out of them all the LORD delivers him;
he watches over all his bones;
  not one of them shall be broken.

READING II   Ephesians 5:21–32

A reading from the Letter of Saint Paul to the Ephesians

[**Brothers** and **sisters:**]
Be **subordinate** to one another out of **reverence** for **Christ**.
Wives should be subordinate to their **husbands** as to the **Lord**.
For the **husband** is head of his **wife**
  just as **Christ** is head of the **church**,
  he **himself** the savior of the **body**.
As the **church** is subordinate to **Christ**,
  so **wives** should be subordinate to their **husbands**
    in everything.
[**Husbands**, love your **wives**,
  even as **Christ** loved the **church**
  and handed himself **over** for her to **sanctify** her,
  cleansing her by the bath of **water** with the **word**,
  that he might **present** to himself the **church** in **splendor**,
  without **spot** or **wrinkle** or any such **thing**,
  that she might be **holy** and without **blemish**.
So also **husbands** should love their **wives** as their own **bodies**.
He who **loves** his wife **loves** himself.] »

who freed them from Egypt and continues to free them from all types of forced subordination. The Lord provided water for them in the wilderness where none could be seen. He rained down the manna that they saw but did not realize could be eaten, until the Lord opened their eyes. They reached the Promised Land because all along the way the Lord protected them from danger.

READING III The shorter form of today's reading begins with material from an earlier part of Ephesians (5:2a) than the rest of the reading. This decision

situates the rest of the reading in a particular context, namely, the mutual life in Christ that all the baptized share. A consequence of this new status is that how they view and treat each other manifests how they view and treat Christ. Specifically, they must be kind—or also in Greek "useful, good, benevolent"—to one another, tenderhearted or compassionate, and forgiving. They must be imitators of God and live like beloved (a form of *agapē*) children of God. For all of these, Christ is their model.

The rest of the reading is part of a "household code," a literary genre which

gives instructions for an ordered household in the Greco-Roman world of the first century AD. The text, therefore, reflecting the views of that place and time, names the husband (the *paterfamilias*) as the one responsible for regulating the lives all those who live under one roof—usually his wife, children, and slaves.

The code opens with a fundamental command to all members of the Body of Christ. Each of them must "be subordinate" to others out of reverence for Christ. In other words, all must be deferential to, or see themselves as inferior to, every other

For no one **hates** his own flesh
　　but rather **nourishes** and **cherishes** it,
　　even as **Christ** does the **church**,
　　because we are **members** of his **body**.
　　*For this **reason** a man shall **leave** his father and his mother*
　　　　*and be **joined** to his wife,*
　　*and the **two** shall become **one flesh**.*
This is a great **mystery**,
　　but I **speak** in reference to **Christ** and the **church**.

[Shorter: Ephesians 5:2a, 25–32 (see brackets). This shorter version adds 2a as the first line: "Live in love, as Christ loved us."]

It might not be inappropriate to allow a little irony to tinge your expression of the word "mystery."

GOSPEL   John 6:60–69

A reading from the holy Gospel according to John

Many of Jesus' **disciples** who were **listening** said,
　　"This saying is **hard**; who can **accept** it?"
Since **Jesus** knew that his **disciples** were **murmuring** about this,
　　he said to them, "Does this **shock** you?
What if you were to **see** the Son of Man **ascending**
　　to **where** he was **before**?
It is the **spirit** that gives **life**,
　　while the **flesh** is of no **avail**.
The **words** I have **spoken** to you are **Spirit** and **life**.
But there are **some** of you who do not **believe**."
Jesus **knew** from the **beginning** the ones who would not **believe**
　　and the **one** who would **betray** him.
And he said,
　　"For **this reason** I have told you that **no one** can **come** to me
　　unless it is **granted** him by my **Father**."

A narrative reading with a dramatic interplay. It's possible to read this passage either as a confrontation or as an expression of Jesus' confidence. As ever, a straightforward proclamation of the reading will allow its meaning to resonate with your assembly.

When Jesus asks this question, he is seeking the attention of his audience.

In the Gospel of John, Jesus repeatedly makes such claims about the Father, which suggest something of his foresight.

---

person in the community because Christ dwells within him or her. This outlook does not come naturally to human beings; it requires conscious change because it is divine, the stance of Christ himself.

Therefore, it is a given that wives should "be subordinate" to their husbands. Most of the passage, however, elaborates how the husband must treat his wife and especially on why. Notably, this household code expands the code in Colossians where a single verse instructs the husband (Colossians 3:19). Ephesians elaborates that he is the head of his wife just as Christ is

head of the Church. And his mission is to love her as Christ loved the Church.

And how was that? Christ "handed himself over" or "betrayed" his own interests and died for all the baptized. Therefore, a husband who loves like Christ will set aside his concerns for those of his wife, even if it kills him! He must also love her as he loves his own body. He must nourish her and cherish her even as Christ does the Church because all the baptized are members of his Body.

The quote from Genesis 2:24 shows that a married couple is in a unique position

to experience how divine love works and to be drawn together ever more deeply into it. The mystery of their life together, of a man loving his wife like himself and a woman respecting Christ in him, displays to all who see them the great mystery of Christ's love for the Church.

GOSPEL   In the preceding unit of this Gospel, John 6:52–59, Jesus insists that disciples must eat the flesh of the Son of Man (Jesus' self-designation) and drink his blood to have life within them. When Jesus sees them struggling to accept

Express this question without any added drama.

When Peter speaks, he speaks for the whole assembly.

As a **result** of this,
 many of his disciples **returned** to their **former** way of **life**
 and no **longer accompanied** him.
Jesus then **said** to the Twelve, "Do you **also** want to **leave**?"
Simon Peter **answered** him, "**Master**, to **whom** shall we **go**?
You have the **words** of eternal **life**.
We have **come** to **believe**
 and are **convinced** that **you** are the **Holy One** of God."

this teaching, he raises an even more shocking issue when he asks, "What if you were to see the Son of Man ascending to where he was before?"

What he means is not exactly clear. His disciples seem to accept that he is the Bread come down from heaven, that God is with him. But his humiliating death on the cross convinced most of his followers that he was only human. John's audience, using only their mind of flesh, fails to grasp that the Father raised him up and that he lives on among them.

Comprehension of Jesus' real presence in daily life begins with a decision to believe in him. Faith deepens as disciples put his teachings, which are "Spirit and life," into practice. They have new experiences that deepen awareness of the closeness and intermingling of the spiritual and physical realms in daily life. Like Peter, they "come to" believe and be convinced that Jesus is the Holy One of God.

But, for most of his disciples, this is too much to accept. With a deep sigh of disbelief—and of relief that they can retreat

into familiar and comfortable routines—they reject the Lord of Life. They reckon their days are "full enough" and shamble off to rejoin the unbelieving crowd.

Today, Jesus asks each of us, "Do you also want to leave?" Eternal life with him hinges on our response. E. N.

TWENTY-SECOND SUNDAY IN ORDINARY TIME

LECTIONARY #125

READING I   Deuteronomy 4:1–2, 6–8

Deuteronomy = doo-ter-AH-nuh-mee
statutes = STACH-oots

An exhortatory reading in which Moses presents to the Israelites the nature of their God.

A reading from the Book of Deuteronomy

Moses said to the **people**:
    "Now, **Israel**, hear the **statutes** and **decrees**
    which I am **teaching** you to **observe**,
    that you may **live**, and may enter **in** and take **possession**
        of the **land**
    which the LORD, the **God** of your **fathers**, is **giving** you.
In your **observance** of the **commandments** of the LORD,
        your **God**,
    which I enjoin **upon** you,
    you shall not **add** to what I **command** you nor **subtract** from it.
Observe them **carefully**,
    for **thus** will you give **evidence**
    of your **wisdom** and **intelligence** to the **nations**,
    who will **hear** of all these **statutes** and **say**,
    '**This great nation** is truly a **wise** and **intelligent** people.'
For what great nation **is** there
    that has **gods** so close to it as the LORD, our **God**, is to **us**
    whenever we call **upon** him?
Or what **great nation** has **statutes** and **decrees**
    that are as **just** as this whole **law**
    which I am **setting** before you **today**?"

Note the rhythm from "observance" to "commandments" to "Lord" to "God."

Again, note the rhythm from "wisdom" to "intelligence" to "nations."

Moses concludes by contrasting "gods" to "God," uplifting Israel in its worship of the one true God.

READING I | In the earthly realm, nations who have great military power, wealth, scientific and business acumen, and such attract worldwide attention and accolades. In contrast, it is the wisdom and understanding, or intelligence, of God's people that should draw the notice and admiration of other nations. What transforms Israel into a "great" nation is God's closeness to them and the divine gift of the Torah. As they put divine teachings into practice, they become more perfect images of God and reveal him to the world around them.

Wisdom (ḥokmah) begins with fear of or respect for the Lord and the conviction that he is always present and active in daily life. Consequently, ḥokmah results, not from appealing to metaphysical logic, but by engaging reality and pondering what God is doing within it. Wisdom is grounded in what is real and is often practical.

Understanding, or intelligence, in Hebrew binah, results from a serious process of discernment. This search for insight always begins with questioning appearances and challenging personal assumptions and opinions. Binah presumes that

one cannot immediately and completely grasp what God is doing in any situation—much less know how God is using circumstances to fulfill long-range divine plans. Intelligent people do not speak and act as if they were God.

READING II | James reminds his readers that all good or beneficial giving and every perfect gift (like wisdom in James 1:5) come from God. "The Father of lights" depicts God as the Creator of the heavenly bodies that make life possible. James seems to be contrasting their light,

For meditation and context:

RESPONSORIAL PSALM   Psalm 15:2–3, 3–4, 4–5 (1a)

R. The one who does justice will live in the presence of the Lord.

Whoever walks blamelessly and does justice;
   who thinks the truth in his heart
   and slanders not with his tongue.

Who harms not his fellow man,
   nor takes up a reproach against
     his neighbor;

by whom the reprobate is despised,
   while he honors those who fear the Lord.

Who lends not his money at usury
   and accepts no bribe against the
     innocent.
Whoever does these things
   shall never be disturbed.

An exhortatory reading in which James urges us in the ways of becoming good followers of God.
Parallel emphasis on "all good giving" and "every perfect gift."

READING II   James 1:17–18, 21b–22, 27

A reading from the Letter of Saint James

Dearest brothers and **sisters:**
All good giving and **every perfect gift** is from **above,**
   coming **down** from the **Father** of **lights,**
   with whom there is no **alteration** or **shadow** caused by **change.**
He **willed** to give us **birth** by the **word** of **truth**
   that we may be a **kind** of **firstfruits** of his **creatures.**

Humbly welcome the **word** that has been **planted** in you
   and is **able** to save your **souls.**

Contrast "doers" and "hearers." Delusion comes from only hearing and not doing.

Be **doers** of the word and not **hearers** only, **deluding** yourselves.

Religion that is **pure** and **undefiled** before **God** and the **Father**
   is this:
   to **care** for **orphans** and **widows** in their **affliction**
   and to keep **oneself unstained** by the **world.**

Emphasis on "stained" in "unstained."

A narrative reading in which Jesus uses a confrontation by the Pharisees to exhort his followers towards a more open, less rule-bound faith.

GOSPEL   Mark 7:1–8, 14–15, 21–23

A reading from the holy Gospel according to Mark

When the **Pharisees** with some **scribes** who had come
   from **Jerusalem**
   gathered around **Jesus,** »

---

which varies with the seasons, to the consistent and unwavering stream of divine gifts.

The Father's greatest and most perfect gift is the word of truth, the Gospel which is implanted in believers at Baptism for the salvation of their "souls"—the Greek *psyche* here denoting one's entire being. Christians are the first to experience this destiny that God intends for all, "a kind of firstfruits" of the crop to come.

James enjoins his readers to "humbly welcome" the word of truth. Merely acknowledging it betrays a lack of "under-standing." Those who comprehend must also "be doers of the word." The Greek translated as "be" carries here the sense of "become," intimating that the baptized are not as active as they could be. James warns them that if they are "hearers only"—if they continue to live with the same attitudes and follow the same routines after hearing the word as they did before—they delude themselves that they are being saved.

Pure religion obliges believers to care for widows and orphans and to shun the world's ways to follow the Lord's. James echoes the teaching of biblical prophets that, in God's view, two things are mutually exclusive—worship and social injustice. In the biblical world, widows and orphans were groups who had no one to advocate for their rights and care for their needs. They come to represent all those members of society who have fewer advantages and opportunities than others, and who consequently are easily ignored or exploited. "Pure and undefiled" religion requires churchgoers to "care for" these less fortunate people whose quality of life matters to God. The Greek for this caring, *episkeptomai*, involves personal contact and the intention

The reading opens with a description of Jewish purity rituals. These are important to note so that the point Jesus makes in his exhortation hits home.

they observed that some of his **disciples** ate their **meals**
with **unclean**, that is, **unwashed**, hands.
—For the **Pharisees** and, in fact, all **Jews**,
do not **eat** without carefully **washing** their hands,
keeping the **tradition** of the **elders**.
And on **coming** from the **marketplace**
they do not **eat** without **purifying** themselves.
And there are many other **things** that they have
    traditionally observed,
the purification of **cups** and **jugs** and **kettles** and **beds**.—

Slight pause between "scribes" and "questioned."

So the **Pharisees** and **scribes questioned** him,
"Why do your **disciples** not follow the **tradition** of the **elders**
but **instead** eat a **meal** with unclean **hands**?"
He responded,

Prophesy = PROPH-eh-sigh.

"Well did Isaiah **prophesy** about you **hypocrites**, as it
    is **written**:
This people honors me with their **lips**,
    but their **hearts** are **far** from me;
in **vain** do they **worship** me,
    teaching as **doctrines** human **precepts**.
You disregard God's **commandment** but cling to
    human **tradition**."

Jesus insists that for the Pharisees the rules are more important than the heart of God's commandments.
With "Hear me" begins Jesus' general exhortation to his followers. that a blessed, rule-bound rage for order can corrupt, even defile, a believer. This is a wild claim in the face of a faith for which the law of obedience to rules and tradition is paramount.
All the elements in this list are important.

He summoned the **crowd** again and **said** to them,
"**Hear** me, **all** of you, and **understand**.
Nothing that enters one from **outside** can **defile** that person;
    but the **things** that come out from **within** are what **defile**.

"From **within** people, from their **hearts**,
    come **evil thoughts**, **unchastity**, **theft**, **murder**,
    adultery, **greed**, **malice**, **deceit**,
    licentiousness, **envy**, **blasphemy**, **arrogance**, **folly**.
All these **evils** come from **within** and they **defile**."

Give "defile" added emphasis.

---

to improve the situation of those visited, that is, to bring them salvation.

GOSPEL The Law of Moses required only priests to perform ritual washings and only when they celebrated Temple liturgies. But, since all God's people are commanded to "be holy" (Leviticus 11:44–45; 19:2; 20:7; etc.), the requirement was extended to everyone. Over time, people forgot that the call to holiness entails difficult and continuous change. Religious leaders fell into the habit of operating as if their rules could replace

God's commandments. Jesus calls them hypocrites because they talk for God and about God, but they water down divine teachings and thus render their liturgical activities "useless."

Jesus tells the crowds that nothing from the world around them can make them unworthy of God's service. Only what comes from within them can do this (vv. 14–15). Later he gives his disciples a list of examples that elaborates his point (vv. 21–23).

Most of these sins translate easily into English, but the Greek for some of them carries other nuances. "Unchastity" can be

specified as fornication. "Greed" evokes thought about self-indulgent insatiability. Where there is "deceit or fraud" there are also cunning and treachery. "Envy," a translation of the idiom "the evil eye," can also convey stinginess. "Blasphemy" can be speech that injures another. "Folly" results from mental laziness, from not trying to understand divine teachings. All of these come, not from the outside world, but from one's own heart and mind. E. N.

TWENTY-THIRD SUNDAY IN ORDINARY TIME

LECTIONARY #128

READING I   Isaiah 35:4–7a

A reading from the Book of the Prophet Isaiah

Thus says the LORD:
　　Say to those whose **hearts** are **frightened**:
　　　　Be **strong**, fear **not**!
　　Here is your **God**,
　　　　he **comes** with **vindication**;
　　with divine **recompense**
　　　　he **comes** to **save** you.
　　Then will the **eyes** of the **blind** be **opened**,
　　　　the **ears** of the **deaf** be **cleared**;
　　then will the **lame leap** like a **stag**,
　　　　then the **tongue** of the **mute** will **sing**.
　　Streams will burst **forth** in the **desert**,
　　　　and **rivers** in the **steppe**.
　　The burning **sands** will become **pools**,
　　　　and the **thirsty ground**, **springs** of **water**.

Isaiah = ī-ZAY-uh
An exhortatory reading of nearly unbounded jubilance. This passage from Isaiah reads like a poem with deliberate rhythms and resonance, as well as a sense of gathering meaning. Read it slowly, surely, and at a volume slightly higher than normal.

vindication = vin-dih-KAY-shuhn = clearing from blame
recompense = REK-uhm-pens = compensation for wrongs suffered

Emphasize "opened" and "cleared." These words capture Isaiah's exhortation.
Slight pause between "lame" and "leap."

steppe = step = grassland

READING I　Isaiah preaches to people who live in a world of international upheaval. In the eighth century BC, the Assyrians conquer the Northern Kingdom of Israel, exile its inhabitants, and make the Southern Kingdom of Judah a vassal. By the end of the seventh century, the Babylonians crush the Assyrians and Judah. God's people worry not only about the uncertain future of their nation, they also suffer the disappointments and physical limitations that attend every human life. Their hearts, that is, their minds, imagine the worst. Isaiah tells them that, in the face

of conditions that naturally cow and paralyze the masses, they must be fearless and strong. Amid panic and chaos, they must demonstrate their belief that their God is on the way.

The prophet announces that God is coming "with vindication (*naqam*), with divine recompense." What God's coming will look like varies for the parties involved. Israel's enemies will experience it as divine vengeance for their treatment of God's people. In support of this understanding, the entire preceding chapter of Isaiah is an

oracle of judgment against Judah's longtime foes, the Edomites.

The effects of God's advent for Judah are deliverance from all kinds of oppression, here especially from physical limitations. The healing of the blind, the deaf, the lame, and the mute shows that the God who judges nations also cares about the quality of every person's life. When God comes, the land, whose fate the prophets tie to that of the people, also experiences new life as deserts and wilderness areas become pools and springs of water.

For meditation and context:

RESPONSORIAL PSALM   Psalm 146:6–7, 8–9, 9–10 (1b)

R. Praise the Lord, my soul! or R. Alleluia.

The God of Jacob keeps faith forever,
  secures justice for the oppressed,
  gives food to the hungry.
The LORD sets captives free.

The LORD gives sight to the blind;
  the LORD raises up those who were
  bowed down.

The LORD loves the just;
  the LORD protects strangers.

The fatherless and the widow the
  LORD sustains,
  but the way of the wicked he thwarts.
The LORD shall reign forever;
  your God, O Zion, through all
  generations. Alleluia.

READING II   James 2:1–5

A reading from the Letter of Saint James

My **brothers** and **sisters**, show no **partiality**
  as you **adhere** to the **faith** in our **glorious Lord** Jesus **Christ**.
For if a **man** with **gold rings** and **fine clothes**
  comes into your **assembly**,
  and a **poor person** in **shabby clothes also** comes **in**,
  and you pay **attention** to the one wearing the **fine clothes**
  and say, "**Sit here**, please,"
  while you say to the **poor one**, "Stand **there**,"
    or "Sit at my **feet**,"
  have you not made **distinctions** among **yourselves**
  and become **judges** with evil **designs**?

Listen, my beloved **brothers** and **sisters**.
Did not God choose **those** who are **poor** in the **world**
  to be **rich** in **faith** and **heirs** of the **kingdom**
  that he **promised** to those who **love** him?

A didactic reading, in which James insists all people are worthy of their faith, no matter how they look.
Even emphasis on "show no partiality."

Slight pause between "shabby clothes" and "also."

Even emphasis on "Did not God choose."

> **TO KEEP IN MIND**
> The words in bold are suggestions for ways to express the meaning of the reading. Consider using them as you practice the reading, then choose to stress them or to find your own way of proclaiming.

READING II   James writes to a Christian community that is still spiritually immature. The baptized continue to live too much by the world's standards instead of by the Lord's teaching and example. To open their eyes to this shortcoming, James sets before them two vignettes that describe the receptions of a rich and a poor man in the assembly. He puts words on the lips of community members to vivify each scenario. The respectful "Sit here, please," which greets the bejeweled person who sports fine clothes, ridicules believers who automatically fawn over the wealthy simply because they are wealthy. The "Stand there" and "Sit at my feet," meaning "there's no seat for you," conveys an ingrained snooty remoteness toward poorer people whose clothes are shabby or dirty.

James declares that persisting in judging others by appearances and treating some people as more important fosters the designs of evil within the community. He tells them that the riches that should elicit their respect are found in the poor who believe in and love God. They are the ones God chooses to be the heirs of his kingdom.

GOSPEL   Today, Jesus' healing fulfills one of Isaiah's signs of God's activity in the human realm. The man brought to him is deaf and speaking with difficulty. Jesus takes him away from the crowd to be alone with him, puts his finger into the man's ears, spits, touches the man's tongue with his saliva, looks heavenward, groans, and commands, "Be opened."

In the Greco-Roman and Jewish worlds, putting fingers in ears and using saliva, which was thought to have healing properties, were elements of medical treatment. The Greek for "Be opened," *dianoigō*, can

Tyre = tīr
Sidon = SĪ-duhn
Decapolis = dih-KAP-uh-lis

A narrative reading that explicitly depicts Jesus' healing powers, specifically, how he healed in terms of the gestures he makes and the words he says. Quite powerful.

Emphasis on "off" and "away," to indicate the separation of the deaf man from the crowd. The depiction of Jesus' healing powers. Emphasis on "finger," "ears," "spitting," and "tongue."

Ephphatha =
EPH-PHAH-THA (even emphasis).

This expresses the "Messianic secret" that runs through Mark's Gospel; Jesus, for some reason, doesn't want people to know what he's doing. But the people can't help themselves from telling everyone what they've seen.

Parallel emphasis on "deaf hear" and "mute speak."

GOSPEL   Mark 7:31–37

A reading from the holy Gospel according to Mark

Again **Jesus** left the district of **Tyre**
  and went by way of **Sidon** to the Sea of **Galilee**,
  into the **district** of the **Decapolis**.
And **people** brought to him a **deaf man** who had a
    speech impediment
  and begged him to **lay** his **hand** on him.
He took him **off** by himself **away** from the **crowd**.
He put his **finger** into the man's **ears**
  and, **spitting**, touched his **tongue**;
  then he **looked up** to **heaven** and **groaned**, and **said** to him,
  "***Ephphatha***!"—that is, "**Be opened!**"—
And **immediately** the man's **ears** were **opened**,
  his **speech** impediment was **removed**,
  and he spoke **plainly**.
He **ordered** them not to tell **anyone**.
But the **more** he ordered them **not** to,
  the more they **proclaimed** it.
They were **exceedingly** astonished and they **said**,
  "He has done **all things well**.
He makes the **deaf hear** and the **mute speak**."

also convey spiritual opening, as it does in Luke 24:32, when Jesus "opens" the Scriptures to the disciples on the road to Emmaus and they recognize him. In today's Gospel, the heavenward glance of Jesus signals that, in him, the spiritual and physical realms connect.

At his command, the deaf man's hearing is "opened," his speech impediment is removed, and he speaks clearly. The Greek for "clearly," *orthōs*, can also denote hearing "correctly or rightly" (as "*ortho + dox*" denotes a "straight or right opinion"). Here,

the use of *orthōs* reinforces the idea that the man's healing is spiritual as well as physical.

Jesus' order that those who witness this event not tell anyone about it is an example of the so-called messianic secret in Mark—a confidence referred to by some scholars as one of the worst-kept secrets of all time. They point out that in numerous passages of this Gospel, bystanders are astonished by what Jesus says and does. All kinds of people seek Jesus out because his fame has spread throughout Galilee, Jerusalem, and the bordering lands. Given

this disjunction, some scholars suggest that Jesus' command to silence shows that he is not one among other healers in the biblical world. The secret is that there is more to him than people see, more that can only be understood after he is raised from the dead. E. N.

TWENTY-FOURTH SUNDAY IN ORDINARY TIME

LECTIONARY #131

READING I   Isaiah 50:5–9a

Isaiah = ī-ZAY-uh

An exhortatory reading that presents Isaiah's faith in God's powers. It reads like a poem with great verbal and rhythmic energy.

A reading from the Book of the Prophet Isaiah

> The **Lord GOD** opens my **ear** that I may **hear**;
>   and I have **not** rebelled,
>   have **not** turned back.
> I gave my **back** to those who **beat** me,
>   my **cheeks** to those who **plucked** my **beard**;
> my **face** I did not **shield**
>   from **buffets** and **spitting**.

This second stanza parallels the first. Emphasize "God" and "help."

> The Lord **GOD** is my **help**,
>   **therefore** I am not **disgraced**;
> I have set my **face** like **flint**,
>   knowing that I shall **not** be put to **shame**.
> He is **near** who upholds my **right**;
>   if anyone wishes to **oppose** me,
>   let us **appear** together.
> **Who** disputes my **right**?
>   Let that man **confront** me.
> **See**, the Lord **GOD** is my **help**;
>   **who** will prove me **wrong**?

Repeated emphasis on "God" and "help."

TO KEEP IN MIND

Pay attention to the pace of your reading. Varying the pace gives listeners clues to the meaning of the text. The most common error for proclaimers new to the ministry is speaking too fast.

READING I   Most of the prophecies in the work known as Second Isaiah (Isaiah 40—55) are oracles of salvation or good news. But, interwoven through these are four poems that trace the life of the "Servant of the Lord," a man who suffered and died to fulfil his divine calling. Some of these poems identify him as Israel, but others as an enigmatic figure who is rejected, killed, and assigned a grave among the wicked (Isaiah 53:8–9). In today's reading, which is part of the third poem, the servant insists that his teachings come from the Lord; "the Lord opens [or awakens] my ear." Though his call places him in danger, he does not "rebel" and does not "turn away."

What gives the servant the courage to fulfill his mission no matter the personal cost, to "set [his] face like flint"? He is convinced that the Lord God is with him, "helping" (Hebrew `āzar) him. `Āzar almost always denotes divine assistance, help that no human could imagine, much less provide. For the Servant, his experience that God is helping him to persevere, moment by moment, is more desirable than the transient peace and security that would be his if he abandoned his call.

The Servant wants his persecutors and contemporaries to know that he does not see himself as disgraced and shamed. He is not a "help-less" victim. He "gives" his back to those who beat it, his cheeks to those who pluck his beard, his face to their punches and spit. The servant lays down his own life, blindly trusting that the Lord is using his suffering and death to accomplish a divine purpose. For this, he was born.

For meditation and context:

RESPONSORIAL PSALM Psalm 116:1–2, 3–4, 5–6, 8–9 (9)

R. I will walk before the Lord, in the land of the living.
or
R. Alleluia.

I love the Lord because he has heard
   my voice in supplication,
because he has inclined his ear to me
   the day I called.

The cords of death encompassed me;
   the snares of the netherworld seized
      upon me;
   I fell into distress and sorrow,
and I called upon the name of the Lord,
   "O Lord, save my life!"

Gracious is the Lord and just;
   yes, our God is merciful.
The Lord keeps the little ones;
   I was brought low, and he saved me.

For he has freed my soul from death,
   my eyes from tears, my feet
      from stumbling.
I shall walk before the Lord
   in the land of the living.

READING II   James 2:14–18

A didactic reading whose theology is at the core of our faith: You cannot have faith without comparable works. James specifically aligns this teaching with the treatment of the poor.

With "If . . ." begins the example on which this reading hinges.

With "So also . . . ," James seeks to embolden faith with deeds.

Emphasis on "from" and "works."

A reading from the Letter of Saint James

What **good** is it, my **brothers** and **sisters**,
   if **someone** says he has **faith** but does not have **works**?
Can that faith **save** him?
If a **brother** or **sister** has **nothing** to **wear**
   and has no **food** for the **day**,
   and one of you **says** to them,
   "Go in **peace**, keep **warm**, and eat **well**,"
   but you do not **give them** the **necessities** of the **body**,
   what **good** is it?
So also **faith** of **itself**,
   if it **does** not have **works**, is **dead**.

Indeed someone might **say**,
   "You have **faith** and I have **works**."
Demonstrate your **faith** to me **without works**,
   and I will **demonstrate** my faith to you **from** my **works**.

READING II Today James warns Christians that profession of faith alone is not "saving" (Greek *sōzō*) them. Words are cheap. In contrast, a living faith entails at least inconvenience and usually great effort.

To impress this reality on his readers, James asks them to imagine a scenario. In it, they notice or hear about someone who is poorly clothed and ill fed, someone whose biblical "peace" or "well-being" requires their immediate action. Instead of providing food or clothes for the destitute person, they say heartily, "Go in peace. Keep warm.

Eat well." James insists that such expressions of faith devoid of action will not save believers.

GOSPEL In Mark's Gospel, after Peter acknowledges that Jesus is God's Messiah, or Christ, Jesus begins to talk about the path his life must take. He will suffer greatly, be rejected by the religious leaders, be put to death, and rise in three days. Mark notes that Jesus is now speaking "openly" or "plainly," not metaphorically as in his earlier parables.

The divine plan for Jesus greatly disturbs Peter. It conflicts with his presumptions about God and divine ways. Shouldn't God reward those who carry out his will with a peaceful pleasant life? Shouldn't God save those who love him from suffering? Jesus rebukes Peter because he is not thinking like a disciple but like the crowds. Further, Jesus reveals that Satan is using Peter's well-intentioned concern for him to try to sway him to reject God's will.

Jesus' final saying clarifies the core and the cost of discipleship. Whoever wishes to follow him must "deny," "disown," or

Caesarea Philippi = sez-uh-REE-uh fih-LIP-ī

A narrative reading that begins with Jesus asking his disciples to describe him or to say what other people are saying about him. The answers establish a prophetic connection between Jesus and those who came before him but also insist upon his unique qualities.

Slight pause between "anyone" and "about." This sentence once again expresses the "Messianic secret."

Jesus prophesies his own death; this news shocks his disciples. Emphasis on "openly."

Jesus' response is hard. "Get behind me, Satan" is a challenging thing for Peter to hear. Emphasis on "not."

Pay attention to the parallels: save/lose, loses/sake, gospel/save.

GOSPEL   Mark 8:27–35

A reading from the holy Gospel according to Mark

Jesus and his disciples set **out**
     for the **villages** of Caesarea **Philippi**.
Along the **way** he asked his **disciples**,
     "**Who** do people **say** that I **am**?"
They said in reply,
     "John the **Baptist**, others **Elijah**,
     still **others** one of the **prophets**."
And he **asked** them,
     "But who do **you** say that I am?"
Peter said to him in **reply**,
     "You are the **Christ**."
Then he **warned** them not to tell **anyone about** him.

He began to **teach** them
     that the **Son** of **Man** must suffer **greatly**
     and be **rejected** by the **elders**, the **chief priests**, and the **scribes**,
     and be **killed**, and **rise** after **three days**.
He spoke this **openly**.
Then **Peter** took him **aside** and began to **rebuke** him.
At **this** he turned around and, **looking** at his **disciples**,
     rebuked **Peter** and said, "Get **behind** me, Satan.
You are thinking **not** as God does, but as human **beings** do."

He **summoned** the **crowd** with his **disciples** and **said** to them,
     "Whoever wishes to come **after** me must **deny** himself,
     take up his **cross**, and **follow** me.
For whoever wishes to **save** his life will **lose** it,
     but whoever **loses** his life for **my** sake
     and that of the **gospel** will **save** it."

"renounce" him- or herself for Jesus' sake. Disciples must accept that their life will somehow unfold like his did. They too must be prepared to suffer greatly, be rejected, and even be put to death —all the while proclaiming their hope that they will be raised up and live on with the Lord for all eternity.

Jesus' next saying elaborates what "saving" and "losing" one's life means for a disciple. The multiple meanings of the Greek words for "save" and "lose" suggest how these concepts can play out in human experience. For example, those wishing to

"save" (Greek *sōzō*) their life could be wanting to be healed from a physical or mental condition, or to be delivered from tiresome or painful situations. They could be making every effort to save or preserve a pleasant lifestyle or routine. While these are perfectly normal desires and good things to pray for, Jesus' point is that the unique and integral mission that every disciple is given for Jesus' sake and the sake of the Gospel supersedes them.

Jesus' disciples must aim to lose their life in his risen life, so that he can continue

his mission on earth through them. The Greek for "lose," *apollumi*, can also convey that disciples permit their life to "disappear," "perish," or "be ruined." Few can suddenly do this. Heroic suffering takes practice. For example, one can bear the weaknesses of others or their ill-timed or otherwise inconvenient needs, or a common cold, or chronic illness. Like Isaiah's servant, disciples "give" their bodies over to all that is "ruining" it so that the risen Lord can work through them. E. N.

TWENTY-FIFTH SUNDAY IN ORDINARY TIME

LECTIONARY #134

READING I   Wisdom 2:12, 17–20

A reading from the Book of Wisdom

The **wicked** say:
Let us **beset** the **just** one, because he is **obnoxious** to us;
    he **sets himself against** our **doings**,
reproaches us for **transgressions** of the **law**
    and **charges** us with **violations** of our **training**.
Let us **see** whether his **words** be **true**;
    let us find **out** what will **happen** to him.
For if the **just one** be the **son** of **God**, **God** will **defend** him
    and **deliver** him from the **hand** of his **foes**.
With **revilement** and **torture** let us put the **just one** to the **test**
    that we may have **proof** of his **gentleness**
    and **try** his **patience**.
Let us **condemn** him to a **shameful death**;
    for **according** to his own **words**, **God** will take **care** of him.

An exhortatory reading spoken in the voice of the wicked. Avoid the temptation to dramatize the reading by spicing up these claims of the wicked. Give the words their emphasis. This line is in an iambic meter: he SETS himSELF aGAINST our DOings.

"Let us" orients the reading: You will speak this phrase three times. This is the second.

"Let us" once again for the third time.

For meditation and context:

RESPONSORIAL PSALM   Psalm 54:3–4, 5, 6–8 (6b)

R. The Lord upholds my life.

O God, by your name save me,
    and by your might defend my cause.
O God, hear my prayer;
    hearken to the words of my mouth.

For the haughty have risen up against me,
    the ruthless seek my life;
    they set not God before their eyes.

Behold, God is my helper;
    the Lord sustains my life.
Freely will I offer you sacrifice;
    I will praise your name, O LORD,
      for its goodness.

TO KEEP IN MIND
Be careful not to swallow your words. Articulate carefully, especially at the end of lines.

READING I   The book of Wisdom presents stereotypical portraits of the just and the wicked. Today's entire reading, placed on the lips of the wicked, displays their innate hostility and disdain for the just who try to do what is right in every situation. The wicked mock the just one who calls himself a "child of the Lord," boasts that "God is his Father" (omitted vv. 13, 16), and trusts that God will defend him. To the wicked, God's faithful are "obnoxious" and their Torah lifestyle is an indictment of evil, narcissistic routines.

Especially grating on the wicked are the persistently patient and gentle ways of the just—ways that highlight the strident methods of slanderers and blunt the effectiveness of their arrogant pronouncements. The wicked simply cannot leave the just alone. They must test them. They try to break the gentle spirit of the just with evil's default weapons—violence, cruelty, insults. When these don't work, they condemn the just to a shameful death which, in their eyes, will prove that God does not defend them.

READING II   James' view of wickedness within the Christian community is more nuanced than that depicted in Wisdom. For him, no one always acts justly, nor is anyone irredeemably evil. Everyone must work on rooting out personal wicked habits. Here, James targets envy and selfish ambition or rivalry as the sources of "every foul practice" . He writes that those who seek recognition or insist on getting their own way are not yet living by wisdom "from above." They still follow human inclinations and ape the behaviors

A didactic reading that consists mostly of a condemnation. The traits that James condemns in this letter are as relevant today as they were when he first wrote them. Jealousy and ambition are the sources of disorder and foul practices.

"Passions" connects to "jealousy" and "ambition" at the beginning of the reading.

Here, James begins to condemn: You covet, you kill and envy, you fight, you wage. Strong words.

READING II   James 3:16—4:3

A reading from the Letter of Saint James

Beloved:
Where **jealousy** and selfish **ambition** exist,
    there is **disorder** and **every foul practice**.
But the **wisdom** from **above** is **first** of all **pure**,
    then **peaceable**, **gentle**, **compliant**,
    full of **mercy** and good **fruits**,
    without **inconstancy** or **insincerity**.
And the **fruit** of **righteousness** is **sown** in **peace**
    for **those** who cultivate **peace**.

Where do the **wars**
    and **where** do the **conflicts** among you **come** from?
Is it not from your **passions**
    that make **war** within your **members**?
You **covet** but do not **possess**.
You **kill** and **envy** but you cannot **obtain**;
    you **fight** and wage **war**.
You do not **possess** because you do not **ask**.
You **ask** but do not **receive**,
    because you ask **wrongly**, to **spend** it on your **passions**.

of those whose worldly position or influence they desire for themselves.

Divine wisdom is first of all pure—holy or different from the wisdom of the crowd. It is innocent or untainted. Those who live by divine wisdom do not enshrine personal opinions and foist them off on the community. Rather, they prize the peace and well-being of all. With deliberate gentleness or courtesy, they work to resolve disagreements. They give in to others and show mercy. They are impartial and consistent in their treatment of everyone. They do not, for example, welcome those who agree

with them but ignore those who do not. All that they say or do is sincere or genuine.

Instead of being at "war" (Greek *polemos*, English "polemics") "with each other," James wants the baptized to make war on their inner cravings and passions, which are tearing the community apart. To vanquish these, they need the divine guidance for which they no longer pray and so do not receive. They pray, but for the wrong things. They ask God to do their will, to champion their cause. Therefore, their prayers go unanswered.

GOSPEL   As the disciples travel around Galilee with Jesus, basking in the light of his growing reputation, they conclude that following him will ensure a similarly successful and mostly pleasant life. In this Gospel, Jesus is trying to deepen their understanding of what discipleship entails. He tells them again that the Son of Man will be betrayed to men who will kill him, but after three days he will be raised from the dead. Though his disciples do not understand this saying, they are afraid to ask Jesus for clarification. It seems that they cannot even entertain

GOSPEL Mark 9:30–37

A reading from the holy Gospel according to Mark

Jesus and his **disciples** left from **there** and began a **journey**
    through **Galilee**,
  but he did not wish **anyone** to **know** about it.
He was **teaching** his disciples and **telling** them,
    "The **Son** of **Man** is to be handed **over** to **men**
    and they will **kill** him,
    and **three days** after his **death** the **Son** of **Man** will **rise**."
But they **did not** understand the **saying**,
    and they were **afraid** to **question** him.

They **came** to **Capernaum** and, **once** inside the **house**,
    he began to **ask** them,
    "**What** were you **arguing** about on the **way?**"
But they remained **silent**.
They had been **discussing** among themselves on the way
    who was the **greatest**.
Then he sat **down**, called the **Twelve**, and **said** to them,
    "If **anyone** wishes to be **first**,
    he shall be the **last** of **all** and the **servant** of **all**."
Taking a child, he **placed** it in their **midst**,
    and putting his **arms** around it, he **said** to them,
    "Whoever receives **one child** such as **this** in my **name**,
        receives **me**;
    and whoever receives **me**,
    receives not **me** but the **One** who **sent** me."

A narrative reading that hits several different tones: confidence, assurance, anxiety, fear, arrogance, foolishness, and chastisement among them. It opens with yet another expression of the "Messianic secret."

After Jesus once again foretells his death, the disciples find themselves knotted with fear. This perhaps explains what they will argue about.

Capernaum = kuh-PER-nee-*m

Their argument seems foolish: Why, after hearing Jesus tell them that he will die, do they argue about who among them is greatest? Perhaps they cannot accept the reality of what Jesus has told them.

Jesus chastises the disciples with the example of the child in their midst. He is trying to make them see who he is. The implication is they cannot yet see him.

the idea that he must suffer and die, much less that if they follow him, they must expect the same fate.

The twelve turn their thoughts to a more engaging topic: Who among them is the greatest? Who is the most important? After they settle in that evening, Jesus exploits their discussion about worldly eminence to deepen their understanding of gospel greatness. He tells them that if any of them want to be first, they shall be the last of all and the servant of all. No exceptions—in every situation, anyone who wants to be noticed makes himself the slave of everyone else. He never welcomes being treated as a lord.

To illustrate his point, Jesus places a child in the midst of his disciples and embraces it. His actions must have surprised them, for in the biblical world children were seldom noticed, much less served by men. His words must have astounded them even more: "Whoever receives one child such as this in my name, receives me; and whoever receives me, receives not me but the one who sent me." The fourfold repetition of "receive" reminds Jesus' disciples—and all who desire to be his disciples in every age—that their relationship with him grows through encounters with others. His disciples will be especially surprised to discover him and the one who sent him in those whom they tend routinely to ignore or slight because they deem them unimportant. E. N.

TWENTY-SIXTH SUNDAY IN ORDINARY TIME

LECTIONARY #137

READING I Numbers 11:25–29

A reading from the Book of Numbers

The LORD came **down** in the **cloud** and spoke to **Moses**.
Taking **some** of the **spirit** that was on **Moses**,
   the LORD bestowed it on the **seventy** elders;
   and as the **spirit** came to **rest** on them, they **prophesied**.

Now **two men**, one named **Eldad** and the other **Medad**,
   were **not** in the **gathering** but had been **left** in the **camp**.
They **too** had been on the **list**, but had not gone **out** to the **tent**;
   yet the **spirit** came to **rest** on them **also**,
   and they **prophesied** in the **camp**.
So, when a **young man** quickly told **Moses**,
   "**Eldad** and **Medad** are **prophesying** in the **camp**,"
   Joshua, son of **Nun**, who from his **youth** had been
     Moses' **aide**, said,
   "**Moses**, my **lord**, **stop** them."
But Moses **answered** him,
   "Are you **jealous** for my **sake**?
Would that **all** the people of the LORD were **prophets**!
Would that the LORD might bestow his **spirit** on them **all**!"

A narrative reading that presents some of the operation of God's prophetic power, as well as a correction on Moses' part when that power is misunderstood as a result of jealousy.
Prophesied = PROPH-eh-side.

Eldad = EL-dad; Medad = MEE-dad

Emphasis on the words "left" and "out."

Emphasis on "stop." This word expresses the jealousy at the heart of the reading.

Moses' answer is a correction.

READING I When Moses complains that leading the Israelites is too much of a burden for him alone to bear (Numbers 11:14–17), the Lord takes some of the Spirit that is on him and bestows it on elders who then assist him by prophesying. Like all biblical prophets, their main task is to persuade the people to follow the Lord and divine teachings with more integrity.

Two Israelites, Eldad and Medad, apparently were on the list but do not attend the ceremony at the Tent of Meeting, the portable sanctuary that symbolizes God's presence with the people in the wilderness. The elders who do show up for the rite prophesy briefly and only by the Tent. Eldad and Medad, however, keep on prophesying "in the camp," out among the people. This anecdote (last edited c. 400 BC) seems to reflect the tensions that existed during the monarchy between court prophets, who were appointed by the king, and "lay" prophets whom the Lord called but who held no official position.

Joshua's concern is the unofficial status of Eldad and Medad, who were not liturgically "installed." When he hears of their prophesying, he urges Moses to stop them. But Moses, who has learned that the Lord traditionally acts in untraditional ways, expresses his deep desire that all the Lord's people live as spirit-filled prophets. His wish eventually comes to fruition in Christian Baptism where believers receive the Spirit and are anointed "prophets," not for a temporary mission, but for life. Not only around the "Tent," but out "in the camp."

READING II Though James seems to single out business people as an example of disciples who stray from the Lord's ways and walk their own path,

For meditation and context:

RESPONSORIAL PSALM Psalm 19:8, 10, 12–13, 14 (9a)

R. The precepts of the Lord give joy to the heart.

The law of the LORD is perfect,
  refreshing the soul;
the decree of the LORD is trustworthy,
  giving wisdom to the simple.

The fear of the LORD is pure,
  enduring forever;
the ordinances of the LORD are true,
  all of them just.

Though your servant is careful of them,
  very diligent in keeping them,
yet who can detect failings?
  Cleanse me from my unknown faults!

From wanton sin especially, restrain
  your servant;
  let it not rule over me.
Then shall I be blameless and innocent
  of serious sin.

A didactic reading full of condemnation, agitation, and judgment. Its lesson is as relevant today as it was in the first century.

Emphasis on the word "corrosion," which captures the greed and venality James is railing against.
Emphasis on the word "devour."

TO KEEP IN MIND
Pause to break up separate thoughts, set apart significant statements, or indicate major shifts. Never pause in the middle of a thought. Your primary guide for pauses is punctuation.

This conclusion is especially striking. Who is the murdered righteous one? Let this claim resonate.

READING II James 5:1–6

A reading from the Letter of Saint James

Come now, you **rich**, **weep** and **wail** over your
    impending miseries.
Your **wealth** has rotted **away**, your **clothes** have become
    moth-eaten,
  your **gold** and **silver** have **corroded**,
  and that **corrosion** will be a **testimony against** you;
  it will **devour** your **flesh** like a **fire**.
You have **stored up treasure** for the last **days**.
Behold, the **wages** you **withheld** from the **workers**
  who **harvested** your **fields** are **crying** aloud;
  and the **cries** of the **harvesters**
  have reached the **ears** of the **Lord** of **hosts**.
You have **lived** on earth in **luxury** and **pleasure**;
  you have **fattened** your **hearts** for the **day** of **slaughter**.
You have **condemned**;
  you have **murdered** the **righteous** one;
  he **offers** you no **resistance**.

---

his target audience is all Christians whom he would persuade to examine the integrity of their witness to Christ. It is important to realize that James is not condemning business per se or all enterprising people. He specifies those entrepreneurs who work mainly to accumulate wealth and material possessions and who, in the process, abuse those who work for them. Even as these unjust rich enjoy their excesses, the Lord hears the cries of their workers who lack the necessities of life, and plans justice for them.

James assembles a collage of images that he hopes will haunt his readers to change. He draws on the familiar experiences of clothes fading and wearing out, and prized possessions breaking down or rotting away. He declares that such paltry residues of wealth will bear witness against those who live for them and will, in the end, devour their flesh like fire. This last image evokes a smoldering corpse whose emergent bones are covered with moldy rags and dusted by the rust of trifles and trinkets.

James also envisions the practice of extravagant living as the "fattening" of the

self-indulgent (like an animal for sacrifice) for "the day of slaughter," in other words, the final judgment. In the Lord's view, when the prosperous "murdered" their righteous workers and "condemned" them to a miserable existence, they also condemned themselves to eternal destruction.

GOSPEL This Gospel reminds us that the Kingdom of God is catholic, or all-embracing, and larger than the Church. In God's kingdom, the Spirit works uniquely, as it wills, and in an infinite variety of people. Already during Mark's

GOSPEL   Mark 9:38–43, 45, 47–48

A reading from the holy Gospel according to Mark

At that time, **John** said to **Jesus**,
   "**Teacher**, we saw **someone** driving out **demons** in your **name**,
   and we **tried** to **prevent** him because he does not **follow** us."
Jesus replied, "**Do not prevent** him.
There is **no one** who **performs** a mighty **deed** in my **name**
   who can at the **same time** speak **ill** of me.
For **whoever** is not **against** us is **for** us.
Anyone who gives you a **cup** of **water** to **drink**
   because you **belong** to **Christ**,
   amen, I say to you, will **surely** not **lose** his **reward**.

"**Whoever causes** one of these **little ones** who **believe** in me
      to **sin**,
   it would be **better** for him if a great **millstone**
   were **put** around his **neck**
   and he were **thrown** into the **sea**.
If your **hand** causes you to **sin**, cut it **off**.
It is **better** for you to **enter** into life **maimed**
   than with two **hands** to go into **Gehenna**,
   into the **unquenchable** fire.
And if your **foot** causes you to sin, cut it **off**.
It is **better** for you to **enter** into life **crippled**
   than with **two feet** to be **thrown** into **Gehenna**.
And if your **eye** causes you to sin, pluck it **out**.
Better for you to **enter** into the **kingdom** of God with **one eye**
   than with **two eyes** to be **thrown** into **Gehenna**,
   where 'their **worm** does not **die**, and the **fire** is not **quenched**.'"

An exhortatory reading with two components: First, a statement of inclusiveness when it comes to people doing things in Jesus' name; and, second, a statement about the abusive nature of sin. In this second part, Jesus pulls no punches.

Emphasis on "against" and "for."

Here, Jesus shifts his attention to sin by way of a series of examples. Each example includes an "If" clause followed by an "it is better" clause, as well as a mention of Gehenna, a Hebrew place-name that became associated with eternal damnation.

Gehenna = geh-HEN-nah

Emphasis on "worm" and "die," "fire" and "quenched."

---

time, there was a tendency among some of Jesus' followers to make God's kingdom an exclusive club, limited to like-minded people. Like the disciples in this Gospel, they think they can control how and where the Spirit acts—an arrogant presumption which Jesus rejects. In his view, "whoever is not against us is for us."

Jesus' subsequent teachings are linked by the fourfold repetition of *skandalizō*—a Greek verb which denotes "to cause or lead to sin, to cause to fall away," or "to put a stumbling block before another." The first two sayings concern how people treat Jesus' followers, the "little ones." Those who provide for their simplest need receive divine, not merely human, rewards. Those who weaken a disciple's commitment are better off thrown into the sea with a huge stone hung around their neck.

The rest of Jesus' sayings urge disciples to root out whatever causes them to sin and remind them that Jesus offers a life beyond human imagining, a life that begins on earth and continues beyond the grave. His mention of the legal penalties of limb amputation for stealing and eye-removal for adultery emphasize both the immense appeal of the life he offers and the drastic measures that disciples should be willing to take to avoid losing it. The threefold mention of Gehenna, Jerusalem's perpetually smoky and smelly garbage dump, metaphorically evokes the alternative destiny of those who fail to take action. E. N.

TWENTY-SEVENTH SUNDAY IN ORDINARY TIME

LECTIONARY #140

READING I Genesis 2:18–24

A reading from the Book of Genesis

The LORD God said: "It is not good for the **man** to be **alone**.
I will **make** a suitable **partner** for him."
So the LORD God **formed** out of the **ground**
    various **wild animals** and various **birds** of the **air**,
    and he **brought** them to the **man** to see what he would
        call them;
    whatever the **man** called **each** of them would be its **name**.
The **man** gave **names** to all the **cattle**,
    all the **birds** of the **air**, and **all wild animals**;
    but **none** proved to be the suitable **partner** for the **man**.

So the LORD **God** cast a **deep sleep** on the **man**,
    and while he was **asleep**,
    he took **out** one of his **ribs** and closed up its **place** with **flesh**.
The LORD God then built **up** into a **woman** the **rib**
    that he had **taken** from the **man**.
When he **brought** her to the **man**, the man said:
    "**This** one, at **last**, is **bone** of my **bones**
        and **flesh** of my **flesh**;
    this one shall be called '**woman**,'
        for out of '**her man**' this **one** has been **taken**."
That is why a man **leaves** his **father** and **mother**
    and **clings** to his **wife**,
    and the **two** of them become **one** flesh.

Genesis = JEN-uh-sihs
A narrative reading, deeply familiar, and filled with expressions that are part of our collective consciousness. No need to overdo it. Read slowly, with care, sounding out the names of things as they come, and let them resound for your assembly.

Almost even stress on the opening phrase, "The Lord God said: 'It is not good . . .'"

A little slower through all these details.

Equal emphasis on "deep" and "sleep."

TO KEEP IN MIND
Make eye contact with the assembly. This helps keep the assembly engaged with the reading.

Proclaim the conclusion of this passage clearly; you are setting up the Gospel reading.

READING I This simple narrative presents a sophisticated theological view of why there are men and women and why they marry. God originally makes a single entity, "the human being" (Hebrew *ha* "the" + *adam*, which here is not a proper name but the general term "human being"). Seeing that it is "not good" for *ha adam* to be alone, God resolves to find an *ezer kenegdō* (Genesis 2:18, 20) for this being. In the Hebrew Scriptures, *ezer* denotes "a helper" and almost always refers to God or to the help that only God can give. The phrase *kenegdō* qualifies this helper as one who "corresponds to" or is the "counterpart" of the human being.

Like a potter, God goes to work forming animals, birds, and sea creatures "out of the ground" (*adamah*), just as in Genesis 2:7 the potter "formed" *ha adam* out of dust from the earth (*adamah*) and made it a "living being." None of the new creatures, who are also called "living beings," are the *ezer kenegdō* that God seeks for the human, the loftiest creation.

The detail that God casts *ha adam* into a deep sleep veils the creation of the woman with divine mystery. The human being is unaware that God takes a rib, literally, "something from his side," and "builds" it into the woman. With this scene, the narrator reveals that though a man and a woman are sexually different, they are made by God of the very same stuff. Neither men nor women are "more" than the other—not more noble, superior, significant, reasonable, or anything. This divine view challenges especially the patriarchal views of men and women that were held by the contemporaries of this inspired biblical author.

The human's reaction to the woman reinforces the sameness of their make-up.

For meditation and context:

RESPONSORIAL PSALM   Psalm 128:1–2, 3, 4–5, 6 (5)

R. May the Lord bless us all the days of our lives.

Blessed are you who fear the LORD,
  who walk in his ways!
For you shall eat the fruit of your handiwork;
  blessed shall you be, and favored.

Your wife shall be like a fruitful vine
  in the recesses of your home;
your children like olive plants
  around your table.

Behold, thus is the man blessed
  who fears the LORD.
The LORD bless you from Zion:
  may you see the prosperity of Jerusalem
  all the days of your life.

May you see your children's children.
  Peace be upon Israel!

READING II   Hebrews 2:9–11

A reading from the Letter to the Hebrews

A didactic reading whose core teaching expresses Christ's humanity, insisting that he was one of us.

Emphasis on "taste death" and "everyone."

Brothers and **sisters**:
He "for a little while" was made "**lower** than the **angels**,"
  that by the **grace** of God he might **taste death** for **everyone**.

For it was **fitting** that he,
  for whom and **through whom** all things **exist**,
  in **bringing** many **children** to **glory**,
  should make the **leader** to their **salvation perfect**
    through **suffering**.
He who **consecrates** and those who are being **consecrated**
  all have one **origin**.
Therefore, he is not **ashamed** to call them "**brothers**."

Slight pause between "salvation" and "perfect."

Emphasize "consecrates" and "consecrated."

GOSPEL   Mark 10:2–16

A reading from the holy Gospel according to Mark

A narrative reading with teachings about divorce and the nature of the kingdom of God. While the second topic is not controversial, the first topic is more challenging. Ordinarily, Jesus overturns religious law; here, he affirms it.

[The **Pharisees** approached **Jesus** and **asked**,
  "Is it **lawful** for a **husband** to **divorce** his **wife**?"
They were **testing** him.

"Bone of my bone and flesh of my flesh" is an expression which conveys kinship and mutual loyalty in biblical contexts of commitment or covenant (see Genesis 29:14; Judges 9:2; 2 Samuel 5:1; 1 Chronicles 1:11; 2 Samuel 19:13). Sameness is also conveyed by the masculine and feminine forms of the Hebrew words for "man" and "woman": "This one shall be called 'woman' (*ishshah*) for out of man (*ish*) this one has been taken." The two human beings are reunited in marriage. Becoming "one flesh" refers to more than sexual union; it also conveys the new existence that a couple share and the life they create together.

READING II | The quotation of Psalm 8 ("for a little while" "lower than the angels"), here applied to Jesus, originally expressed a poet's wonder at the high position that fragile human beings hold amid the grandeur of the cosmos. The psalmist marvels that God notices and cares for people and even crowns them with the divine attributes of "glory" and "honor."

The author of Hebrews applies the psalm to the Incarnation of the Son of God in the fragile human being Jesus. His suffering and death make it possible for the entire race to finally and fully reflect the "glory" and "honor" that God bestows on them at birth. Because Jesus and those whom he consecrates have a common origin, Jesus gladly acknowledges that every man and woman is his brother or sister.

GOSPEL | The Pharisees approach Jesus and try to trip him up with a question about divorce: "Is it lawful for a husband to divorce his wife?" The Torah allowed a man to write out a "bill of

He said to them in **reply**, "What did **Moses** command you?"
They replied,
> "**Moses** permitted a **husband** to write a **bill** of **divorce**
> and **dismiss** her."

But **Jesus** told them,
> "Because of the **hardness** of your **hearts**
> he **wrote** you this **commandment**.

But from the **beginning** of **creation**, *God made them **male***
> *and **female**.*
*For this **reason** a man shall **leave** his **father** and **mother***
> *and be **joined** to his **wife**,*
> *and the **two** shall become **one flesh**.*

So they are no longer **two** but one **flesh**.
Therefore what **God** has joined **together**,
> no human **being** must **separate**."

In the **house** the disciples again questioned **Jesus** about this.
He **said** to them,
> "Whoever **divorces** his wife and **marries another**
> commits **adultery against** her;
> and if she **divorces** her **husband** and **marries another**,
> **she** commits **adultery**."]

And **people** were bringing **children** to him that he might
> **touch** them,
> but the **disciples rebuked** them.

When Jesus **saw** this he became **indignant** and **said** to them,
> Let the **children come** to me;
> do not **prevent** them, for the **kingdom** of **God** belongs to such
> as **these**.

Amen, I **say** to you,
> whoever does **not** accept the **kingdom** of **God** like a **child**
> **will not enter** it."

Then he **embraced** them and **blessed** them,
> placing his **hands** on them.

[Shorter: Mark 10:2–12 (see brackets)]

Margin notes:

This quotation from Genesis repeats the conclusion of the first reading.

Slight pause between "adultery" and "against."

Here the topic shifts to children and the kingdom of God.

Slight pause between "disciples" and "rebuked."

Slight pause between "children" and "come."

---

divorce," thus freeing his wife to leave and remarry (Deuteronomy 24:1–4), and in Jesus' day Judaism permitted divorce. The rabbis, however, disagreed on the grounds for it.

While the evangelist Matthew and the apostle Paul make exceptions for divorce, Mark presents Jesus' most radical teaching on it. In Jesus' view, the instruction in Deuteronomy is a concession that Moses makes because of the "hardness of people's hearts": because they refuse to "change their thinking." They refuse, even, to inform themselves about God's view of marriage and persist in following their own opinion and will.

Refusing to argue about legal loopholes, Jesus reminds his listeners of God's original plan for "the human being." They are the only creatures that God makes, both male and female, in the divine image and likeness. Neither human being is more God-like than the other (Genesis 1:26–27). Whereas Genesis 2 insists that men and women are made of the same stuff, Genesis 1 emphasizes that together they reflect a unique image of God. Their mutual commitment in marriage also has the potential to reveal God's patient longing and determination to live in union with—to make a life together with—humankind.

In the second section of today's Gospel, Jesus is indignant or angry that his followers keep the children from him, that they decide whom he should welcome. Jesus declares that children, who depend on others for life's necessities and simply accept what is given to them, are models for how to receive and experience life in God's kingdom. E. N.

TWENTY-EIGHTH SUNDAY IN ORDINARY TIME

LECTIONARY #143

READING I   Wisdom 7:7–11

A short but powerful exhortatory reading, with the intensity of a poem, full of praise and discernment. As you proclaim, attend to its rhythms, allowing the passage to resonate with your assembly.

Note the details here and those to follow: "scepter," "throne," "a priceless gem," "silver." The details give the reading its texture.

mire = muck

Emphasis on "her." This is wisdom, embodied.

A reading from the Book of Wisdom

I **prayed**, and **prudence** was **given** me;
  I **pleaded**, and the spirit of **wisdom came** to me.
I **preferred** her to **scepter** and **throne**,
and deemed **riches nothing** in **comparison** with her,
  nor did I liken **any priceless gem** to her;
because **all gold**, in **view** of her, is a little **sand**,
  and **before** her, **silver** is to be accounted **mire**.
Beyond **health** and **comeliness** I **loved** her,
and I chose to have **her** rather than the **light**,
  because the **splendor** of her never **yields** to **sleep**.
Yet all **good things** together **came** to me in her **company**,
  and **countless riches** at her **hands**.

For meditation and context:

RESPONSORIAL PSALM   Psalm 90:12–13, 14–15, 16–17 (14)

R. Fill us with your love, O Lord, and we will sing for joy!

Teach us to number our days aright,
  that we may gain wisdom of heart.
Return, O Lᴏʀᴅ! How long?
  Have pity on your servants!

Fill us at daybreak with your kindness,
  that we may shout for joy and gladness all
  our days.
Make us glad, for the days when you
  afflicted us,
  for the years when we saw evil.

Let your work be seen by your servants
  and your glory by their children;
and may the gracious care of the Lord our
  God be ours;
  prosper the work of our hands for us!
Prosper the work of our hands!

TO KEEP IN MIND
The attention you bring to your proclaiming enables you to pray the Word of God with the assembly.

READING I The author of Wisdom presents his work as the legacy of King Solomon, who in several biblical passages is renowned for his wisdom. In this reading, the king prays for "prudence" (Greek *phronaesis*). The Greek denotes both an uncommon way of thinking or of framing life experiences, and the understanding and insight that flow from these practices. God hears the king's plea and bestows on him prudence and the "spirit of wisdom."

The king learns that the things that humans naturally value, pursue, and consider essential for a good life do not, in fact, produce the desired results. He comes to prefer prudence to "scepter" or "throne," objects that represent the power that he exercises over others. He sees that wealth and luxuries do not enrich his life in the ways that wisdom does, that for a profoundly full and memorable life gold is as valuable as sand, silver as useful as "mire" or "mud." He seeks wisdom more avidly than health and good looks because the brightness that wisdom sheds on his path never "sleeps." Wisdom, not what humans call "light," illumines his way. In the end, it surprises him that along with wisdom and prudence came all good things and "countless riches."

READING II Today's reading marvels at God's dynamic presence, here portrayed as the "Word of God" in the human realm. This Word has an unparalleled ability to know human beings. It penetrates even between soul and spirit, joints and marrow. God alone can "discern reflections and thoughts of the heart." In this passage, "heart" represents the mind, the place where a person weighs options and makes decisions. God perceives one's most

A short, potent didactic reading. That the word of God is living and effective is a credo for any proclaimer of the Word.

Note the parallels: soul/spirit; reflections/thoughts; naked/exposed.

Emphasis on "creature."

READING II   Hebrews 4:12–13

A reading from the Letter to the Hebrews

Brothers and **sisters**:
Indeed the word of **God** is **living** and **effective**,
   sharper than any **two-edged sword**,
   penetrating even between **soul** and **spirit**, **joints** and **marrow**,
   and **able** to discern **reflections** and **thoughts** of the **heart**.
No **creature** is **concealed** from him,
   but **everything** is **naked** and **exposed** to the **eyes** of him
   to **whom** we must **render** an **account**.

A narrative reading with teachings crucial to our faith and to the Church but often easily lost in the getting and spending that make up our days. It's hard to give up your possessions.
Jesus' refutation begins with the man's first word, "Good." Emphasis on "good."

GOSPEL   Mark 10:17–30

A reading from the holy Gospel according to Mark

[As **Jesus** was setting out on a **journey**, a **man** ran up,
   knelt down **before** him, and **asked** him,
   "**Good teacher**, **what** must I **do** to **inherit** eternal **life**?"
Jesus answered him, "**Why** do you call me **good**?
No one is **good** but **God alone**.
You **know** the commandments: *You shall not* **kill**;
   you shall not commit **adultery**;
   you shall not **steal**;
   you shall not bear **false witness**;
   you shall not **defraud**;
   honor your **father** *and your* **mother**."
He **replied** and **said** to him,
   "**Teacher**, all of these I have **observed** from my **youth**."
Jesus, looking at him, **loved** him and **said** to him,
   "You are **lacking** in **one thing**.
Go, **sell** what you **have**, and **give** to the **poor**
   and you will have **treasure** in **heaven**; then **come**, **follow me**." »

After all of the "thou shalt nots," emphasize the word "loved." The hard thing Jesus is about to tell this man is said out of love.

intricate calculations as well as the conscious and unconscious motivations that spawn them. No creature can hide anything from this all-seeing God before whom every human being will one day stand alone and give an account of his or her life.

GOSPEL The three parts of this Gospel focus, respectively, on how to inherit eternal life, on how difficult it is for those who are rich in earthly possessions to enter the kingdom of God, and on how the experience of eternal life begins on earth.

A man, whom the evangelist Mark does not initially describe as rich and never calls young, comes to Jesus because he wants "to inherit eternal life." Though he keeps the commandments, he still longs for a deeper experience of God. Recognizing the man's sincerity, Jesus looks at him with love and gives him three more commands: Go, sell what you have, and give to the poor. In effect, Jesus tells the man to exchange his transitory wealth for lasting treasure in heaven. Jesus also teaches that discipleship entails more than keeping rules. His followers must not value and

work for what most people do. Rather, they seek what will last beyond the grave.

The man is "shocked" or "appalled" (Greek *stugnazō*) at Jesus' response. *Stugnazō* can also denote that his eager joyful countenance droops suddenly into gloomy sadness or that his joy darkens. Then, "sad" or "grieving" (Greek *lupeō*), the man walks away from Jesus. *Lupeō* can also convey that he is somewhat irritated or insulted; Jesus simply demands too much. Only at this point in the narrative does Mark give the reason for the man's reactions: he has many possessions.

At **that statement** his **face** fell,
and he went away **sad**, for he had **many possessions**.

Jesus looked around and **said** to his **disciples**,
"How **hard** it **is** for **those** who have **wealth**
to **enter** the **kingdom** of **God**!"
The **disciples** were **amazed** at his **words**.
So **Jesus** again said to them in **reply**,
"**Children**, how hard it is to **enter** the **kingdom** of **God**!
It is **easier** for a **camel** to pass through the **eye** of a **needle**
than for **one** who is **rich** to **enter** the **kingdom** of **God**."
They were **exceedingly** astonished and said among themselves,
"Then who can be **saved**?"
Jesus looked at them and said,
"For **human beings** it is **impossible**, but **not** for God.
All things are **possible** for **God**."]
Peter began to **say** to him,
"We have given up **everything** and **followed** you."
Jesus said, "Amen, I say to you,
there is **no** one who has given up **house** or **brothers** or **sisters**
or **mother** or **father** or **children** or **lands**
for **my** sake and for the **sake** of the **gospel**
who will not receive a **hundred times more now** in this
present age:
houses and **brothers** and **sisters**
and **mothers** and **children** and **lands**,
with **persecutions**, and eternal **life** in the **age** to come."

[Shorter: Mark 10:17–27 (see brackets)]

This famous saying of Jesus' deserves to be heard. He is making a striking claim.

Emphasize "All things."

The details give this passage its texture: "mother," "father," "children," "houses," "brothers," "sisters." Give each detail its due.

Jesus uses the incident to teach about the danger of earthly riches. He declares that wealth "is"—he does not say "can be," but "is"—an enormous obstacle to entry into God's kingdom. His words amaze his disciples, probably because in Scripture riches are a blessing or sign of God's favor and a reward that God grants to those who keep the commandments. Jesus stresses his point with the intentionally absurd and hyperbolic example of a camel passing through the eye of a needle. When they hear this, his disciples are "exceedingly astonished." They ask, "Who then can be saved?" In response, Jesus reminds them, and Mark's readers, that saving is something that only God can accomplish.

Peter and other disciples spend their time and energy, not on protecting, increasing, and worrying about their possessions, but on carrying on Jesus' mission. Rather than work for wealth, they voluntarily live with less. Their choices challenge the beliefs of those who have not yet grasped Jesus' teaching about eternal life. Sometimes, their choices lead to discon-nection and even alienation from their families—situations which always entail suffering and even persecution. Jesus promises that his disciples become a new family (see Mark 3:20–21, 31–35), one that will live together forever. E. N.

TWENTY-NINTH SUNDAY IN ORDINARY TIME

LECTIONARY #146

READING I   Isaiah 53:10–11

Isaiah = ī-ZAY-uh

An exhortatory reading from Isaiah's prophecy about the Suffering Servant, a figure with an essential, anticipatory role in the theology of the Church.

Note the rhythm of this line: da-da-DAH da-da-DAH . . .

Emphasis on "servant."

A reading from the Book of the Prophet Isaiah

The LORD was **pleased**
    to **crush** him in **infirmity**.

If he **gives** his life as an **offering** for **sin**,
    he shall see his **descendants** in a long **life**,
    and the **will** of the LORD shall be **accomplished**
        through **him**.

Because of his **affliction**
    he shall **see** the light in **fullness** of **days**;
through his **suffering**, my **servant** shall **justify** many,
    and their **guilt** he shall **bear**.

For meditation and context:

RESPONSORIAL PSALM   Psalm 33:4–5, 18–19, 20, 22 (22)

R. Lord, let your mercy be on us, as we place our trust in you.

Upright is the word of the LORD,
    and all his works are trustworthy.
He loves justice and right;
    of the kindness of the LORD the earth
    is full.

See, the eyes of the LORD are upon those
        who fear him,
    upon those who hope for his kindness;
to deliver them from death
    and preserve them in spite of famine.

Our soul waits for the LORD,
    who is our help and our shield.
May your kindness, O LORD, be upon us
    who have put our hope in you.

READING I   Woven into the joyous good news of Second Isaiah (Isaiah 40—55) are four passages that trace the life of an enigmatic figure called "The Servant of the Lord." While in one passage the prophet names the servant Israel (Isaiah 49:3), in others his identity is uncertain; he could be a prophet like Moses or Jeremiah, a king, or any one of God's people.

During his lifetime, the Servant went unnoticed or was shunned. The verses preceding this reading describe him as a man with no bearing or beauty to catch the eye. He endured great suffering, which people viewed as divine punishment for his private sins. Only after he dies a shameful death and is buried among the wicked (Isaiah 53:2–9) do his contemporaries realize that the Servant suffered for them, that it was the Lord's will that he bear their guilt, take their punishment, and thus justify them.

After Jesus' Resurrection, his disciples —steeped in his teaching and filled with his Spirit—saw a deeper meaning in Second Isaiah's theological explanation of the mysterious Servant's life and death. Their prayerful reflections led them to understand that Jesus suffered and gave his life to take away the punishment due for the sins not only of Israel but of all humanity.

READING II   In Judaism, the high priest passed through the Temple curtain once a year on the feast of Yom Kippur or the Day of Atonement and entered the holy of holies. There he interceded to God on the people's behalf (Hebrews 9:1–9). Today's reading announces that when Jesus, our great high priest, died on the cross, he "passed through the heavens" once and for all and opened the way to direct, continuous access to God.

READING II   Hebrews 4:14–16

A reading from the Letter to the Hebrews

An exhortatory reading about the direct connection we have to Jesus.

Brothers and **sisters:**
Since we have a **great high priest** who has **passed** through
    the **heavens,**
    Jesus, the Son of **God,**
    let us hold **fast** to our **confession.**
For we do **not** have a high **priest**
    who is **unable** to **sympathize** with our **weaknesses,**
    but **one** who has similarly been **tested** in every **way,**
    yet **without** sin.
So let us **confidently** approach the **throne** of **grace**
    to receive **mercy** and to find **grace** for timely **help.**

Note the ways in which the author of Hebrews connects our experience to Jesus'. The one difference: He is without sin. (A big difference.)

Emphasize "mercy," "grace," and "help."

GOSPEL   Mark 10:35–45

A reading from the holy Gospel according to Mark

Zebedee = ZEB-uh-dee

A narrative reading that includes teachings embedded in conversation between Jesus and the disciples. Jesus is testing the disciples' (natural) desire to be first, to be superior. He wants to redirect that desire toward service.

James and **John,** the sons of **Zebedee,** came to **Jesus** and **said**
    to him,
    "**Teacher,** we want you to **do** for us whatever we **ask** of you."
He replied, "**What** do you wish me to **do** for you?"
They answered him, "**Grant** that in your **glory**
    we may sit **one** at your **right** and the **other** at your left."
Jesus said to them, "You **do not know** what you are **asking.**
Can you **drink** the cup that I **drink**
    or be **baptized** with the **baptism** with which I am **baptized?**"
They said to him, "We **can.**"

Gentle as Jesus often seems, he must surely have felt impatience, especially when receiving requests like James' and John's.

This passage emphasizes the compassion and understanding that Jesus has for us because he is like us in all ways except sin. He experienced all the difficulties that attend every human life. Tested in every way that we are, he "gets" human weakness. Therefore, we can confidently approach his throne of grace, certain that he will receive us not with aloof disapproval but with empathy and mercy, and give us the divine help that we seek.

GOSPEL | Immediately preceding this Gospel, Jesus declares for the third and last time that he must suffer, die (like the servant in Isaiah), and rise. Now, as he nears the end of his journey from Galilee to Jerusalem, which Mark depicts as his way to the cross, he knows the time has come to fulfil the most difficult part of his mission. James and John, more concerned with their personal ambitions for glory, ask Jesus for the top places of honor in his kingdom. He tells them bluntly that they do not realize that the eminence they seek comes only at the great personal cost entailed in doing God's will. He uses the metaphors of his "cup" and his "baptism" to elaborate his point.

In Scripture, the cup can represent one's lot or fate. Here, as in the description of Jesus' agony in the garden, it represents the work that the Father assigns him. Taken in the context of the expiatory suffering of the Lord's servant in the first reading, Jesus' cup also evokes the cup of wrath which Second Isaiah uses to convey Jerusalem's punishment for its sins (Isaiah 51:17), and

Jesus said to them, "The **cup** that I **drink**, you will **drink**,
and with the **baptism** with which I am **baptized**, you will
be **baptized**;
but to **sit** at my **right** or at my **left** is not **mine** to **give**
but is for **those** for whom it has been **prepared**."
When the ten **heard** this, they became **indignant** at James
and John.
[Jesus **summoned** them and **said** to them,
"You **know** that those who are **recognized** as **rulers** over
the **Gentiles**
lord it **over** them,
and their **great ones** make their **authority** over them **felt**.
But it shall not be so **among** you.
Rather whoever **wishes** to be **great among** you will be
your **servant**;
whoever **wishes** to be first **among** you will be the **slave** of **all**.
For the **Son** of **Man** did not **come** to be **served**
but to **serve** and to give his **life** as a **ransom** for **many**."]

[Shorter: Mark 10:42–45 (see brackets)]

Even stress on "But it shall not be so . . ."

Slight pause between "great" and "among"; and between "first" and "among."

Emphasis on "serve."

which Jeremiah employs as a metaphor for the destruction of Jerusalem and other nations for the evil that they did (Jeremiah 25:15–38). When Jesus drinks his own cup, he also drinks "the cup of wrath" that is destined for all sinners. He takes their (our) punishment on himself, as he does also by undergoing the "baptism" with which he is to be baptized. Those who desire fame in his kingdom must likewise be willing to share in his suffering for others.

The anger of the rest of the disciples suggests that, like James and John, they fail to grasp that the way to glory in Jesus' kingdom is the cross. Christian leaders especially must proclaim this essential teaching by making themselves the slaves of the people they encounter in every situation. Their model is Christ on the cross, not the world's arrogant, self-aggrandizing rulers who flaunt their power. Jesus insists, "Not like this can it be among you." The great among his disciples must put the concerns and needs of others before their own. Like Jesus, they show up not to be served, but to serve.

Jesus often asks people, "What do you wish me to do for you?" His humble deference to the will of others trained him for his final act of service on the cross. His entire life of voluntary servitude is the ransom that he paid to release humankind from captivity to sin. Disciples who seek greatness will make themselves the servant of others because that is what he did. E. N.

THIRTIETH SUNDAY IN ORDINARY TIME

LECTIONARY #149

READING I Jeremiah 31:7–9

A reading from the Book of the Prophet Jeremiah

> **Thus** says the LORD:
> **Shout** with **joy** for **Jacob**,
>   **exult** at the **head** of the **nations**;
>   **proclaim** your **praise** and **say**:
> The LORD has **delivered** his **people**,
>   the **remnant** of **Israel**.
> **Behold**, I will bring them **back**
>   from the **land** of the **north**;
> I will **gather** them from the **ends** of the **world**,
>   with the **blind** and the **lame** in their **midst**,
> the **mothers** and **those** with **child**;
>   they shall **return** as an immense **throng**.
> They **departed** in **tears**,
>   but I will **console** them and **guide** them;
> I will **lead** them to **brooks** of **water**,
>   on a **level road**, so that **none** shall **stumble**.
> For I am a **father** to **Israel**,
>   **Ephraim** is my **first-born**.

Jeremiah = jayr-uh-MĪ-uh

An exhortatory reading of rhythmical intensity and proclamatory power. Read it like a poem, allowing its words and its rhythms to sound out as you proclaim it. There are three beats in these lines, for instance: SHOUT with JOY for JACob. This is part of this reading's poetry.

Emphasis on "father." A parent is Jeremiah's analogy for God's love for humankind.

TO KEEP IN MIND
Use the pitch and volume of your voice to gain the attention of the assembly.

READING I | Jeremiah prophesies in Judah in the seventh century BC, following the fall of the Northern Kingdom Israel (referred to in this reading as "Ephraim"), to the Assyrians. These conquerors, in order to impede the efforts of their new subjects to rebel, mixed the Israelites with other populations throughout their realm.

In today's reading, Jeremiah announces that the Lord will gather this scattered people and bring them back to Zion or Jerusalem. Among this "remnant"—"an immense throng"—Jeremiah mentions the blind, lame, and pregnant, people whose way would be especially difficult. The prophet assures them that the Lord will provide water, which is never a certainty in biblical lands, all along an easy road home. Upon hearing this divine promise, the people should rejoice.

The responsorial psalm expresses Israel's longing for the promised reversal of their situation, with one verse highlighting the abruptness that often marks divine activity: "Restore our fortunes, O Lord, like the torrents in the southern desert," the Negeb. This area of uncertain rainfall lies between the Judean wilderness and the Sinai peninsula. When rains do come here, they collect in dry stream beds and suddenly bring life where none seemed possible.

READING II | Most of this reading is about the Jewish high priest who represents the people before God. Because, like them, he is imperfect, he can be patient with the ignorant and the erring. The Greek word for "deal patiently" or "gently," *meriopathein*, denotes showing consideration for others by tempering

For meditation and context:

RESPONSORIAL PSALM   Psalm 126:1–2, 2–3, 4–5, 6 (3)

R. The Lord has done great things for us; we are filled with joy.

When the LORD brought back the captives
  of Zion,
    we were like men dreaming.
Then our mouth was filled with laughter,
    and our tongue with rejoicing.

Then they said among the nations,
  "The LORD has done great things
    for them."
The LORD has done great things for us;
    we are glad indeed.

Restore our fortunes, O LORD,
    like the torrents in the southern desert.
Those that sow in tears
    shall reap rejoicing.

Although they go forth weeping,
    carrying the seed to be sown,
they shall come back rejoicing,
    carrying their sheaves.

READING II   Hebrews 5:1–6

A reading from the Letter to the Hebrews

A didactic reading in which the writer of Hebrews provides instruction about how to approach and understand the priests who serve God on behalf of the people.

The word "himself" repeats four times in this reading. Emphasize it: himSELF.

The analogy compares Jesus and his sacrifice to the sacrifices of priests.

Brothers and **sisters**:
Every high priest is **taken** from among **men**
    and **made** their **representative** before **God**,
    to offer **gifts** and **sacrifices** for **sins**.
He is **able** to deal **patiently** with the **ignorant** and **erring**,
    for **he himself** is **beset** by **weakness**
    and **so**, for this **reason**, must make **sin offerings** for **himself**
        as **well** as for the **people**.
No one takes this **honor** upon **himself**
    but **only** when **called** by **God**,
    just as **Aaron** was.
In the **same way**,
    it was not **Christ** who glorified himself in becoming
        high **priest**,
    but rather the **one** who **said** to him:
    You are my **son***:
        this* **day** *I have* **begotten** *you;*
    just as he **says** in another **place**:
    You are a **priest** *forever
        according to the* **order** *of Melchizedek.*

Melchizedek = mel-KEEZ-uh-dek

---

one's feelings or emotions, often anger. The Jewish high priest well understands how slowly humans come to see where their ways differ from God's ways. Finally, he must offer gifts and sacrifices for both his own and the people's unintentional sins.

The last verses declare that neither the Jewish high priests nor Jesus take the honor of mediating between the people and God on their own initiative. The references to Psalms 2:7, "You are my son," and 110:4, "You are a priest forever," underscore the Lord's choice and appointment of Jesus. Originally, these psalms were recited

at the installation liturgy of an Israelite king whose task, like that of the high priest, was to represent God to the people and the people to God.

Melchizedek, whose name means "king of justice," appears in Genesis 14:17–20, where he is called the king of Salem (Hebrew *shalem*), which most probably means "king of peace" (reading *shalem* as the equivalent of Hebrew *shalom*). In Genesis, Melchizedek functions as a Canaanite priest who blesses Abraham. For the author of Hebrews, Jesus is both the Lord's eternal king and king / high priest

who uninterruptedly mediates justice and peace from God to humankind.

GOSPEL   Two narratives of Jesus' healing of a blind man frame the journey that he makes with his disciples from Galilee to Jerusalem (Mark 8:22—10:52), a journey which Mark depicts as the "way" of the cross. As they travel, Jesus tries to open the eyes of his followers to "see" what discipleship entails. Near the journey's end, today's encounter with a blind beggar emphasizes that faith is needed for full understanding.

GOSPEL   Mark 10:46–52

A reading from the holy Gospel according to Mark

As **Jesus** was leaving **Jericho** with his **disciples** and
        a sizable **crowd**,
    Bartimaeus, a **blind** man, the son of **Timaeus**,
    sat by the roadside **begging**.
On **hearing** that it was **Jesus** of **Nazareth**,
    he began to cry **out** and **say**,
    "**Jesus**, son of **David**, have **pity** on me."
And many **rebuked** him, telling him to be **silent**.
But he kept calling **out** all the **more**,
    "Son of **David**, have **pity** on me."
Jesus stopped and said, "**Call** him."
So they **called** the blind man, saying to him,
    "Take **courage**; get **up**, **Jesus** is **calling** you."
He **threw** aside his **cloak**, sprang **up**, and came to **Jesus**.
Jesus **said** to him in reply, "**What** do you want me to **do**
        for you?"
The blind man **replied** to him, "**Master**, I want to **see**."
Jesus told him, "Go your **way**; your **faith** has **saved** you."
Immediately he received his **sight**
    and **followed** him on the **way**.

A narrative reading depicting the miraculous healing of a blind man by Jesus.

Jericho = JAYR-ih-koh
Bartimaeus = bahr-tih-MAY-uhs
Timaeus = tih-MAY-uhs or tī-MEE-uhs

The words of the blind man resonate through the ages; we want Jesus to have pity on us.

The blind man's wish also resonates: "I want to see." Its direct statement seems to lead to his healing.

As Jesus is leaving Jericho and heading up to Jerusalem—the city of David where the Lord will gather Jeremiah's "remnant" —Bartimaeus hears that "Jesus of Nazareth" (a necessary qualification since Jesus was a common name) is passing by. Bartimaeus addresses him, "Jesus, Son of David." The royal title, which appears only here in Mark, identifies Jesus as the long-awaited Davidic descendant.

Bartimaeus is determined to meet Jesus. All the verbs for "calling" in the drawn-out series of exchanges that lead to their encounter subtly show that more than hearing is involved in understanding Jesus. Specifically, Bartimaeus calls out; people try to silence him; he cries out even more; Jesus tells his disciples to call him; they call him, telling him that Jesus is calling him. Finally, when asked by the Lord what Bartimaeus wants him to do, he replies, "Lord, I want to see."

Jesus' response, "Go your way," seems to give Bartimaeus the option of returning to the life he knows. But Mark tells us that as soon as he receives his sight, Bartimaeus follows Jesus on the way. Meeting Jesus convinced him that his faith is not mis-placed. Jesus, whose teachings are like Jeremiah's brooks of water along a level road, will henceforth be his sure guide. In effect, Mark presents Bartimaeus as one of the remnant that Israel's Lord gathers and leads to the "promised land," or in Jesus' terms, to the kingdom of God. E. N.

THIRTY-FIRST SUNDAY IN ORDINARY TIME

LECTIONARY #152

READING I Deuteronomy 6:2–6

A reading from the book of Deuteronomy

Moses spoke to the **people**, saying:
  "**Fear** the LORD, your **God**,
  and **keep**, throughout the **days** of your **lives**,
  all his **statutes** and **commandments** which I **enjoin** on you,
  and **thus** have **long life**.
Hear then, Israel, and be **careful** to **observe** them,
  that you may **grow** and **prosper** the **more**,
  in **keeping** with the **promise** of the LORD, the **God** of
      your **fathers**,
  to give you a land **flowing** with **milk** and **honey**.

"**Hear**, O Israel! The LORD is our **God**, the LORD alone!
Therefore, you shall **love** the LORD, your God,
  with all your **heart**,
  and with all your **soul**,
  and with all your **strength**.
Take to heart these **words** which I **enjoin** on you **today**."

Deuteronomy = doo-ter-AH-nuh-mee
An exhortatory reading in which Moses declares to the Israelites the nature of their covenant with God.
The covenant involves keeping God's commandments. The imperative to "fear" is notable here.

Emphasize "flowing," "milk," and "honey."

These are the words of the Great Commandment, to be repeated in the Gospel reading.

TO KEEP IN MIND
When you proclaim the Word, you participate in catechizing the faithful and those coming to faith. Understand what you proclaim so those hearing you may also understand.

READING I This passage stresses the responsibilities that each generation has not only to "fear the Lord," i.e., to respect the Lord as the most powerful being that exists, but also to instill this respect for the Lord in their children and their grandchildren. People learn to fear the Lord as they make choices and decisions that are based on divine statutes and commands, and then observe carefully what happens next. Parents and elders bear witness to the Lord's fidelity by retelling their experiences of God's presence with them in the ups and downs of family life.

For example, they pass on the surprise of discovering the Lord's care for them manifested in unexpected people and places. Each generation of God's people must persuade the following one that the way to the fullest life possible—to life in a "land flowing with milk and honey"—is to heed and follow the Lord alone. The "land of milk and honey" originally referred to a wilderness area that could support only small animals, like the goats favored by Israel's seminomadic ancestors. The honey is wild honey.

Israel's famous *Shema* (Hear, O Israel . . .), which faithful Jews repeat two or three times daily, carry in amulets, or place on doorposts, constantly reminds them of their calling to live as God's people in the world. The repetitions of "all" in the *Shema* underscore the consuming nature of this vocation. The "heart," which for Israelites is the seat of the intellect, must concentrate on ways to demonstrate loyalty to the Lord. The "soul" (Hebrew *nephesh*) denotes one's entire being, i.e., every gift, quirk, and penchant that marks a person as a uniquely crafted image of God. All this *nephesh* and

For meditation and context:

RESPONSORIAL PSALM   18:2–3, 3–4, 47, 51 (2)

R. I love you, O Lord, my strength.

I love you, O LORD, my strength,
  O LORD, my rock, my fortress,
    my deliverer.

My God, my rock of refuge,
  my shield, the horn of my salvation,
    my stronghold!

Praised be the LORD, I exclaim,
  and I am safe from my enemies.

The LORD lives! And blessed be my rock!
  Extolled be God my savior,
you who gave great victories to your king
  and showed kindness to your anointed.

READING II   Hebrews 7.23–28

A reading from the Letter to the Hebrews.

levitical = lih-VIT-ih-k*l

A didactic reading about the nature of the priesthood in relation to Jesus' eternal priesthood.

The contrast is being made between the priests of the law on earth and Jesus' eternal priesthood in an implied heaven. Slight pause between "God" and "through."

These are the attributes of Jesus the eternal priest.

Once again, Jesus as eternal priest is contrasted to mortal priests and their weaknesses.

Brothers and **sisters**:
The **levitical priests** were **many**
    because they were **prevented** by **death** from **remaining**
      in **office**,
    but **Jesus**, because he remains **forever**,
    has a **priesthood** that **does not** pass **away**.
Therefore, he is **always** able to **save those** who **approach God**
      through him,
    since he lives **forever** to make **intercession** for them.

It was **fitting** that we should have such a high **priest**:
    holy, **innocent**, **undefiled**, **separated** from sinners,
    higher than the **heavens**.
He **has** no need, as did the **high priests**,
    to **offer** sacrifice **day** after **day**,
    first for his **own sins** and **then** for those of the **people**;
    he did that **once** for **all** when he **offered** himself.
For the **law** appoints men **subject** to **weakness** to be **high priests**,
    but the **word** of the **oath**, which was **taken** after the **law**,
    appoints a **son**,
    who has been made **perfect** forever.

---

all one's "strength" or "energy," which for some scholars includes one's wealth, must be put at the Lord's disposal.

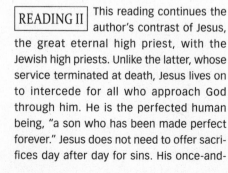 This reading continues the author's contrast of Jesus, the great eternal high priest, with the Jewish high priests. Unlike the latter, whose service terminated at death, Jesus lives on to intercede for all who approach God through him. He is the perfected human being, "a son who has been made perfect forever." Jesus does not need to offer sacrifices day after day for sins. His once-and-

for-all sacrifice on the cross accomplished God's plan for humankind. Finally, Jesus' authority comes from God, not from "the law." He is appointed by "the word of the [Lord's] oath," a reference to the citation from Psalm 110 in last Sunday's section of the letter to the Hebrews.

GOSPEL   In contrast to the religious authorities who oppose and challenge Jesus in two earlier confrontations (Mark 11:27 and 12:18), the scribe in this Gospel is impressed by Jesus' deep understanding of Torah. A teacher himself,

the scribe seeks Jesus' opinion about what matters the most to God, about what is God's greatest or most fundamental commandment. Jesus, an orthodox Jew, recites the *Shema*. However, he adds to it a second commandment that ties loving God to loving one's neighbor as oneself (Leviticus 19:18). Then, to reinforce the inseparability of these two statutes, he declares, "There is no other commandment greater than these."

Jesus' answer evokes a remarkable declaration from the scribe: love of God and love of neighbor are *perissoteron*, "worth more than" all whole-burnt offerings

A narrative reading that include a core teaching—perhaps *the core teaching*—in Christian faith, the so-called Great Commandment.

Here begins the Great Commandment, quoting from Deuteronomy, followed by Jesus' addition (antecedents for which can also be found in the Torah). What follows Jesus' teaching is the affirmation of the scribe to whom he tells the Great Commandment, effectively repeating and reinforcing the teaching.

Even emphasis on "no other commandment."

Even emphasis on "are not far."

GOSPEL Mark 12.28-34

A reading from the holy Gospel according to Mark.

One of the **scribes** came to **Jesus** and **asked** him,
    "**Which** is the **first** of all the **commandments**?"
Jesus **replied**, "The first is this:
    Hear, *O Israel!*
    *The **LORD** our God is **Lord** alone!*
    *You shall **love** the **LORD** your **God** with all your **heart**,*
    *with all your **soul**,*
    *with all your **mind**,*
    *and with all your **strength**.*
The **second** is this:
    *You shall **love** your **neighbor** as **yourself**.*
There is **no other commandment** greater than **these**."
The **scribe** said to him, "Well **said**, teacher.
You are **right** in saying,
    'He is **One** and there is no **other** than **he**.'
And 'to **love** him with all your **heart**,
    with all your **understanding**,
    with all your **strength**,
    and to love your **neighbor** as **yourself**'
    is worth **more** than all burnt **offerings** and **sacrifices**."
And when Jesus **saw** that he answered with **understanding**,
    he **said** to him,
    "You **are not far** from the **kingdom** of **God**."
And no one **dared** to ask him any more **questions**.

(the most costly and altruistic ones) and sacrifices. It is noteworthy that Jesus' exchange with the scribe takes place in the Temple where priests preside over daily sacrifices, and that much of the scribe's professional work would deal with sacrificial regulations. Further, both the scribe and Jesus would be familiar with the writings of the prophets who preached that the Lord rejected Temple worship unless it was accompanied by demonstrated concern for one's neighbors (such as Isaiah 1:10–17; Amos 5:21–24; Jeremiah 7:1–7). In this Gospel, Jesus' linking of the two command-

ments leads the scribe to realize that love of God, which entails incarnating God's concern for people, is more important than the correct performance of long-standing liturgical rituals.

In his rendition of the *Shema*, the scribe changes one word of Jesus' version. He replaces "soul"—in Greek, *psychās*, which here means "one's whole being"—with the Greek *sunesis*, which means "understanding." This change stresses the intellectual effort that God's people must make to uncover personal biases and convictions that run counter to divine com-

mands. Jesus appreciates the openness and the honest mental discipline of another teacher. When he sees that the scribe answers "with understanding" or "thoughtfully" (Greek *nounechos*), Jesus declares that the scribe is "not far from the kingdom of God." E. N.

ALL SAINTS

LECTIONARY #667

READING I   Revelation 7:2–4, 9–14

A reading from the Book of Revelation

Revelation = rev-uh-LAY-shuhn
A narrative reading of visionary power and enticing detail. Revelation has inherent drama in its language and imagery. You only need to proclaim the passage with clarity and directness; its power will express itself through your voice.
Note the repetitions: "damage, land, sea."

I, **John**, saw another **angel** come up from the **East**,
   holding the **seal** of the living **God**.
He cried **out** in a **loud voice** to the four **angels**
   who were given **power** to **damage** the **land** and the **sea**,
   "Do not **damage** the **land** or the sea or the **trees**
   until we put the **seal** on the **foreheads** of the **servants**
      of our **God**."
I heard the **number** of those who had been **marked** with the seal,
   one **hundred** and forty-four **thousand** marked
   from every **tribe** of the children of **Israel**.

Even stresses on the words in this line.

After **this** I had a **vision** of a great **multitude**,
   which **no one** could count,
   from every **nation**, **race**, **people**, and **tongue**.
They stood before the **throne** and before the **Lamb**,
   wearing **white robes** and holding **palm branches** in
      their **hands**.
They cried out in a **loud voice**:

Emphasis on "Lamb," which will be repeated at the end of the passage.

   "**Salvation** comes from our **God**, who is **seated** on the **throne**,
   and from the **Lamb**."

All the **angels** stood around the **throne**
   and around the **elders** and the four living **creatures**.

TO KEEP IN MIND

As you prepare your proclamation, make choices about what emotions need to be expressed. Some choices are evident from the text, but some are harder to discern. Understanding the context of the Scripture passage will help you decide.

READING I | The setting for this reading is the heavenly throne room from which God and his Christ rule over all creation. Those who remained faithful to Jesus during their earthly life stand before the throne and acclaim the Lamb's victory over evil and death. The scenes set before us today are from John's vision of the opening of seven seals on a scroll that is in God's right hand (Revelation 5:1—8:2). The contents of the scroll symbolically describe "the time of great distress" which will accompany the final destruction of evil on earth at the end of time. The detail that the scroll is in God's hand conveys divine control over this event. The seven seals—seven being a perfect number—indicate that God's plan is completely hidden from humans until the Lamb, by his death and resurrection, "opens the seals" and reveals it.

An angel halts this process so that God's seal can be placed on the foreheads of those who serve him, indicating that they belong to God, who will preserve them. The identities of the "144,000" and the "great multitude" are unclear. The former is

They **prostrated** themselves before the **throne**,
   worshiped **God**, and **exclaimed**:

   "**Amen. Blessing** and **glory**, **wisdom** and **thanksgiving**,
      honor, **power**, and **might**
      be to our **God** forever and **ever. Amen**."

Then one of the **elders** spoke up and **said** to me,
   "**Who** are these wearing **white robes**, and **where** did they
      come from?"
I said to him, "My **lord**, you are the one who **knows**."
He said to me,
   "**These** are the **ones** who have **survived** the time
      of great **distress**;
   they have **washed** their **robes**
   and made them **white** in the **Blood** of the **Lamb**."

RESPONSORIAL PSALM   Psalm 24:1bc–2, 3–4ab, 5–6 (6)

R. Lord, this is the people that longs to see your face.

The LORD's are the earth and its fullness;
   the world and those who dwell in it.
For he founded it upon the seas
   and established it upon the rivers.

Who can ascend the mountain of the LORD?
   or who may stand in his holy place?

One whose hands are sinless, whose heart
      is clean,
   who desires not what is vain.

He shall receive a blessing from the LORD,
   a reward from God his savior.
Such is the race that seeks him,
   that seeks the face of the God of Jacob.

---

a symbolic number for a great crowd. Since the omitted verses, Revelation 7:5–8, name the twelve tribes, it most probably represents Israelites who acknowledge the Lamb.

The "great multitude," which includes people from every community on earth, stands (an early Christian liturgical posture of praise) and carries palms to celebrate Christ's victory. These survivors of the great distress wear robes that are white

because they washed them "in the blood of the Lamb," a washing that, Revelation 12:11 will clarify, entails personal participation in Christ's suffering. Unless Christians are taught and accept this consequence of Baptism, their faith remains immature. They see Christianity as a ticket to "heaven" and a promise that the Lord will protect them and those they love from suffering. They know that some Christians endure

persecution for Christ, but they expect to avoid it. Then, when indescribable sorrow does come their way, they often conclude that God is not faithful. In contrast, informed Christians recognize that their earthly troubles constitute a unique "ministry" that is entrusted to them by Christ their king. As they persevere on their distinct path to sainthood, their sufferings whiten their robes in the blood of the Lamb.

READING II 1 John 3:1–3

A reading from the first Letter of Saint John

Beloved:
See what love the **Father** has **bestowed** on us
  that we may be **called** the children of **God**.
Yet **so we are**.
The **reason** the world does not **know** us
  is that it did not know **him**.
Beloved, we are **God's** children now;
  what we shall **be** has not yet been **revealed**.
We **do know** that when it is **revealed** we shall be **like** him,
  for we shall **see** him as he **is**.
Everyone who has this **hope** based on him makes himself **pure**,
  as **he** is pure.

GOSPEL Matthew 5:1–12a

A reading from the holy Gospel according to Matthew

When **Jesus** saw the **crowds**, he went up the **mountain**,
and after he had sat **down**, his disciples **came** to him.
He began to **teach** them, saying:

  "**Blessed** are the poor in **spirit**,
    for **theirs** is the **Kingdom** of **heaven**.
  Blessed are they who **mourn**,
    for **they** will be **comforted**.
  Blessed are the **meek**,
    for they will **inherit** the **land**.
  Blessed are they who **hunger** and **thirst** for **righteousness**,
    for they will be **satisfied**.

An exhortatory reading proclaiming the mysterious nature of God's revelation.

Emphasis on "know." In the next line, on "him."

Note the interplay between "revealed" and "see."

An exhortatory reading whose expressions are familiar but whose specifics are helpfully reintroduced to your assembly. This Gospel reading is an opportunity to teach the Beatitudes anew.

Blessed = BLES-uhd

Note the rhythmical emphases. The first word in each beatitude is stressed, as is the last word in each line. Let that rhythm guide your proclamation.

READING II John's image, "children of God," reminds believers that Baptism changes one's status. Through this sacrament, a person becomes part of the most powerful royal family on earth and in heaven. Full understanding of this privilege, however, will come only with the Lord's return. Until then, those who hope to see the Lord "as he is" live by his teachings —especially his command to love one another—rather than by the world's ways.

God's children grow in likeness to their brother and look forward to knowing him completely, to being "at home" with him for eternity.

GOSPEL The Beatitudes set out the behaviors and attitudes of those who believe that Christ lives and reigns. When the baptized shape their life by these fundamental teachings, they make his rule visible in the space they occupy, and in the relationships and events that make up their life. They become "the salt of the earth" and "the light of the world (Matthew 5:13–16).

Living by the Beatitudes does not come naturally. It requires a sustained effort because it entails changing one's automatic reactions to people and events. As believers practice the Beatitudes, they gradually see where their opinions and priorities, which generally agree with those of

Blessed are the **merciful**,
> for they will be shown **mercy**.

Blessed are the clean of **heart**,
> for they will see **God**.

Blessed are the **peacemakers**,
> for they will be called **children** of God.

Blessed are they who are **persecuted** for the sake
> of **righteousness**,
> for **theirs** is the **Kingdom** of **heaven**.

Blessed are you when they **insult** you and **persecute** you
> and utter every kind of evil **against** you falsely **because**
> of me.

Rejoice and be **glad**,
> for your **reward** will be **great** in **heaven**."

most people, run counter to the teachings that Jesus sets before us today.

For example, disciples become "poor in spirit" as they concede that they cannot control God or divine timing and ways. They accept what comes, trusting that God is present and active—reigning—in the mix. When disciples realize that some people are treated unfairly or do not have the opportunities that they take for granted, they get "hungrier" and "thirstier" for justice for all. They become more merciful as they try to understand the situation of their "offenders" and give them the benefit of the doubt.

The baptized become "clean of heart" as they focus on God's kingdom above all else. They become peacemakers even though doing so disrupts their own pleasant pastimes. They do not merely endure insults, persecution, and every kind of evil talk for Jesus' sake, they "rejoice" and "are glad" when these come their way. Grateful to be in the fray, they stand with the risen Christ and fight the evils around them. They are honored to bear the seal of the living God, to be called children of God—to be among the saints whose lives we celebrate today. E. N.

THE COMMEMORATION OF ALL THE FAITHFUL DEPARTED (ALL SOULS' DAY)

LECTIONARY #668

READING I   Wisdom 3:1–9

A reading from the Book of Wisdom

An exhortatory reading, one whose tone is conciliatory and hopeful.

The **souls** of the **just** are in the **hand** of **God**,
   and no **torment** shall **touch** them.
They **seemed**, in the view of the **foolish**, to be **dead**;
   and their passing **away** was thought an **affliction**
   and their going **forth** from us, utter **destruction**.

Emphasize "peace."

But they are in **peace**.
For if before **men**, indeed, they be **punished**,
   yet is their **hope** full of **immortality**;
chastised a little, they shall be greatly **blessed**,
   because God **tried** them

Emphasize "himself." God gathers all the souls offered to him, transforming them.

proved = tested

   and found them **worthy** of **himself**.
As gold in the furnace, he **proved** them,
   and as sacrificial **offerings** he took them to **himself**.
In the time of their **visitation** they shall **shine**,
   and shall dart **about** as **sparks** through **stubble**;
they shall judge **nations** and rule over **peoples**,
   and the LORD shall be their King **forever**.
Those who **trust** in him shall understand **truth**,
   and the **faithful** shall abide with him in **love**:

Emphasize "grace," "mercy," and "holy."

because **grace** and **mercy** are with his **holy** ones,
   and his **care** is with his **elect**.

There are options for today's readings. Contact your parish staff to learn which readings will be used.

| READING I | Today's readings remind believers of the relation- |

ship that God desires to have with them on earth and after death. For the author of Wisdom, this intertwined existence, this mixing of divine and human life, is both constituted and evidenced by the just acts that a person performs. In other words, unless a person works to carry out God's justice on earth, there is no relationship between him or her and God, no bond that can continue after physical death.

This passage contrasts the divine and human views of the life and death of "the just." The "foolish" misperceive the "passing away" (Greek *exodos* = *ex* "out of" + *hodos* "way," thus a "way out" of earthly life) of a just person as an affliction or divine mistreatment. And, their "going forth" (Greek *poreia* denotes a journey or pursuit) from the human realm an "utter destruction." Both *exodos* and *poreia* convey that, in the divine view, physical death is not an end but a way out of the bondage and trials that attend every human life. Death is the next leg of a trip that gives the just new experiences with God. Wisdom depicts these experiences as living "in the hand of God," as being sheltered by the omnipotent God from any further pain, as "resting in peace."

The foolish also misread the earthly trials of the just as divine punishment for their obvious or hidden sins. As usual, appearances mislead the foolish. For the sufferings of the just are not punishment but spiritual training or education in divine ways. The simile of gold tested in the furnace reflects a business practice common

For meditation and context:

RESPONSORIAL PSALM   Psalm 23:1–3a, 3b–4, 5, 6 (1)

R. The Lord is my shepherd; there is nothing I shall want.
or
R. Though I walk in the valley of darkness, I fear no evil, for you are with me.

The LORD is my shepherd; I shall not want.
  In verdant pastures he gives me repose;
beside restful waters he leads me;
  he refreshes my soul.

He guides me in right paths
  for his name's sake.
Even though I walk in the dark valley
  I fear no evil; for you are at my side
with your rod and your staff
  that give me courage.

You spread the table before me
  in the sight of my foes;
you anoint my head with oil;
  my cup overflows.

Only goodness and kindness follow me
  all the days of my life;
and I shall dwell in the house of the LORD
  for years to come.

READING II   Romans 5:5–11

A reading from the Letter of Saint Paul to the Romans

An exhortatory reading in which Paul locates the source of hope in Jesus himself.

Brothers and **sisters**:
Hope does **not** disappoint,
  because the love of **God** has been poured **out** into our **hearts**
  through the Holy **Spirit** that has been **given** to us.

Emphasize "Christ."

For **Christ**, while we were still **helpless**,
  died at the appointed **time** for the **ungodly**.
Indeed, only with difficulty does one die for a just **person**,
  though **perhaps** for a **good** person
  one might even find **courage** to die.
But **God** proves his **love** for us
  in that while we were still **sinners** Christ **died** for us.

Emphasize "through." This indicates the direction/tendency of our salvation, sparing us from wrath.

How much **more** then, since we are now **justified** by his **Blood**,
  will we be saved **through** him from the **wrath**. ❯❯

---

to the biblical world. Payments of metal for goods or services rendered were melted down to remove impurities and confirm their supposed value. For example, in one fourteenth century BC Amarna Letter (part of an archive of diplomatic correspondence on ancient tablets), a Babylonian king complains to another ruler that "the twenty minas of gold" that he submitted in payment of a bill "were not pure," for when they were put in the furnace, they produced "only five minas."

  For Wisdom, the death of the just is their "sacrificial offering" that God takes

completely to himself. As fire transforms and transports an animal sacrifice out of the human realm, so does death transform the just man or woman into a being who can know God completely, who can experience a love beyond human knowing, and who will enjoy God's presence, mercy, and care for all eternity.

READING II **Romans 5.** This reading emphasizes the love that God has for people. Christ displayed the depth of this love by his death, which reconciled or brought all humanity into right

relationship with God. Paul stresses that humans did nothing to attract or merit divine love. Before Christ died for them, people were "helpless" or "weak," unable to free themselves from millennia-old, ingrained, human inclinations and pursuits. Unmindful of God's love, they floundered around in a world shaped by the egocentric desires and drives of small-minded earthbound leaders.

  Before Christ's death, humanity was also "ungodly" or without adequate reverence for the invisible God. Sinners all, people followed their whims and "missed the

Indeed, if, while we were **enemies**,
    we were **reconciled** to God through the **death** of his Son,
    how much **more**, once **reconciled**,
    will we be **saved** by his **life**.
Not only **that**,
    but we also boast of **God** through our Lord Jesus **Christ**,
    through whom we have now **received reconciliation**.

Or:

READING II   Romans 6:3–9

A reading from the Letter of Saint Paul to the Romans

Brothers and **sisters**:
Are you **unaware** that we who were **baptized** into Christ **Jesus**
    were **baptized** into his **death**?
We were indeed **buried** with him through **baptism** into **death**,
    so that, just as **Christ** was raised from the **dead**
    by the **glory** of the **Father**,
    we too might **live** in newness of **life**.

For if we have **grown** into **union** with him through a death
        like **his**,
    we shall **also** be united with him in the **resurrection**.
We know that our old **self** was **crucified** with him,
    so that our sinful **body** might be done **away** with,
    that we might no longer be in **slavery** to **sin**.
For a dead person has been **absolved** from sin.
If, then, we have **died** with **Christ**,
    we **believe** that we shall also **live** with him.
We know that **Christ**, **raised** from the **dead**, **dies** no more;
        death no **longer** has **power** over him.

A didactic reading, somewhat dense in its considerations. Give them space in your proclamation to be heard. Don't rush through any portions of the reading.

Note the analogy, introduced here by "so that." Paul is connecting our eternal life to Jesus', prepared for us by his death and Resurrection.

From here until the end of the reading, Paul intensifies the analogy between us and Jesus, relating it to metaphors of life and death as well as the body and sinfulness. The material is dense; pace yourself as you proclaim it.

mark," i.e., the noble and divine life that their Creator desired to share with them. They stumbled through their days, never completely satisfied, always seeking more. God and humans were also at odds with each other, "enemies" who seemed unable to communicate enough to coexist and thrive in peace.

God makes the first move to "fix" this relationship, a move that was neither hesitant nor probing. God did not trickle a few acts of loving kindness on the human race to see how they would respond. No, God "poured out" his love—the Greek perfect tense conveys that the effects of this pouring out perdure—by sending the beloved Son to die that humans might live fully. Christ is God's love poured out into our hearts through the Holy Spirit who lives with and in the baptized. In his *Anchor Bible* commentary on Romans, Joseph Fitzmyer describes this outpouring as "the divine energy manifesting itself in an overwhelming embrace of once godless creatures who are smothered with his openness and concern for them . . . in a way unparalleled by any human love." If Christ's death accomplished all this, Paul asks, how much more will we be saved by his (resurrected) life?

Romans 6. Paul asks us if we are "unaware" that we were baptized into Christ Jesus' death *so that*, just as he was raised from the dead by the glory or action of the Father, "we too might live in newness of life?" "Live" here translates the Greek *peripateo*, which denotes "to walk around." In the Hebrew Scriptures, "walking" in God's ways is a common metaphor for covenant fidelity, which Paul reapplies to Christian life. He is frustrated that the baptized stroll along the same paths as

A powerful and assertive exhortatory reading that expresses one of John's favorite themes, the will of the Father.

Will is the operative word in this reading. It is repeated four times (as a noun). Give it weight each time you say it.

For John, will is connected directly to the Father, toward which Jesus, as Son, is utterly obedient and which clearly empowers him. Emphasize "this," "will," and "Father."

GOSPEL   John 6:37–40

A reading from the holy Gospel according to John

Jesus said to the **crowds**:
"**Everything** that the Father **gives** me will **come** to me,
    and I will not reject **anyone** who **comes** to me,
    because I came **down** from heaven not to do my **own will**
    but the **will** of the **one** who **sent** me.
And **this** is the **will** of the **one** who **sent** me,
    that I should not lose **anything** of what he **gave** me,
    but that I should **raise** it on the last **day**.
For **this** is the **will** of my **Father**,
    that **everyone** who sees the **Son** and **believes** in him
    may have eternal **life**,
    and I shall raise him up on the **last day**."

their non-Christian contemporaries. They still amble after the crowd, letting it set their goals, tell them what they "need," and how to spend their time. They mosey through life unmindful that their old self was "co-buried with Christ," and that now he opens new experiences, foretastes of his resurrected life.

To die to self and rise with and in Christ—that is, to live as people freed from slavery to sin—require focus, discipline, imagination, and a constant questioning of personal opinions and habits. The struggles that ensue are themselves signs of one's growing union with Christ "through a death like his." At the same time, new experiences provide evidence that the baptized are also sharing in Christ's resurrected life. Paul urges Christians to trust the Lord and live more boldly, to demonstrate more vividly their conviction that since death no longer has power over their Lord, it no longer has power over them.

GOSPEL   When Jesus, the Son of God, came into the human realm, he made visible what Wisdom calls the divine love that God has for those whom he chooses to live intimately on earth and for all eternity. Today, Jesus announces that all human beings are so chosen. He insists that he came into the world not to do his own will but the Father's, which is that he "not lose" anything that the Father gave him. Humans, however, must cooperate with this divine plan. They must stake their life on Jesus' words that everyone who sees the Son and believes in him will have eternal life. And that Jesus will raise them up on the last day. E. N.

THIRTY-SECOND SUNDAY IN ORDINARY TIME

LECTIONARY #155

READING I   1 Kings 17:10–16

A reading from the first Book of Kings

In **those** days, **Elijah** the prophet went to **Zarephath**.
As he **arrived** at the **entrance** of the **city**,
    a **widow** was gathering **sticks** there; he called **out** to her,
    "**Please bring me** a small **cupful** of water to **drink**."
She left to **get** it, and he called out **after** her,
    "**Please bring** along a bit of **bread**."
She answered, "As the LORD, your God, lives,
    I have nothing **baked**; there is only a **handful** of flour
        in my **jar**
    and a little **oil** in my **jug**.
Just **now** I was collecting a couple of **sticks**,
    to go in and prepare **something** for myself and my **son**;
    when we have **eaten** it, we shall **die**."
Elijah said to her, "**Do not be afraid**.
Go and do as you **propose**.
But **first** make me a little **cake** and **bring** it to me.
Then you can prepare something for **yourself** and your **son**.
For the LORD, the God of Israel, says,
    'The **jar** of flour shall **not** go empty,
    nor the **jug** of oil run **dry**,
        until the **day** when the LORD sends **rain** upon the **earth**.'"
She **left** and did as Elijah had **said**.

Margin notes

Elijah = ee-LĪ-juh
Zarephath = ZAYR-uh-fath

A narrative reading in which the power of God extends through his prophet Elijah to the poor and needy, in this case, a woman and her son. It's a compelling, compressed story with a happy ending, emphasizing the message of trust in God.

Emphasize "Please" and again two lines below.

Don't overdo the woman's fatalism. She is stating her death as a fact.

The words Elijah attributes to God are repeated at the conclusion of the reading, which underscores the power of the Lord's foretelling.

READING I

The context for this short anecdote is a famine brought on by a years-long drought. To take care of Elijah, the Lord commands him to settle in Zarephath, where a widow will feed him (1 Kings 17:9). The small details in this passage (in italics below) show how the simplest human needs and gestures can reveal divine activity in the human realm. Specifically, when Elijah arrives at Zarephath, he sees the widow gathering *a few sticks* and asks her to "bring me a *little water in a vessel*." As she goes off to get it, Elijah asks her to "bring *a little bit of bread in your hand*." Speaking for the first time, the woman explains that she has *a mere handful of flour in her "kad,"* (a large pottery jar used to store grain and water), and *a little oil in a juglet*. Her plan is to collect a few sticks, feed herself and her son, and then the two of them will wait together to die.

But Elijah reveals that the Lord has another plan for her. First, she must stop being afraid, stop worrying. Then she must take care of Elijah's need before her own by making him *a little cake* (like a pita). Ultimately, we hear that her thrice-repeated *flour jar* does not go empty nor her *juglet of oil* go dry before the Lord brings rain.

READING II

This passage sets out differences between the sacrifices offered by the Jewish high priests and the single sacrifice offered by Christ, *the* high priest. While generations of Jewish ministers repeatedly offered animals, Christ offered himself on the cross in a once-and-for-all offering that took away the sins of humankind. Also, while the high priests entered a sanctuary made by hands —a "copy" or representation of the true

She was able to **eat** for a **year**, and **he** and her **son** as well;
  the jar of **flour** did not go **empty**,
  nor the jug of **oil** run **dry**,
  as the LORD had **foretold** through **Elijah**.

For meditation and context:

RESPONSORIAL PSALM   Psalm 146:7, 8–9, 9–10 (1b)

R. Praise the Lord, my soul! orR. Alleluia.

The LORD keeps faith forever,
  secures justice for the oppressed,
  gives food to the hungry.
The LORD sets captives free.

The LORD gives sight to the blind;
  the LORD raises up those who were
  bowed down.

The LORD loves the just;
  the LORD protects strangers.

The fatherless and the widow he sustains,
  but the way of the wicked he thwarts.
The LORD shall reign forever;
  your God, O Zion, through all generations.
  Alleluia.

READING II   Hebrews 9:24–28

A reading from the Letter to the Hebrews

Christ did not enter into a **sanctuary** made by **hands**,
  a **copy** of the **true** one, but heaven **itself**,
  that he might now **appear** before **God** on our **behalf**.
Not that he might offer **himself** repeatedly,
  as the **high priest** enters each **year** into the **sanctuary**
  with **blood** that is not his **own**;
  if that were **so**, he would have had to suffer **repeatedly**
  from the **foundation** of the **world**.
But **now** once for all he has **appeared** at the end of the **ages**
  to take away **sin** by his **sacrifice**.
Just as it is **appointed** that human **beings** die **once**,
  and after this the **judgment**, so also **Christ**,
  offered **once** to take away the sins of **many**,
  will appear a **second time**, not to take away **sin**
  but to bring **salvation** to those who eagerly **await** him.

A didactic reading with a complex teaching cunningly stated. The teaching itself uses the analogy of Jesus as high priest to anticipate the Second Coming.

Emphasize "Not." This word anticipates "But" a few lines below. Initially, the author of Hebrews sets up his claim about Jesus by describing something Jesus did *not* do.

Emphasize "now," which follows "But." The verb tenses in this sentence are ingenious. "Now" suggests the present but "has appeared" is in the present perfect, which combines the present with something that has already happened. "At the end of ages" suggests something to happen in the future. Jesus' sacrifice encompasses all of time. Emphasize "second time." This is the Second Coming.

---

one—at his death Christ entered "heaven itself" where he continually intercedes with God on behalf of the baptized of every age. Another difference—while other high priests offered the blood of animals in a traditional holy place, Christ poured out his own blood on the cross. In short, the author of Hebrews reinterprets Jesus' ignominious execution on the cross as a "sacrifice," a ritual in which Jesus is both the sacrificial victim and the high priest who offers it.

Finally, the author emphasizes that Christ will return, not to take away sins—he already did that on the cross—but to lead those who eagerly await him into the full experience of life with God.

GOSPEL   One day while teaching in the Temple precincts, Jesus warns his disciples to "beware" (Greek *blepete,* which denotes "to look at closely and discover" or "to see with open eyes") of some pretentious scribes who like to walk around in the religious garb that identifies them as men who are knowledgeable about God's ways. These scribes also welcome the attention of others in public places and accept prominent seats in the synagogue—where all can gaze upon them while worshipping God—and at banquets. Jesus' "beware" stresses that his disciples must see through and not be misled by pietistic façades.

But what bothers Jesus even more than the esteem that certain scribes cultivate for themselves is that they think they can both put on long displays of piety and arrogantly and with impunity exploit the less advantaged—like widows who are especially vulnerable in the biblical world because they have no man to ensure their

A narrative reading stating clearly Christ's teachings about wealth and its accumulation, a relevant topic.

The meter of this line reads: reCITE LENGTHy PRAYers.

Emphasize "Amen." Here Jesus states his teaching about wealth, putting it as clearly as possible.

GOSPEL   Mark 12:38–44

A reading from the holy Gospel according to Mark

In the **course** of his teaching **Jesus** said to the **crowds**,
    "**Beware** of the **scribes**, who like to go around in long **robes**
    and accept **greetings** in the **marketplaces**,
    seats of **honor** in **synagogues**,
    and places of **honor** at **banquets**.
They devour the **houses** of **widows** and, as a pretext
    recite lengthy prayers.
They will receive a **very severe** condemnation."

[He sat **down** opposite the **treasury**
    and **observed** how the crowd put **money** into the **treasury**.
Many **rich people** put in large **sums**.
A poor **widow** also came and put in **two small coins** worth
    a **few cents**.
Calling his **disciples** to **himself**, he said to them,
    "**Amen**, I say to you, this **poor widow** put in **more**
    than **all** the other contributors to the **treasury**.
For they have **all** contributed from their **surplus** wealth,
    but **she**, from her poverty, has contributed **all she had**,
    her **whole livelihood**."]

[Shorter: Mark 12:41–44 (see brackets)]

just treatment. Jesus warns such scribes to expect severe condemnation at judgment

Then Jesus plants himself opposite the treasury, probably one of several collection chests in the Temple court. Some scholars suggest that these receptacles were trumpet shaped—like those mentioned in the Jewish *Mishnah* (written c. AD 200, *m. Sheqalim* 2:1; 6:5)—to amplify the clatter that donations made. As Jesus watches people tossing in various coins, he notices that "many" rich people toss in large ones that broadcast their generosity.

But, summoning his disciples, Jesus does not praise the largesse of the rich but calls attention to "a poor widow" who drops in two very small thin coins which together are perhaps worth a penny. He uses her unpretentious openhandedness to teach that in the matter of religious giving, God notices the cost of the gift to the donor more than its objective value. Jesus wants his disciples to see that while the rich gave from their surplus, the widow gave, not "from" her whole livelihood, but "*her whole livelihood*." Jesus' solemn "Amen, I say to you" stresses how important it is that disciples adopt his view. E. N.

THIRTY-THIRD SUNDAY IN ORDINARY TIME

LECTIONARY #158

READING I   Daniel 12:1–3

A reading from the Book of the Prophet Daniel

In **those** days, **I, Daniel,**
  heard **this word** of the **Lord**:
"At that **time** there shall **arise**
  Michael, the great **prince**,
  guardian of your **people**;
it shall be a **time unsurpassed** in **distress**
  since **nations** began until that **time**.
At that **time** your people shall **escape**,
  everyone who is found **written** in the **book**.

"**Many** of those who **sleep** in the dust of the **earth** shall **awake**;
  some shall live **forever**,
  others shall be an everlasting **horror** and **disgrace**.

"But the **wise** shall shine **brightly**
  like the **splendor** of the **firmament**,
and those who lead the **many** to **justice**
  shall be like the **stars** forever."

An exhortatory reading of what amounts to an apocalyptic vision by Daniel. (Though Christians classify Daniel as a prophetic book, Jews regard it as an apocalypse.) Daniel makes vivid claims about what might happen in the future.

The meter of this line runs: it shall be a TIME unsurPASSED in diSTRESS.

Emphasize "horror" and "disgrace." These comprise the apocalyptic vision. Emphasize "wise" and "brightly," which sound a note of hope.

TO KEEP IN MIND
Recognize how important your proclamation of the Word of God is. Prepare well and take joy in your ministry.

READING I   As we approach the end of the liturgical year, these Scriptures remind us that we live in the final stage of humankind's story, the stage that began with Jesus' death and Resurrection. This reading is an apocalyptic work whose aim is to display God's consistent involvement in all creation, including political and international affairs on earth. Taking the long view, apocalyptic writers emphasize that while worldly kingdoms and governments rise and fall, God's kingdom is invincible and unending.

The author of Daniel writes about signs that will mark the end of time as we know it. These include earthly and cosmic upheavals and the persecution of those who remain faithful to God. A figure called Michael, who is identified here as the great prince and guardian of Israel, will play an unspecified role in these events.

The "wise who shall shine brightly" are sages who, like Daniel, work to persuade others to live by God's decrees. The notion that these wise teachers shall live forever is a rare allusion to resurrection in the Old Testament, though other Jewish apocalyptic works of this period ponder some form of life after death.

READING II   The author of Hebrews presents Jesus as *the* high priest and contrasts his ministry to that of other Jewish high priests. This passage focuses on Christ's one-time sacrifice for sins—his priestly act of dying on the cross —and on his enthronement at God's right hand. There he waits until his enemies —earthly rulers whose actions demonstrate their opposition to him—"are made his footstool." This image comes from art in

289

For meditation and context:

RESPONSORIAL PSALM   Psalm 16:5, 8, 9–10, 11 (1)

R. You are my inheritance, O Lord!

O LORD, my allotted portion and my cup,
   you it is who hold fast my lot.
I set the LORD ever before me;
   with him at my right hand I shall not
     be disturbed.

Therefore my heart is glad and my soul
   rejoices,
   my body, too, abides in confidence;

because you will not abandon my soul to the
   netherworld,
   nor will you suffer your faithful one to
     undergo corruption.

You will show me the path to life,
   fullness of joys in your presence,
   the delights at your right hand forever.

READING II   Hebrews 10:11–14, 18

A didactic reading comparing priests of the world with the high priesthood of Christ himself.

A reading from the Letter to the Hebrews

Brothers and **sisters**:
Every **priest** stands daily at his **ministry**,
   offering **frequently** those same **sacrifices**
   that can never take away **sins**.

"This one" is Christ.

But **this one** offered one sacrifice for **sins**,
   and **took** his seat **forever** at the right **hand** of **God**;
   now he **waits** until his **enemies** are made his **footstool**.

Emphasize "one" and "offering."

For by **one offering**
   he has made perfect **forever** those who are being **consecrated**.

Emphasize "forgiveness," which transforms our lives.

Where there is **forgiveness** of these,
   there is no longer offering for **sin**.

---

the biblical world which depicts a king resting his feet on the heads of vanquished foes.

     The baptized stake their life on the reality that Christ is alive and reigning. As they live ever more radically by this teachings, they experience the freeing effects of his sacrifice. All of this is their "being consecrated," or in Greek, *hagiazomenous*, which means literally "being made holy, different, or other."

 GOSPEL In the verses preceding this passage, Jesus' disciples marveled at the construction of the Temple

in Jerusalem. Indeed, it was probably the tallest building in the city and Jesus' announcement that not one of its stones would be left atop another would have been hard to imagine. When he arrives at the Mount of Olives, which even today provides a splendid view of the Temple complex, his disciples ask him when the destruction of the Temple will occur.

     Chapter 13 of Mark is often referred to as this evangelist's "apocalypse" because its themes, symbolic language, and images are like those found in Daniel and in Jewish apocalyptic writings of Mark's time (before

AD 70). Jesus announces that cosmic disturbances will herald the universal realization of God's kingdom on earth. The sun, the moon, and the stars that God created to light the earth and to mark age after age its seasons, days, and years (Genesis 1:14–18) will be darkened. The stars will fall from the sky. The forces that these lights exert over earth or represent in various religions— forces that are greater than human but lesser than divine power— will be shaken. Amid this upheaval, Jesus' disciples will see the Son of Man coming in the clouds with great power and glory and know that he is

GOSPEL   Mark 13:24–32

A reading from the holy Gospel according to Mark

Jesus said to his **disciples**:
"In **those days** after that **tribulation**
    the **sun** will be **darkened**,
        and the **moon** will not give its **light**,
    and the stars will be falling from the **sky**,
        and the **powers** in the heavens will be **shaken**.

"And **then** they will see the '**Son** of **Man** coming in the **clouds**'
    with great **power** and **glory**,
    and then he will send out the **angels**
    and **gather** his elect from the four **winds**,
    from the **end** of the **earth** to the **end** of the **sky**.

"Learn a **lesson** from the **fig** tree.
When its **branch** becomes **tender** and sprouts **leaves**,
    you **know** that summer is **near**.
In the **same way**, when you see these things **happening**,
    know that he is **near**, at the **gates**.
Amen, I **say** to you,
    this generation will not pass **away**
    until **all these things** have taken **place**.
Heaven and **earth** will pass away,
    but my **words** will **not** pass away.

"But of that **day** or **hour**, no one **knows**,
    neither the angels in **heaven**, nor the **Son**, but **only**
        the **Father**."

An exhortatory reading, which consists of Jesus' apocalyptic prediction of coming days of tribulation.

Emphasize "sun," "moon," and "stars." Note what they are connected to: "darkened," "light," and "sky." These give a sense of the cosmic totality of the tribulation.

Jesus compares the coming of the Son of Man to the signs that announce spring, in this case, buds on a fig tree. This is not, however, a natural order. Instead, it's something else.

Emphasize "knows" and "Father."

about to send out angels to gather his elect of every place and time.

Jesus uses a fig tree growing on the Mount of Olives as a visual aid to reinforce his teaching. Unlike ubiquitous evergreen trees, fig trees display seasonal changes. When people see their branches sprouting leaves in April, they know that summer is near, and that their figs will ripen in June. Just so, when Jesus' disciples see the signs that he announces come to pass, they will know that the return of the Son of Man is at hand.

Jesus' teaching that "this generation will not pass away until all these things have taken place" is unclear. "All these things" could refer to the signs mentioned above, in which case Jesus' prediction was not fulfilled. It could, however, also refer to Jesus' coming passion, death, and Resurrection. What *is* clear is Jesus' declaration that *no one* can say when heaven and earth as we know them will pass away— *not* the angels, *not* the Son, Jesus himself— *only* the Father.

The Gospel's final verse begins an exhortation which compares Jesus' disciples to servants of a household whose master left them in charge until he returns. He reminds his followers that their mission is to watch constantly for his coming, that is, to live like he will come back this evening, or this midnight, or dawn tomorrow, or tomorrow morning . . . (Mark 13:33). E. N.

OUR LORD JESUS CHRIST, KING OF THE UNIVERSE

LECTIONARY #161

READING I   Daniel 7:13–14

A reading from the Book of the Prophet Daniel

As the **visions** during the night **continued**, I saw
   one like a Son of **man coming**,
     on the **clouds** of **heaven**;
   when he reached the **Ancient** One
     and was presented **before** him,
   the **one** like a Son of **man** received **dominion**, **glory**,
       and **kingship**;
   all **peoples**, **nations**, and **languages serve** him.
His **dominion** is an **everlasting** dominion
   that shall not be taken **away**,
   his **kingship** shall not be **destroyed**.

A short, high-powered, brilliant narrative reading full of apocalyptic intensity. Proclaim this reading at an even pace; its passion will come clearly through your voice. Note "like a Son of man"; this phrase is repeated a few lines below.

Here begins a sequence of nouns, each of which should be equally weighted: dominion, glory, kingship, peoples, nations, languages.

Emphasize "destroyed."

For meditation and context:

RESPONSORIAL PSALM   Psalm 93:1, 1–2, 5 (1a)

R. The Lord is king; he is robed in majesty.

The LORD is king, in splendor robed;
   robed is the LORD and girt about with
   strength.

And he has made the world firm,
   not to be moved.
Your throne stands firm from of old;
   from everlasting you are, O LORD.

Your decrees are worthy of trust indeed;
   holiness befits your house,
   O LORD, for length of days.

TO KEEP IN MIND
Read the Scripture passage and its commentary in *Workbook*. Then read it from your Bible, including what comes before and after it, so that you understand the context.

READING I The book of Daniel, like most Jewish-Christian apocalyptic literature, reminds believers that while earthly kingdoms vie for power and territory, the omnipotent God reigns over them all and works with their machinations to accomplish divine plans. In this literature, God reveals these plans to human intermediaries, like Daniel.

Today's passage presents Daniel's vision of the throne room of "the Ancient One," which is a title for God. As Daniel watches, someone like "a Son of man" enters. The identity of this figure is unclear.

While the phrase "son of man" denotes "a human being," some scholars find that in Daniel the figure also has a supernatural character. In the synoptic Gospels, Jesus uses "Son of Man" as a self-designation, and for the evangelists it is a Christological title which recognizes that Jesus is the one who received from God "dominion, glory, and kingship" over all peoples and nations.

READING II This reading calls Jesus the (God's) faithful witness, the firstborn of the dead, and the ruler of the kings of the earth. He is also the one who

loves the baptized, freed them, and made them "into a kingdom, priests for his God and Father." In Exodus 19:6, Moses declares that Israelites who are faithful to God's covenant will become a "kingdom of priests" and Isaiah 61:6 announces that after the Lord brings Israel back to the land from Babylon, the people will be called "priests of the Lord" and "ministers of our God." For the author of Revelation (and in the baptismal rite), all the baptized are anointed "priests" and thus called, wherever they find themselves, to be intermediaries between earth and heaven. In the language

READING II   Revelation 1:5–8

A reading from the Book of Revelation

Jesus **Christ** is the faithful **witness**,
   the firstborn of the **dead** and ruler of the kings of the **earth**.
To **him** who loves us and has **freed** us from our **sins** by
      his **blood**,
   who has made us into a **kingdom**, priests for his **God**
      and **Father**,
   to him be **glory** and **power forever** and **ever**. **Amen**.

   Behold, he is coming amid the **clouds**,
      and every **eye** will **see** him,
      even those who **pierced** him.
   All the **peoples** of the **earth** will **lament** him.
      Yes. Amen.

"I am the **Alpha** and the **Omega**," says the Lord God,
   "the one who **is** and who **was** and who is to **come**,
      the **almighty**."

of the early Church writers, Christians are called to be other Christs through whom God's grace flows into the world around them. Their faithful witness to the risen Christ manifests his kingship on earth.

The Lord God is "the Alpha and the Omega," the first and last letters of the Greek alphabet which here convey the beginning and the end of all creation and everything in between. The Lord God was, is, and will be active in every place and time. "The almighty," in Greek *ho pantokrator* (a common icon of Christ), emphasizes God's omnipotence.

GOSPEL   Often, the reason that people give for an action—the truth behind it—is not the real reason, not "the truth." As in this passage, the real reasons that the religious authorities of the Jews want to get rid of Jesus are that his interpretation of Torah often undermines their own teaching, and his integrity challenges their personal witness, the comfortable routines into which they have settled. Also, Jesus claims not only to speak for God, but also to be God's Son. But this is not what they tell Pilate. They tell him that Jesus must die because he claims to be

King of the Jews. Since Rome chooses its client kings—local rulers like Herod Antipas in Galilee and Herod Philip in Philippi—such a claim marks Jesus a rebel with whom Pilate must deal.

Though Pilate recognizes the deceit and ploy of the Jewish authorities, he does not challenge them for fear of political repercussions. Ironically, he does not realize that, as scholars note, he is the one on trial here—on trial before God. Pilate is guilty of not acknowledging the truth to which Jesus bears witness in John's Gospel, namely, that God loves all human beings

A narrative reading, part of John's Passion. It consists of a conversation between Pilate and Jesus. Treat the parts of the dialogue equally; proclaim them evenly.

The crucial question. Don't exaggerate it. Pilate, a government official, is asking an earnest question.

Even emphasis on the words in this question.

Jesus' answer is completely mysterious but supercharged with confidence. Read these words clearly and plainly.

Again, mysterious and confident.

GOSPEL   John 18:33b–37

A reading from the holy Gospel according to John

Pilate said to **Jesus**,
   "**Are you** the King of the **Jews**?"
Jesus answered, "Do you **say** this on your **own**
   or have others **told** you about me?"
Pilate answered, "I am not a **Jew**, **am** I?
Your own **nation** and the chief **priests** handed you **over** to me.
What have you **done**?"
Jesus answered, "My **kingdom** does not **belong** to this **world**.
If my kingdom **did** belong to this world,
   my **attendants** would be **fighting**
   to **keep** me from being handed **over** to the Jews.
But as it **is**, my **kingdom** is not **here**."
So Pilate **said** to him, "Then you **are** a king?"
Jesus answered, "You **say** I am a **king**.
For **this** I was born and for **this** I came into the **world**,
   to **testify** to the **truth**.
Everyone who **belongs** to the truth **listens** to my **voice**."

TO KEEP IN MIND
The attention you bring to your proclaiming enables you to pray the Word of God with the assembly.

and that Jesus came to lead them into everlasting communion with God. Pilate also fails to see that he has no real power over Jesus. Jesus will die, not because Pilate condemns him but because Jesus chooses to lay down his own life (John 10:18).

Groomed to promote politics as usual, Pilate cannot imagine a kingdom that "does not belong to this world." The Greek behind this phrase indicates a kingdom that is not from this world, did not originate on earth, is not humanly conceived, and does not operate like other political entities. A distinctive feature of Jesus' kingdom is that it is not sustained by violence. He tells Pilate that, if his kingdom were of this world, his followers would be fighting (Greek *agonizomai*, struggling with all their physical and mental energy like athletes) to keep him from being handed over to the religious authorities.

Jesus' kingdom is a spiritual one that exists in people of every nation who have a personal relationship with him and thus with each other. The primary mission of this global community is to bear witness to the truth for which Jesus died, namely, that God loves all peoples, seeks their common good, and desires to live with them forever. E. N.